PREACHING THE LUMINOUS WORD

Preaching the Luminous Word

Biblical Sermons and Homiletical Essays

Ellen F. Davis

with

Austin McIver Dennis

WILLIAM B. EERDMANS PUBLISHING COMPANY

GRAND RAPIDS, MICHIGAN

Wm. B. Eerdmans Publishing Co.
2140 Oak Industrial Drive N.E., Grand Rapids, Michigan 49505
www.eerdmans.com

22 21 20 19 18 17 16   1 2 3 4 5 6 7

ISBN 978-0-8028-7423-8

Library of Congress Cataloging-in-Publication Data

Names: Davis, Ellen F., author.
Title: Preaching the luminous word : biblical sermons and homiletical essays /
    Ellen F. Davis with Austin McIver Dennis.
Description: Grand Rapids : Eerdmans Publishing Co., 2016. |
    Includes bibliographical references and index.
Identifiers: LCCN 2016024703 | ISBN 9780802874238
Subjects: LCSH: Preaching. | Bible—Sermons. | Episcopal Church—Sermons.
Classification: LCC BV4211.3 .D38 2016 | DDC 252/.03—dc23
    LC record available at https://lccn.loc.gov/2016024703

Contents

CONTENTS

Contents

Contents

Foreword

Ellen Davis has the gift to help us recover the oddness of the everyday. That is particularly true of her sermonic works that we are fortunate to have collected in this book. The burden of my remarks in this foreword is to suggest why I think these sermons help us recover the significance of preaching for the church. One may well wonder why the significance of preaching needs to be recovered. After all, the everyday presumption by most Christians when they go to church is that they will hear a sermon. But that is just the problem. Because the sermon is taken for granted we seldom ask why we need a sermon; nor do we ask what a sermon in the Christian tradition is or should be. Because these questions remain unasked it is assumed, particularly in our day, that the sermon is more like a lecture by someone who may have some insights to help us negotiate the hard spots of life. A "good sermon" so understood is one that has some entertaining and/or heart-warming stories that distract us from the everyday cares of life.

The sermonic practice Ellen Davis employs is a fundamental challenge to the tendency to understand the sermon as one or another kind of lecture or talk. Her sermons are anything but "information" or "helpful hints for being happy." Instead her sermons are rigorously exegetical, which means she refuses to make the sermon "a thing in itself." In form and content her sermons mimic Peter's great sermon in the second chapter of the book of Acts. Peter's sermon is the paradigm for all subsequent Christian preaching because his sermon makes clear that Christians are a people whose lives are determined by a story. To be sure, the story Peter tells is a complex one, but that is why the story must be repeated over and over again. Stories must be repeated over and over because stories, at least the stories we call Scripture, live through memory.

That Christians gather every Sunday is an indication that we live through memory and narrative. Christianity is not a collection of generalizations about life that can be known by anyone. We have to show up Sunday after Sunday to hear again the stories that make us who we are. We are a people whose lives are determined by the stories of the people of Israel and a particular Jewish man named Jesus. The sermons of Ellen Davis are hewn from the texts of our Scripture in a manner that helps us remember that we are a people who live by words born from stories of pain, suffering, and the glory of God. The Word that is known through words is no generalized truth that must exist because "something must have started it all." No, this is a God who is known on his own terms. The sermon as the genre of Christian speech is but a reflection of such a God.

In the introduction to her book *Wondrous Depth: Preaching the Old Testament,* Davis writes:

> The . . . essays in this volume address what I regard as the gravest scandal in the North American church in our time—namely, the shallow reading of Scripture. Such reading results from the assumption that we already know just what the Bible says; therefore, our reading is a simple rehearsal of what (we think) we know rather than an attempt to probe deeper. The assumption of prior knowledge that is fully adequate to new challenges seems to be widely held by "conservative" and "liberal" Christians alike. Ironically, that common assumption may account for the sterility of the arguments between them. However heated and divisive those arguments may be, they do little to advance the church's understanding of its Scriptures, or even to provoke curiosity about what fresh insight the Bible might offer into the multiple situations that perplex or disturb us, or what new possibilities for our life it might disclose.[1]

Davis's exasperated remarks about how Scripture is generally read in contemporary times should not be taken to indicate that she is given to polemics. She cares about her craft, that is, the craft of reading, because that craft she rightly thinks is crucial for the church if we are to recover from the habits that have made us shallow readers of Scripture. Shallow readings of Scripture too often lead to sermons driven by the desire to "make a point." By contrast, Davis preaches in a manner that trusts the "take home" benefits are found in the text itself.

1. Ellen F. Davis, *Wondrous Depth: Preaching the Old Testament* (Louisville: Westminster John Knox, 2005), xi.

If Davis seems angry in her critique of shallow readings of Scripture, she is so because she is a person in love with God and with the Bible. Her criticism, therefore, of the way many currently read Scripture is first and foremost a gesture of love meant as a constructive gift. The sermons in this book are the material form that gift takes in the hope that they may provide exemplifications enabling us to become better readers and hearers of the Bible in order that we might reflect the holiness of God.

It is important to remember that Ellen Davis is first and foremost a scholar of the Old Testament, though her scholarship is in service to the church. For some, that she reads Scripture in a confessional manner may imply that she pays less than full attention to the scholarly issues surrounding the text. But that way of understanding her "method" would do her a profound injustice. Rather, what Davis seeks to do is help us read Scripture with eyes ready to be surprised by the God whom Scripture reveals as the Lord of surprises.[2] Historical scholarship is often an aid in that endeavor. But she is at her best when she focuses our attention on those aspects of the text we are most likely to miss because we are so desperate to have the text confirm what we already think we know. For example, consider her extraordinary sermon on Genesis 22, in which she suggests that God tests Abraham because God needs to know whether Abraham is devoted to God. In short, God needs to know if Abraham can be trusted.

Though her scholarship is meant to help us read Scripture more deeply, it is through her preaching, which is of course shaped by her scholarship, that her ability to awaken our scriptural sensibilities is clearly on display. Again, that is one of the reasons we should be grateful to have this book. You can talk all you want about the need to recover a theological reading of Scripture, and I have been one of those who have indulged in such talk, but such talk does not help us accomplish what a theological reading actually looks like. With these sermons Ellen Davis not only provides the exemplification of a theological reading of Scripture but also demonstrates the power of such a reading when articulated by someone of depth and elegance. She has a talent for word care—a finely cultivated craft—resulting in sermons that allow the words of Scripture to stop us in our tracks. She does that by forcing us to attend not only to what is said but to how it is being said.[3]

2. See, for example, her chapters in *The Art of Reading Scripture*, ed. Richard Hays and Ellen F. Davis (Grand Rapids: Eerdmans, 2003), 9-26 and 163-80. See especially her chapters entitled "Teaching the Bible Confessionally in the Church" and "Critical Traditioning: Seeking an Inner Biblical Hermeneutic."

3. Davis, *Wondrous Depth*, 11.

Moreover, she writes and speaks with beauty even while attending to those passages in Scripture that are ugly and/or tragic. For example, consider her use of repetition in her sermon on Jeremiah, in which she repeatedly says, "No one should ever see what Jeremiah saw." But Jeremiah did see his people forced into exile and the destruction of his home. In a fashion not unlike Jeremiah's world, we live in a world that is being destroyed by our habits. Yet we do not register the destruction that surrounds us, so the question becomes how to get our attention. Davis does so by placing us in Jeremiah's story using the trope, "No one should see mountains exploding in Kentucky."

Her use of repetition is a poetic device not uncommon among great preachers—think of Martin Luther King Jr. But then sermons are an art—minor poems—that require great care and time. Davis takes the care and time to help us see how the texts of Scripture illumine our world. In other words, she does not assume that the world is self-interpreting, but rather knows that the world needs the narration that only Scripture can provide.

I have noticed that Ellen Davis often says things I've tried to say but wish I had said much better. This may be because we share a common history. We both did our graduate work at Yale, though at different times and in different subjects. Ellen did her graduate work in Old Testament under Brevard Childs. I did my graduate work in Christian ethics under James Gustafson. That we were both at Yale does not mean we were drawing on the same intellectual currents, but I suspect we represent theological developments at Yale at that time that were simply "in the air." I was more directly shaped by Hans Frei and George Lindbeck than was Ellen, though Dr. Frei was on her dissertation committee. However, I think Frei and Lindbeck would recognize themes in her work that they represented. I am happy to say that I was fortunate to have Professor Childs for my first semester at the Divinity School at Yale.

One reason Ellen gave for why she would like me to introduce this book is my avowed love of preaching. In my "later years" I have discovered that what I most like to do is preach. Ellen, an Old Testament scholar, and I, a theologian and ethicist, share the conviction that we find preaching the most theologically enlivening thing we do. I love to preach because in preparing and delivering sermons I often discover theological convictions I did not know I had.[4] Just as Ellen has discovered that preaching makes her a better scholar of the Old Testament, so I have discovered that preaching makes me a better theologian

---

4. I emphasize the importance of preaching for me in several collections of my sermons, but particularly in *Without Apology: Sermons for Christ's Church* (New York: Seabury, 2013), xi–xxxii.

and ethicist. Preaching does so because when preaching there is no way to avoid the fact that if God does not matter then what we are about as Christians cannot help but be an elaborate lie.

I'm deeply appreciative of Ellen Davis's calling attention to Hugh of St. Victor's suggestion that sermon preparation and delivery are best understood through an analogy to stone masonry. As a person who was raised a bricklayer I am particularly drawn to Hugh's analogy. In particular, Davis points out Hugh's observation that the upper levels of theological meaning are only possible if they rest on stones that often cannot even be seen, given the necessity that they secure a firm foundation. Once such a foundation is laid, the even harder work begins, requiring that the stone mason find the right size and color of stones that must be laid in relation to other stones that have already been laid. Davis similarly suggests that sermons depend on the interconnections demanded by the text, interconnections between the great story of God's calling of Israel and the life, death, and resurrection of Jesus.[5]

I was never particularly good at building stone walls. My father, however, was a genius when it came to laying stone. Laying brick and laying stone are dramatically different skills. Bricks are sufficiently uniform that you do not have to see each brick in its particularity in order to lay brick well. When you lay stone, and bricklayers actually use the language of "setting stone," each stone has to be seen in relation to other stones. If that vision is not maintained the stone mason risks getting all the small stones in the same place in the wall. I was tempted to make that mistake because I was in too much of a hurry. Setting stone is an exercise in an imagination schooled by the patience required to see each individual stone for its beauty while also seeing how that stone will enhance and be enhanced in relation to the surrounding stones. I hope I have learned to be a better preacher than I was a stone setter. What I know, however, is that Davis's preaching is the art of a master mason.

Let me try to make explicit why the analogy of stone masonry is so suggestive for illuminating how Davis works as a preacher: just as masons do not need a blueprint to know how to set the stone they have been given, so Davis assumes the work demanded by the text precedes any theory about what makes a sermon a sermon. Put differently, her sermonic practice is blessedly free of theory. Davis is simply not a theory-driven person. She does not worry whether this or that theologian will or will not agree with her reading of a text. What she cares about is reading the text in a such manner that we can recognize our lives in and through the text. She has obviously read widely and her

5. Davis, *Wondrous Depth*, 71.

sermons reflect her reading, but her reading is first and foremost determined by long and patient attention to the text of the Bible.

In a very illuminating way she characterizes her "method" as an exercise of the imagination. Contrary to many of the characterizations of the imagination as a faculty associated with fantasy, Davis argues that the imagination makes possible a precision otherwise unavailable. The imagination provides precision because for her the imagination is shaped by close attention to the words—and, in particular, the words of Scripture—in a manner that makes possible readings that otherwise would be missed.[6] The poetic character of her sermons, therefore, reflects the subject that is every poet's subject, that is, words.

Davis does not need a homiletical theory because she has something far more significant: the text and her exegetically informed imagination. She observes that to read with the precision exercised by a well-formed imagination enables the preacher to recognize that scriptural texts are sometimes very blunt. Oftentimes the texts challenge our "accustomed notions about God and our place in the world that God has made. Yet at the same time, they affirm that the Old Testament in all its parts speaks to us in ways that are Christianly coherent, guiding us toward an intimate yet unsentimental relationship with the God whom Christians know best as the Father of our Lord Jesus Christ."[7]

Davis's understanding of the precision that comes from an imagination so formed reflects what I take to be one of the fundamental commitments that shape her sermonic practice; that is, her presumption that we should never try to protect God. Too often the god we try to protect is the god that is the projection of our sentimental presumptions that have been born by our denial that suffering and death are an undeniable reality. From Davis's perspective, the great enemy of a truthful reading of Scripture that results in equally horrific sermons is sentimentality. Atheism is preferable to sentimentality because atheists at least have the virtue of thinking God to be worthy of denial. The god of sentimentality cannot be the God whose Son can say on the cross, "My God, my God, why have you forsaken me?"

Above I quoted Davis's observation that the greatest challenge facing us today is the shallow reading of Scripture. That such readings prevail is due, I believe, to the presumption that the gospel makes us safe. That presumption, a presumption that is a denial of the reality we rightly call "sin," cannot help but distort how Scripture is read. We live in a dangerous world. Our worship

6. For her account of "imaginative precision" see Davis, *Wondrous Depth*, 68-72.
7. Davis, *Wondrous Depth*, 68.

of God does not make that world safe. Our worship of God, our sermonic practice, does, however, make the world endurable.

As a number of these sermons indicate, Ellen Davis has a deep commitment to serve the church of South Sudan. Having traveled to South Sudan many times, she knows that to be a Christian can and often does put your life in peril. Preaching takes on new urgency when we need the truth in order to endure whatever form our survival may take. For example, Davis was pleasantly surprised to discover that Hebrew was one of the first subjects the Christians of South Sudan wanted taught as part of their ministerial formation. At least one of the reasons for this was that they could see themselves in the struggles of the people of Israel.

Davis's commitment to exegetical sermons, her critique of the use of illustration, and her awareness of the concrete place and time in which the sermon is to be delivered are closely interrelated. An accommodated church, a church that no longer remembers that to be a Christian is to recognize the fragility of life, cannot help but produce and reproduce sermons that reinforce the presumption that things are "all right." The church operating on this false assumption is now dying. That is why the sermons in this book are so important. They are paradigms for a future when we will need all the help we can get to sustain the worship of the Lord of Israel. That Lord, a king who died on a cross, demands an encounter with the world through sermons chastened by a relentless honesty. The sermon so understood will not need illustrations or sentimentality.

I can illustrate what I take to be Davis's discovery that illustrations often get in the way of the text in this way. When a preacher says, "As my twelve-year-old said to me recently," you are justified in thinking you need to listen no further. What such sermonic practices do is let the preacher gesture to the congregation that she or he has a family and that's what really matters. Illustrations are a way preachers underwrite the sentimentalities that many come to church to have reinforced.

Thus the oft-repeated sermonic bottom line: when it is all said and done what is really important is that we love one another. That profound "truth" is then illustrated by an example of someone making sacrifices for a family member or even a stranger. Usually what anyone who has been subjected to such a sermon remembers is the illustration. The problem with such preaching is exactly what Davis suggests: namely, that such truths and illustrations could be used whether Jesus has been raised or not.

Sentimentalities can be avoided if we remember, as Davis emphasizes, that preaching is participation in an ongoing conversation with the text and the readings of the texts by Jews and Christians through the centuries. As she makes clear, her own sermonic style developed from close attention to past Christian preachers such as John Donne who freed her from the presumption that the preacher has to have an illustration if the sermon is to be compelling. She also discovered that she has little use for thematic preaching because that form of preaching has the tendency to legitimize and reproduce established viewpoints. As a result, the primary purpose of preaching—that is, to initiate change by introducing the community of faith to challenges that may force the church to move in new directions—will be lost.[8]

"Words matter." I think no sentence is more indicative of Ellen Davis's approach to preaching than that short sentence. Words, moreover, come with a history, which means the preacher must resist the temptation to translate the words we have been given into "the univocal language of modern rationalism."[9] The demand for translation results in the shallow readings of Scripture Davis finds so characteristic of contemporary preaching. That very demand, moreover, reflects the social and political accommodation of a church whose primary function is to convince Christians that the way things are is the way things are supposed to be.

Davis is well aware of the challenge to those who occupy the sermonic office to resist having their sermons reproduce the way things are. She suggests one way to resist that outcome is for preachers to understand themselves as an "elementary language teacher." Accordingly, a preacher's most important responsibility is to educate "the imaginations of her hearers so that they have the linguistic skills to enter into the world which Scripture discloses, and may thus make a genuine choice to live there."[10] For example, in her sermon on Genesis 1, "Being a Creature Means You Eat," she begins with the simple and straightforward observation that to be a creature means you eat for a living. That turns out to be the essential difference between ourselves and God because God does not need to eat.[11] What an interesting way to identify the difference between God and ourselves. That difference is often put metaphysically by the claim that only in God are existence and essence one. But Davis's observation that only God does not need to eat— also a metaphysical observation—is a powerful way to make clear the difference God is. And it helps us to better inhabit our own creaturehood.

8. Ellen F. Davis, *Imagination Shaped: Old Testament Preaching in the Anglican Tradition* (Valley Forge, PA: Trinity Press International, 1995), 256.

9. Davis, *Imagination Shaped,* 253.

10. Davis, *Imagination Shaped,* 250.

11. Davis also makes this point in her Easter sermon of April 7, 1999 (see pp. 271–75 below). I call attention to this point because it is surely an interesting and fundamental theological claim to suggest that the God of Israel, in contrast to the gods that surrounded Israel, had no physical needs.

Davis acknowledges that even though she had read Genesis for many years it was her growing concerns about the environment that forced her to notice how important food is, not only in Genesis but throughout the Bible. She finds this extremely important because Scripture clearly presumes that eating and agriculture are constitutive of our relationship to God. Yet we miss that relationship despite its being so clearly *in* the text because we live as a people who see no relationship between God and food. How odd that a Eucharistic people should fail to comprehend that how and what we eat makes a difference for our relation with God. It is as if we reproduce our first ancestor's rebellion against God in which food played a decisive role.

Davis acknowledges that this reading of Genesis 1 is not a typical reading of our lives from the contemporary pulpit. Yet that should make such readings all the more important. They are so because they provide ways to "read our cultural situation in the light of Scripture." This is the antithesis of reading Scripture in light of our cultural situation. To read our situation in light of Scripture means allowing Scripture to open our eyes and reveal what realistic hopes we might have. Davis's reading of Genesis is informed by her concern about our degrading of the environment—as she herself acknowledges—but it was Scripture in the first place that led to her growing concern and conviction, which then fostered her research into how the environmental crisis might help her read Genesis as our story. If you need an exemplification of what Lindbeck meant by "intratextual theology," that is, what it means for the biblical text to "absorb" the world rather than the world the text, Davis's reading of our lives through Genesis is a worthy example.[12]

It may be that "absorb" is too strong a word to characterize Davis's "method." She is acutely aware that the "world" is more than capable of resisting being absorbed by scriptural display. Yet she masterfully has the ability to draw on the stories of Israel and the life, death, and resurrection of Jesus to help us recognize the often unacknowledged narratives that subject us to destructive ways of life. In that respect her preaching has a prophetic character that is remarkable.

The prophetic character of her preaching draws on the absolute majesty and glory of God. God's glory, God's holiness, is for Davis manifest in creation. God's glory and God's holiness are not some ideas about God, but attributes of God that reflect God's refusal to abandon his promise to the people of Israel.

---

12. For Lindbeck's account of intratextual theology see his *The Nature of Doctrine: Religion and Theology in a Postliberal Age*, 25th anniversary ed. (Louisville: Westminster John Knox, 2009), 104-8.

This God, the God who covenants with Israel, is always the central character in Davis's sermons, and Israel's God is not ephemeral. This is the God of creation who is ever-present in his creation, including those whom he called into existence and with whom he shared his law. Davis's text-determined sermons reflect her profound sense that God's glory and holiness are as near and as far as the coal that cleansed Isaiah's lips; and it turns out that coal is Scripture itself.

One of the great gifts Davis has given us in this collection is examples of how to preach *on*—or, perhaps better put, *with*—the Old Testament. For it must surely be the case that the shallow reading of Scripture Davis so deplores can be partly attributed to how seldom we hear sermons from the Old Testament. Even if a sermon is on an Old Testament text the result is often less than it should be. The sermon is less than it should be because too often preachers think they need to "explain" why the God of the Old Testament is not the God we find in Jesus Christ. As a result Christians lose any sense that we are a people like Israel who must learn to survive in a world by relying on the God who makes us intelligible in the first place. Like Israel and the Jews, Christians must learn to live by their wits, for we are fundamentally a people whose worship of God makes us a people who must learn to live out of control.

To learn to live out of control may be but another name for being a people who reflect God's holiness. For it is surely the case that Israel's calling to be a people who worship the God of glory is the basis for what it means for the church to be holy, a suggestion I think present in Ellen Davis's baccalaureate sermon at Yale Divinity School in 1992 (pp. 38–43 below) in which she calls attention to Moses's request that God show him God's glory. Davis rightly draws from Moses's presumption that God's glory is to be found in God's unrelenting love of Israel and the church.

Davis's preaching on the Old Testament is nowhere more eloquently exemplified than when she preaches on the Psalms. For her the Psalms have a unique potential for connecting those who sing the Psalms to the larger biblical story. Moreover, the Psalms were and are Jesus's prayer book, which means we must learn to pray the Psalms with Jesus. Accordingly Davis, who is acutely aware that heavy-handed Christological readings of the Old Testament help no one, suggests that if we attend to the Psalms we will learn to read our lives with the humility the Psalms demand and Jesus embodies.

I suggested above that Ellen Davis is a master of locating our lives in the drama of salvation through the sermon. To be sure, she does this in diverse ways because she is sensitive to the different occasions and contexts in which she preaches. Consider, for example, the short but powerful memorial sermon for Joseph Taban Lasuba. The pathos of his death hangs in the air like thick fog. Yet, drawing on Psalm 116, Davis narrates his life and death in a manner that at once gives voice to the sadness of his death without that voice becoming maudlin. She rightly argues that his death means he is no longer bodily present in our lives, but because through death he has been drawn closer to God we now share in an intimate relation with him.

Her sermon for Joseph Taban Lasuba is absent the sentimentality that preachers find almost impossible to avoid, particularly at funerals. I suspect one of the reasons Davis is so drawn to the Psalms is the absence in the Psalms of even a hint of sentimentality. According to Davis, the Psalms were written by and for people who pray prayers that indicate a passion to know God. That passion, however, is one that cannot be truthful if the mystery of our suffering and death, a suffering and death that are often inexplicable, is denied. Her sermons on the Psalms, therefore, are meant to teach us to pray the Psalms and thus be united with our ancestors who refused to hide the anguish of their lives from themselves or from God. As she notes, by praying the Psalms in the company of Jesus we hope to learn to pray boldly yet without sentimentality or self-deception.

I have emphasized Ellen Davis's attention to the text, but I haven't yet mentioned the attention she pays to how the biblical story is told according to the church's liturgical year. The church year matters for how the text is to be received. In attending to liturgical time we are better able to see how one text is related to other texts. Though Davis's focus is always on the texts assigned for the day, she never forgets that there is "a larger biblical story." That story must be constantly tested by the smaller stories throughout Scripture. Accordingly these sermons make fascinating reading as we watch her negotiate that delicate task of showing the relation between the larger story and the text for the day.

These sermons need no introduction by me or anyone else. I regard it a great honor, however, that Ellen asked me to write this foreword. It has provided me with the opportunity to say why I find her such a powerful preacher. I do so, I believe, because, as she says in her preface, through preaching she has discovered "the conviction that the Bible is in a meaningful sense the word of the living God, given to us in human words so that we may 'live by them'" (Lev. 18:5). How odd of God to be willing to be so known. We are in Ellen Davis's debt for helping us recover that "oddness."

STANLEY HAUERWAS

On Not Worrying about Sermon Illustrations

The sermons here exemplify what I often call "biblical preaching," which means preaching that takes its primary impetus from scriptural texts. I stay close to a given text (occasionally, more than one) and, correspondingly, I make light use of sermon illustrations. That is the only way I know how to preach, although it is not what I took away from my seminary courses in homiletics. I do not presume to know now what my teachers actually *said* about how we should preach, but I remember giving a lot of attention then to finding the right story to fill out or carry a sermon—either in response to explicit instruction or because the admired preachers I heard or read made much of illustrations.

I know exactly when I stopped thinking about illustrations, and why. It was 1983, my final year in seminary, when I first encountered John Donne's spectacular sermons on the Psalms. (To this day, I consider that seventeenth-century poet and priest to be the greatest English-language preacher of the Psalms; because of his example, the Psalms have become my own most favored preaching texts.) Donne's sermons came as a revelation to me. Here was a style of preaching that was theologically probing, emotionally engaged, eloquent, even entertaining—and entirely focused on the Bible. The preaching text he explicitly identified was never more than a single verse. However, he would read it in relation to any and every other verse of Scripture—roaming through the two Testaments as he might have strolled through London, observing with familiarity and endless fascination the particularities of the language and the local characters. Repeatedly, Donne reminded his audience of their stories, and when he used a contemporary illustration, it was drawn in just a few words. Its purpose was to engage his hearers directly with the scriptural witness and thus enable them to see their own lives more clearly.

Thus Donne showed me what it was to enter fully into the textual world of the Bible, and from there to articulate a worldview clearly and confidently, with no anxiety that such a reading of reality might not be sufficiently interesting or relevant to hold an audience's attention for fifteen minutes. In a word, John Donne gave me assurance; he modeled firm reliance on the text, and that gift has stayed with me ever since. Without it, I doubt very much that I would still be preaching at all. The anxiety of finding something wise or "spiritual" to say on my own would have defeated me, probably sooner rather than later.

The main phrase of my title, "the luminous word," is inspired by the New Testament scholar Krister Stendahl, who was also a distinguished preacher and bishop. He offered me encouragement and practical counsel in the early years of my own teaching and scholarship, as I was trying to figure out what I as a professor of Old Testament might contribute to the education of preachers. My first encounter with his own thinking about preaching was in 1983, when Bishop Stendahl gave the Lyman Beecher Lectures on Preaching at Yale Divinity School. I remember just one thing he said on that occasion, an informal remark over lunch. I remember, because it so profoundly challenged the preaching culture of the day and of that place, and of most other places known to me then and now:

> Be careful about using an example that is too good, too "unforgettable." If your preaching is doing what it should do, then people probably won't remember what you said, and it doesn't matter. Your goal should be that the next time they turn to that part of the Bible, *it* will say a little more to them. *The purpose of preaching is to give the text a little more room to shine.*

Those words gave me a point of orientation and confirmed what I had seen in Donne's sermons. Based on that witness from two great preachers some three-and-a-half centuries apart, I dispensed with illustrations and took up exegesis as the anchor for my own preaching.

Exegesis is also the anchor for my work as a biblical scholar, and so each form of work, preaching and scholarship, is indispensable for the other. The immediacy of the response to preaching—seeing the surprise, joy, gratitude with which people receive the gift of the text as it is unfolded—has kept the Bible luminous for me. Thus preaching has kept me alive and reasonably well as a biblical scholar. It has sustained me in my study and teaching, and also in my faith. Turning regularly to the Bible, not for an academic purpose but with the need to discover what *this* text (usually chosen for me by the lectionary) has to say to *this* audience on *this* occasion—that concrete and particularizing practice has repeatedly renewed in me the conviction that the Bible is in a meaningful sense the word of the living God, given to us in human words so that we may "live by them" (Lev. 18:5).

Almost all my work as a teacher and scholar has been directed toward narrowing the gap between academic theology and what I understand to be the proper concerns and ministries of the church. Publishing a collection of exegetically based sermons may be the most direct intervention of that kind I have yet attempted. I undertake it now, after many years of thinking it might be worth trying, because I have been blessed with the right partner for this work. Austin McIver Dennis selected some fifty sermons from the several hundred I had preached over a quarter-century, and he wrote a brief introduction for each of them, as well as the concluding essay in this volume. I am an exegete who teaches Old Testament and preaches, in that order. Mack Dennis is an ordained Baptist preacher, a theologian, and a trained homiletician, perhaps in that order. What that means to me is that he thinks full time and knowledge-ably about the work of preaching, in a way that I do not think, and cannot. It is not only that he is sensitive to technique and method; much more importantly, he is able to articulate from a broad and well-considered perspective what are the essential elements of the kinds of preaching the church most needs at this time in its life. He thinks as an experienced pastor, as the instructor of young preachers, as a person with (God willing) several decades of active ministry ahead. Seeing my sermons through Mack Dennis's eyes is for me an education and a gift.

One of the greatest joys of my academic life during the past fifteen years has been regular and often probing conversation with Stanley Hauerwas, my colleague and friend. In recent years, much of that conversation has concerned the sermons we happened to be writing at any given time. His companionship in this work is a steady source of encouragement that enables me to believe that serious preaching is the best possible use of a theologian's time.

Three skilled editors, Judith Heyhoe of Duke Divinity School and Michael Thomson and Jenny Hoffman of Eerdmans, have each contributed a great deal to shaping and polishing this book. I am grateful.

Finally, I thank my husband, Dwayne Huebner, who read almost every one of these sermons as it was being written and often gave me the criticism it required in order to preach. This volume is dedicated to him.

Being a Creature Means You Eat

First Baptist Church, Greensboro, North Carolina
January 10, 2010

GENESIS 1

The first chapter of the Bible offers a vantage point for situating the ecological crisis theologically. Thus it makes possible a new ecological imagination, anchored in God's creational design for humanity and the world.

Being a creature means you eat for a living; it is that simple. As the Bible understands it, one of the major differences between God and ourselves is that we need to eat, and God doesn't. "If I were hungry, I wouldn't tell you," God comments acidly in one psalm.[1] And the essential corollary is that God, who does not eat, provides food for all the creatures, who do. As we just read in Genesis 1, verses 11–12, God is stocking the pantry, you might say. If we had read the whole chapter, you might have noted that there is a shift in style at the point when God makes the dry land ready for life on the fifth day. Up until that point, the description of each divine act is terse: " 'Let there be light': and there was light" (v. 3). But the narrator becomes positively verbose in describing the food sources available on the earth, with grains "setting seed heads" and fruit trees setting "fruit with the seed inside them" (vv. 11–12). This is a precise, botanically correct description of the remarkable variety of edible plants native to the Middle East, the region where dry-land agriculture originated.

Reading the Bible is my line of work, yet for years I hardly noticed all this detailed attention to the food supply in its first chapter. And once I did notice, I still had no idea what to make of it—and the scholarly literature

---

1. Psalm 50:12.

1

was of no real help. I now realize that this general cluelessness about food sources among modern professional readers of the Bible points to a deep and worrisome difference between a modern cultural mindset and the culture that all the biblical writers represent. The difference comes down to this: for them, eating and agriculture have to do with God, and for us they do not. We might think carefully about what food we buy; some of us I dare say are "foodies," for reasons of health or personal taste. Yet I doubt we consider eating to be a genuinely religious activity. We might bless the food on our plates, but rarely does that provoke any serious thought about the mystery that underlies it. For the biblical writers, however, God's provision of food is a key mystery and a core theological concern; eating is at the heart of our relationship with God and all that God has made. That is why the first chapter of the Bible says more about what the creatures eat than about any other aspect of earthly life.

So Scripture stands against us, in our obliviousness to the theological significance of eating. The weight of history is also against us: the vast majority of cultures and individuals who have preceded us on the planet, up until the last three generations perhaps, have been intensely aware that getting food from field to table is the most important religious act we perform. Every day, taking our sustenance from the earth and from the bodies of other animals, we enter deeply into the mystery of creation. Eating is practical theology, or it should be; daily it gives us the opportunity to honor God with our bodies. Our never-failing hunger is a steady reminder to acknowledge God as the Giver of every good gift. When we ask our heavenly Father for an egg, we do not get a scorpion (Luke 11:12; see also v. 3).

Genesis 1 is a theological statement about food, and at the same time it is an ecological statement. Eating is practical ecology, the most important ecological act we perform. For it is through eating that we enter most fully into the delicate complex of interactions among living creatures, exchanging the energy that keeps us alive for a time, consuming until in the end we are consumed. We are, as Genesis says, "dust to dust," taking from the soil and in the end becoming part of the fertile soil that yields more food for God's creatures.

"Dust to dust"—in this way we are no different from the other creatures, yet Genesis says we have a special status among them: we are charged to "exercise dominion." That notion of human dominion is suspect to many ecologically sensitive people, since it has been used as a license to kill, to exercise power in wantonly destructive ways. However, the key Hebrew verb suggests power, yes, but also skill. A better translation might be that we are charged to exercise "skilled mastery among the creatures." And our best clue to what skilled mastery might mean comes immediately after the charge is given, when in the very next verse God says, "Look, I have provided food for every creature: for humans, fruit trees and grains; and green plants for all animals and birds and creeping critters."

God never wastes a word in Genesis 1. So if God charges humans to exercise skilled mastery, and then with the very next breath says that there is food enough for all, I would guess that those two divine statements are connected in this way: As the creature made in the divine image, humans are meant to exercise mastery by maintaining the food supply for all creatures. To use contemporary language, the integrity of the food chains may well be the test of whether or not we are fit to exercise a special place of power and responsibility among the creatures.

And the Bible never says we have passed the test. As you know, in Genesis 1, nearly every divine commandment is followed directly by a notice of fulfillment: " 'Let there be light' . . . and there was light . . . ; 'Let there be a firmament' . . . and it was so"—*et cetera*. But no such notice of fulfillment follows the charge for humans to exercise skilled mastery; we are never told "And it was so." So we readers are left in a position—maybe with an obligation—to render judgment on ourselves. If indeed our dominion has something to do with maintaining the God-given abundance of food for all creatures, then we might well find ourselves guilty, living as we all do in the Sixth Great Age of Species Extinction, when food chains and natural systems have been disrupted worldwide. Knowing that this latest tidal wave of extinctions is driven largely by human activity, we might well conclude that we have failed to exercise the skilled dominion with which we were charged. Genesis 1 suggests that this failure of ours is the one outstanding gap in God's design for the world, and it is the gap that threatens to undo all the rest.

It may surprise us to hear that very much of our failure has to do with the seemingly innocent and certainly necessary practice of food production. The "waving fields of grain," in our land and others around the world, are the source of catastrophic erosion rates; in the last sixty years or so, half the topsoil of Iowa has gone south. The chemicals we put on our fields have made it unsafe to drink the water in some rural communities and produced hundreds, maybe thousands of dead zones in our oceans. Modern industrial agriculture also consumes water in vast quantities: great rivers such as the Colorado have been drained to the point that in some seasons they no longer reach their mouths. Forests on this continent and around the world have been razed for cropland, much of it for animal feed. Our dominant agricultural practices are thus a major driver of global warming and species loss. Maybe half our plant and animal species will disappear within the next century.[2]

God's creatures are dying, in numbers incalculable, because for the better part of a century, we in the industrialized world have been eating ignorantly and dangerously. We have been eating against the laws of the biosphere. To put that in theological language, we are eating against the design of creation. Paradoxically, an *ancient* text gives us the best insight into our contemporary and completely unprecedented situation. The first human sin, as Genesis tells it, is an eating violation; God sets a limit—the humans may take food from any tree except one—and they override that limit. The Eden story underscores the point made already in the creation account: the way we get our food lies at the heart of our relationship with God. Therefore eating against the design of creation is the first step in turning away from God.

In eating against God's express command, the first humans are refusing to be the creatures of God. As far as we know, we are the only species capable of that refusal. A muskrat cannot refuse to be the muskrat-creature she is, but we can in a real sense refuse to be the creatures God made us to be. In the past century, largely through the catastrophic agricultural practices of industrial culture, we have done so to an extent that the earth can no longer bear.

I realize that this is not a typical topic for the pulpit. But it is a necessary one. We need to read our cultural situation by the light of Scripture in order to see just where we are, and even more, to lay hold of realistic hope. A scripturally and scientifically informed reading of our situation indicates that it is bad, but not yet hopeless. As we have seen, Genesis begins with the hopeful charge that we humans might by God's grace take note of the biological integrity of the world and preserve it by our actions. That view of the human role in the world is reinforced by another radically ecological view of creation, at nearly the opposite end of the Bible: the letter to the Colossians calls us to stand firm in "the gospel that was preached to every creature under heaven" (Col. 1:23). "The gospel that was preached to every creature under heaven"—now consider the scope of that vision of the gospel, which is preached this very Sunday in the hearing, not of *Homo sapiens* only, but of monkeys and hardwood forests, of mighty rivers and earthworms and microbes. The gospel of Jesus Christ, the One in whom and through whom and for whom all things were created, is preached to and for every one of us.

What that means is that we can hear the whole truth of the gospel only in

2. James Gustave Speth, *The Bridge at the End of the World* (New Haven: Yale University Press, 2008), 36.

the full company of creatures. We can hear the gospel truth only if we listen to it as creatures, among other creatures. But if the art of being creatures is now a nearly lost art,[3] if we have forgotten how to be creatures, then how can we learn again, so that our ears may be opened to the truth and realistic hope of the gospel?

Being a creature means eating within the limits that God has set in the design of creation. And so the most hopeful task for us is to learn all over again how to eat, within the limits of our fertile, yet fragile and compromised, planet. The genuinely hopeful news is that better choices about eating are becoming more widely available to us, better choices than many of us have had in a lifetime. Here in this area, there are community gardens and, increasingly, church gardens. Urban gardens grow in formerly derelict lots, providing skills-training for youth and nutritious food for the poor. Through farmers' markets and membership farms we can personally support farmers who treat their land not as an industrial site but as a home for people and other living things. Nationally, there is work on a fifty-year farm bill (not a five-year farm bill) that directly addresses erosion, toxic pollution, and the destruction of rural communities.

These are partial solutions, of course. Creating a global food economy that is adequate for the long term will not be done by any quick or easy fix. The current moment is frightening, as we awaken from our long slumber about our destructive ways of eating, for we are awakening to widespread damage and serious danger. But the good news is that we—probably all of us here today—now have opportunities to eat in response to the gospel that was preached to every creature under heaven. A fuller response may be as close to us as our next meal; it should be as routine as filling our dinner plates. It must become so, in order that our grandchildren and their children may live in a lovely fertile world, and God may be glorified in our eating.

Amen.

---

3. See Rowan Williams, "On Being Creatures," in *On Christian Theology* (Oxford: Blackwell, 2000), 63-78.

Radical Trust

Duke Chapel, Durham, North Carolina
June 26, 2011

GENESIS 22

Drawing on the interpretation of Holocaust survivor Eliezer Berkovits,
this sermon attends to the complex interweaving of terror and trust that
lies at the heart of this unique and formidable passage.

A thought experiment: If they had asked me to edit the Bible (whoever "they" might be—perhaps the Holy Spirit, or the heavenly Council on Divinely Inspired Works) . . . if they had made me the original editor of the Bible, I would have made some substantial changes, and the very first change would have been to get rid of the twenty-second chapter of Genesis, the story of the near-sacrifice of Isaac. "It's way too off-putting," I would have argued. "Just listen to this: *And God said, Take your son, your only son, the one you love, Isaac, and take him to some as yet unspecified place, and offer him there as a burnt offering.* This is exactly the kind of story that gives the Old Testament a bad name," I would have said. "It gives God a bad name. If you put this story just twenty-two chapters into the Bible, who is going to read the rest? Even if the story is true, who would want to believe in a God like this?"

Mine is a commonsense argument, which must have occurred to countless sensible people through the ages. Certainly the literary and theological geniuses who put together the book of Genesis must have considered this argument, and dismissed it. Raising my sights, I imagine making my argument to the heavenly Council on Divinely Inspired Works, and after they had listened politely, they would tell me that I had completely missed the point. The point of this story is *not* to make people want to believe in Abraham's God—who is of course also Jesus's God and Father. Rather, this harrowing story exists to

6

help people who already believe make sense of their most difficult experience, when God seems to take back everything they have ever received at God's hand. In other words, the Holy Spirit and the heavenly Council would tell me, the point is not to draw people in but rather to help people who are already in stay in, stay in relationship with the one true God, even when their world turns upside down.

This story appears front and center in Genesis, where no reader of the Bible can miss it, because the hard truth is that the world turns upside down for the faithful, more often than we like to admit. I remember the words of my young friend, a devout Roman Catholic, just a few hours after his first child had died in birth, strangled in her umbilical cord, "I could say, Why me? But why not me? I knew this happens to people, and it never made me doubt God before. So why should I doubt God now? But still, I do not understand."

The twenty-second chapter of Genesis is the place you go when you do not understand at all—Why does God allow us to suffer like this? Are we really expected to bear this?—and the last thing you want is a reasonable explanation, because any reasonable explanation would be a mockery of your anguish. This story of Abraham and God and Isaac is the place you go when you are out beyond anything you thought could or would happen, beyond anything you imagined God would ever ask of you, when the most sensible thing to do might be to deny that God exists at all, or deny that God cares at all, or deny that God has any power at all. That would be sensible, except you can't do it, because you are so deep into relationship with God that to deny all that would be to deny your own heart and soul and mind. To deny God any meaningful place in your life would be to deny your own existence. And so you are stuck with your pain and your incomprehension, and the only way to move at all is to move toward God, to move more deeply into this relationship that we call faith. That is what Abraham does: without comprehension, nearly blinded by the horror of what he has been told to do, Abraham follows God's lead, for the simple and sufficient reason that it is God who is leading—to what end, Abraham has no idea.

It is quite common for theologians to hold up Abraham as a model of unquestioning obedience to God, but I think this is misleading and possibly even damaging to Abraham's character. After all, obedience is a virtue only if it serves a just cause. Obedience in service of an unjust cause is servile, cowardly, even criminal; that we learned definitively from Nuremberg and, in our own country, from the My Lai massacre. If it is purely out of obedience that Abraham submits to God's command, then his willingness to submit is monstrous. But there is another option. What if Abraham follows God's command, not out of obedience, but out of faith—which is to say, what if Abraham *trusts* God, even now, when what God asks of him seems to run counter to everything God has promised? (For the child Abraham is called to sacrifice is the child through whom God's promise of blessing is meant to unfold.)

It is trust, not obedience, that binds Abraham to God; this is something I learned from the great twentieth-century Jewish theologian Eliezer Berkovits, who is one of the leading thinkers in Jewish theology after the Holocaust. In his probing and wrenching book *With God in Hell,* Berkovits asks this question: Why did so many Jews keep their faith in the ghettos and the Nazi death-camps? Why did they gather to say prayers and keep Sabbath, or circumcise their children as a sign of the covenant, even as the SS literally beat down the door? Why did they keep blessing God as the Holy One of Israel, instead of cursing the God who seemed to have abandoned the Jews?

As he puzzles over this question, Berkovits turns to this story of Abraham, and what he discovers is the bottomless trust that holds Abraham together with God. Here is what Berkovits imagines Abraham saying to God during those three days of hell, as he follows God to Moriah, the place of unspeakable sacrifice:

> In this situation I do not understand You. Your behavior violates our covenant; still, I trust You because it is You, because it is You and me, because it is us. . . .
>
> Almighty God! What you are asking of me is terrible. . . . But I have known You, my God. You have loved me and I love You. My God, you are breaking Your word to me. . . . Yet, I trust You; I trust You.[1]

What Berkovits shows, better than anyone I know, is how intimate is the relationship between God and Abraham. Abraham is with God in hell, the way two long- and well-married people are together in the worst moments of the life they share. The marriage metaphor is apt, because Isaac is the child of this union between God and Abraham, the miraculous child of the promise of blessing and offspring. And in the strangest of all paradoxes, that is why Abraham is ready to do what God asks, even to the point of taking a knife to his child. Abraham trusts God totally with the life of the child they share, the life that God has given. In the midst of this life-shattering thing that he does not understand at all, Abraham knows only this: life and life with God are

---

1. Eliezer Berkovits, *With God in Hell: Judaism in the Ghettos and Deathcamps* (New York: Sanhedrin, 1979), 124.

the same thing. Like the Jews who risked their lives to observe Sabbath in the deathcamps or to circumcise children in the ghetto, Abraham is incapable of choosing survival—even his child's survival—over life with God. For better, for worse, it is simply too late for him to live apart from God.

Total, radical trust—this is the only thing that makes any sense of Abraham's submission to God. But still you have to ask, Is God trustworthy? What kind of God would submit Abraham to this appalling "test," as our story calls it? There are just two possible answers, and both are difficult. One answer is a sadistic deity who takes pleasure in human pain, but that answer is biblically impossible. If God is a sadist, then the rest of the Bible is a lie, and so is everything we say and sing here in this chapel.

And so I am forced to choose the only alternative: God calls for this test because God needs to know, desperately needs to know whether Abraham is completely devoted to God. It is theologically unconventional to say that God Almighty needs to know something God does not already know, but that is the clear logic of this test. Remember, Abraham is the person on whom God has chosen to rely completely. After the flood, when God almost gave up on humanity, after we had filled the whole world with violence, God decided to move forward in relationship with the world, but on this condition: from now on, Abraham and his seed will be the one channel for the dissemination of God's blessing. Abraham is like a prism: he focuses God's blessing and then spreads it through the world like a rainbow stream of light.

So now we see: God has staked everything on Abraham, even the whole world. Yet there is serious reason to doubt that Abraham has staked everything on God. Abraham and God have been in relationship for decades now—it is already a long marriage—and there are signs that Abraham still does not totally trust God, that he is still looking out for his own interest. You might remember those stories of Abraham passing off his beautiful wife Sarah as his sister, when they are traveling in foreign territory. So Sarah gets taken into the royal harem as a concubine—not once but twice (Gen. 12:10–20 and ch. 20), and Abraham gets protected status as her "brother." God never told Abraham to do that. He did it because he was scared; he might get killed if someone wanted Sarah, knowing she was his wife. Abraham put Sarah in that terrible situation because he did not trust God to pull them through the danger.

Abraham's lack of trust puts God in a terrible situation, too. Look, God is counting entirely on Abraham as the channel for overcoming evil in our world with divine blessing. But if Abraham does not entirely trust God, then all hope is lost. If Abraham tries to secure his own well-being *apart from God,* if he holds back anything, even his beloved child, and tries to protect him *from*

God, then it would be better if the world had never been made. That is what this test is about: trust, the delicate yet potentially durable link between God and ourselves, on which everything, even the whole world, depends.

Placed front and center in the Bible, this story makes it clear that the thing we call faith is not in the first instance a matter of what we *think* about God, any more than a good marriage or our deepest friendships are held together by what we think about the other. No, in every case the relationship endures only because two hearts are bound together through mutual trust. And trust is of course the very opposite of compulsion. Trust is how you relate to others when you don't try to control them by force or manipulation. The astonishing truth this story reveals is that God chooses to relate to the world not by compulsion but by trust. Yet trust is inherently a condition of vulnerability. You can be disappointed by the one you trust, and deeply, deeply hurt. God's own trust makes God vulnerable; God is "grieved to the heart" by human evil, as the flood story in Genesis tells us (Gen. 6:6). We do not often think of God as needing to be courageous, yet it must take courage for God to stay in relationship with the world, as it takes courage for each of us to stay in relationship with God. We have already experienced grievous disappointment, and we know that more pain lies ahead, in ways we dare not and should not try to imagine. Everyone and everything we love in this world is passing away, later or sooner, we do not know.

Now you have to ask, What kind of way is this for God to run the world—a way that is inevitably fraught with so much disappointment and pain on both sides? And the answer is: This is the way of love, for mutual trust is the only environment in which love is wholly free to act. We know this from the earliest intimacy, the relationship between parent and child. Trust is the only environment in which love is wholly free to act for our good. It is the same way in the relationship between the divine Parent and the Son. The absolute trust between God and Jesus is the environment in which divine Love is wholly free to act for the good of the world. The God who is wholly Love chooses to trust us, so that the fullness of divine power may be unleashed to work through the lives of those who trust God wholly. This is what we see in Jesus's cross, death, and resurrection: trusting love that suffers on both sides; and, working through that love, God's boundless power to save. As Christians have always seen, there is a storyline that runs straight from Abraham, Isaac, and God at Moriah, to the cross and resurrection; it is the story of trusting Love on which the whole world depends.

Caution: relationship with the real God, the God of Abraham and Jesus, is not for the risk-averse. The book of Genesis puts it to us straight: sometimes being in relationship with the real God hurts like hell. Sometimes it's bewildering; we'll be inching along in the dark, with no vision of where this relationship is taking us. But the gospel also puts it to us straight: it is taking us to the cross, and on to resurrection. It is taking us straight into the arms of God. The paradox of risky faith delivering us into the arms of God—that is the paradox at which artist Margaret Adams Parker hints in the print on the front of your bulletin. See, Abraham has one hand behind his back, holding the knife—but the other he stretches out as if to caress his bound child, curled up as though asleep on the cloth his father laid down to protect him from the rough wood. And above them both we see what Abraham does not see: the angel stretching out strong protective hands to enfold them. It is a picture of a child's radical trust, a parent's aching yet indomitable love, and the divine Love that will not let us go—ever, not ever. You can put your trust in that.

Amen.

What Does Moses Do?

St. David's Episcopal Church, Friday Harbor, Washington
March 7, 2010

EXODUS 3:1–15

This sermon on Moses's faithful response to God explores multiple facets
of the story of the burning bush, revealing at each point how demanding
an encounter with the divine presence can be.

Do you remember those bracelets kids used to wear: WWJD ("What would Jesus do?")? Even as an adult, I found the implications of that question overwhelming—comparing one's conduct to that of the Word made flesh. "What would Jesus do?" It's a good question, I suppose, as long as you don't forget that the Bible offers us more attainable models of holiness: flawed people more or less like ourselves, who still manage to draw close to God and serve God well. And of all those fairly ordinary models of holiness in the Bible, Moses is the first among equals. We know more about him than about anyone except Jesus himself; the long, detailed, and really interesting story of Moses from birth to death stretches over four whole books. The fact that we know his words and actions in such detail suggests to me this measure for our behavior: WDMD? What does Moses do?

What does Moses do? This is a good thing to think about during Lent, when we are trying to adjust our behavior, in ways however small, so that we too may come closer to God. And our lesson this morning gives us the best place to start: at the beginning of the long, intimate relationship between Moses and God. That relationship will last for forty years; and, like all intimate relationships of long duration, it will have its stresses and strains, especially when it comes to sharing responsibility for the children—the children of Israel, that is. Sometimes Moses and God sound like an old married couple, bickering about the kids. They won't ever give up on each other, but you cannot always tell that from the way God and Moses argue.

However, our story today takes us to the moment when the spark of intimacy first gets ignited between them, at the burning bush. Notice, this story does *not* begin with Moses out in the desert seeking God. He is just tending his sheep, out in the middle of nowhere, and then God makes a play for Moses's attention, so to speak: flaming in that bush without burning it up. And the way Moses responds must be pleasing to God, who then strikes up a conversation and . . . well, the rest is biblical history. So let's look at the story from the angle of Moses's response: *What does Moses do* that draws God into lasting relationship with him?

I see three things here.

First, *Moses turns aside* from his regular business to see what God is up to: "I must turn aside and see this great sight. Why does the bush not burn up?" (Exod. 3:3). That is the signal God was looking for, as the narrator implies: "And when God saw that [Moses] had turned aside to see, *then* God called out to him" (v. 4). What God sees in Moses, it would seem, is someone who has enough healthy curiosity and imagination to set aside his usual business—tending sheep—and let himself be distracted by what God is doing.

In fact, this is not the first time Moses has set aside business as usual for something that turns out to be the business of God. As soon as Moses had grown up, an earlier story tells us, this adopted grandson of Pharaoh left the palace. He went out to where his fellow Hebrews, the slaves, were laboring, "and he looked upon their burdens" (Exod. 2:11). He saw their burdens and something more, an Egyptian beating a Hebrew slave, and you remember what happens: Moses kills the Egyptian to save his brother. That episode is the end of Moses Prince of Egypt. Suddenly Pharaoh recognizes him as an enemy inside the palace, a Hebrew sympathizer, and Moses has to flee for his life. From that story we learn that God and Moses have something in common: they see the affliction of the weak, and they do something about it, even if it costs them a lot. In the end, it costs Moses and God everything to deliver the weak from their suffering. The book of Exodus is the beginning of the Bible's long story of God's work of deliverance and of how God gets help from flawed but nonetheless holy people who share God's costly compassion. So here, just at the beginning of God's work of deliverance, we see one important thing that attracts God to this man in particular: Moses "turns aside"; he sets aside his ordinary work to see the work of God.

WDMD—What does Moses do? A second thing: *he wonders.* "Why does the bush burn and burn yet not burn up?" Moses wonders.

You at St. David's know how important it is to wonder about the things of God. Every Sunday your children engage in "Godly Play," and the essence of that wonder-full program is wondering out loud, just as Moses does in this story. Godly Play may be the best form of biblical education I know for people of any age (I do it with my adult divinity school students), because it gives us all the chance and the freedom to wonder out loud about why things happen as they do: Why is it this way in God's story, and not that way?

That is the most religiously significant thing we do in our lives: wonder about God and the story of God's ways with us. Godly Play does not even try to come up with the one right answer to every question we might ask. But by encouraging us to ask questions about the ways of God, Godly Play, like the Bible itself, honors this truth: it is by our imagination more than anything else that we stretch our minds and hearts toward God. A good answer to a question about God is one that stretches your imagination toward God.

There is an ancient story about a man who wondered about the burning bush: "Why," he asked, "why did [God] speak to Moses out of a thornbush?" He brought his question to a great rabbi, who offered him one possible answer: "To teach you that there is no space free of the divine presence, not even a thornbush."[1]

That is an answer with some stretch to it: there is no space free of the divine presence. Certainly this island [San Juan Island] is not free of God's presence—I know that is why some of you have chosen to live here. Especially in this season of Lent, it is good to notice how the divine presence is felt in the places where we find ourselves physically, and also in the places where we find ourselves going in our prayers. How is God's presence felt

> . . . in your kitchen or your garden, your workshop or your office?
> . . . in your favorite chair, where you read and pray, think and dream, and
>   sometimes feel your pain?

How is God's presence felt

> . . . in the room where your child is sleeping, or where someone you love
>   lies ill?
> . . . in the place where someone else may lie dying, alone and unloved?

---

1. Nahum N. Glatzer, ed., *Hammer on the Rock: A Short Midrash Reader* (New York: Schocken Books, 1962), 36.

Can we feel the reality of God's presence in those places? Through our prayers and actions, can we make God's presence real for others? "There is no space free of the divine presence, not even a thornbush."

WDMD—What does Moses do? First, he turns aside from his business to pay attention to God's business; and second, he wonders about God. There is a third thing, and this is the most difficult: *Moses gives his life over to the mystery of God.* Moses lets himself be claimed by a God he hardly knows, whose purposes he only begins to understand. God sends Moses back to Egypt, to bring the Israelites out, and Moses naturally wants to have God's name backing him up: "They're going to ask for your name. What should I tell them?" And God gives Moses that famous non-answer: "I am who I am." *Ehieh asher ehieh.* You could translate that, "I will be who I will be. Tell the Israelites, 'I will be' has sent me to you" (Exod. 3:14). I'm sure Moses thought, "Oh great," but in fact that non-answer has a lot of truth to it. "I will be whoever I will be"—thus God declines to be packaged for neat consumption by Moses or anyone else, anyone who is eager to put a label on God and market the product, as religious professionals are perennially fond of doing (and there were plenty of religious professionals in the biblical world, just as in our own). "I will be who I will be"—that divine non-answer should make us wary of ourselves when we are too sure of what God is doing, especially what God is doing in the lives of those whom we oppose or despise—as when Pat Robertson explained that the earthquake in Haiti was divine punishment for those who had supposedly made a pact with the devil. Robertson is a broad and easy target, but probably we all can think of some group within the church whose view of what God is doing we abhor, whose view on church order and politics we consider hopelessly benighted. That kind of certainty, on both the right and the left, currently threatens the existence of the Anglican Communion as a global church.

But the God who burns in the thornbush mocks all such certainties: "I will be who I will be." The true measure of Moses's holiness is that he accepts the challenge offered by this unpredictable and never fully comprehensible God, and he steps into an ever-deepening mystery. Out there in the wilderness, the former Prince of Egypt steps into a world of power more wondrous even than the empire of his grandfather Pharaoh. At the bush that burns but is not consumed, Moses steps into the kingdom of God.

The kingdom of God is a vast territory stretching out on both sides of death; this is the territory that the Bible charts for us. The Bible is a sort of map, a fantastically detailed, multidimensional map of the kingdom of God, seen from every angle from which we can view it on this side of death. If we use the map for our exploration, and use it well, then gradually we will draw closer to God, and God will have some companionship in this world. That is what the Bible is for: to make us good companions for God.

To be a competent explorer of the kingdom of God, you don't need to be a card-carrying saint, but you do need some imagination, and also the capacity to be surprised by what God is up to. We need that capacity all our life long, from childhood to adulthood and into old age—especially in old age, because cultivating the capacity to be surprised by God is how we prepare for our own deaths; and preparing for death has traditionally been part of the work of each Christian during Lent. Maybe that is why we read the story of the burning bush in Lent, because death will be the burning bush for each of us, the point of entry into the fuller mystery of God. A dear friend said this to me, a year or so after the death of her husband: "I have seen just enough to wonder more. I don't know what life will be like on the other side of death, but I am sure of this: When I get there I will say, 'I had no idea . . .'"

WDMD—What does Moses do, and how does he offer us a model for holiness?

- He turns aside from business as usual to share the concerns and compassion of God.
- He opens himself in wonder to what God is doing.
- He enters deeply and fearlessly into the mystery of God.

May we too learn these ways of holiness, so that with Moses and all the saints we may become good companions for God.

Amen.

Witnessing to God in the Midst of Life:
Old Testament Preaching

....

ESSAY

Old Testament preaching was nonexistent in my childhood experience of the Episcopal Church in the United States, where Old Testament "lessons" (a term with unfortunate moralistic overtones) were heard no more than a few times a year. Happily, lectionary revisions have changed that, but preaching habits among North American Anglicans appear to be much the same. Moreover, reports I hear from the field indicate that, in this respect, there is little difference among the so-called mainstream denominations, or between them and churches that self-identify as nondenominational or evangelical. Robust Old Testament preaching remains a rarity.

A recent comment from one of my students gave me fresh insight into what may account for this. About halfway through a year-long course on Old Testament interpretation, Amanda, a young ordinand, came to me with a problem: "I'm having a hard time figuring out how I could preach from the Old Testament. My pastor preaches from the New Testament; he sets forth a passage as representing an ideal and then tries to show us how to live into it. But I don't see how that would work with most of the Old Testament." When she put it that way, I could see why she was having difficulty. That understanding of the preacher's task may not be completely wrong, and probably it is widely shared among those who preach and those who listen to sermons. Certainly it is more commendable than what I would take to be another common view, namely that the main aim of preaching is to entertain and thus befriend the congregation—a view that precludes any serious engagement with the Bible in either Testament.

Nonetheless, the understanding that biblical texts should be seen or preached chiefly as representing ideals seems to me somewhat misleading, and

17

therefore the goal of getting people to live into such ideals is almost certainly doomed to failure, for both preacher and hearer. I am convinced that the Bible in both Testaments is not idealistic at all. Rather, it is rigorously realistic with respect to human character and all the various conditions and contingencies of human life, and above all life with God as we experience it in this world. The Old Testament spends few words and less imaginative energy on depicting "paradise," "heaven," or whatever we might call the ideal. (I suspect that the situation for the New Testament is only marginally different, although that argument exceeds my brief here.)

Among modern Christian theologians, Dietrich Bonhoeffer may be the one who has focused most perceptively on the realism of the Old Testament as what makes it indispensable to Christians aspiring to spiritual maturity—a desirable and attainable goal that every preacher should seek to advance, with every sermon. The letters Bonhoeffer wrote as a political prisoner in Tegel (Berlin) show the extent to which he is, in his own words, "thinking and perceiving things in line with the Old Testament," as a foundation for a proper understanding of the language and promises of the gospel:

> Only when one loves life and the earth so much that with it everything seems to be lost and at its end may one believe in the resurrection of the dead and a new world. Only when one accepts the law of God as binding for oneself may one perhaps sometimes speak of grace. And only when the wrath and vengeance of God against God's enemies are allowed to stand can something of forgiveness and the love of enemies touch our hearts. Whoever wishes to be and perceive things too quickly and too directly in New Testament ways is to my mind no Christian.[1]

This memorable crescendo, with its astonishing conclusion, articulates the truth that the Christian faith is too readily "spiritualized." In every age, from antiquity to postmodernity, proclamation of the faith has often been disconnected from a serious reckoning with the limitations and relationships, formative and sometimes painful, which are inevitably part of our material and social existence. As Bonhoeffer sees, such a spiritualized Christianity is more fantasy than faith. By contrast, the Old Testament "bars the way to all escapism in the guise of piety," since it consistently represents "God [as] the beyond in

---

1. Dietrich Bonhoeffer, letter to Eberhard Bethge, December 5, 1943, in *Letters and Papers from Prison*, in *Dietrich Bonhoeffer Works*, vol. 8 (Minneapolis: Fortress, 2010), 213.

the midst of our lives."[2] Therefore a genuinely Christian "this-worldliness" means "living fully in the midst of life's tasks, questions, successes and failures, experiences, and perplexities." It is in such a life that "one throws oneself completely into the arms of God."[3]

Although Bonhoeffer is not here reflecting on preaching, his remarks point to the best reason to preach frequently from the Old Testament: it offers an incomparable vehicle for witnessing to God in the midst of life, in circumstances that are much less than ideal. Thus preachers may develop and offer a moral vision—not a "lesson"!—that is faithful and may be compelling, precisely because it is not false in its simplicity. In what follows I focus on two aspects of a vast topic, preaching Old Testament characters and preaching psalms, because I enjoy doing both. Moreover, the opportunities are abundant; even preachers whose choices are generally determined by a lectionary encounter one if not both options on a weekly basis.

Preaching Biblical Characters

The best justification for preaching Old Testament characters is simply that we know a lot about them—the major characters and many of the minor ones—because they are drawn with such striking clarity. For this reason, I know of no better place to begin than with Moses, who is of course the most developed, and his representation shapes those of other characters to follow, including Elijah, Jeremiah, and Jesus. One reason I preach on Moses to my divinity school students is that his story gives much-needed theological content to our understanding of "leadership." Yet Moses is for everyone; probably no other story has so much to teach us about what an intimate, long-term relationship with God may look like, for better and for worse. In other words, his story speaks about the long road to spiritual maturity.

A baby floating in a basket on a river sounds to us like a fairy tale; in its own ancient Near Eastern setting, it echoes the birth story of the legendary Mesopotamian king Sargon the Great, from the third millennium BCE, a story already ancient by the time the Bible was written. Characters in fairy tales and royal legends are generally static; we might derive a "lesson" from their two-

---

2. Letter to Eberhard Bethge, April 30, 1944, in *Letters and Papers from Prison*, 367.

3. Letter to Eberhard Bethge, July 21, 1944, in *Letters and Papers from Prison*, 485. This letter was written the day following the failed coup attempt that Bonhoeffer had helped to plan although he did not yet know the outcome.

dimensional stories, but we are not drawn into them in any deep way. Royal legends do not preach. It is different with Moses's story; many of the events are on a larger-than-life scale, yet because his character is recognizable to us, we can enter into the ways he struggles with God, with members of his own community, and with his own weaknesses.

The very first scene of the young man Moses reveals a crucial aspect of his character: he sees (the Hebrew word *ra'ah*, "see," is extremely common in these first few chapters of Exodus) what others do not see, and especially the suffering of others. As we shall learn at the burning bush, the ability to see what others suffer and the inability to ignore it is the single most important characteristic that Moses shares with God (see Exod. 3:7). On his first reported excursion outside Pharaoh's palace, Moses "looks upon" (*ra'ah b-*) the burdens of the Hebrew slaves (Exod. 2:11); the verbal phrase denotes an experience of seeing that is deep enough to have consequences. Thus, when he "sees" an Egyptian beating one of his "brothers" (whether or not Moses knows of their kinship), he strikes and kills—and that marks the end of the Prince of Egypt. Moses has "fallen," we might say, out of the realm of royal legend and into the world of anguish, hardship, and rejection, the real world that biblical narrative treats.

If there is any one thing that definitively stamps Moses's life story with the feeling of reality rather than legend, it is his failure to enter the Promised Land with the people for whom he has spent himself over forty years, interceding for them time and again, sometimes arguing with God as two parents might argue over their deeply disappointing children. Exactly why Moses has to die short of the Land is not as clear as we might like—and that in itself is part of the aura of reality here; that sad outcome is not quickly moralized. The Deuteronomic tradition says that it was on account of Israel's sin that Moses was held back (Deut. 4:21), making this the first biblical instance of vicarious suffering unto death on behalf of the people. There may even be some truth to Kafka's observation that Moses suffers this most bitter disappointment simply because he is human, and to be human is to inhabit a world that does not match our dreams and desires.[4]

Yet the Priestly account of Moses's action at Kadesh suggests a different reason, one that seems to me critical for understanding the temptations and the costs that attend leadership in any religious community. In that waterless place, God had commanded Moses and Aaron to speak to a certain rock

4. See Gabriel Josipovici, *The Book of God: A Response to the Bible* (New Haven: Yale University Press, 1988), 194.

before the people, and it would yield its water. However, the only speech recorded is when Moses says to the people, "Shall we bring forth water for you from this rock?" (Num. 20:10). As the great rabbinic commentator Rashi observes, he was just one letter off; he should have said, "He"—God—not "we."[5] Is it possible that, after all this time, Moses has come to think, at least in this moment of extreme pressure, that the people's survival depends ultimately upon him? God's response is swift and unyielding: "Because you did not show faith in me so as to sanctify me in the eyes of the Israelites, therefore you shall not bring this congregation into the land that I have given them" (v. 12). By "speaking rashly" out of an embittered spirit, as the psalmist describes this moment (Ps. 106:33), Moses becomes an obstruction and danger to the people he is meant to bring, not just to the land of Canaan, but to God. With that, his own fate is sealed, although Moses's work and words continue; his death outside the land does not occur for some fifty more chapters (Deut. 34:4–5).

Living closely enough with Moses's story to preach and teach it faithfully, all the way to the sobering yet not hopeless end, would be a significant step toward realism and maturity in the life of any worshiping community, including its leadership. "The church cannot make the difficulty of reality less difficult," states Stanley Hauerwas. "What I hope . . . the church can do is help us bear the difficulty without engaging in false hopes."[6] Patient, truthful engagement with the biblical story may well be the single best way for Christians to gain that kind of spiritual strength, and some of the most helpful parts of the story may well be those that are not obviously encouraging.

I once preached on the prophet Jeremiah at an ordination.[7] While Jeremiah's call narrative is specifically given as an option for ordinations in the American *Book of Common Prayer,* it is in some ways an odd choice, since Jeremiah had probably the least enviable ministry of any prophet: forty years of futile warnings and summons to repentance, of intercessions for the people and laments over his own desperate situation, and all that ending in the destruction of Jerusalem and Judah. Nonetheless, the choice is justified, because more explicitly than anyone else in the Bible except Jesus, Jeremiah shows us what it is to live solely on the strength of God's word. God says to him, "Look, I put my words in your mouth" (Jer. 1:9). And Jeremiah tells us just how that

---

5. The difference in the Hebrew verb would be just one letter: *notsi'* vs. *yotsi'*.

6. Stanley Hauerwas, "Bearing Reality: A Christian Meditation," *Journal of the Society for Christian Ethics* 33, no. 1 (2013): 3–20, at 17.

7. See "Swallowing Fire," pp. 204–8 below.

feels: like swallowing fire and feeling it burn until he can no longer hold it in (20:9), or swallowing a hammer that pounds inside, hard enough to shatter rock (23:29). Yet for all that, Jeremiah remains the true friend of God, never growing cold or indifferent. On the contrary, he burns hot, even against God, yet he never burns out. What distinguishes Jeremiah from the masses of burnt-out ministers, lay and ordained, in the church is that he never tries to fuel his ministry with his own vision, enthusiasm, and creativity, with the clever answers he has devised to the conundrums of life. God's word is the only source of power behind every word the prophet utters and everything he does, and his spiritual courage is demonstrated as he opens himself repeatedly to that word, through decades of unimaginably difficult ministry.

After I had preached, a priest expressed disappointment in a message he took to be dispiriting: "I just wish you had spoken about Jesus." Someone else had a different response: "I was ordained earlier this year. If you had preached that at my ordination, I would have had no idea what you were talking about. But now I can tell you it is the most helpful thing I have heard in these nine months." If listening deeply to Jeremiah comes as a relief to some Christians, perhaps that is because he models what it is to hold together in one "heart" (one of Jeremiah's own favorite words) acute suffering, outrage over undeserved suffering, and unshakable faith in God. Indeed, in him we glimpse the truth that faithful suffering is itself participation in the life of God in this world. "Sharing in God's suffering in the worldly life" is what "makes someone a Christian," declares Bonhoeffer, whose own sense of vocation was profoundly shaped by Jeremiah's witness.[8] "That is *metanoia*"—a profound change of mind.[9]

Recently I saw Jeremiah's prophetic witness work a change of mind in one accomplished and highly successful preacher. I had spoken about Jeremiah's "art of lament" to a group of experienced clergy, suggesting that it is our responsibility as preachers and teachers to help other Christians become more adept at a mode of speech that is common in the Bible, though not in contemporary church culture. One of them, the senior pastor of a church with some 19,000 members, protested that people in his church find it a relief to get away from their troubles for a little while, via worship at 97 decibels. I did not attempt to persuade him otherwise, so I was surprised when he took the initiative to reopen the subject before the whole class the next day: "I thought

8. On Bonhoeffer's identification with Jeremiah, see Eberhard Bethge, *Dietrich Bonhoeffer: Man of Vision, Man of Courage* (New York: Harper & Row, 1970), 82–83, 273–74.
9. Letter to Eberhard Bethge, July 18, 1944, in *Letters and Papers from Prison*, 480.

and blogged about it last night, and I realize that I have been withholding something from my people, because I didn't want to deal with their pain, or even my own. But I am depriving us all of genuine comfort. So this has to change." It took courage to say that before a group of peers to whom he would be accountable over a period of two years or more. It was the witness of Scripture that exerted coercion on this biblically centered preacher, pressuring him to change his mind.

Preaching the Psalms

Turning now to a second aspect of Old Testament preaching, I confess my bias at the outset: were I to be confined to a desert-island pulpit with only one book of the Bible, it would be the Psalms. I preach from it more often than from any other book, and not only because psalms are recited in virtually every worship service I attend. That only points to the deeper reason to preach them frequently, namely, that as a resource of theology, prayer, and pastoral care, the Psalter is inexhaustible; not for nothing did Martin Luther speak of it as a Bible in miniature. Yet psalms do something that other biblical texts do not: they speak directly for us in the presence of God. As prayers (or, in some cases, calls to prayer and meditations on prayer) that are themselves scriptural, they instruct us when we do not know how to pray as we ought. Luther describes their distinctive witness thus:

> Thus the Psalter lays before us . . . [the saints'] very hearts and the inmost treasure of their souls, so we can look down to the foundation and source of their words and deeds. We can look into their hearts and see what kind of thoughts they had, how their hearts were disposed, and how they acted in all kinds of situations, in danger and in need.[10]

Even for contemporary preachers who may not share Luther's view that many of the psalms were written by David and other biblical "saints," they make accessible to us the world of thought and feeling that is the biblical story. They lend themselves to preaching, just because so many psalms are formulated as first-person speech and thus make a ready connection with our

---

10. Martin Luther's *Preface to the Psalter* (1528/1545), in Martin Luther, *Faith and Freedom: An Invitation to the Writings of Martin Luther,* ed. John F. Thornton and Susan B. Varenne (New York: Random House, 2002), 26.

experience. John Calvin, one of the greatest pastoral preachers of the Psalter, treasured it as "An Anatomy of all the Parts of the Soul," drawn "to the life" by the Holy Spirit and revealing "all the griefs, sorrows, fears, doubts, hopes, cares, perplexities"—in short, every disposition of the heart, with the blessed exception of hypocrisy![11]

Great preachers of virtually every age—among them Augustine, Chrysostom, John Donne, and Bonhoeffer, as well as Luther and Calvin—have often expressed a particular affinity for the Psalter, and many of their sermons on this favorite book survive. Yet my experience is that people are often surprised, even mildly shocked, when I choose a psalm as a preaching text. So what has changed to make preaching psalms a foreign practice? I would suggest that the core of the problem may well be that they are poems. As schoolchildren, many of us had negative experiences with poetry—or more accurately, with the tortuous way poetry was taught, so that its energy was lost in pitiless examinations of rhyme and rhythm and expressions that seemed so indirect as to be deliberately antagonizing.

But the psalmist's expression is anything but indirect; this should be heartening to those who might once have been put off by a teacher who would, in Billy Collins's memorable image, beat a poem "with a hose / to find out what it really means."[12] Rather than dwelling on rhythmic patterns, which are obscured by translation anyway, the prospective preacher is well advised to focus on what Murray Lichtenstein insightfully identifies as the "peculiar genius" of biblical poetry, its capacity "for effecting the direct, immediate involvement of its audience in a kind of emotional dialogue." Biblical poetry is essentially "a relational phenomenon. It both derives from interaction and has the marked capacity to generate more of the same."[13] This genius for interaction is most fully evidenced as psalms speak for us, like someone with the gift for prayer, and also to us, like a good pastor or teacher:

> When I call out, answer me, my righteous God.
>   In the straits, you set me free.
>   Have mercy upon me and hear my prayer.

. . . .

11. John Calvin, *Commentary on the Book of Psalms,* trans. James Anderson (Grand Rapids: Eerdmans, 1949), 1:xxxvii.

12. Billy Collins, "Introduction to Poetry," in *The Apple That Astonished Paris* (Fayetteville: University of Arkansas Press, 1988), 58.

13. Murray H. Lichtenstein, "Bible: Biblical Poetry," in *Back to the Sources: Reading the Classic Jewish Texts,* ed. Barry W. Holtz (New York: Summit Books, 1984), 120-21.

In peace, all whole, let me lie down and sleep.
For You, LORD, alone, do set me down safely. (Ps. 4:2, 9 [4:1, 8 Eng.])

Near is the LORD to the broken-hearted,
and the crushed in spirit He rescues.
. . . .
The LORD ransoms His servants' lives,
they will bear no guilt, all who shelter in Him.
(Ps. 34:19, 23 [34:18, 22 Eng.])

Do not fling me from Your presence,
and Your holy spirit take not from me.
Give me back the gladness of Your rescue
and with a noble spirit sustain me. (Ps. 51:13–14 [51:11–12 Eng.])

LORD, save my life from lying lips,
from a tongue of deceit.
What can it give you, what can it add,
a tongue of deceit? (Ps. 120:2–3)

Any pastor or preacher will instantly recognize that there is a drama, or a trauma, underlying each of these passages, which are chosen nearly at random. Taken as a whole, the Psalter bespeaks intense and fluctuating emotions, and many individual psalms testify to the important truth that we can feel and think different things at one time, especially about the things that matter most. "Part of the spiritual greatness of Psalms," as Robert Alter observes, "part of the source of its enduring appeal through the ages, is that it profoundly recognizes the bleakness, the dark terrors, the long nights of despair that shadow most lives, and against all this, evokes the notion of a caring presence that can reach out to the broken-hearted."[14] The verses here I cite from Alter's indispensable recent translation, which renders at exactly the right pitch the Psalter's characteristic emotional vibrancy, yet without loss of dignity and control.

In order to bring hearers fully into the drama in the short space of a sermon, my most frequent approach to a psalm is to focus on a guiding image or emotion, sometimes a single line or phrase, which becomes a point of orientation as I trace through the psalm its shifting moods and developing

14. Robert Alter, *The Book of Psalms: A Translation with Commentary* (New York: W. W. Norton, 2007), 120.

thought. Psalms are characteristically dynamic—another aspect of their relationality, since no genuine relationship is static. Therefore I always preach a whole psalm (Psalm 119 being the one exception!), not the fragments that are often presented in lectionaries and liturgies. I usually request that it be read as a lection, by a skilled reader, so the congregation has a chance to hear the text in a way they likely have not done before.

The first lines of Psalm 27 are very familiar. Taken out of context, as they generally are, they would seem to dismiss the elemental terror to which Alter points:

> The LORD is my light and my salvation: of whom would I be afraid?
> The LORD is my life's strength; whom would I dread? (v. 1)[15]

But read in context, those questions do not seem to be merely rhetorical; the next verse suggests that the psalmist is not dismissing anxiety but rather actively battling against it. Surrounded by enemies ready "to eat my flesh" (v. 2), the psalmist takes a stand:

> If a battalion encamps against me, my heart will not fear.
> If war breaks out against me, in this I am secure. (v. 3)

In just a few lines the psalmist sums up the faith dynamic of the whole Bible and of every person who tries to believe: either we see God as "my life's strength," or we are defeated by a host of fears, until we are finally undone by the fear of death itself. There is no third possibility.

Yet taking a position in battle is not the same as holding it, and if we follow the movement of the psalm we see just how precarious this position is. In one moment, the psalmist is sure that "[God] will hide me in the shelter of his tent" (v. 5); in the next, she pleads:

> Do not hide your face from me!
> . . . Do not forsake me nor abandon me, O God of my deliverance! (v. 9)

That sudden shift from confidence to abject pleading has prompted some modern commentators to propose that two originally separate prayers, a strident lament and a psalm of thanksgiving, have been somewhat awkwardly joined

---

15. The translation of verses of Psalm 27 is my own, as it was read as a lection in the service at which I preached it.

together here. However, a much more plausible perspective comes from Luther's insight into the First Commandment, which, he observes, "claims the two parts of your heart: fear God and trust him."[16] So fear is finally indivisible from faith; certainly this is one of the core spiritual insights of the Old Testament altogether, where "fear of the LORD" is the ordinary term for faith. Our psalmist speaks from both parts of the heart.

Firm faith comes only through battling with our deepest fears, subjecting them and ourselves to rigorous examination: "Do I really need what I am so afraid of losing?" Engaging in that most difficult spiritual task is what brings the psalmist to the point of utter clarity, to naming the one thing that must not be lost—and therefore (as Luther sees) the one thing we can trust God to give us:

> One thing I ask of the LORD; it is what I seek:
> that I may dwell in the LORD's house all the days of my life,
> to gaze upon the loveliness of the LORD and to frequent his sanctuary. (v. 4)

The spiritual sight of God's "face" (v. 8) is the one vision that can lift us out of our small frightened selves, hold us up and give us a life with a view. "On a rock he will lift me high" (v. 5). Whenever any psalmist speaks of "rock," it is likely that "the Rock of Israel," God's protective presence (see Isa. 30:29 and 2 Sam. 23:3; cf. 22:2–3 = Ps. 18:3), is in view. During the Epiphany season, in which this psalm appears in the Revised Common Lectionary, one might see Christ as the Rock on which we are lifted high (see 1 Cor. 10:4); he is God's strong protective presence revealed to all the world.

My understanding of Psalm 27 was first shaped, in the early years of my teaching, by a student who chose this text for an exegesis assignment. He was drawn to a line that most of us would take as simple hyperbole: "Though my father and my mother abandon me, the LORD takes me in" (v. 10). For him, that line was testimony, witness. As a child he had been sexually abused by both parents, and the psalm enabled him both to face the horror of his childhood and to move beyond it, over and over again. His face appears in my mind whenever I hear this line:

> If I were not sure of looking upon the LORD's goodness in the land of the
> living . . . (v. 13)

---

16. Martin Luther, "Ten Sermons on the Catechism" (1528), in *Luther's Works*, vol. 51, ed. and trans. John W. Doberstein (Philadelphia: Fortress, 1959), 139.

The thought remains incomplete even in the context of the psalm. Drawing back from the temptation to imagine even for a moment what it would be to lose hope of seeing God's goodness in this life, the psalmist concludes with a forceful imperative addressed to the psalmist herself as much as to us:

> Hope in the LORD; be strong and let your heart take courage, and hope in the LORD! (v. 14)

The aim of Old Testament preaching, as I understand and try to practice it, is to enter into the biblical story—not just the twists and turns of plot, but also the thoughts and feelings, the kind of faith that informs its manifold witness. The aim is to enter in such a way that both preacher and hearers are sobered or comforted, as the need may be, and all of us are strengthened in our life with God. That does not happen if the preacher merely sets forth ideals with the exhortation to live into them. Such an approach distances preacher from hearers, at the same time as it obscures the bracing yet expansive moral vision of Scripture. Entering into the story world of the Bible is a matter not of resolve but rather of *seeing*, differently and more deeply, and that is why idealistic or moralistic exhortations do not work. Yet we may acquire the habit of this different and consequential way of seeing as we seek out and indeed befriend the deeply human characters of the Old Testament. We may become, as medieval theologians put it, *capax Dei*—capacious enough to receive something of God—as we persistently and even courageously take on our own lips and into our hearts the words of psalmists, words both revealing and revelatory, in such a way as to allow our relationship to God to be changed.

The Manna Economy

Crescent Hill Presbyterian Church, Louisville, Kentucky
July 13, 2010

EXODUS 16

Egypt's economic practices mirror our own, and they call us to reckon with the most destructive food economy in world history. In spite of impending human and environmental catastrophes, we learn how judgment, hope, and a "manna economy" may nourish Israel and the church.

Moving inside the story we just heard from Exodus 16, it is now just six weeks since God brought Israel out of Egypt with a strong hand and an outstretched arm. On that day Israel watched the hand of the Lord pile up the waters of the sea, so Israel passed through on dry ground. Then the divine hand released the walls of water, and they collapsed on Pharaoh's army. All this just six weeks ago, and now . . . what are the Israelites saying? "If only we had died by the hand of the LORD in the land of Egypt, while we were sitting by the stew pots, eating till we were stuffed!" (Exod. 16:3).

That one sentence is enough to tell us what happened to Israel during their generations in Egypt. Slaves though they were, they learned to rely on the deceptive abundance of empire. The fertile Nile Valley was the green miracle of the ancient Near East. The Nile provided food in abundance, and Pharaoh the god-king controlled the Nile—or so he thought. Pharaoh's agricultural agents took in so much food, he needed whole storage-cities to hold the surplus, and slaves to build the storage-cities, Rameses and Pithom. So Israelites built those cities, serving Pharaoh's purposes well enough—that is, until by God's grace Israel, too, prospered from the bounty of the Nile. When the slaves "became fruitful . . . and multiplied" (Exod. 1:7), *then* Pharaoh became frightened. To him they looked like so many "swarmers" (1:7)—insects, reptiles—and so he ground them under a crushing workload and threw their boy-babies into the Nile. Then the people of Israel cried out to God, and God's mighty hand took them out of Egypt.

Who could forget that, the horror and the deliverance? But the ex-slaves did forget. No sooner were they out of Egypt than the Israelites started longing for the slave economy that had been steadily killing them off: "If only we'd died happy, sitting by the stewpots, eating until we were stuffed! For you [Moses and Aaron] have brought us out into this wilderness to kill this whole congregation by starvation!" So now we see that, deep in their hearts, the Israelites had bought into the economic system of Pharaoh's empire, whose basic principle is typical of every empire: namely, maximize profit at the top, get as much as you can, share it with as few as you can, but convince everybody that they somehow benefit from the system. This mode of economic operation is in our news every day.

Now listen to how God responds to Israel's forgetfulness: "Look, I am about to rain down for you bread from heaven, and the people shall go out and collect just enough for each day, so that I may test them, whether they will walk in my Torah (my Teaching) or not" (16:4). With this grace-filled instruction, God begins to outline for Israel a totally different kind of economic system. Interesting: here on the far side of the Red Sea, the very first thing God needs to get straight with Israel is the economics of eating. The manna economy is the precise opposite of the killing economy of empire. Israel gathers manna one day at a time (no storing the stuff; it gets wormy and rotten overnight)— now contrast *that* with Pharaoh's vast cities of grain silos.

The key question, of course, is where we think our food comes from. To the Egyptian slaves, the answer seemed to be that bread came from Pharaoh, who owned all those wheat fields along the Nile and took all the grain into his silos. But the manna economy rests on the nonnegotiable truth that bread comes from God; always and everywhere food is God's gift. That is why the manna economy incorporates within itself the practice of keeping Sabbath, a day for remembering that God is the Creator of heaven and earth (20:11) and thus the source of every good material gift, food included. That is why the Israelites collect a double portion on Friday, and on Sabbath they stay home; they have time for gratitude, time to rest in God's sufficiency. These two simple practices—no hoarding the manna, keeping Sabbath—these are the practical means by which Israel is meant to remember that its life is totally and blessedly dependent on God.

However, the Israelites don't get it. Some of them try to store the manna.

We can sympathize, can't we? They've been slaves; they are living on the edge in the wilderness. Who can blame them for wanting to have a small margin of security? Again, some of them go out to collect on Saturday—just to get a little extra. And God shows zero-tolerance for these infractions. For the first time God becomes angry with the Israelites, really angry: "How long will you refuse to keep my commandments and my teachings?" (16:28). From our perspective, God has tolerated much worse than this: all that whining, even that insulting innuendo of divine malevolence: "You have brought us out here to kill us. . . ." But what pushes God over the edge is Israel's inability or refusal to live by the rules of the manna economy and thus acknowledge that all food is the daily gift of God. If they can't do that, then there will be no deal, no covenant, between God and Israel.

Now, what is at stake for us in this long and detailed story about Israel's ideal food economy? The manna economy is no less confrontational for us than for the Israelites fresh out of Egypt. It may in fact be more confrontational for us than any previous generation, because we are enmeshed, all of us, in a global food economy whose size and power are unprecedented in history, and whose basic principles are exactly opposed to those of the manna economy. The manna economy is governed by actual human need; its rhythms are God-centered, punctuated by Sabbath. By contrast, we get our food via a system of ceaseless industrial-scale production. It is a system of huge rotting surpluses in one place and starvation in another. Everywhere it shows a dangerous disregard for the earth as God's own creation. Across the globe, industrial agriculture is a machine spinning crazily out of control, effecting massive erosion of our land, drastic draining of rivers and underground water supplies, and widespread poisoning of water systems. Some 38 percent of the world's agricultural land is now degraded;[1] soil erosion rates far outpace replacement. We are robbing the future, but let's put a face on that: we are robbing the young, our own children and grandchildren and their children. Damage on this scale will be repaired only in geological time.

We who live in big farming states know from our local news sources, we see with our own eyes, that even now the suffering of land and people and animals is immense, beyond calculation. Farm workers suffer from chemical poisoning, food-factory workers from massive injuries on the ever-accelerating production lines. Factory-farmed animals are psychotic from toxins and confinement; their effluents poison air, water, and perhaps even the crops

---

1. Wes Jackson, "Right Livelihood Award Acceptance Remarks," Stockholm, December 8, 2000.

on which the still-raw manure is too often sprayed. In contrast to the manna economy, in which everyone has enough and no one has too much, this is a system of glut and dearth, in which a few giant multinational corporations get immensely rich, while the vast majority of farmers, in this country and around the world, are driven out of business, off the land, into desperation and increasingly into violence against their families and themselves.

In our present situation, the manna story presses us to consider how we as Christians might assume some responsibility for how we and our culture as a whole eat. If indeed our food economy is part and parcel of our life with God and one another, then the first thing necessary is to learn more about the real cost of our food. Does the food that is cheap at the supermarket or McDonald's entail inhumane treatment of people and animals, permanent loss for the soil, depletion of safe seed and water supplies? Does its chemical history make you nervous about your long-term health, and even more your children's? Will our children look back at this generation and accuse us of reckless waste of their food security?

The book of Exodus tells us that Pharaoh ultimately destroyed his own empire through blind refusal to acknowledge the God who is Creator of all. Through ten devastating plagues, Pharaoh pits his puny and deluded power against the true God, who answers his delusion by turning Egypt's dusty soil into lice and the life-giving waters of the Nile into blood. Pharaoh is a royal fool who uses his power to destroy his own land. After the seventh plague, Pharaoh's courtiers shake their heads in brokenhearted amazement and ask: "Do you not yet know that Egypt is history—it's gone!?" (10:7).

As a member of the reckless generation, I am haunted by those words: "Do you not yet know that Egypt is history?" Do we not yet know that a large swath of the Gulf Coast is history? That some five hundred mountains in Appalachia, along with their creeks and valleys, are history? That the High Plains Aquifer, the Colorado River, countless more rivers and streams are on their way to being history?

So the biblical story condemns us for our grossly destructive practices, and this is terrible news. But the reason for bringing this story into a place of good news, into our worship today, is that it also encourages us, guides us in putting our food production practices on the church's agenda. The Bible asserts repeatedly, starting with the first chapter of Genesis, that eating is part of our life with God. And this manna story gives us permission—more, it gives us a mandate—to bring food into our faith life, to talk, as the people of God, about how we are eating. The principles of the manna economy—take only what you need, remember that all food comes from God—these are to be the permanent principles of every godly economy. That is why, when the Israelites get to the Promised Land of Canaan, a jarful of manna is set in the sanctuary, right in front of the Ark of the Covenant, as a keepsake for all generations. Eating faithfully is the basic covenantal act; indeed, it is the fundamental act of every healthy community. The Bible cares how we get our food, because this is the very first place that justice establishes itself in our lives, or else it departs from us as we eat against the principles of the divine economy.

That simple understanding of food justice underlies these remarkable lines from Psalm 85, the work of a poet who surely comes from the Israelite heartland, knows the social realities of food production, and knows also that, always and everywhere, food comes from God:

> Surely [God's] salvation is near to those who fear him,
> that Glory may dwell in our land.
> . . . .
> Righteousness and peace kiss;
> faithfulness springs up from the earth.
> Yes, the LORD gives what is good,
> and our land yields its bounty. (Ps. 85:9–13)

May it be so for us, in this land and throughout the earth, generation to generation.

Amen.

Beautifying Heaven

Baptism of Aaron Gill, Yale Divinity School, New Haven, Connecticut
May 7, 1996

EXODUS 28:1–4A, 15–23, 28–30, 36–38; JOHN 1:1–18

With its central image of Aaron's exquisite breastplate, this sermon
shows how, in the burnishing light of God, judgment becomes "a horizon
of hope" and a powerful demonstration of the beauty of redemption.
The priestly duty of "wearing one another" before God signifies the true
work of judgment.

Come, people, Aaron is about to be dressed. In a few minutes, Aaron Gill will "put on Christ" (Gal. 3:27; see also Rom. 13:14)—"holy in [his] head, perfect and light in [his] dear breast."[1] Of course, the ceremony itself won't look like much: a little water and oil, some tender mumbling, maybe a shout of protest or sociability from Aaron. You have to listen carefully to the words in order to enter into the riveting drama that is unfolding here, when Aaron is enlisted in the cosmic battle against "Satan and all the spiritual forces of wickedness that rebel against God," when he is initiated into the intimate life of God: "buried with Christ in his death" and "reborn by the Holy Spirit" so that he may "continue for ever in the risen life of Jesus Christ our Savior," as the great poem of the liturgy says.[2] Every line of the baptismal liturgy is fraught with tension and inexhaustible hope. But one of the best lines has already been delivered behind the scene, and it is important for our understanding of what we are doing this evening. Some time ago, a bishop

---

1. George Herbert, "Aaron," in *The Temple* (London: Cassell & Co., 1893), 169 (lines 21–22). This poem was read as a "lesson" in the service.
2. *The Book of Common Prayer* (New York: The Church Hymnal Corporation, 1979), 306.

consecrated the oil with which Marilyn Adams will anoint Aaron. At that time, the bishop prayed that "those who are sealed with it may share in the royal priesthood of Jesus Christ."[3]

So Aaron Gill and all of us who have put on Christ in baptism are to share in his royal priesthood—obviously an immense privilege and responsibility, but what does it mean? I believe that the best answer to that question lies in the fancy-dress portrait of Aaron, brother of Moses and Israel's first high priest, from the book of Exodus. The verbal picture of Aaron in his liturgical robes is one of the most striking snapshots from Israel's family album. Recall the scene: the Israelites are camped at the foot of Sinai, in that moonscape of dust and jutting rock, and here is Aaron the High Priest, tricked out in enough embroidered linen and precious metal to make the fussiest Anglo-Catholic drool. Blue, purple, and scarlet pomegranates at the hem, alternating with gold bells, so he will tinkle when he goes in and out of the sanctuary, and God won't be startled by human presence and inadvertently strike him dead. A turban with a gold rosette at the forehead, engraved with the words, "holy to the LORD." But the centerpiece of the whole costume is that drop-dead piece of sacred jewelry called, enigmatically enough, "the breastplate of judgment"—all goldwork, and studded with twelve great jewels, each engraved with the name of one of the tribes of Israel. Aaron is to wear the breastplate of judgment each time he goes into the sanctuary, literally wearing the people of Israel into God's presence, "wearing the judgment of the Israelites over his heart before the LORD perpetually" (Exod. 28:30).

"Judgment" is not one of our favorite words in the liberal church, but it is a frequent and very important word in Scripture. This image of the breastplate of judgment urges us to consider what is in fact one of the most positive concepts of biblical faith. When the biblical writers evoke judgment, their aim is not primarily to scare us into submission, but rather to set the horizon of hope for our lives. And Aaron's breastplate gives us insight into the nature of that hope. The first thing to notice is that it is an object of beauty, and the people of Israel are identified with its beauty; each glowing stone on the breastplate of judgment is inscribed with the name of one of the tribes. Think of that—jewels are precious because they reflect light so clearly. They break it into brilliant colors—emerald, amethyst, topaz, sapphire—showing how wondrously complex is the phenomenon of light. And light is, you might say, God's outstanding physical characteristic, the first element of God's being imparted to the world at creation. But, as John's Gospel attests, God's light has not fared well among us. It has become badly diffused by sin, so that to our sad eyes the world is

---

3. *The Book of Common Prayer*, 307.

a shadowy place; the exquisite lines of God's handiwork are distorted. Most of the time we see even ourselves only in vague outline, our own identities confused and fragmented.

God's judgment aims precisely at the clarification of our identities. For God's judgment—and this is the difference between God's judgment and our own—is not a neurotic rehearsal of the sinful past. God hates sin, but the whole point of judgment is to separate us from our sins (see Ps. 103:12), to restore us to the wholeness for which we first were made. Judgment is not, then, something that takes place only when you die. It begins in this life, as God works with us, stripping away the thick, hardened overlay of sin, our own sins and those of others who have hurt us, stripping us clean so that at last we may appear in our true identity, shared with every human being, which the Priestly writer of Genesis calls "the image of God" (Gen. 1:26–27). Polished gemstones are a good image for the work of judgment, in which we are held in God's firm, loving hands, cut severely and rubbed hard, until each one achieves the form and clarity intended especially for us, until each of us is perfect in reflecting some aspect of the infinitely varied light of creation.

Cutting and burnishing, the real work of judgment, is God's work. The priestly work in which we all share through Jesus Christ is to wear Aaron's breastplate, to wear one another over our hearts before the Lord perpetually—that is, to bear one another up before God, so that everyone may catch and reflect some of God's light as it pours into the world. And what does that mean, in concrete terms? Most of our Aaronic actions are small and require no professional expertise. You hold up someone for God's healing judgment whenever you offer a prayer for him, or forgive her rather than hold a grudge, or listen or speak out of your compassion instead of your impulse to condemn. Less personally but no less importantly, you hold others before God whenever you seek to establish the social conditions in which they may dwell free, as God's beloved children.

Often we perform these priestly actions in the dark, with no particular insight into the heart of the other. Yet each small act of kindness flickers with a little of heaven's light, brightening the world, gradually dispelling the false ideas we hold about ourselves and others, dispelling the shadows that obscure our real, heaven-bound identity as those creatures formed in the image of God. And what is our priestly responsibility toward this child? To wear him before God. We, Aaron's parents and brother, relatives, friends, will fulfill our responsibility whenever, through our words and actions, he feels how infinitely precious he is in God's sight, whenever we enable him to glimpse something of God's dream when forming him in the womb, when through us he glimpses the beauty that he, and he alone, can contribute to the glory of heaven.

36

To beautify heaven—that is finally the purpose of what we do this evening in helping Aaron put on Christ in baptism. Indeed, it is the purpose of this royal priesthood we are meant to share, the final purpose of wearing each other before God, time and again—so that heaven may be more beautiful. This we learn from another biblical snapshot, the one with which the family album concludes, namely St. John's vision of the heavenly Jerusalem, where those twelve jewels from Aaron's breastplate appear a second time, now mounted as the chief decorations on the foundations of the celestial city, where they catch the full light of God's glory and glow with the pure light of Christ the Lamb (Rev. 21:19–20). Since that is our goal, let us then pray for this child Aaron and for ourselves, that when all our work of ministry and God's healing work of judgment are done, each of us may be grown into the full stature of Christ and thus be found worthy to glorify our God, to whom be "worship and praise, dominion and splendor, for ever and for evermore" (cf. Rev. 5:13).

Amen.

Living Icons

Yale Divinity School Baccalaureate, New Haven, Connecticut
May 24, 1992

EXODUS 34:1–9, 28–35; PSALM 111; EPHESIANS 3:7–21

Graduating divinity students, on the cusp of ministerial service and leadership, are challenged here to incorporate the daily disciplines of Torah so that they may become "living icons" of God's holy splendor. Seasoned ministers, too, will hear an invitation to rededicate themselves to essential habits that sustain them as faithful servants of the church.

And [Moses] was there with Yhwh forty days and forty nights . . . and when [he] came down from Mount Sinai—the two tablets of the Covenant were in Moses's hand when he came down from the mountain—Moses did not know that the skin on his face shone, from his talking with [God]. (Exod. 34:28a, 29)

When Moses came down the mountain that second time, bringing the tablets of the Law, his face was shining. This is one of the Bible's unforgettable verbal snapshots: Moses coming down from Sinai, visibly aglow with the divine fire. Moses burned clear, burned to transparency during forty days and forty nights in the heat of God's presence. The people were afraid when they saw how he shone, and with good reason. It was because of them and their sin that Moses had been called up the mountain a second time to write the Law as he heard it from God's own mouth. You remember what happened to the first tablets: Moses smashed them at the foot of the mountain; he smashed them in rage when he saw the golden calf that the people had made. When he saw them dancing in a frenzy about the idol, Moses shattered the stone tablets against the mountainside—shattered them in despair, I suppose, for how could that foolish, undisciplined people ever bear upon their hearts the steady pressure of God's word?

So the tablets were broken, and the people were punished, and then God decided to try once more. Again God told Moses to carve tablets of stone, and again called Moses up Sinai to hear the teaching given for Israel's sake. But this time Moses returned from that encounter visibly changed, his face radiant with God's electrifying holiness. No wonder the people shrank back in fear. Yet Moses called them to come to him; he sat and taught them all that he had heard in those forty days and nights on Sinai, when God spoke to Moses "face to face, as one speaks to a friend" (Exod. 33:11).

There is tremendous force in that image of Moses at the very point when his greatest power and greatest gentleness converge. It is this moment that Michelangelo captured in his massive marble portrait of Moses with horns, as the Hebrew has it, horns of light standing out from his head. Yet despite the horns, despite its size, Michelangelo's statue somehow is not daunting; it does not impose itself upon us but seems instead to await our attention. I think it is the fact that it is a seated figure: Moses does not tower over the people but sits almost at their level, waiting to instruct them.

Moses's beaming countenance was for the apostle Paul a kind of emblem of the Christian life. Writing to the Corinthians, he suggests that every Christian is now experiencing a transformation like Moses's: "For all of us, with unveiled face, contemplating the glory of the Lord, are being changed into his very likeness, from glory into glory; thus it is from the Lord, the Spirit" (2 Cor. 3:18). With a boldness that characteristically borders on presumption, Paul trumps Moses even at the height of his spiritual powers: in Christ, all of us become images of a divine glory that, better than Moses's, never fades away. I would give Paul's exegesis of Moses's veil (which supposedly hides the fading glory) no more than a high pass, but as usual he is dead right about the potential for the Christian life: the church is like a hall of mirrors in which a candle has been set, Jesus Christ; and all of us reflect that light, making the world bright with God.

Because this biblical portrait of Moses is crucial for our understanding of how we as Christians are to be in the world, I want to examine it with you, to trace more closely the lines of that image. What can we learn of the character of this man Moses, to whom God spoke "mouth to mouth" (Num. 12:8), and through whose mouth God spoke to Israel with full command and infinite gentleness? The question of Moses's character has particular relevance to us on this occasion. As we celebrate the grace of your calling and preparation for leadership in the church, it is appropriate to consider what kind of man was this who first brought God's word to Israel. As you steward the education you have received in this place, it will be your task to work with God's people, as Moses does, so that they may (first) stand firm and wait to hear the word of God, and (then) respond with courage and eagerness when that word comes.

The first thing we learn of Moses's character is that he was a man of monumental and sometimes problematic passions. We see that immediately—the intensity of both his compassion and his rage—in the first story of the young man Moses, then still a prince in Pharaoh's household, who killed an Egyptian slavemaster for beating a Hebrew slave. Even in maturity, Moses never learned fully to govern his temper; the tradition says that it was rash speaking that disqualified him from entering the Promised Land (Ps. 106:33). Moses offended God in the wilderness—it's not quite clear how, but probably he took a little too much personal credit for bringing forth water from the rock for the grumbling congregation.

Yet I wonder if it was not Moses's very passion that drew God to him in the first place. God seems often to take a fancy to people whose emotions are not quite under control—people who have some crazy gleam in their eye and their feet slightly off the ground. God seems always to have an eye open for the place where the lid is not screwed all the way down, where God can make an opening into our hearts. And if it is our passion that draws God to us, it is also passion that carries us to God. The playwright Paddy Chayefsky says, "Passion is the very fact of God in man."[1] "Passion is the very fact of God in man": it is passion that carries our sight beyond the immediate and moves us to commit ourselves to non-molecular realities such as beauty, love, hope: those deep but not quite rationally defensible investments of ourselves that we must make, if ever we are to know God. Still, there is something about Moses that distinguishes him from other intensely human figures whose passions we come to know through the stories of the Hebrew Bible—especially I think of Jacob and David. We sense that, unlike them, Moses's deepest passion remains hidden from us; his real life is closed off from our sight by the clouds that surround the mountaintop. For it is up there that Moses comes fully alive. Shining Moses sits at the foot of Sinai and teaches the people. Yet that time always has the quality of an interlude. For when Moses finishes speaking, he covers his face; he withdraws and waits for another call to enter into God's presence. When Moses is not teaching, he veils his face and waits, his eyes riveted on God, waits until God should choose to speak again.

---

1. Paddy Chayefsky, *Gideon*, Act 1, scene 3, in *The Collected Works of Paddy Chayefsky: The Stage Plays* (New York: Applause Books, 1995).

Without passion, we cannot come to God. Yet passion alone will never direct our hearts surely, for they are willful and balky beasts. And so Moses's passion needs to be disciplined, trained to go the way that leads to God. Rabbinic legend has it that it was for the sake of Moses's own discipline that he spent those forty days and forty nights on the mountain with God. The one who received the Law on behalf of Israel needed first to receive it into his own heart. So all day long he studied Torah, as he heard it from God's mouth, and by night he wrote down what he had learned, in order that he might teach those who waited below.

The fact that you are sitting here today suggests that, in the last few years, you have with some frequency followed Moses's holy discipline of spending all day in class and chapel and all night bent over your desk. Many of you have experienced also the discipline of living in community, finding pleasure and doubtless also irritation in the close company of the faithful. You have lived under the further discipline of straitened finances, and many leave with debts that will be with you for some years. All of these things are sources of discomfort; less obviously, they are crucial for your growth in God, and I would urge you not to free yourself entirely of these discomforts when you leave this place. For those who have thought long and deeply about the discipline that fosters spiritual growth—and I mean the monastics—they have come up with something remarkably close to the lifestyle you have had to adopt here: a regulated program of study and prayer, material simplicity, and more personal accountability than our culture generally regards as healthy. Monastics choose this lifestyle, quite simply, because it increases their freedom. Observing a discipline that orients us to God—for isn't that what we mean by Torah from Sinai?—accepting a holy discipline frees us from the burden of continually making new decisions about how to live. It frees us from the tyranny of our own whims, which are so often dictated by our deepest fears. Discipline delivers us from the tedious search for novelty, so that something genuinely new can happen in our hearts. It gives stability to our daily lives, so that the transformation of which Paul speaks may take place: gradually we become living icons, each one of us a clear image of God's splendor. It is said that the "angels began to shine when they learned discipline."[2]

Standing at the top of the mountain before God, Moses, that "monumentally impassioned man,"[3] acquired discipline. And when he sits at the foot of

2. Rumi, "Praising Manners," in *The Soul Is Here for Its Own Joy: Sacred Poems from Many Cultures*, ed. Robert Bly (Hopewell, NJ: Ecco Press, 1995).
3. Chayefsky, *Gideon*, Act 1, scene 3.

the mountain with the people, then we see the fruit of that refined passion. We see it in his patience: for Moses does not keep his anger forever. Like God (see Exod. 32:9–14), Moses is able to withdraw his terrible anger over the abominable metal cow, and work again to draw this people into obedience to the one living God. This is surely the greatest challenge to his leadership: to bring Israel out of abject fear and into obedience, wean the people from an idolatrous obsession with their own desires, and enable them to hear the real demand and promise of God. And if they are able to hear God at all, perhaps it is because Moses teaches them patience along with the Law. He imparts to them some of his own patience, so that they may accept the terrible failures of the past, and still try to obey. In a lovely phrase, the Jesuit poet Gerard Manley Hopkins calls patience "natural heart's ivy."[4] "Natural heart's ivy": patience insinuates itself into our hearts, winding its strong tendrils round the wreckage of our old ambitions and self-serving purposes, softening their abrupt outlines, allowing us to look upon those ruins, with sadness perhaps, yet without horror.

So we have identified something of the character of Moses: his passion, his discipline, his patience. But do those qualities explain why God chose this man Moses to be Israel's leader and greatest teacher? No, of course not. God's peculiar choice, of Moses, of each of us, remains finally a mystery; and each of God's choices is mysterious most of all to the one on whom it falls.

The rabbis tell that God once granted Moses the extraordinary privilege of looking into the future of his people. God allowed Moses to sit for a while in the classroom of the greatest teacher of Judaism, Rabbi Akiva. (Akiva was that phenomenon most rare in history, a genuine academic martyr: he was arrested by the Roman occupiers of Palestine because he would not desist from teaching Torah, and was flayed alive at the age of ninety; he died exegeting the Shema: "And you shall love the LORD your God with all your heart and with all your soul and with all your might.") So Moses, they say, transported in time to the second century, watched Akiva match wits with his adroit students on minute points of the teaching that Moses himself had received at Sinai, and the prophet understood nothing. When Moses again appeared before God, he poured out his despair: "LORD, you've made a terrible mistake. If you could create a brilliant mind like that, you should never have entrusted the treasure of Torah to me. Akiva understands your commandments much better than I do. He even understands what I said better than I do. You could have chosen a scholar like Akiva, LORD, to be your prophet. Why did you ever pick an ig-

---

4. Gerard Manley Hopkins, "Patience, Hard Thing! The Hard Thing but to Pray," in *The Major Works* (Oxford: Oxford University Press, 2009).

norant man like me?" And God shrugged and said, "Shhh, Moses—I wanted it that way."

Today we celebrate the mystery of the way God wanted it, in calling you to this responsibility of service and leadership to the people of God—some of you perhaps still burdened with Moses's rashness, probably none of you (or any of us, for that matter) quite so theologically acute or so saintly as old Akiva, yet every one of you called to grow into an ever-sharper image of the glory of God, as we have seen it most clearly in the face of Jesus Christ. Glory be to God, whose power, working in you, can do infinitely more than you can ask or imagine. Glory be to God from generation to generation in the church, and in Christ Jesus for ever and ever.[5]

Amen.

5. Compare Ephesians 3:20–21 and *The Book of Common Prayer* (New York: The Church Hymnal Corporation, 1979), 102.

The Humility of Moses

Commencement Address, Virginia Theological Seminary, Alexandria, Virginia
May 23, 2013

NUMBERS 12

After God rebukes Moses for "speaking rashly" on Mount Sinai, we discover a new dimension of the prophet's faithfulness: Moses walks humbly with God even in the wake of his greatest disappointment. Moses epitomizes genuine humility by being thoroughly transparent to God's will. Even more, he reveals how the disappointments and failures of ministry can bring us closer to God than we ever thought possible.

When I received Dean Markham's invitation to preach today, the words that came immediately into my mind are that remarkable sentence from the twelfth chapter of Numbers: "Now the man Moses was utterly unassuming (*'anav me'od*), completely humble, more so than any other person on the face of the fertile earth" (v. 3). I found that I could not get these words out of my mind, whenever I thought of you and this day, so perhaps this text was given me for you. Pray with me, then, if you will:

In this hour, in this place, may God's word only be spoken,
and God's word only be heard. Amen.

Class of 2013, although I do not know you as individuals (with a few happy exceptions), I know something of the work to which you are called—as recognized leaders in the church, with an education in the things of God that distinguishes you from most. No wonder Moses came to mind, who above all others is given us as a model of what leadership can and should look like among the people of God, over the long haul—or the long slog, as it often is.

Today we focus, through the book of Numbers, on Moses's total humility. For the rabbis of antiquity, this defining characteristic of Israel's greatest leader was also the essential principle of religion altogether. "Be exceedingly, exceedingly lowly of spirit" (*Pirke Avot* 4:4), they taught, because as soon as your heart begins to puff with pride, then at the very same time you begin to forget God. (They learned that from Deuteronomy [8:14].) So you might say that humility is nothing other than your capacity for remembering God, always and everywhere remembering God, and, further, your capacity for being transparent to God, so when people look at you what they see is the power and action and compassion of God. Isn't this what Paul has in mind when he writes to the Philippians of the humility of Christ? One might say that, from the perspective of the whole Christian canon, Jesus is the only one whose humility is greater even than that of Moses; when we look at Christ, we see God with no opacity, no distortion at all. But Moses shows us the deep yet imperfect humility to which we ourselves might aspire, humility demonstrated over the long haul (forty years, as you know, is the biblical round number for a hell of a long time), humility exercised, yes *honed*, in a tough place, namely, the near presence of God.

Now let's be clear: Moses's humility has nothing to do with timidity before God. Just a few verses back in the book of Numbers we hear Moses challenging God over the pressure of his position, caught as he is between a people whining for a more gourmet diet and an impatient Deity. "Did *I* birth this people?" Moses asks God. "Look, if this is how you are going to do me, then just do me a favor and kill me now!" (Num. 11:12–15). Moses's humility is, you might say, robust—the kind of tough disposition for ministry that might make any one of us useful to God over a lifetime. Looking then to Moses as a model of humility, I see three things, and all are crucial for us:

> *First,* in the story that was just read from Numbers 12, we see Moses's humility demonstrated in how he handles *power* and *conflict,* those twin phenomena that figure so centrally in the life of ministry—like it or not.
> *Second,* if we read on a few more chapters in the story, we see the one instance when Moses's characteristic humility fails him, the moment of presumption that tragically bars his entrance into the Promised Land.

But that is not the end of the story.

> So *third,* we see Moses's habit of humility renewed and deepened when God disappoints his greatest personal hope, the hope that inspired

his whole ministry and kept him going. We see how humble Moses keeps faith, when God lets him down.

First, then, power and conflict—how does a genuinely humble leader handle them? The story begins when Miriam and Aaron raise that incendiary question: "Is it only through Moses that YHWH has spoken—really? Hasn't [God] also spoken through us?" (12:2). Moses's siblings are tired of playing second and third fiddle to their little brother. They even make some kind of slur against Moses's Ethiopian or Sudanese wife, but it's the power issue that really bothers them. Yet, in fact, Moses does not hold all the power in the community. You remember that just before this God took some of the prophetic spirit that was upon Moses and shared it among seventy hand-picked elders. There was even a little extra that spilled over onto some other folks, and Moses was thrilled: "If only all YHWH's people were prophets, that he would put his spirit upon them!" (11:29).

Note this: Moses doesn't care about being unique in God's eyes. Just the opposite: "If only all God's people were prophets!" That is his humility speaking. Moses has the wit to see that his spiritual stature cannot be measured directly, by looking at him, but rather by looking at everybody around him, as they all share the spirit that empowers them in God's service. How different would the church look if all our leaders had *that* kind of understanding of power?

It is just at this point, when the divine spirit is overflowing into the community, that Miriam and Aaron get up and say, "Well, what about us; aren't we just as special as he is?" And Moses says nothing in response, not a mumblin' word. That, too, is his humility. He doesn't say who ought to be speaking for God . . . because he doesn't know, and he knows he doesn't know. So Moses leaves an empty space for God to speak and act freely, and I have to believe that is why (to put it crudely) God craves Moses's company. Just because he assumes nothing, claims nothing for himself, God is able and eager to get up close to Moses, even "mouth-to-mouth" (12:8)—because Moses isn't running his own mouth, asserting his own distinctiveness all the time.

So Aaron and Miriam make their bid for spiritual power, and God gets angry, really angry. As a result, Miriam gets scale-disease, while Aaron just gets egg on his face—a high priest's immunity, I suppose. There is nothing especially fair about that, but I can't clean the Bible up for you. As you know, fairness as we reckon it is not a big part of the divine economy, and I am sure on the whole that is lucky for us. But the point of this story is elsewhere, namely, on what godly leadership looks like in the face of conflict, and so it is notable that as soon as Miriam is stricken, Moses cries out to God for her to be healed. Now think about that for a moment, and think about it again, sometime in the future. Remember this story when the people who have stood with you and struggled alongside you suddenly become jealous of whatever has prospered under your hand. (It happens.) Remember it when they say hurtful things about you, when they make your job so much more difficult—and yet, and yet, these troubled individuals stand in need of your compassion. Then, like Moses, you must pray God's mercy upon them. "Love is not irritable or resentful. . . . It bears all things, believes all things, hopes all things, endures all things" (1 Cor. 13:5–7). When Paul wrote that, he might have been meditating on the humility of Moses, who claims nothing for himself, who in the midst of conflict leaves space for God to act, who in the face of mean-spiritedness implores God to act in mercy.

Moses is the best of us, in many ways, and the great value of his long story is that it shows us how the very best of us can and will go wrong, terribly wrong, in our service to God. That is a good thing to consider on this commencement day, as you begin a new stage of your life with God, so you will not waste precious energy contending with the fear of failure. It happened to Moses; it will happen to you. What you must fear is falling utterly away from God, and Moses can help you with that.

You remember the story of what God names as Moses's worst failure in ministry—just a few chapters further on in Numbers, when he strikes the rock to bring forth water for the people. "He spoke rashly with his lips," as the psalmist says (Ps. 106:33): "Shall we bring forth water for y'all?" (Num. 20:10). "Shall *we*"—that's where Moses went wrong. He was just one letter off the mark (as the rabbis taught); Moses should have said, "Shall *he* [God] bring forth water . . . ?" For one rash moment, Moses thought it all depended on him, and so he spoke foolishly with his lips, the very lips that had nearly touched God's own. He takes credit, even if just for an instant, for what only God can do—that is how Moses's humility fails him.

But after all Moses had done with and for God, couldn't we call this an understandable error? So why does divine judgment fall like a sledgehammer on Moses and Aaron both? "Because you did not keep faith with me to show my holiness in the eyes of the Israelites, you shall not bring this assembly into the land which I have given to them" (Num. 20:12). This is one of the hardest sayings of God in the whole Bible. "Because you did not keep faith with me and show my holiness. . . . Because you were not fully transparent to *my* action in the life of this people, you, Moses and Aaron, will not enter the land of promise." Lack of humility in the leaders—that has to die in the wilderness, along with the whole generation that came out of Egypt. God is unrelenting on this point, precisely so we can be clear on it. At the moment when we in our self-absorption cease to be transparent to God, we cease to be useful in the ministry to which we have been called.

We might suppose that at this point Moses's story would end: he has failed God publicly and terribly, and he is done. But of course it's not like that. Moses's story and his service to God go on for years after this, almost as though nothing had changed: God continued to trust in Moses, and Moses continued to trust in God. And what does this say about Moses's unconditional humility? It is just because Moses claims nothing for himself that he can endure disappointment and continue the ministry to which he is called. Because he is more humble than any other person on the face of the earth, he can endure loss of the goal to which his whole adult life seemed to point, loss of the hope for which he has sacrificed so much—and still, Moses will serve God totally. "Leaders have to be people who give up things." That's what Moses says to Aaron in Zora Neale Hurston's novel about Moses. "Leaders have to be people who give up things. They ain't made out of people who grab things."[1]

Leaders have to be people who have learned, inevitably through much pain, to wait upon God with open hands and boundless patience—and something even beyond that. Think of the remarkable prayer of thanksgiving we have just said, written by Charlie Price, a beloved teacher at the seminary: "We thank you also for the disappointments and failures that lead us to recognize our dependence on you alone."[2] Moses himself might have written that prayer. You can pray it only when you know beyond the shadow of a doubt that everything is gift, every single thing and hope you cherish is pure gift, given just for a time. "Leaders have to be people who give up things. They ain't made out of people who grab things." This is a wise saying of Ms. Hurston's, yet we could and must add just one thing more: leaders *for the church* ain't made out of people who grab *things,* but rather out of people who grab onto God and hold fast, people who through suffering, yet with fathomless humility and gratitude, are led to recognize their dependence on God alone. That you should be people like that—that is our prayer for you, Virginia Seminary Class of 2013. May your humility, like Moses's own, be a source of overflowing blessing for the church in this generation, giving glory to God, whose power working in you can do infinitely more than we can ask or imagine. Glory to God from generation to generation in the church, and in Christ Jesus, forever and ever.[3]

Amen and amen.

---

1. Zora Neale Hurston, *Moses, Man of the Mountain* (New York: HarperCollins, 1991), 214.

2. *The Book of Common Prayer* (New York: The Church Hymnal Corporation, 1979), 836.

3. Compare Ephesians 3:20–21 and *The Book of Common Prayer,* 102.

Perfect Love

Opening Convocation, Duke Divinity School, Durham, North Carolina
August 25, 2015

DEUTERONOMY 6:4–13

Loving God with our entire mind requires an ever-deepening commit-
ment to rigorous academic pursuits. As we seek the sanctification of
our intellect, the possibility that our minds may become darkened to
God's ways is an appropriate fear that perfect love should not cast out.

Hear, O Israel, Yhwh our God, Yhwh is One. And you shall love Yhwh
your God with your whole heart and with your whole being and with
everything you've got. (Deut. 6:4–5)

Perfect love—that is what Moses is talking about, when he makes his great
speech at the edge of the Jordan Valley, just across the river from Canaan (Deut.
4:45–46). Bring up the scene in your imagination, in the eye of your heart, and
put yourself, and all of us, into that scene. Here we are, gathered before our great
teacher, almost within sight of the land where we are promised that we will have
rest—that is, we will dwell there, settle down at last, in committed relationship
with God. We're not there yet, but we're close. We've come a very long way to
here. Out of Egypt, running for our lives, with Pharaoh hot on our trail, and
through the Red Sea on dry land, in a way we still don't quite fathom. Then the
divine teaching at Sinai—that was the beginning of our education in the things
of God, when we first glimpsed a whole new dimension of reality. But even that
unmistakable encounter with God didn't make everything clear, or easy. Still
we wandered in the wilderness for years, often hot and thirsty and weary and
frustrated and sometimes, yes, angry. There was so much loss in the wilderness;
so many died. All that is part of our common history before coming to this place.

And today we are gathered here together on the verge of something huge and demanding and, please God, beautiful beyond imagining. We know that our whole lives are about to become different, and we are looking to Moses, that incomparable teacher, to help us get ready. Moses, of whom God said, "Mouth to mouth I speak to him, in plain sight" (Num. 12:8). Mouth to mouth, eyeball to eyeball—this man Moses knows more about intimacy with God than any other ordinary person in the Bible, except the young girl Mary of Nazareth—but hers is a history for another day. There is no one we could or should trust more than Moses, when he speaks to us about love:

> You shall love Yhwh your God with your whole heart (*bekhol levavekha*) and with your whole being (*uvekhol nafshekha*) and with everything you've got (*uvekhol me'odekha*)—with all your muchness. (Deut. 6:4–5)

The commandment to love God is of course very familiar to us, because Moses's teaching is central to Jesus's teaching. Therefore it would be easy for us not to see how weird is this instruction—to put that in more scholarly terms, how unparalleled is this commandment in the context of Torah. No other of the 613 commandments in Exodus, Leviticus, or Numbers tells us to love God. We have been instructed to love our neighbor, to love the stranger—both of those in Leviticus. Of course, there is considerable emphasis on *obeying* God—that goes back to Genesis and the Garden of Eden. But this is a new commandment, to love God totally, "with your whole heart and with your whole being and with everything you've got"—that is, to love the way Moses does. And since this is unprecedented, you have to ask: Why suddenly now, Moses? Why speak to us at this particular moment, and so urgently, about loving God perfectly, like you do, with everything we've got?

The answer becomes clear when you remember where we are in the story— just across the Jordan from Canaan. Moses is giving us this commandment now, because if we don't learn to love God that way, we'll never make it in the land of promise. We won't have the stamina for all that committed relationship with God demands, for all that ministry requires of us, in the many different forms in which different ones of us are called to it. The kind of love Moses is talking about isn't an emotion merely, although our emotions are drawn into it, sometimes at the highest pitch of intensity. But much more basically, this love is a survival skill in the situation in which we now find ourselves—a skill we have a chance to use and hone every single day in this place, in good times and in bad. In other words, loving God perfectly is a matter of daily practice, a habit that is sustained by will more than by any warm feelings you may have toward God on a given day. It is a habit of the heart, as Moses's instruction suggests—*bekhol levavekha*, "with all of your heart"—and remember, in the metaphorical physiology of the Bible, the heart is where your will resides. For people like us, loving God—or at least working on loving God daily—is the one habit of the heart that makes possible anything and everything we are called to do. Absent that habit, anything we do in God's name is likely to be a sham, or a confusion about what we are genuinely called to do. It is possible to deceive ourselves and others, to be visited by a passion and call it a vocation. Passion and vocation are related, but they are not the same.

So how do we keep from being deceived about what we are called to do for God? Well, for starters, you have to know who God really is. Notice that Moses's instruction does not start with us; it starts with God, and so should we: "Listen, Israel, Yhwh our God, Yhwh is One." That declaration of the Oneness of God is the basis for any theological statement in any of the monotheistic faiths. If you ask any responsible Muslim, Jewish, or Christian theologian what it means to say that God is One, they will ask you in turn, "How much time do you have?" The implications are inexhaustible, and we have about ten minutes, so let me pick one thing that may help us think about what it would be to love totally this God who is One—as we understand it, One in Three and Three in One. Oneness denotes the utter incomparability and sufficiency of our God, who is sufficient to meet all our real needs. Therefore the Oneness of God puts a certain healthy pressure on us to identify what are our real needs, as well as to name the real needs in the world and in our communities and families that we must address in order to be faithful. If we are honest and discerning, that probably eliminates quite a lot of things that might otherwise occupy our heart and mind, our will and emotional energy and time. Putting it another way (and this is something I learned from one of my students some years ago), this declaration that God is One puts pressure on us to be single-minded and wholehearted toward God. Divine Oneness requires human integrity, if we are to have a real relationship.

Claiming our integrity fully is for each of us the work of a lifetime; it takes however many years are given us to give back to God a life wholly shaped by love. That is why Jews have for centuries observed the practice of daily reciting this declaration of God's Oneness, and especially reciting it near the time of death. In doing so, they follow the example of Rabbi Akiva, the great second-century teacher who was thrown into a Roman prison and condemned to death for violating the imperial decree that forbade Jews from studying or practicing Torah. (The Romans would not have esteemed Duke Divinity School.) It was the hour for prayer when they led the elderly Akiva out of his cell to be executed by flaying. As they stripped the skin from his ninety-year-old body, he recited the words in a steady, clear voice: *Shema Yisrael, Adonai Elohenu, Adonai Ehad*—"Hear, O Israel, Yhwh our God, Yhwh is One." His disciples standing by cried out in their own agony and bewilderment, *Rebbe, ad kan*—"Teacher, even to this point?" And Akiva replied: "Always I have been troubled by the words, *uvekhol nafshekha*, 'with your whole life.' I wondered, When shall I have the opportunity to fulfill it? Now that I have the opportunity, shall I not fulfill it?" He died with the word *Ehad*—"One"—on his lips (Babylonian Talmud Berakhot 61b).

Matthew gives us Jesus's version of Moses's great teaching. I turn to that now, because Jesus highlights something that is especially crucial for us in this place: "You shall love the Lord your God with your whole heart and your whole soul and your whole *dianoia*—your mind, your understanding, your intellect" (Matt. 22:37). For many of you, these years at Duke are your first and best opportunity to learn what it means to love God with all your intellectual capacity. This is the time for sanctification of your intellect. For most of you preparing for ministry outside the academy, this may be your last extended opportunity before retirement to express that love fully—every single day. Don't miss that opportunity. It will wear you out at times; love does that. But even so, you, all of us, are privileged to take our place among Christians—not so very many through the millennia—who are called to manifest our love of God through the sanctification of our intellects.

That is the chief purpose for which you were called here, the sanctification of your intellect. I do *not* mean that you should all set your sights on getting a string of A's. In most cases making that your goal would be beside the point, and possibly sinful, especially if you are balancing study with other demanding work that cannot be deferred, such as raising young children. Nonetheless, for each of you, sanctification of your intellect must be your aim, and that work begins here and now, this week. Hear this, O Israel. Loving God with your whole mind means giving your intellect over to the things of God, learning as deeply and widely as you can, simply for the sake of giving God joy. And take joy in it yourself; the joy with which you bear the yoke of study may well be your most important witness of faith during your years here.

Study as a witness of faith—hold that thought, treasure it up in your heart, because you will encounter opposition. Intellectual devotion is sadly countercultural in the church. There will be some who will urge you to be "just a little more practical," who will view a lifetime commitment to study as a form of self-indulgence, even a sign that you are cold-hearted toward God and neighbor. They will tell you that people don't care what you know; they want to know that you care. They will tell you that we need restless prophets working the streets, not intellectuals poring over books. Take courage and resist those too-simple dichotomies, for as Jesus's teaching affirms, it is the *failure* to give our minds generously that bespeaks a tepid love for God and neighbor.

You have been called to serve in a time of deepening difficulty in the church, in this country and around the world. I think we all know this. People are literally dying, as the prophet Hosea saw, for lack of true knowledge of God. "Bloodshed follows upon bloodshed" (Hos. 4:1–2), the earth itself is in mourning (4:3), because the will of God does not govern our actions. The situation is urgent. If the church is to be a light and not a stumbling block on the way to God, then there is no room here or anywhere else for sloppy theology, intellectual laziness or rigidity, ignorance of either the rich Christian tradition or the various kinds of fresh and well-disciplined work that stand to enrich the tradition further in your own generation.

Today we at Duke Divinity School are re-forming ourselves as a new community, pledged to study and prayer and active love of God and neighbor. That is going to take strength, physical and intellectual, moral and spiritual—more of each than you know you've got. So you are going to have some anxiety here (it goes with the territory). Therefore I want to close by giving you a prayer from someone who can help you, one of our closest brothers within the Bible, the young theology student who gave us the 119th Psalm. It is a long and beautiful poem or song that could provide much comfort for you in the coming years, as it expresses both the longing and the anxiety that all of us feel when we commit ourselves to loving God totally with our minds.

"My whole being melts away from anguish" (119:28), our psalmist says, and then this prayer: "The way of lies take from me, and in your teaching be gracious to me" (v. 29). "The way of lies take from me"—our psalmist fears darkness in his mind, living by all the lies that are daily in the air, about

   ... what matters after all,
   ... what constitutes our worth as human beings,
   ... what love really requires of us,
   ... what genuine power looks like, the power to create and sustain the world, to save it from sin and death.

To fear being deceived in these things is a wise fear, indeed the best of all possible fears. God grant that that excellent anxiety may extinguish in us all lesser fears and free us to love God perfectly, with heart and soul and mind and might.

Amen.

Receiving the Gift of Rest

All Saints Cathedral, Khartoum, Sudan
June 13, 2004

JOSHUA 1:1–18; MARK 2:1–22

The gift of rest for war-weary people comes in the form of freedom from fear. Devotion to God's word in Scripture will be their new weapon, as their courage is renewed and sustained by the conviction of God's continuing presence.

Grace to you and peace in the name of our Lord Jesus Christ.

It is a great joy and a privilege to worship with you this morning. Seven years ago, I promised Bishop Daniel Deng Bul that when peace came to the Sudan, so would I. I know that the prayers and the faithfulness of many Sudanese sisters and brothers have helped prepare the way for peace to come to this land, and I am honored to join with you today in offering praise to our God. Halleluia!

Almost four hundred years ago, the great English poet and preacher John Donne said this about the Bible: It's like a closet full of clothing in different sizes. When we read the Bible, we're looking for a piece of clothing that fits, so we can "put on Christ," as St. Paul says (Gal. 3:27). We're looking for the "fit" between God's word and our lives, our situation.

Our Old Testament reading this morning is from the first chapter of Joshua, when Israel is about to enter the Promised Land. At a first reading, it is not easy to see the fit between this text and this congregation. For we know from the book of Deuteronomy that the Israelites are entering a land that already has people in it. So the Israelites will displace the first people of the land of Canaan (v. 4). That would seem to be the exact opposite of your situation, for *you* have been displaced. Many of you who are adults have not seen your first home for more than twenty years. Many of the children among you have never seen the home of their ancestors. From that perspective, Joshua's instructions to the Israelites do not seem to fit your situation.

But from another perspective, I believe that the text does speak to the displaced people of the Sudan. Consider this: Joshua speaks of the Promised Land as a place where God will give the people *rest* (v. 15). Rest—that does not mean that the people will not have to do any work in the Promised Land. It does not mean that they will not have to make any effort to live there. Rather, it means that the land is the home that God has prepared for them. When God gives the people rest, they will no longer have to be afraid of their enemies (v. 9). They will be safe, at home with God. "I will not let you go; I will not abandon you," God says (v. 5). When the people are at rest in the land, they will raise their children in confidence, not despair. They will look to the future with hope, rather than looking back with grief.

Probably this description of rest for God's people sounds familiar to you. It's what you've long been praying for: freedom from fear, a place where you can relax and be at home with God. So perhaps this passage from Joshua is indeed the right clothing for the church in Sudan at this time. It will enable us to clothe ourselves in Christ as we pray toward the future of this beloved country. It will, I pray, guide your feet into the way of peace.

And specifically what guidance does Joshua offer, as you prepare to enter the Promised Land of peace? This crucial message: living in the land of rest is a privilege granted only to those willing to do the hard work of listening for God's word. Rest is granted only to those who listen and obey God's will, first of all as we hear it in Scripture.

There is something very strange about Joshua's instructions to the Israelite soldiers as they prepare to cross the Jordan River. We might expect Joshua to tell them to get their weapons ready, to sharpen their swords—but he doesn't. We might expect him to command the destruction of homes and cattle—but he doesn't. We might expect him at least to outline a battle plan. But he doesn't do that either.

In fact, the only equipment these soldiers are told to carry into battle is not a sword but a book, the book of God's instruction to Moses. Listen again: "Be strong and of very great courage to do everything . . . that Moses my servant commanded you. Don't let this book of instruction depart from your mouth. Go over it and over it day and night. That way you will succeed" (vv. 7–8).

Joshua doesn't sound at all like an army general here. He sounds much more like a Bible teacher. This is what I tell my students: read the Bible day and night; read very carefully. Let God's word shape your words, your thoughts, your actions. That takes discipline, so be strong. It is hard to follow God's word when it calls you to change, or to depart from the custom of your family, your tribe. So be of very great courage, and you will prosper in the way that God is calling you to go, into the land of rest and peace.

This chapter from Joshua gives a second instruction that may guide you in the months and years ahead. The people of Israel are to receive God's gift of rest in *solidarity* with one another, not one tribe here or another there. Remember, the tribes who have their allotments of land on the east side of the Jordan are not allowed to settle down comfortably while the others continue to struggle. No, Reuben, Gad, and Manasseh must cross the Jordan and help their brothers; they cannot rest until all the tribes have rest together. God's people are called to be a community of solidarity and mutual help. They must not yield to the temptation to let the claims of one tribe suppress the claims of another. They cannot receive God's gift of rest if they do not have peace and unity among themselves.

"Be strong; have courage," Joshua tells the people over and over as they are poised to enter the land of rest. Those words fit the people of this nation well as you prepare to enter the Promised Land of peace. Already you know that the challenges of peace will be many. You will be challenged to extend your hand to others in forgiveness, in mutual help. You will be challenged to find new ways of living with old rivals, old enemies, finding a way forward together, walking as brothers and sisters along the paths of peace. "Be strong; have very great courage"; "I will not let you go; I will not abandon you," says your God.

Amen.

"All That You Say, I Will Do"

"The Book of Ruth," interfaith conference sponsored by the Luce Program in Scripture and Literary Arts, Boston University, Boston, Massachusetts May 8, 2003

BOOK OF RUTH

Ruth epitomizes what it means to show deference to both the needs and the wisdom of the other. We see in her a model for enriching Jewish-Christian relationships, for bearing one another's burdens, and for embarking upon a mutually upbuilding journey toward the "covenanted future" God intends for us.

The first words of Ruth: "In the days when the judges were judging, there was a famine in the land." "The days when the judges were judging . . ."—if you have read the seventh book of the Bible, then you know that it was a time of political chaos, with Philistine enemies pressing hard on Israel's flank, and the "national leadership" (if you can call it that) worse than a bad joke. Yes, early on there was Deborah, a great judge, but things deteriorated pretty steadily after that. By the end of the period of the judges, when our story is set, we see the perpetually adolescent Samson, too preoccupied with his sexual misalliances to give proper attention to the people's needs, and also "Jephthah the Gileadite, . . . a mighty warrior" (Judg. 11:1), who during his six years in office managed to stir up civil war, killing 42,000 Israelites, in addition to his own daughter. Of this grim period when the judges were judging, the biblical narrator comments caustically, "there was no king in Israel, and everyone did what was right in their own eyes" (17:6).

Against that background of deterioration and disaster on a national scale, the small domestic tale of Ruth, Naomi, and Boaz unfolds. "And after the fire, a still small voice" (1 Kings 19:12). Through all those burning events reported in the book of Judges, there isn't much of God's action to be seen—but rather

Israelite murdering Israelite; women kidnapped, raped, killed; bodies piled high at the fords of the Jordan. Ironically, it seems, "in the days when the judges were judging," the action of God in and for Israel was gradually obscured, eclipsed. It was as Elijah experienced at Horeb: God's presence is not to be found in the events that break up rocks and mountains and nations. For YHWH was not in the wind, nor the earthquake, nor the fire. But "after the fire, a still small voice." The book of Ruth is the *qol demamah daqqah* (1 Kings 19:12), the still small voice in the canon. It quietly refutes "the great-man theory of history," the notion that all the really important events occur in war rooms or on battlefields or even on holy mountains. After all the machinations of those great (or at least powerful) men in the book of Judges, it is an experience of grace to turn to Ruth and dwell on the small and not-evidently earthshaking interactions among three quite ordinary people. We watch as they help each other grow through and beyond the lamentably common tragedies that mark many, even most lives: for Naomi and Ruth, displacement, bereavement, childlessness, poverty; for Boaz, some unexplained loneliness in an otherwise prosperous and respectable life.

I think it is the ordinariness of the characters that explains why people love this story so. Everywhere else the biblical history tells us about patriarchs and matriarchs, prophets and kings; people whose lives are marked from the get-go by blessing, anointing, a special calling from God; people who shape history, for better or for worse. Ordinary people show up in those stories only as occasional foils for the main, extraordinary characters. But this little story is not about movers and shakers. At most these three generated a low buzz in Bethlehem ("Is this Naomi?! Oy, has she lost her looks!"), a little eddy of local news for a few months ("Older man falls for younger woman; pillar of the local community takes up with Moabite laborer without a green card"). Naomi, Ruth, and Boaz are people sort of like us—or better, perhaps, people we might grow to resemble, if we should order our lives to that end.

And that is further reason to love this story, because it gives us hope and direction for ourselves, and hope also for something beyond our own lives. The story gives hope, because it shows ordinary people helping each other grow through and beyond personal tragedy. And what opens up, through acts of generosity and mutual regard, is something far beyond their own small sphere, beyond what they could know or imagine. Probably none of them ever saw the grandbaby (the great-grandson, to be precise) whose name is the last word—literally, the last word—of their story. Yet what opens up through David is the future God intends for Israel. After the spectacular failures of the days of the judges, this itself is amazing: God still intends a future for Israel. The full story of that future isn't yet known to any of us, even now. We have read far enough and lived far enough beyond that promising end of Ruth to know that what lies beyond their story is an imperfect future, marked by sin and much suffering and punishment for sin. Nonetheless, it is a covenanted future; it is a future with God—and all of us here, Gentile Christians along with Jews, dare to believe that we have some share in the covenanted "afterlife" of the story of Naomi, Boaz, and Ruth.

If Ruth stands in the canon as a gracious counter to the book of Judges, it also speaks a word of grace to times such as our own. In pondering Ruth again through recent weeks, I have come to see it somewhat differently than I did before. For me, at least, the world situation has revealed more deeply the need for Ruth, and what I want to suggest this morning is that this little book is Torah for socially and politically disordered times. Like the Israelites in the time of the judges, we are worn down and worn out by "great events," on a national and international scale. In this country, in Israel and Palestine, in Afghanistan and Iraq, in Africa, maybe in China, and also in the ecosphere, we are witnessing cataclysmic events that seem to offer only the most uncertain hope of a better and safer future for any of the people of God. And so, perhaps the Torah of this book of Ruth is especially apt now, for its essential message is this: in a time of widespread disorder and personal loss, simple acts of mutual regard—the Hebrew word for that is *hesed,* the discipline of generosity that binds Israelites to one another and to God—acts of *hesed* can open up the future God intends. This is something considerably more than a sop to those who are discouraged by their inability—our inability—to see the way out of some fearful situations. For the future that this book begins to open has the broadest scope possible. It encompasses Jews and Christians, and through our communities, we believe, it points to the repair and redemption of the whole world. This little book of Ruth teaches us, more concisely perhaps than any other book of the Bible, what the Swiss theologian Karl Barth calls, in a lovely phrase, "the simplicity and comprehensiveness of grace."[1]

"The simplicity and comprehensiveness of grace"—yet the *credibility* of grace depends on its concrete expression.[2] The ultimate concrete expression of divine grace in this book is, of course, the birth of a child. Probably there

1. Karl Barth, *The Word of God and the Word of Man,* trans. Douglas Horton (New York: Harper & Row, 1957), 92.
2. See Walter Brueggemann's comment on the Psalms and other texts that reflect liturgical affirmations of God's power: "The new tales based in the credibility of concreteness lead to a different world" (*Israel's Praise: Doxology against Idolatry and Ideology* [Philadelphia: Fortress, 1988], 86).

is no miracle that so regularly and powerfully speaks of God's grace manifest in our world. The conception and birth of a child is powerful to move even the most spiritually inert parent or close loving observer—it moves us, for a time at least, to some degree of inchoate wonder. Notably, in the whole four chapters of Ruth, we hear of only one direct divine action, and that at the very end: "Yнwн gave [Ruth] a pregnancy" (Ruth 4:13).

So God's action is clear only at the end of the story, but acts of *hesed* enter the picture and shape it from the outset. Listen to Naomi's very first words, addressed to Orpah and Ruth on the road between Moab and Bethlehem: "Go on, go back, each of you to her own mother's house, and may Yнwн do *hesed* with you, as you have done with the dead and with me" (1:8). Ruth is indeed the still small voice in the canon; all its literary effects are subtle. This blessing by Naomi of her "bride-daughters" (*kalloteyha*) affords the first delicate surprise in the book: *hesed,* the foundational virtue of Israelite community and culture, enters the story from what is, biblically speaking, an unlooked-for direction: from the East, from Moab. You will recall that everywhere else in the Bible, Moabites are well known to be heathen no-good-niks. But now two young Moabite women are distinguished for their covenantal kindness toward their Israelite husbands, now dead, and their ravaged mother-in-law. And God is called upon to take special note of these Moabite women—even to follow their example?!

Hesed is the keynote of this book, in a way that is distinctive in the Bible. As you know, Moses and the Prophets often enjoin the practice of *hesed,* but Ruth's story is altogether *torat hesed,* the teaching of *hesed,* to use a phrase from the book of Proverbs (Prov. 31:26). Ruth's story teaches in the way only a great narrative can do, by taking a quality, a virtue of which we often speak in the abstract, and then showing us what that quality looks like when it is concretized in life. Isn't it always the case that when a virtue assumes flesh, the effect is much more interesting than you expected? I think this is why Jews and Christians have traditionally loved to tell stories about holy and righteous men and women: because there is invariably a surprising angle to holiness or true virtue when you see it in a life—or in this case, in several intertwined lives.

Ancient hearers of this story would be surprised to see a Moabite modeling *hesed,* but I think we, who have no particular animus against Moabites, might be more struck by something else about Ruth: namely, by her generous regard for Naomi, when she can so ill afford to be generous. She takes an incalculable and completely unnecessary risk: leaving home, over Naomi's objections, to accompany the old woman to Bethlehem, a small town where a foreign woman who does not clearly belong to anyone—a woman with a tattoo, as Peggy Parker has imagined her—can only be viewed with suspicion, if not outright hostility.

Looking hard at Ruth, we see that, for all her courage and physical strength, for all her determination to protect and provide for the old woman whose life has been shattered, Ruth is herself extremely vulnerable. She is the vulnerable protector. In that role, she stands for countless women throughout history and around the world who, though living in precarious situations, take on the additional risk and struggle of caring for the very old or the very young or the sick or the permanently frail. As a model practitioner of *hesed,* Ruth teaches us something about covenant relationship that might not otherwise be clear, although I am convinced that many parts of the Bible point to it: namely, that the real test of covenant relationship is how one vulnerable person treats another who is likewise vulnerable; or (by extension) how one people, one nation that is troubled, frightened, terrorized, takes the risk of recognizing its kinship with another vulnerable, beleaguered people.

What we see in the course of this story is that Ruth's practice of *hesed* moves others into the incalculable risk and joy of covenanted relationship. First, there is the old, spent woman Naomi, who has loved and lost two "boys," as the narrator poignantly calls her two dead sons (*yeladeyha,* 1:5). At the beginning of the story she is ready to be done with God and with life (1:13). Yet gradually she reinvests herself in another young life, as she plots how to secure the future, how to secure a good husband for this foreign "daughter" of hers. Then Boaz, the well-to-do man (*'ish gibbor hayil,* 2:1) who seems to lack no comfort but that of love, finds himself unexpectedly in emotional debt to the woman who asks him to marry her. Boaz, like Ruth herself, is a vulnerable protector.

The quality of relationship that has grown between Ruth and Naomi, Ruth and Boaz, is revealed in one phrase, uttered at two key junctures: "All that you say (to me),[3] I will do." Ruth says it first, when Naomi gives her instructions for the threshing floor night. Knowing that her reputation and therefore (in that small-town world) her whole life hangs on the success of Naomi's highly risky scheme, Ruth entrusts herself completely to the old woman's wisdom: "All that you say, I will do" (3:5). Shortly thereafter, when Ruth whispers to a startled Boaz, "Spread your wing [your cloak] over your maidservant," Boaz answers with the same words: "All that you say, I will do for you" (3:11).

It is a statement of complete trust and deference. It sums up *torat hesed* as we see it in Ruth, all the acts of mutual regard that bind these three:

3. The Hebrew records variant readings, with or without "to me."

"All that you say, I will do"—each one recognizing the other's genuine needs, spoken or unspoken, and letting those needs determine her (or his) actions;

"All that you say, I will do"—each one, knowing the situation is precarious, taking on the still-unmeasured burden of the other; each one accepting as wisdom the considered judgment of the other;

"All that you say, I will do"—each one honoring the risk undertaken by the other; each tough, determined individual giving up the impoverished security of "going it alone" and entrusting the future into the hands of a now-beloved other.

I have suggested that Ruth may be Torah for disordered, even desperate times. If that is so, it must not be because it turns us away from concern for the public sphere, enclosing each of us in our own little domestic world. Rather, it must be because Ruth teaches us the quality of relationship that enables life with others to be decent, secure, even (dare we say it?) happy. Mutual deference to the genuine needs and the wisdom of the other—we know this is essential if our families, our congregations, our schools, and our offices are to be places of *shalom,* well-being, and genuine peace.

We know this to be true on a small scale; is it also true on a larger one? As we look beyond our immediate communities, it seems to me that what we are doing today is one example of, or at least one opportunity for, mutual deference in a wider public sphere. When Jews and Christians agree to read Scripture together, that is a significant act of mutual deference, since we come together after a bitter and, for Christians, shameful history of violent disagreement about the texts that mark us as siblings and, at the same time, divide us. Today we come together to read Ruth, knowing that we do not entirely agree on what even this little book might mean for our own communities and for the world. But we sing it, see it, pray and interpret it in each other's presence—exploring an almost unused model of peace, believing that there is grace in the endeavor, even daring to hope that it may orient us more surely to the covenanted future God intends for us all.

Amen.

God's House

Duke Chapel, Durham, North Carolina
July 23, 2006

2 SAMUEL 7:1–17; MARK 6:30–46; HEBREWS 3:1–6

Despite being God's most intimate friend, King David is plagued by restlessness that harms others and himself and prevents him from fully resting in God. Jesus-Son-of-David's relationship with God, however, opens David's story wide to hope, finally revealing and fulfilling what it means to rest in "God's house." We find this pattern of rest in those around us who, despite their own troubles, dwell at home with God in joy and gratitude.

From the letter to the Hebrews: "We are [God's] house, if we hold fast the confidence and the pride that belong to hope" (3:6).

If I could pick only one story that reveals the possibilities and problems that people like us encounter in our life with God, it would be the story of David as told in the book of Samuel, the deeply moving and ultimately tragic story of someone who is in many ways like us: intelligent and well placed, possessed of a certain charm or even charisma. In a word, David is powerful—like us, but more so. David is a much bigger character than any of us, and it is just because he is larger-than-life that we can see in him something of ourselves, especially the unresolved tensions and contradictions in our life with God. The story of David and God is surely one of the greatest love stories ever told. It is accurate (if unconventional) to call it a love story, for God chooses David to be an intimate, "a man after his own heart" (1 Sam. 13:14), as the prophet Samuel says. At the outset, God's hopeful love casts David in the best possible light, just as ours does when we are newly in love.

Yet, as the story unfolds, it becomes evident that David's heart can never be one with God's, because he is so full of himself. Once David becomes king, his life is governed far less by devotion to God than by all the other passions of his heart—chief among them imperial ambition—so even though God gives David rest from his enemies all around (2 Sam. 7:1), nonetheless he continues his wars of aggression (2 Sam. 10–11). David is ruled also by self-indulgence, so he permits himself to bed and impregnate the wife of his closest friend, and then David has to murder him to cover it up; and he spoils his royal sons, with the result that there is constant strife in his household and his kingdom. Furthermore, David is ruled by the desire for vengeance, a desire so strong that on his deathbed he busies himself ordering the executions of those against whom he still holds a grudge (1 Kings 2:5–9). And always, always, David is gripped by the anxiety that is the surest sign of a human heart not fully joined to God's heart. David's anxiety is what emerges in our passage this morning—and if we listen with spiritual alertness, I think we can discern how God's own heart even now begins to ache over David, with an ache that only deepens as their story goes on.

The passage we have just heard from 2 Samuel 7 comes early in David's kingship. Significantly, this is the first verbal exchange, the first conversation (you might say) between God and David, although it is mediated by Nathan the prophet. As you know, a good storyteller (and this writer is a great one) gives you clues especially at the beginning of a tale. And so it is here, in the very first verse: "Now when the king sat in his house, and YHWH had given him rest all around from all his enemies . . ." (2 Sam. 7:1). Thus the scene is set for what follows: David is secure on the throne; God has "given him rest." "Rest"—it's one of the most important words in the whole Bible, something like a code word, summing up all that God longs to give us. Rest is a *given* for King David, or it should be—something given and assured by God. Maybe all the tragedy that marks his life comes down in the end to just this one thing: never can David let himself rest in God.

As is typical of the restless, David has a plan to make himself more secure, and like all pious ambitious people, he includes God in his plan. "So the king says to Nathan the prophet, 'Look here, I am sitting in a house of cedar, while the Ark of God is sitting in a cloth tent.'" You can tell that David has set his heart on building a proper temple, a royal chapel, and Nathan his court prophet falls right in line with that suggestion: "Go on; do it; God is with you." It is well to remember that even competent religious leaders like Nathan (and Nathan is certainly a good-enough prophet) don't always know what God is up to. That very night God comes to Nathan and says, "You tell David this for me: 'Did I ask you to build me a house? I've always lived in a tent, ever since I brought Israel out of Egypt. In all this time, hundreds of years, have I ever said, Why haven't you built me a house of cedar?'" (2 Sam. 7:2–7).

A house of cedar—that is the key term in this exchange between David and God. They're talking giant timbers, not cedar shakes. Great cedar trees, suitable for building a house for a king or a god, were found not in the hills immediately around Jerusalem but rather a hundred miles to the north, in the mountains of Lebanon. David and other ancient Near Eastern kings imported cedars of Lebanon as routinely as national leaders in our age import Middle Eastern oil, and for exactly the same reason: access to power. In David's world, if you could get cedar, you could be a player. You could build tall-masted ships and engage in international trade on a grand scale. Cedar was the luxury building material for public buildings, elegant palaces and temples that carried the fragrance of the great north woods. According to the ancient pagan mythology of Canaan, the gods themselves lived in the cedar forests of Lebanon. In that world, then, the aroma of cedar was the smell of power. That is why David wants to build God a big cedar house like his own and install God in conspicuous splendor right next door to the palace. He is counting on God to be a prestigious and useful neighbor.

So God's word to David is this: "I, God, am building a house for you, David, not vice versa" (2 Sam. 7:11). What God wants is a faithful royal house, faithful leadership for the people of Israel, not architectural power-enhancement as David imagines. Indeed, the book of Samuel shows a God who is immensely powerful and at times unpredictable, resisting containment either in a house of cedar or in the political program of any king. And already young King David has witnessed something of God's uncontainable power. Just before the present encounter, he brought up to Jerusalem the Ark of the Covenant. For Israelites, that Ark was the most holy artifact, the centering place of God's power. But during the move someone touched the Ark of God incautiously, and power flashed out, deadly as the charge from a hot wire (2 Sam. 6). Maybe that is another reason why David wants to build a cedar temple for God. Maybe he imagines it will render God's high-voltage presence safe for the consumer; it would be useful to have a god who is powerful yet tame enough to do his bidding. In other words, David would like a god just slightly less powerful than he himself is. Probably most of us religious people spend some portion of our lives wishing for, even worshiping, that kind of tractable, highly employable God, who is contained by our desires and takes direction from our prayers. The idea is initially attractive, of course, but the sad irony is, if you hold onto that false image of a tame god, then you will be perpetually anxious. For if you believe that you are managing and directing God's power, then everything depends on you, as far as you can see. So as long as you hold onto that false image, there is nothing the real God can ever do or say to take away your anxiety.

Exactly so here: no assurance, no promise from God can relieve David's anxious self-concern. Having already given David rest from his enemies, God now promises him everything else, everything: "My steady love will not depart from you. . . . Your house and your kingship will be secure forever . . . ; your throne will be established forever" (2 Sam. 7:15–16). God might have saved the breath, for David responds with a prayer that shows he has heard nothing. He goes on (I am filling you in on what happens after the part we just read) to cajole God, asking for what has already been granted: "You've given me a house, LORD, but that's a little thing for you. Now bless it; make it last forever" (2 Sam. 7:18–19). Poor David; he doesn't get it. This is the moment for gratitude, for resting on God's promise of faithfulness to the royal house and the people of Israel. But even the God who is all faithfulness cannot satisfy the need for assurance in this restless heart. David demands more promises from God, more military victories. Compulsively he tries to secure what has already been freely granted, relying on himself more than on God's power and faithfulness. In the end, of course, David only destabilizes what God secured. The man whose heart was to be bound to God's own heart acquires the habit of perpetual fear. By the end of his life, King David, like King Saul before him, is terrorized even by God (2 Sam. 24). It is a tragic end for the one to whom God promised rest from all his enemies.

Why do you suppose the Bible tells us so much about David, and so much of it not edifying? His is the most detailed story of anyone in the Bible, except for Jesus. Perhaps we need to know David well because we share so many of his dispositions. Like him, we trust ourselves more than we trust God; we prefer our plans for the future over God's; and as a consequence we live in perpetual anxiety. I have some years of personal experience in this; probably some of you do as well. But thanks be to God, David's personal history is not the whole story of God's faithfulness to the house of David, nor is it the best part. A thousand years later, Jesus, born to the royal house of David, reopens this story and opens it wide to hope.

Like his great ancestor, Jesus-Son-of-David (Mark 10:47) works to establish a house, a kingdom that will endure forever in God's sight, but with this difference: in all Jesus's work he rests in the power of God. Recall that story we heard a few weeks ago, when Jesus sleeps peacefully in the middle of a killer windstorm on the Sea of Galilee. The boat is being swamped, the disciples are panic-stricken, and there lies Jesus on that infuriating cushion in the stern, wholly at rest in God (4:35–41). Again, in today's Gospel lesson, the apostles come back from a mission trip, full of "all that they have done and taught," and Jesus says to them, "OK, fine. Now come away to a quiet place, by yourselves, and rest a little" (6:30). And out of that rest, even that small but perfect rest in God, flows power and abundance, enough to meet the needs of all the crowds who follow them in hunger and confusion. And again, after all have eaten their fill, Jesus goes up on a mountain to pray, to rest in God (6:46). This is the pattern of Jesus's ministry, and the pattern he would have us learn so that we may be free enough to let God's power flow through us:

first, rest in God;
then, serve God's people;
then, again, rest in God.

In our culture, the resting-in-God bit is the harder one to learn. We talk a lot about service at a chapel and university like this one, and that is good, very good—but sometimes you have to go out of the way to learn about resting in God. Ultimately, I suppose, you must learn about rest from Jesus, but it helps very much to know an ordinary person, a neighbor, who is in the habit of resting in God. So look around you; look for someone who seems to be relaxed, spiritually speaking, taking pleasure in the company of God. This is perhaps the most surprising thing about people who are very close to God: they are much less serious than we would expect. They have a joy and lightness about them, even though their responsibilities may be weighty, their troubles real and deep.

Two years ago I made my first trip to Southern Sudan, to visit the church there, which has been persecuted for half of its one hundred years of existence. I had fortified myself emotionally for what I expected to be the teeth-gritting experience of a lifetime. It never once occurred to me that I would have fun among the Christians of Sudan. But I did. For day after day I was surrounded by joy and laughter and outpourings of love. Of course, everyone I met, except for the tiniest children, had suffered terribly. By then peace accords had been signed, but the suffering produced by twenty years of genocide was not over, and for many it will never be entirely over. Yet everyone spoke to me of the goodness of God—because they were alive, because they could now see the beginning of an answer to their prayers for peace, because I had been able to come to Sudan and we could study the Bible together, because today there was food enough for everyone to eat. If you are a Sudanese Christian, you don't waste your spiritual energy trying to contain God's power. Having so little control over many aspects of your life, you learn to trust in God's power, to rejoice daily in every evidence, small and great, that God's faithfulness is something more than a scam, a bad biblical joke. Day by day you cultivate in your heart the habit that the letter to the Hebrews calls "the confidence and the pride belonging to hope." That is how we become God's house, by "hold[ing] fast the confidence and the pride that belong to hope" in God (Heb. 3:6).

People like the Christians of Sudan know they must be *God's* house, for the simple reason that they are still standing, and they lack the strength to stand on their own against all their enemies. They are a striking yet far from isolated example of people who have found rest in God, who rest in God's faithfulness with confidence and pride. If you open your eyes you will begin to discover other such people here and there, who have relaxed their power grip and are now enjoying the good company of God. Like the Sudanis, many of those well-rested people have come home to God by way of bitter anguish and loss. Yet in God's house there is joy, the joy of gratitude and hope. Why don't you go over and join that company? I bet you could use a little rest.

Amen.

The View from Mount Elijah

Baccalaureate, Duke Divinity School, Durham, North Carolina
May 14, 2011

1 KINGS 17:1–24; MARK 9:2–8

At his best, Elijah epitomizes prophetic trust and courage in the most desperate situations. At his worst, he is too arrogant to discern God's voice. But God speaks to Elijah again in an unexpected way—not in the wind, earthquake, or fire, but in "a sound of a finely textured silence." With renewed clarity for his own vocation, Elijah comes nearer to God's presence, and ultimately shows how essential to God are those who carefully listen in obedience.

Direct us, O Lord, with your most gracious favor, and further us with your continual help, that in all our works begun, continued, and ended in you, we may glorify your holy name, and finally, by your mercy, obtain everlasting life. Amen.

The Old Testament is a mountainous landscape, whose rugged peaks we climb in order to get a closer look at God. That metaphor is crude, but I think everyone in the class of 2011 knows what I mean. Most of you have spent a year or more traversing, in English and sometimes in Hebrew, the rough terrain that runs from Genesis through Chronicles. You have climbed many of its peaks, starting with Mount Abraham and Mount Sarah. And if you haven't gotten all the way up some of them, you have at least gained enough climbing experience to lead others on exploratory expeditions. There are challenging ascents enough to last you a lifetime, and the views from the top are spectacular.

Now, if you stand in the middle of the land of the Old Testament and look around, or if you cross the open border into New Testament country and look back, you'll see a few peaks that tower over all the rest, and Mount

Elijah is one of them. Elijah is the highest mountain in the range we call the Prophets—maybe just a little less grand than Mount Moses itself. That's how the landscape appears in the passage we just heard from the ninth chapter of Mark's Gospel: Moses and Elijah, those twin peaks, each standing in a direct line of sight with "the high mountain" where Jesus was transfigured. Moses and Elijah, those servants who stood in such close proximity to God that at the last they were taken up fully into the divine presence—from Moses and Elijah, you can see Jesus.

Just a moment ago we all prayed that after a lifetime of work in God's name, we too might be taken up into God's presence for all eternity. So it is apt for us to linger a little on Mount Elijah this evening, as we celebrate your work at Duke Divinity School and bless you on to the next work, big or small, currently known to you or not, recognized by church officials as ministry or not—we bless you to the next work you will do in God's holy name. Now we'll look at three moments in Elijah's memorable story: the beginning of his ministry, his mid-career despondency, and finally his ascent into heaven. We could linger and talk all night about the view from this place, but those three moments will be enough; they will help us see what it is to serve the God before whom Elijah stands.

But first, a word about his personal style, which is distinctive. Personal style is certainly a component of ministry, although not the most important component, thank God. Elijah is feisty. You know the type: he is one of those people who is constitutionally disposed to run up hard against power and against the majority. Some of you may even be his type. Elijah confronts Ahab, Jezebel, and all Israel with their sins of idolatry; he kills the 850 prophets of Baal and Asherah and announces that it's going to be real ugly for all who align with them. And because Elijah is characteristically confrontational, it is striking that the first extended story of his prophetic ministry is not about confrontation but about community. It's not a public story but a rather private one, that takes place not even in the land of Israel but in the unpromising location of Zarephath in the land of Sidon—a little town just eight miles down the road from the city where Jezebel's daddy Ethbaal reigns as king. This is not exactly a plum appointment for the young prophet of Israel's God; they worship Baal in Zarephath. Still, this is where Elijah is called, in the third year of a killing drought, on the strength of this divine promise: "I have commanded a widow-woman there to provide for you" (17:9).

Maybe this widow-woman didn't get the message, because when Elijah shows up she is not standing at her front door, eagerly awaiting another mouth to feed in the midst of a famine. No, she is out "gathering a couple of sticks" so she can make a final supper out of the handful of meal left in the jar, and then she and her young son will just lie down and die. Her despair is deep enough that you might expect the prophet to perform a miracle right then and there, refilling the meal jar and the vat of olive oil. But instead of performing a miracle himself, Elijah asks her for one. This demanding stranger asks her to feed him, before she feeds her own starving child. Somehow, astonishingly, she does just that, and the meal and the oil do not run out, "and they all ate for a long time" (v. 15).

Now notice the strange order of events here: her miracle of hospitality to the stranger makes way for the divine miracle of more food. The woman's unflinching heroic generosity with the last she has opens a channel through which God's power begins to flow. And God's power-for-life flows for months in that little household, sustaining them with food, and then, climactically, God's power is manifested in life-breath itself, flowing from Elijah into the still body of the widow-woman's child, restoring him to life.

So, class of 2011, standing on Mount Elijah and looking toward Zarephath, what do we learn about ministry that might be called prophetic? This: you have to trust in God's ability to create out of the most unpromising raw material a community of mutual caring. Like Elijah, you have to be willing to be called into a desperate situation, with no clue as to how to improve it. Like him, you have to go among strangers, as needy as you and even more clueless, with nothing more substantial to offer than a word that you trust is from God. Like Elijah, you have to go to people who don't seem to know God at all, and risk everything on God's ability to speak into their profound deafness—the deafness not just of individuals but of a whole culture. You have to trust that God's Word and Spirit can awaken in them a capacity for generous and faithful action, so they will make your work fruitful in that unpromising place.

Let's go now to a second lookout point here on Mount Elijah and look over toward Horeb (Sinai). You remember this story from the middle of Elijah's career, just after his famous confrontation with the 450 prophets of Baal on Mount Carmel, when he exposed them as religious frauds, and God answered Elijah with a consuming fire. Then all the people fell on their faces proclaiming, "The LORD alone is God!" Elijah topped off the day by killing all those prophets of Baal who ate at Queen Jezebel's table (18:19), and then he proclaimed the end of the three-year drought, and they all got good and wet. It was an incomparable prophetic performance . . .

. . . But Jezebel did not appreciate it. The queen went after Elijah and he fled, running for his life and at the very same time wishing to God that he could die (19:4); the highest point of Elijah's career was followed immediately by the lowest. He fled as far away as he could, from the North of Israel all the way down the Sinai Peninsula, walking forty days and forty nights until he came to the great Mountain of God, where he crawled into a certain cave and waited—waited, I dare say, for his own personal Sinai theophany. He was having a Moses moment. And sure enough, soon there came a word from God's mouth to his ear: *mah-lekha foh 'eliyahu*, "What are you up to *here*, Elijah?" (v. 9).

Now you know it as well as I do from reading the Bible, and some of us know it also from personal experience: when God shows up and starts asking pointed questions—"Where are you? Why are you *here*? What have you done?"—it's a strong indication that God is speaking to someone who stopped listening a while ago. It is a sign that I am in a place, literally or metaphorically, to which I have not been called, a place I did not get to by accident. It took Elijah forty days and nights to walk to Horeb. You can spend energy, determination, ingenuity, and a lot of time getting someplace to which you were not called by God. You might even be fueled by a certain self-righteousness, as Elijah was. Do you remember how he answered God's pointed question? "I have been so zealous for the LORD God of Hosts. . . . The Israelites have forsaken your covenant. . . . I am left all by myself, and they seek my life . . ." (v. 10). That's prophetic self-righteousness.

And so God shows him up, just as Elijah earlier showed up the prophets of Baal. God calls him out of the cave for the spectacle he wanted: rock-breaking wind, earthquake, and fire—all the geophysical signs that Moses himself once experienced on Horeb, signs that *might* herald God's presence; but in this case they don't. And then it came, a phenomenon that can be captured only with the paradoxical phrase: *qol demamah daqqah*, literally "a sound of a finely textured silence" (19:12). This is one of the great phrases of the Bible; it denotes a silence that you can almost feel and see, silence like a curtain of fine Egyptian linen that simultaneously discloses and veils (see Isa. 40:22). This gauzy silence draws attention to what is just beyond our senses; it attunes us to the dimension out of which God speaks.

And once Elijah is listening, God repeats the question—"What's with you *here*, Elijah?" (v. 13). "Now get back on the road!" And God sends him packing off to where the people are, to do a proper prophet's business: in this case, anointing a king or two; and then (here's the kicker) Elijah is to anoint his own successor as prophet of the Lord: "Elisha son of Nimshi you shall anoint in your place" (v. 16). In effect, God says: "Stop posturing, Elijah. Stop playing Moses-at-Sinai and do something useful. And for heaven's sake, stop feeling sorry for yourself. You are not alone, and you are not the only faithful person in

Israel. So get over yourself, Elijah. You are not unique and you are not forever. But still you might be useful, if you could just get over yourself."

So now, looking from Mount Elijah toward Horeb, what do we see—any signs marking out the road to a prophetic ministry? Here is one: you can have your greatest success in serving God and God's people, and then the very next day lose your direction. What went wrong for Elijah? Was he too impressed with the crowd's response to his performance on Carmel? Was he too impressed with his own involvement in ending the terrible drought? And what about killing Jezebel's prophets, an action that, as far as we know, was not commanded by God—did Elijah go astray because he stopped with confrontation and did not go on to show mercy, mercy for those he defined as the enemies of God? The Bible does not explicitly say any of these things, but it leaves all of them open as possibilities.

But this it does say: when he heard that Jezebel was after him, Elijah became afraid. It is certainly not the first time he was in mortal danger, but it is the first time we are told Elijah was afraid.[1] Could it be that he lost heart because for a little while Elijah succumbed to envying somebody else's vocation? He wanted the calling that Moses had received instead of his own. Yet after a time Elijah "came to himself" (see Luke 15:17) . . . when his internal clamor was stilled and he heard *qol demamah daqqah*, the palpable silence that speaks for God.

Looking out toward Horeb from Mount Elijah, we see that we will never be so powerful, so good at what we do, as to be put in charge of the work to which we are called. Sometimes, as with Elijah, God stops us short and sends us packing in a direction altogether different from the one we chose. Being important and successful may even make it that much harder to attend to the quiet, insistent presence of God. Yet whenever we do get over ourselves and listen, and follow where God directs, then we inevitably discover that obedience is not the teeth-gritting experience we had supposed. No, obedience is nothing other than the most intense form of listening. The Latin word *obedio* (taken most literally) means "listening toward" someone. Obeying God means leaning into and living into that dimension of experience that our storyteller calls *qol demamah daqqah*, "the sound of a finely textured silence." And as we grow into it, obedience proves to be a source of excitement. In the end, obedience is nothing other than the exhilarating journey into the nearer presence of God.

No wonder, then, that the great saga of Elijah ends with an image of the

---

1. Accepting the emendation to 1 Kings 19:3: "and he saw" is read as "and he was frightened."

prophet's dramatic journey to heaven. This is our third lookout point from Mount Elijah, the point where he ascends in "a chariot of fire with horses of fire" (2 Kings 2:11). The fiery prophet goes by fire to the God who is pure Fire, the glowing Heart of all that is. That final scene conveys a message very different from the one Elijah heard on Horeb, when God told him (in effect): "You can be done without. I have thousands of other faithful followers. I even have another prophet waiting in the wings, to replace you when the time comes." Elijah can be replaced, as can we all; our time for service in every place and in this world will end—sooner or later, we don't know; our times are in God's hands (see Ps. 31:16 [31:15 Eng.]). But the chariot of fire tells us that even as Elisha is succeeding him as prophet, Elijah remains absolutely essential to God. At the moment when he finishes his service on earth, Elijah rises like a flame to heaven, there to burn bright in God's presence for all eternity.

Dearly beloved of God in Christ, as we bid you farewell, we pray that it may be so for each of you. Let us pray now, each of us for ourselves and for one another, that we may spend the rest of our lives in exhilarating obedience, attentive to the quiet, insistent presence of God. And then, when we shall have served faithfully in our generation, may we rise like a flame, and in the company of Elijah and all the blessed be joined for eternity to the Fire that is the glowing Heart of all the worlds.

Amen.

Holy Friendship

Christ Church Cathedral, Nashville, Tennessee
February 15, 2015

2 KINGS 2:1–12; PSALM 50:1–6;
MARK 9:2–9; 2 CORINTHIANS 4:3–6

The story of Elijah's farewell to Elisha represents a crucial dimension of the Christian life that churches too often ignore—friendship. Yet worship's highest aim is the formation of holy friendships, through which we "disciple" one another to become wholly oriented to God. Holy friendships come in many forms, but all share the same characteristics of careful listening, spiritual imagination, and courageous trust that make possible abundant life in Christ.

God is about to take Elijah up into heaven, and everybody knows it. When it happens, it will be an event such as no one has ever seen or experienced. Elijah is the only person in the whole Bible who visibly ascends to heaven without dying first. We watch as he is scooped up in a great whirlwind, with chariot and horses of fire. This is a world-class miracle, entirely unique, which vindicates Elijah's whole prophetic career. He could use some public vindication, since Elijah is almost always in an oppositional situation with the powers that be: Ahab king of Israel and his queen Jezebel, who would like to see the contrary prophet dead. He is also in an oppositional situation with most of the other prophets in the land of Israel, who are content to serve the royals and the gods (or idols) they worship. In a word, Elijah has more than a few powerful enemies. So you'd expect it to be a major public event when God vindicates the true prophet. Yet it seems that only one person sees Elijah's fiery ascent: his disciple, the apprentice prophet Elisha; a single witness, and that not even an influential person—just a kid really, the young man who calls Elijah "my father." The chariot and horses seem like a wasted photo opportunity.

Another wasted opportunity you might wonder about: Why does the narrator focus so little on the dramatic potential of the story? There are not one but two major miracles in this passage: the chariot of fire, and also that bit about Elijah striking the Jordan River with his cloak, parting the waters, so the two of them passed through the riverbed on dry land. It's like Moses parting the Red Sea; this is a sign that Elijah has attained to the status of the father of all the prophets. Yet the narrator passes over the two confirming miracles quickly, giving hardly any details, and dwells on something else entirely—something that hardly seems important at all, in terms of Elijah's public career: namely, the long goodbye between Elijah and Elisha, when Elisha does not want to let his teacher go.

It's a long walk these two take together, in the final days, as they journey from one region or town to the next. Elijah is trying to slip away, to be alone when God takes him. "Stay here," he says to Elisha at Gilgal; "God is sending me to Bethel"—a couple of days' journey away. And Elisha flat-out refuses to be left behind: "As God lives and you yourself live, I am not leaving you!" (2 Kings 2:2). The scene is repeated several times, until at last Elijah realizes why the young man won't let him go: because there is something this disciple still needs from the master. "So ask, [Elisha]—what can I do for you?" "Let a double share of your spirit come to me," the young prophet answers (v. 9). To translate that request into language we can more readily understand: "I want to be devoted to God, as fully as you are—a person whose whole life is shaped and guided by faith. I have been your disciple; now, my father, give me your legacy. Share with me the spirit of God that I see in you."

I confess that, before working on this sermon, I had never before paid any attention to this poignant scene that brings an end to Elijah's stormy story, and I need to ask myself why it never made any impression upon me. Maybe I read past it for the simple reason that this is a story about discipling, and that is not something that Episcopalians talk about very much. I notice that the dictionary lists the term "discipling" as "archaic, obsolete," even as religious language. Strange that discipling, the foundation and heart of Jesus's own ministry, should be an obsolete notion in the church. So let's use another word. My colleague Greg Jones speaks of "holy friendship," or "God-centered friendship," and that is exactly what Jesus's discipling was about: "I have called you friends," Jesus says to the intimate band of twelve (John 15:15). So let's talk about holy friendship, and consider what this story about Elijah passing on a spiritual legacy to the younger prophet might mean for any of us, younger or older, more or less experienced in the life of faith.

One day Elijah had seen the young man Elisha plowing the field on his parents' farm, and Elijah literally threw his prophet's mantle over him. Then Elisha up and followed after him and became his disciple (1 Kings 19:19–21)—in a flash, on a whim, just as one day still long in the future those Galilean fishermen would leave their boats and nets to follow Jesus. As far as we know, they were strangers to each other, yet Elijah glimpsed something in this youth that no one had seen before, and Elisha had the courage to accept the prophet's call, little though he could have understood it. We don't know how long these two were bound together in holy friendship: was it years, or perhaps just a few intense months? We don't need to know, because it is the depth, not the duration, of the friendship that matters. They are together long enough that when Elijah is taken up, he is able to pass on to the younger prophet Elisha the spiritual legacy of a new self, a self that is wholly oriented to God. That is who Elijah was, and who Elisha eventually grew to be under his tutelage: a self wholly oriented to God.

Holy friendship addresses the basic human need to draw close to God. That need and desire receive very little acknowledgment in our general society. Sometimes, even within the church, we may not know how to talk about it, or how to recognize our own desire to be close to God. Yet nurturing that desire and meeting that need are the sole reason for the church's existence. We may provide a few valuable social services and something we rather vaguely call "community," but the purpose of the church is to enable people to grow toward God in Christ. The church does its job in two related ways: first, by organizing worship, and second, by encouraging holy friendship. All the elements of worship—music, prayers, sacraments, preaching—the aim of all this is to create a space and time in which we turn our restless minds toward God, so that we can imagine, if only for a few flickering seconds, the dimension of existence that Jesus called "life in abundance" (see John 10:10). And holy friendship is the complement to worship. If worship is working, if it is creating an environment in which people are beginning to desire the presence of God, wanting to see more deeply into that mystery, then we need friendships in which that desire can be acknowledged and that mystery talked about. Sometimes, like the young man Elisha, we need to spend time with someone much more practiced in the presence of God than we are.

More than thirty years ago, when I was a theology student in England, I met regularly for spiritual direction with Sister Mary Kathleen, a cloistered nun. When I began meeting with her, I did not know what to ask for; I knew only what I lacked: peace of heart. She quickly recognized that I did not know anything about prayer, and so she took it upon herself to teach me how to set aside a quiet space in my life for God to enter and speak. It was slow daily work; there were no dramatic moments when the heavens suddenly opened. Yet one day, at the end of about nine months, I realized that I was no longer confused and restless; undramatically, yet with a certainty that had previously eluded me, I knew what I was meant to do with my life, namely, to preach and teach for the church. I left England soon after that, and Sister Mary Kathleen became a hermit (literally), her life wholly devoted to prayer; I did not see her again until last year, when she had returned from the hermitage to community life in the convent. She is now ninety and did not remember me at first, but after we had sat together for a minute or so, her eyes brightened and focused on me: "Oh," she said, "I did not remember your name. But now that I hear your voice, I know who you are. I remember that young woman, who knew she was called to do something but did not know what it was. I remember her struggle; yes, I know just who you are."

Indeed she knows who I am. Those many years ago, Sister Mary Kathleen knew better than I did who I was struggling to be, and she helped me to become myself. I grew closer to God through holy friendship with this woman, who is so much more fully oriented toward God than I am. You might say, she gave me a double share of her spirit.

You don't have to be someone of Elijah's spiritual stature, or Sister Mary Kathleen's, in order to pass on something of real substance through holy friendship. Most Sundays a small group of women meets for an hour before we go to the 11 o'clock service at Duke Chapel; sometimes there are two or three of us, sometimes four or five, gathered for Christian conversation and prayer. We have been doing it for four years or so. We were summoned into a group, not because we were personal friends (we weren't), but because one common friend asked each of us to offer prayer for her husband, who was gravely ill. So we began, and within a few months another of us lost her house in a fire; elderly parents and adolescent children met with various challenges. Difficulties smaller and larger emerged for us and those we love, and gradually we realized that we are called to stay together, as a tiny but (for now) durable part of the body of Christ. We call it the Heart Circle. There is no leader and no advance agenda; we simply bring to each other whatever is on our hearts, for honest and loving conversation, and for prayer. Sometimes we celebrate together; we also sigh and laugh and grieve. We disciple each other as we try to bring the light of Christ to the dark places we perceive within ourselves and in the world; we name before God the countless things, large and small, for which we are grateful, the places where we sense healing, where we glimpse growth and new possibility.

What I am describing is probably the simplest form of holy friendship.

Among my friends and colleagues and students, I witness other forms of Christian discipling that are much more costly: partnering with someone recently released from prison, for instance; or foster-parenting young children, giving them a safe, peaceful, Christ-centered home for a shorter or longer period of time; or living in Christian community; or in community with mentally and emotionally challenged adults. I know Christians who disciple people at the end of life; they sit with the dying, perhaps playing an instrument or listening to a family member, so together they may experience the goodness of a holy death. Whatever form it assumes, holy friendship involves these three things:

- consistency and availability, and listening carefully to someone over time;
- the spiritual imagination to glimpse new possibility in someone else;
- the courage to be open to new possibility for yourself, courage that comes from beginning to trust God, and beginning to trust how another person sees you.

Whatever might be your personal reason for coming here this morning, this church and every other exists to bring us closer to God through worship and holy friendship. I wonder what might be the form of friendship into which God is calling you particularly at this time. Is it with someone more experienced than you in the journey of faith, who can guide you in identifying your gifts and your direction? Or is it perhaps with someone just starting out, who needs your companionship to take a few small steps? Is your holy friend someone who needs you to name a gift you see in her, which she does not yet have the confidence to claim? Or is it a group of people engaged in a ministry to which you could contribute, and now it is time to offer yourself? You might be called into holy friendship with other Christians, or perhaps with someone outside the church. One of my own holy friends is an Orthodox Jew, another a Muslim; in each case we stand together, united and embraced within the unfathomable mystery of God.

If you are wondering where the call to holy friendship may be for you at this time, then look for where you sense a new possibility beginning to show itself. Right now it may be only a glimmering: a faint hope or stirring you feel in yourself, a yearning you sense in someone else. Yet those glimmerings have God-potential. They are bits of light, the light of Christ, with which God is seeking to penetrate our darkness, our dullness, our confusion, our solitariness, our self-absorption. So follow the light, that it may draw each of us deeper into holy friendship with one another, and closer to God in Christ.
Amen.

Blessing of the Animals

Duke Chapel, Durham, North Carolina
October 3, 2004

JOB 12:7

That we have the ability to love across barriers of species is not only a gift from God, but also a miracle. It is a miracle that our friendship with animals serves as a sign of God's love for all creatures. If we who are imperfect creatures can love other imperfect creatures, how much more confidently can we say that God, who is perfect love, welcomes our kinship with him in Jesus Christ?

We are gathered here today because we have all experienced a miracle in our lives, the miracle of having a friend who is an animal. It is a relatively common miracle, of course, but that doesn't make it any less wondrous, that we can be intimate with these creatures who are in many ways so different from ourselves. They are not like our other friends. We cannot have a conversation with them; we cannot explain things to them or ask their opinion or advice. Yet I am guessing that each of us came today—not just to have our animals blessed, but to have our friendship with them blessed. We came because we all know the wondrous experience of looking into the eyes of an animal friend and recognizing that we understand each other perfectly, that heart is speaking to heart without need for words.

Intimacy across the barrier that divides one species from another—that is a gift of love, as I think we all know. But in calling it a miracle, I am saying something more: it is a sign that points to God. A miracle is a special event that somehow opens our eyes so we can see God more clearly; it touches our hearts so we can find our way closer to God. And so it is with this miracle of our friendship with the animals. So the question I want to ask now is this: What is it about this amazing experience we all share, of having a real friendship with an animal, that helps us understand *God* better?

I'll tell you a story of a great Jewish teacher named Martin Buber, who grew up in the Ukraine a little more than a hundred years ago. As a boy, Martin worked for a time on a farm, where part of his job was to groom the horses, to brush their coats and comb their manes and tails. He loved that job, as probably most kids would, and he grew to love one pony in particular. One day, as Martin was grooming his special pony, he realized that the horse cared for him, too. It wasn't just that he liked being brushed, or he liked the apples and carrots Martin brought. Beyond all that, the pony actually liked *Martin*. Martin felt the horse's affection for him; he felt loved by that pony.

Now Martin was a smart boy, but he was better than plain smart. He was someone whose head was connected to his heart, and both of those were connected to God. So Martin's friendship with the pony gave him an idea about God. He realized that the pony was teaching him something about God's love for him. That may sound weird to you, but think about it. One of the things we learn from our friendships with the animals is that real love does not depend upon similarity. Love can cross the boundary between species and unite beings who are fundamentally different one from the other: a horse and a boy or a girl; a cat and an old man; a poodle and a middle-aged widow.

What Martin saw is that all those small miracles of love between two fundamentally different beings are little models of the great love that connects us with God. When you think about it, God is even more different from us than the animals are. After all, we and the animals are all creatures; God alone is the Creator. We and the animals all have needs, we are in many ways dependent on others; God alone has no needs. We inhabit these small and sometimes frail bodies; God's boundless power and presence extend through the whole universe. God is really quite unlike us humans—most of all because of the huge difference that sin makes in our lives. All of us, deliberately or not, do things that hurt ourselves and others, and we live with the consequences. But God's life is perfect—perfect love, unscarred by sin.

If, then, God is so different from us, how can we dare to say that God is close to us, that God loves us and we love God? Christians often say that, in Jesus Christ, God comes to us as a friend and a brother, but are we just kidding ourselves? One ancient theologian said, "God is closer to me than I am to myself" (Augustine). How could that possibly be true? Well, Martin Buber would answer us, "Ask the animals, and they will teach you." We've just heard that line from the book of Job (12:7), and that is what Martin, the horse-groomer who grew up to be a great theologian, used to say when people asked him whether there can really be love between us and the God who created heaven and earth. "Ask the animals, and they will teach you." Look into the eyes of your animal friend, put your ear next to his or her heart, and ponder the miracle of love that binds us to these creatures who are so different from ourselves. And gradually, let that little miracle teach you about the great miracle that holds our souls in life, the miracle of love that binds each of us frail creatures to the great Lord of Life.

Amen.

Pray with Your Eyes Open

Fort Collins United Methodist Church, Fort Collins, Colorado
April 21, 2013

JOB 42:1–6, 10–17; MARK 10:46–52

The book of Job is Scripture's most extensive exploration of the depths of human misery. Though many who have endured terrible suffering find Job's ending facile, this sermon offers striking demonstrations of modern people who have found themselves, like Job, demanding a hearing with God. Job's conversation with God finally challenges us to see everything anew, and to "abandon ourselves in love" to a world we cannot control.

Recently my friend Jan and I had a serious conversation; she had been reading the book of Job. "I didn't really like the end," she said. "It seemed . . . well, too easy somehow. Not very real." When Jan talks about Job, I listen carefully, because she is an expert witness to the kind of suffering Job endures and survives. Ten days before our conversation, Jan had watched her house burn to the bare outer walls in the hours following a lightning strike. For the third time in less than two years, Jan and her family had watched everything they thought was safe and solid go up in smoke. First, her 15-year-old son David suffered a traumatic brain injury from a bike accident that left his crash helmet cracked open and him in a coma. After months of therapy and recovery, just as life was beginning to look sort of normal again, David was diagnosed with Hodgkin's lymphoma, and so a new kind of therapy began to bring the disease under control. After some further months, a CT scan delivered the happy news that the therapy had been successful—and then a few weeks later, the whole family found itself standing in the driveway, watching their house burn.

Through these two years, Jan and her family have been living at the outer edge of what seemed possible, if you were playing the odds. More to the point for Jan, they are at the outer edge of what she had thought was possible *with God*. "I'm just about this close to losing my faith," she said. That kind of honesty is why, when Jan talks about Job, I listen with respect. It is because of experiences like these that the book of Job has to be in the Bible—because very bad things happen to good, faithful people. Incredibly bad things happen to people who believe in God, and not just in the abstract. They have a relationship with God; they work on that relationship. And then suddenly, as with Job, they don't know what to do with experiences they never expected to have and feelings they never expected to have toward God: hurt, betrayal, distrust, rage. "What was it . . . ," Jan asked, with deep confusion in her face and voice, "what was it I was supposed to learn that I have to learn this way?"

I will say at the outset that I don't think the Bible or the Christian faith teaches that we suffer because we were supposed to learn something. The Bible does not in fact explain why suffering comes to us. But it does affirm that we can and often do grow through the experience of suffering, that we grow in ways that draw us closer to God, and closer to each other in God.

Jan told me a little more about the night of the fire: "As we stood there watching, David said, 'I'm just trying to calculate the odds: traumatic brain injury, Hodgkin's lymphoma, now our house is burning down. The odds against all that have got to be astronomically high.' And then we all laughed." Then David speed-dialed their youth pastor, who came over and sat with them all night on the lawn, saying psalms of lament and watching the house burn. "How is David doing?" I asked, and Jan answered, "You know, he isn't even fazed by this. He says, after all he's been through, this doesn't seem like a very big deal."

As a guest preacher, I do not know your experiences and your responses the way I know those of my friend, but I know that all of us are reeling in the wake of the Boston bombing and the horrible maiming of young healthy bodies, the appalling death by violence of yet another little child. Although I do not know you personally, I would dare say that some of you here today, perhaps many of us, know exactly what Jan means when she says, "I am this close to losing my faith. And it doesn't help me to read that after all Job went through, God gave him more sheep and camels and oxen, and more children to replace the ones he lost. It seems way too easy."

The book of Job speaks directly to our questions, our struggles, and our anger. However, it does not offer pat answers or neat solutions. That's what Job's three so-called friends offer, pat answers (the way pastors and theologians—people like me—so often do), and Job rightly tells them they are full of it—"worthless physicians," he calls them (13:4). No, the book of Job speaks to those who struggle in the way a great story speaks, in the language of the heart. It speaks the truth that a human heart that is seared by pain, torn open by pain, can become open to God in new ways. This truth cannot be explained, but it can be experienced and witnessed; that is what the book of Job is about.

This morning we heard the part of Job that seemed too easy to Jan, with all those replacement sheep and camels and children. But we cannot make sense of that part of the book unless we first go back into Job's story, back to where Job is pretty much in the same place we might be today: totally bewildered, unable to reconcile this dreadful calamity with anything we thought we knew about God.

Job is one of the longest books in the Bible, and it can be tedious to read, because, as you know, there is nothing particularly interesting about misery. Getting through Job, like getting through misery itself, is a long hard slog. So I am going to cut to the chase here and tell you the single most surprising thing about the book. It's this: Job cries out to God, rails against God through chapter after chapter—yet, curiously, Job never asks, "Why me, God?" Job never demands an explanation for how God could have allowed this to happen to him. What Job demands is much bolder—the kind of thing you demand only from someone with whom you have an intimate relationship, however troubled that relationship may currently be. Job demands a *hearing* from God, not an explanation. Job demands that God show up and listen to him. Job is not afraid of dying; what he's already been through makes the prospect of death look like a walk in the park. Job is ready for death, maybe even eager for it, but he will not die without saying his piece to God's face:

In my flesh I will look upon God,
I myself will look; my eyes shall see, and not as a stranger. (19:26–27)

"In my flesh"—Job is determined that God should know how things look from inside his skin; God owes him that much, he figures.

Now God must think that this demand of Job's is fair enough, because God does indeed show up and speak to Job at length, without ever explaining Job's suffering. No explanation could have satisfied him anyway. What Job gets instead is a God's-eye view of the world. God challenges Job to let his imagination go down to the foundations of the earth and up to the heavens, to see how the constellations are set in place and lightning travels across the sky. God speaks to Job of glorious and powerful animals, the mountain goat and the eagle and the ostrich—all of them leading their own wild and perfect lives, paying no attention at all to human beings. God extols the terrible beauty of Leviathan the sea monster and of Behemoth, the super-hippo that no one

85

wants to meet in a dark alley. Of that awesome and scary creature, God says, "*This* is my masterpiece, the best thing I ever did" (40:19).

In sum, God's answer to Job is something like this: "Open your eyes and see the world I have made. You have had eyes only for your own small sphere, and for your own misery. But now look, my friend, at the whole wild and beautiful world. Yes, it's a dangerous world; Leviathan and Behemoth are nothing to mess with. And human evil—that is deep, intractable (40:10–14); we've never yet managed to root it out. Yes, Job, this world is dangerous because it's wild, but it's also exquisitely beautiful. You cannot have the beauty without the wildness. No one *controls* this world—not even I—yet I like what I have made. And now, Job, what about you? Can you accept my world for what it is: wild, dangerous, violent—and at the same time overflowing with beauties large and small? And your own life—can you accept it for what it is? Can you love your 'one wild and precious life?'"[1]

Job demanded that God show up, and God did. God knows Job well, and it seems that this non-explanation is exactly what he needed to hear. Listen to how Job responds: "Ah, I had heard what people say about you, God, but now I have seen you with my own eyes. And I have changed my mind about dust and ashes." Most translations read here, "I repent on dust and ashes," but that is not a very good translation. "Dust and ashes" is a biblical metaphor for the human condition, as we appear before God. So when Job says, "I have changed my mind about dust and ashes," he means, "I have changed my mind about what it is to be human in the presence of God." That is Job's answer to God's great speech out of the whirlwind. Could it be that this is the only way we can ever be sure that God has shown up for us, when we discover that our mind has changed? I know that God has spoken *to me* when I discover that the world looks different, my own life looks different, because my mind has fundamentally changed.

That is how it was for Robin. Some years ago, Robin's thirteen-year-old daughter was suffering greatly from wild mood swings, from a drastic change in her personality that was eventually diagnosed as bipolar disorder. This happened at the time when Robin was studying to be a priest; his whole family had made considerable changes and sacrifices so he could pursue his vocation to serve God, and now they were suffering beyond anything they had ever experienced. And Robin was angry. One day he poured out his heart to his spiritual director, a rather formidable professor at an ancient English university, and she

---

1. The quoted phrase is from Mary Oliver, "The Summer Day," in *New and Selected Poems* (Boston: Beacon, 1992).

gave him this instruction: "Take a long walk and tell God exactly how you feel. Take as long as you like to say everything you have to say, and time it. Then, when you've finished, give God equal time to speak to you."

So Robin walked and talked and raged about his child's affliction and his feeling that God had abandoned them. He went on and on until there was nothing left to say, and then he stopped and said, "All right, God, it's your turn. I am listening." And in the silence that followed, he heard just one thing, one clear sentence: "From now on, I want you to pray with your eyes open." That was all, but it was enough for him. Like Job, Robin knew that God had spoken. "From now on, I want you to pray with your eyes open." "What I understood," he said to me, "is that I was being asked to pay attention, simply to notice what God is doing around me."

Robin knew that God had spoken, because he heard something that fundamentally changed his way of looking at the world and his own life. Like Job, Robin heard God inviting him to abandon himself in love to a world he cannot control. That word from God has now sustained Robin and his family through more than fifteen years of living with serious illness. It has sustained Robin and his wife as creative leaders of a thriving yet demanding church community. They are a strong and healthy family—people who have grown in wisdom and love, grown together, through all they have endured.

Likewise, Job grows in wisdom after he hears God's challenge to look at the world around him. We see Job's new wisdom evidenced in the context of his family life. After all his sufferings, Job becomes a father again—a very different kind of father than he was before the disaster. In the old days, Job was a cautious parent, and especially he was cautious around God. He used to offer sacrifices on behalf of his children, "just in case they had sinned," our storyteller says. Those sacrifices were a kind of protective hedge against God's anger—disaster insurance, you might say. But Job discovered, to his horror, that disaster insurance does not work in the economy of the cosmos.

Yet after God speaks to Job out of the whirlwind, Job "changes [his] mind about dust and ashes"; he changes how he thinks about living in this wild world, at once horrifying and beautiful. In the end, Job himself becomes . . . well, a wild kind of guy. Earlier, Job was ready to die; he wanted only to give God a piece of his mind first. But now he is ready to start life all over again, ready even to become a father again. Think about that; think of what it must have taken for Job to welcome children into his heart, this time knowing he could not protect them against disaster. Yet Job invests himself totally; throwing caution to the winds, Job and his wife have ten more children, and they do it with flair. Contrary to ancient custom, their beautiful daughters receive a full share in the family inheritance. What's more, they give these girls crazy names. You heard them in Hebrew, but translated into English their names mean "Dove," "Aloe," "Horn of Eye-shadow"—names that celebrate their physical loveliness. No one else in the Bible gives their kids names like that. Now Job, who may once have feared God but certainly did not trust God all that much, is letting the good times roll. Job is along for the ride, loving every minute of it, living every minute to the fullest, though now with no illusion that he is in control.

Today in our reading Job says to God: "I had heard of you with the hearing of the ear, but now my eye has seen you." Again, we heard a similar word in the reading from Mark's Gospel: the blind beggar Bartimaeus said to Jesus, "My teacher, let me see again" (Mark 10:51).

Do you hear? It is all about how you see; the life of faith is all about how you see. That is the message God speaks to us through the Scripture lessons today. Contrast that with the saying that has become so popular among us: "It is what it is." That's a kind of verbal teeth-gritting, isn't it? "I'm a realist, and I can face this situation. It is what it is." Now consider: if by that we mean that we know exactly the dimensions and possibilities of this situation, then "it is what it is" runs directly counter to the biblical view of reality. There is much more wisdom, there is infinitely more possibility, in desperate Job's demand to see God. There is more wisdom, because there is more faith, in the prayer of blind Bartimaeus, "My teacher, let me see again."

Do you hear? Life and faith are all about how you see. So from now on, pray with your eyes open, and pray without ceasing.

Amen.

Holy Preaching: Ethical Interpretation
and the Practical Imagination

....

ESSAY

He often tells them that sermons are dangerous things, that none goes out of church as he came in, but either better, or worse; that none is careless before his Judge, and that the word of God shall judge us. By these and other means the Parson procures attention; but the character of his sermon is holiness; he is not witty, or learned, or eloquent, but holy.

George Herbert, "The Parson Preaching"

JOAN OF ARC: "I hear voices telling me what to do. They come from God."
CAPTAIN ROBERT DE BAUDRICOURT: "They come from your imagination."
JOAN: "Of course. That is how the messages of God come to us."

George Bernard Shaw, *St. Joan*

In seventeenth-century England, preaching was the most popular form of public entertainment and sermons the most widely read literature. The great London preachers dazzled theologically sophisticated audiences, and some of them, such as the poet and priest John Donne, Dean of Saint Paul's, drew the common people in crowds of thousands, for religious controversy was the daily news. And like all national celebrities, they had their less talented imitators in the provinces. When George Herbert asserted that the essential character of the country parson's sermon is holiness, he meant that pastors should stop trying to impress their people and instead move them to repentance and an all-involving commitment to the Christian life. The purpose of this essay is to urge a style of contemporary preaching that aims at such a commitment.

89

Specifically, I maintain that "holy preaching" is explicitly oriented toward the biblical text and characterized by a willingness to acquire new habits and categories of thought in order to read it with comprehension. Such a willingness to think in new ways is the disposition essential for ethical interpretation of the Scriptures; it is also the heart of the biblical concept of repentance. The two are in fact closely linked. I use the term "ethical interpretation" to designate an exploration motivated by curiosity about that which is unknown or different from ourselves, curiosity acute enough to open us to the possibility of personal change in response to what we learn. And profound personal change is what the Bible means by "repentance." The concept includes more than contrition for specific sins; it entails a radical reorientation of self (Hebrew *shuv*, "turn"), a reordering of habits of thought (Greek *metanoia*, "change of mind"). Here I shall argue that the preacher's chief task is to establish and maintain within the worshiping community the conditions that make it possible to hear the Scriptures as the Word of God—that is, as an invitation and challenge to change.

Reading the Scriptures as the Word of God is the basic identifying practice of the Christian community. It underlies every other practice, such as the sacraments and mission. The essential form of the common life is in the broadest sense a *conversation* in which members of the community explore and debate the meaning of their sacred texts and find ways to live together in accordance with what they have read. In what follows I stress the need for openness in conversation, so that many voices may be heard: the different voices within the biblical text, within the community, and also the voices of outsiders. Maintaining openness requires not only curiosity but also trust—trust among the members of the community and, even more, trust in the text that they have gathered to hear. Trust expresses itself in a conviction that, no matter how strange or unappealing a given passage may be, there is something in it for us, something to be gained from the work of painstaking, acute listening, which is the fundamental act of obedience (Latin *ob-audire*). While the interpretive conversation is open-ended with respect to the forms that faithful response may take in the present situation, it is nonetheless rooted in a shared conviction of the necessity and finally the safety of listening to the text.

Such trust in both text and community must be based initially on certain common commitments, namely, those made in baptism and nurtured through participation in worship: profession of faith in a triune God, known by the name of Father, Son, and Holy Spirit; in the incarnation of God in Jesus Christ; in the redemptive value for all humankind of his suffering, death, and resurrection, in which we share through baptism; in the presence and power of the Holy Spirit animating the church. These basic commitments must obtain within the community of faith if its readings of Scripture are to be coherent—that is, if they are to be in basic continuity with the theological understandings of Christian communities in other places and times.

Yet continuity does not imply full agreement. Sometimes new historical or philological knowledge brings us into disagreement with formerly established interpretations. Sometimes such disagreement is born out of reading in a changed social context, or with new awareness of elements of our context. We often and legitimately depart from the interpretations of our predecessors, or from our own earlier understandings, because Scripture addresses us conversationally, as the living Word of God, and therefore it does not speak in identical fashion on every occasion. Freshened by the Holy Spirit, it is at each reading a new utterance, directed personally but not privately to each hearer and community.

The conversational nature of scriptural interpretation within the church precludes simple dichotomizing between truth and falsity. Rather, it is better to recognize that we inevitably fall into errors both major and minor *on our way toward truth.* Advancement in any intellectual endeavor, but above all in the journey of faith, depends upon a process of continual exploration, debate, correction, and reorientation. It necessitates learning to live with disagreement—a process that requires trust in the Holy Spirit, as well as in text and community—and being open to aspects of truth that have not been seen before.

In what follows I shall argue that this process involves paying attention to the imaginative language of Scripture and cultivation of a rich critical imagination, which is the chief faculty of moral discernment. Preaching is indispensable to the cultivation of such imagination in Christian communities, and the primary means by which it is to be nurtured and honed are the biblical stories, images, symbols, prayers, and exhortations.

Uses of the Imagination

That there is little serious biblical preaching in mainline churches is most centrally a problem of a neglected and atrophied Christian imagination, to which the language of the Bible is largely unintelligible. I think it is safe to say that the Scriptures are less accessible to the average believer today than before the Reformation, even if most churchgoers own a personal copy in semi-idiomatic English. They are inaccessible, certainly not because we lack historical information about the biblical world, but because we do not have the imaginative skills to probe the subject matter of the Bible: love and forgiveness, suffering and redemption, the persistence of evil and the birth of boundless hope. Mass media and modes of education that focus on information acquisition and measurable outcomes have left us ill-equipped to deal with those non-molecular facts of human existence, which can be verified but not predicted; proclaimed, probed, and understood both with reason and deep in the bones, yet not fully *explained* in terms of causation, a logical and chronological succession of events.

The only language that is adequate to express and draw connections among such more-than-logical phenomena is the poetic language of symbol, including myth, metaphor, proverb, parable, and even the language of legal code—all of which may (in Paul Ricoeur's terms) "redescribe" reality and thus "disclose a world" richer in meaning than the one we had previously inhabited.[1] The language of Scripture, as most premodern interpreters (both Jews and Christians) understood, is predominantly the language of symbol—something that "metaphysical" preachers and poets such as the Anglicans George Herbert and John Donne also comprehended.[2] Precisely that constitutes the gap between its epistemological presuppositions and our own. Modern technological culture, through an almost exclusive concentration on theory and conceptual analysis, is perhaps unparalleled among the "high cultures" of history for its ineptitude and impatience with the ambiguities of verbal symbolism.

With respect to the formulation of a style of "holy preaching," it is most interesting that the Bible itself in numerous instances evidences no opposition between imaginative proclamation and moral instruction, although the tone of the great biblical sermons is not "preachy." Nathan does not harangue David on violations of the sixth, seventh, and tenth commandments (2 Sam. 12); he uses a story, which the king may or may not have taken as fictional, that enables David to see the moral contours of the situation and render an accurate judgment on himself.[3] Isaiah sings a love song about a vineyard (Isa. 5:1-7); Lady Wisdom

---

1. On the question of the function of symbolic language in Scripture, the work of Paul Ricoeur is seminal; see, e.g., *The Symbolism of Evil* (Boston: Beacon, 1967), and "Biblical Hermeneutics," *Semeia* 4 (1975): 27-148.

2. On the highly imaginative "metaphysical" style of preaching, see Horton Davies, *Like Angels from a Cloud: The English Metaphysical Preachers, 1588-1645* (San Marino, CA: Huntington Library, 1986). Since none of Herbert's sermons survive, we must infer his understanding of Scripture from the poems and especially his two sonnets "The Holy Scriptures I and II."

3. See Garrett Green's treatment of this encounter, which he uses to illustrate the principle, "To save sinners, God seizes them by the imagination" (*Imagining God: Theology and the Religious Imagination* [San Francisco: Harper & Row, 1989], 149-50).

(in Prov. 1:20–33; 8:1–9:18) freely mixes prophetic summons, accusations, and promises with the reasonable appeal of a teacher and also womanly allure in order to win the ingénue to the right path. In every case, the preachers within the Bible appeal to the heart, which in biblical physiology is not distinct from the mind. Such an appeal would seem to be what Herbert intended when he commended "ravishing" rather than controversial preaching texts to his contemporaries;[4] it is the heart ravished by just guilt and wholesome desire that is the best moral instructor.

These examples of biblical preaching all demonstrate a quality too little evident even in contemporary preaching that claims to take direct inspiration from the Bible—namely, preaching with an explicit social agenda that is sometimes termed "prophetic." The quality that marks the preaching of the genuine biblical prophets is irony. Many years ago I heard homiletician Charles Rice say that as preachers we need a more "ironic" and less "heroic" mode of discourse.[5] Jeremiah's confrontation with Hananiah may exemplify the contrast. Hananiah is a prophetic hero, speaking confidently of a bright future for Judah and Jerusalem—a prophecy that proves to be false. Jeremiah takes a stance that Rice describes as "ironic"; he accepts his location outside the power structure and there finds the courage to articulate a vision without a program attached. He speaks fearlessly to the present situation and yet admits with all humility that the future remains obscure to him (Jer. 28:5-11). Much that goes by the name of prophetic preaching is in fact heroic: using the Scriptures to endorse our own programs rather than to call the premises of our programs into question. In the memorable terms posed by Dietrich Bonhoeffer, it is reading Scripture *for* ourselves rather than over *against* ourselves.[6]

I propose that the preacher's first and most important responsibility is to educate the imaginations of her hearers so that they have the linguistic skills to enter into the world that Scripture discloses. The biblical preacher is a sort of elementary language teacher, not a conceptual translator, as is often considered

4. In Herbert's words: "But [holiness] is gained first, by choosing texts of Devotion, not Controversy, moving and ravishing texts, whereof the Scriptures are full" ("The Parson Preaching," in *A Priest to the Temple, or, The Country Parson,* ed. John Wall [New York: Paulist, 1981], 63).

5. Oral communication.

6. Dietrich Bonhoeffer, *No Rusty Swords: Letters, Lectures, and Notes, 1928-1936* (New York: Harper & Row, 1965), 185. See the excellent discussion in "Living and Dying in the Word: Dietrich Bonhoeffer as Performer of Scripture," chap. 6 in Stephen E. Fowl and L. Gregory Jones, *Reading in Communion: Scripture and Ethics in Christian Life* (Grand Rapids: Eerdmans, 1991), 135-64.

to be the case. Whether or not preachers have read or remember Bultmann, they often engage in his program of "demythologizing" the Bible, translating it into the terms of modern rationalism. Thus, as I once heard, John's version of the miracle of the loaves and fishes becomes a display of impressive generosity in a child who shared his lunch, moving others in the crowd to do likewise; and we also should emulate him in our own contexts.

The attraction of such an approach is obvious: it makes Scripture conformable to our accustomed categories of thought and supports socially valuable behavior. This combination of effects is what is usually meant by "making the Bible relevant." The problem, however, is that ready applicability has been purchased at the price of the story itself. While there might be some moral force to a story of public sharing of scant resources, the story the evangelist tells is quite different; he says that Jesus made more food on the spot. John invites us to contemplate a world where offering to God all the little we have inexplicably yields more, in "overflowing" abundance (*perisseusanta*, John 6:12). Responding to that invitation requires that we do something both more difficult and more ethically significant than sharing our lunch, namely, that we think in fundamentally new ways about the presence and power of God. As I have noted, the New Testament word for taking on new mental habits is *metanoia*, "a change of mind"—that is, "repentance." The preacher who invites the congregation to contemplate the multiplication of the loaves and fishes or the parting of the Red Sea *without translating away the wonder* calls upon the congregation to repent.

It is evident that rationalizing the biblical story is far easier for both preacher and hearer than sustaining imaginative attention to a text whose thought categories are so foreign to us. As anyone who has ever engaged in language study knows, success requires a dogged patience with the strange. The reward for forgoing a conceptual translation and learning to listen to the Bible on its own terms is that a more spacious world opens to us. There we see exposed the terrible limitations that we previously accepted as givens of the human condition. We see them overcome in God's faithfulness, maintained despite Israel's faithlessness; in the suffering psalmists' utter trust in God, expressed equally in wild hope and bitter accusation; in the incarnation, death, and resurrection of Jesus Christ. The relevance of the Scriptures is that they take account of my genuine needs, my longing, and my despair, not that they conform to my thinking and lifestyle as they are presently constituted.

The miracle stories are parade examples of what is in fact the Bible's regular rhetorical strategy of using imaginative language to jostle us into radically new ways of looking at the world and at ourselves. But it is more customary for Christians to speak of the Scriptures as being "inspired" than as being "imaginative." While so-called mainline Christians may be reluctant to define too closely the nature of the Holy Spirit's inspiration, it seems valid to consider inspired utterance as a special category of imaginative speech, greatly exceeding even the author's own capacity for conceptualization. T. S. Eliot, speaking of secular as well as religious poetry, suggests that "if the word 'inspiration' is to have any meaning, it must mean just this, that the speaker or writer is uttering something which he does not wholly understand—or which he may even misinterpret when the inspiration has departed from him."[7] Certainly the images that Scripture itself uses to describe the Word of God suggest that it can be neither contained nor controlled: a hammer beating within a body until the blows resound in words or a fire raging inside (Jer. 23:29), a baby insistent to be born (Isa. 42:14; see 26:17).

A degree of indeterminacy is part of the character of inspired speech. Put more positively, inspired speech is an inexhaustible store of meaning, a treasure room out of which the scribe who has been trained for the kingdom of heaven brings what is new and what is old (Matt. 13:52). The reticence inherent in symbolic language is not separable from its richness; it begs and begets interpretation. This peculiar susceptibility to interpretation that characterizes imaginative speech, and that is developed to the highest degree in the Scriptures, would seem to be the quality that makes Scripture the source of continually renewed life in the church.

The imaginative character of the biblical witness bears directly on the task of ethical interpretation. The fundamental ethical question is whether we can reckon seriously with that which is different from ourselves.[8] Though often trivialized, curiosity is a virtue, for this is the basis of the ethical stance: a genuine interest in the character and perspective of the other. As I have suggested, the Scriptures are to us an "other";[9] they speak a language and express a view of reality vastly different from our own. There can be no ethical preaching that does not take respectful account of how deeply strange to us is this written witness to the Word of God.

Imagination is the interpretive faculty by which we relate to that which is

---

7. T. S. Eliot, *On Poetry and Poets* (1957; New York: Octagon Books, 1975), 137.

8. The implications of this view of ethics for the study of literature are explored by Wayne Booth in *The Company We Keep: An Ethics of Fiction* (Berkeley: University of California Press, 1988). The study is highly useful for preachers, who must reckon with a text that is often ethically problematic.

9. On the value of seeing Scripture as an outsider for the maintenance of interpretive humility, see Fowl and Jones, *Reading in Communion*, 110-13.

strange, not fully known, or not immediately present to us. And that, of course, is almost everything—past, present, and future. Hence, constant exercise of the imagination is a practical necessity for every healthy human being, and not only the science fiction writer or the religious mystic. Imagination is essential in composing a thoughtful letter or a sermon, each of which is to be received sometime in the future in circumstances at which we can now only guess. We use imagination in designing a garden or an investments portfolio, in figuring out why a teenager is sulking. A healthy, flexible imagination is the "coping mechanism" by which, moment by moment, we make the small extrapolations that give us a history and a world and enable us to envision a future.

Although the imaginative capacity is universal and is employed in count-less quotidian situations, it does indeed have a mystical dimension in the sense of involving us, to a greater or lesser extent, in an apprehension of the totality of life, which is essentially mysterious. As Richard Kroner has argued in a foundational study of imagination as an aspect of religious knowledge, "an image of ultimate truth is included in every practical situation, and . . . this image is truly religious, or, if not, then it is pseudo-religious and superstitious."[10]

For the spiritual life, the most important use of imagination is in coming to know God. The fact that we know God imaginatively is congruent with the way we know all other persons and also ourselves. We do not form a theory about our intimates and others for whom we genuinely care. Theorizing about persons, as a substitute for knowing them, is otherwise known as prejudice; it is the basis of oppression and resentment, not intimacy. Rather, we form an image of those we love based on the limited data of our own contacts and hearsay: a whole picture, although always to some degree incomplete, subject to change and refinement. Similarly, when we want to know about a stranger, we ask someone close to him for an approximation of his character: "What is he like? Tell me about him." We intuitively know not to ask for an objective measure of the person—who or what is she?—but for an impressionistic eval-uation of what she is *like*. The qualifier "like" lends modesty to all assertions; it acknowledges the perspectival character of personal testimony.[11]

The biblical witness to the nature of God is likewise impressionistic and perspectival. Rigor in maintaining the modesty of our assertions would seem to be what underlies the prohibition against graven images. We must not try

---

10. Richard Kroner, *The Primacy of Faith* (New York: Macmillan, 1943), 154.

11. On the importance of the qualification, see Garrett Green, "'The Bible as . . .': Fic-tional Narrative and Scriptural Truth," in *Scriptural Authority and Narrative Interpretation,* ed. Hans W. Frei (Philadelphia: Fortress, 1987), 79-96; see also Green, *Imagining God.*

to show God directly; we can do no more than indicate what God is like. So, for example, when Ezekiel presents his vision of God by the river Chebar, it is so full of qualifying particles that the Hebrew is almost untranslatable:

> There was something like a throne, resembling sapphire; and up above the likeness of a throne was what resembled a human form. And above what resembled his loins I saw the like of gleaming amber, having the semblance of fire enclosing it all around, and below what resembled his loins I saw the semblance of fire, and there was flashing about him. The semblance of the bow in the midst of clouds on a rainy day—such was the appearance of the flashing all about. This was the appearance of the image of the glory of the LORD. (Ezek. 1:26–28a)

The prophet, who had a reputation as a great lyrical stylist (Ezek. 33:32), here willingly trips over his own tongue lest his description of God be taken as objective representation.

The work of interpretation is greatly complicated, and its interest is incalculably increased, by the diversity of perspectives with which the biblical witness presents us. There is an essential coherence, traditionally called "unity," to the Scriptures, which historical criticism has tended to obscure with its isolating emphasis on the (presumed) conditions and process of production lying behind a given text. The unity of the Scriptures derives from the fact that it is one God who is made known to us through Israel's varied witness. God is revealed as a living God, not a stone idol of unchanging demeanor—a being whose character is coherent although (like other living beings) God's behavior is not predictable. The extraordinary diversity of the Scriptures can be accounted for by the partiality of each aspect of its composite witness, and also by the relational character of the interaction between God and Israel. The fact that the scriptural witness emerges out of personal relationship suggests that serious theological use of the Bible entails looking for constancy, not uniformity, in its delineation of God's character, and that demonstrating the normativity of Scripture entails discerning and articulating intelligible patterns in the revelation of God's nature and will for the world.[12]

The aim of all the Scriptures is to give us an inside view of committed relationship with the God of Israel, based upon the testimony of those most

---

12. On the notion of pattern as the key to the unity and normativity of the Scriptures, see David H. Kelsey, *The Uses of Scripture in Recent Theology* (Philadelphia: Fortress, 1975), 192-97; and Green, *Imagining God,* 114-18.

deeply experienced in it. But attempts to expound *the* meaning—single, fixed, objectively determined—of that testimony are inherently unethical, for they fail to respect the character of this "other" that is Scripture. The biblical witness is ineluctably personal, although not private; and the preacher who would be faithful to it must become personally involved in a process akin to the interpretation of poetry, a process to which intellect, emotion, memory, conscience, and will all contribute, and by which all may be transformed. For "sermons are dangerous things"; no one comes out of the interpretive process as she went in, least of all the preacher. Wherever anyone succeeds in doing so, there the scriptural inspiration that animates the community of faith has been temporarily eclipsed.

The homiletical task is not to pronounce the immutable Truth. Rather, the preacher is to articulate the text's multiple voices, over weeks and years, so that those voices may gradually become the background against which the voices within the community are heard and their differences adjudicated. Likewise, they form the background for hearing the threats, accusations, and skepticism of outsiders, which are not wholly unjust. When the character of the sermon is holiness, listeners are invited into a wide-ranging but disciplined conversation, ongoing through the ages, and advancing with each generation of faith and unfaith into new areas of concern. That conversation puts the participants in responsible relation to the whole of the created order. The responsibility is real, though it is assumed through an imaginative extension of themselves, guided by the Scriptures. In practical terms, for ordinary North American Christians, that means being able to relate their present activity to a larger individual and family history, to the Apostles' Creed and the domestic and foreign policies of the current government administration, to the disobedience in the Garden and destruction of the rain forests, to the fall of Jerusalem and acts of terrorism, to the crucifixion on Golgotha and global warming.

The Inclusivity of Interpretation

Preaching that acknowledges the character of the Scriptures as a personal and imaginative witness to faith is genuinely inclusive, in two senses. First, it recognizes that in many or perhaps most cases, people may in good faith genuinely disagree about the correct interpretation of the facts and the right course of action. Through conversation we maintain the common life, which provides the only basis for serious exploration of what in any given situation may be the few options for faithful living. Second, such an acknowledgment facilitates conversation with outsiders and makes room for their voices to be heard within the community of faith, without disguising—indeed, while putting in the foreground—the personal commitment that obtains there. But respectful attention to others who do not share our own views and commitments should not be confused with the too-common error of liberalism in treating the Christian story (including Israel's history) as a matter of private and elective interest to believers. In a time when many elements of the dominant culture (including most universities) categorically deny the public relevance of the church and Christian conceptions of truth, the church is especially pressed within the context of its own shared life to test and criticize interpretations of the multifaceted truth to which the Scriptures attest.

Contrary to a misconception popular among seminary graduates (for it is too often fostered in the teaching of homiletics, theology, and also Bible), exegetical preaching is the surest way to maintain the breadth and openness of conversation within the community of faith. Thematic preaching tends to present and reinforce an established viewpoint. In Dietrich Bonhoeffer's lectures on homiletics to the Confessing Church seminary at Finkenwalde, he warned: "Thematic preaching carries the danger that only the proposed problem and the suggested answer will be remembered; apologetic comes to the fore and the text is ignored."[13] The best argument for exegetical preaching is that it allows the text to function as what it is: inspired speech, potent to introduce to the community of faith new directions for movement and also new problems, which are more fruitful than the ones advanced by our own agendas.

This inspiration becomes an operative force when not just the preacher but the whole community becomes concerned and competent to give close attention to the words and images of the Scriptures. Surprising metaphors challenge our ready categorizations: "Love is strong, like death, passion fierce, like Sheol" (Song of Songs 8:6). This simile leads the preacher of a wedding sermon to consider that love may be more like death than it is death's polar opposite (as we generally think). Their likeness in strength and fierceness suggests that love is the only thing that consumes us as fully as does death; love teaches us to give ourselves wholly and freely, and thus it is the best preparation for death, to which the whole Christian life is directed. Consonant with the gospel and directly contrary to our cultural assumptions, death does not defeat what love has built but rather completes it.

Serious, ongoing exegetical preaching, aimed at identifying patterns of faithful relationship with God and neighbor, exposes the inadequacy of nar-

13. Dietrich Bonhoeffer, *Worldly Preaching: Lectures on Homiletics* (New York: Crossroad, 1991), 129.

rowly issue-oriented resort to the text. In instituting a building program, it may be less effective for a congregation to hear of Solomon's Temple construction than to consider the achievements and failures of the seven churches in the Revelation to John. Or we might follow the example of John Donne when beginning to build a new chapel at Lincoln's Inn (in London): working with the story of Jacob at Bethel, he says: I speak "not merely literally of building material chapels . . . but I speak principally of building such a church, as every man may build in himself: for whensoever we present our prayers, and devotions deliberately, and advisedly to God, there we consecrate that place, there we build a church."[14] Donne considers what it is to make "churches of our houses, and of our hearts,"[15] to awaken from sleep, as Jacob did, and realize that we stand at "the gate of heaven" (Gen. 28:17).

Again, rather than stopping at the citation of the two verses from Leviticus (18:22; 20:13) that proscribe (male) homosexual behavior, congregations might study them in the context of the larger vision of holiness set forth in that book, and further in light of Jesus's understandings of purity and community. There may be no "right answer" to the questions that most deeply trouble us; yet such an approach helpfully confounds the self-serving tendency to proof-texting and opens up the possibility of genuinely new insight.

To a very great extent, then, the church's life is its interpretive conversation. The Roman Catholic theologian Nicholas Lash has suggested that the proper business of the church is to be "an academy of word-care," a guild of skilled if amateur "philologists"—literally, lovers of the Word.[16] This business is carried on in worship and private prayer; in vestry meetings, hospitals, and classrooms; as well as in the pulpit. In those settings and countless others, scriptural language is probed and its sense tested in light of all that we experience and know from other sources. Reciprocally, our experience is scrutinized in light of the revealing images; the words of the Scriptures provide a measure against which the coherence of our thought and action is to be tested. Over the course of years, the disciplined care of words challenges the identity and commitments of every participant.

The opposite of ethical interpretation, which is fundamentally characterized by respectful curiosity about what is strange, is moralism—that is, insistence that one's own view is incontrovertible and stands in no need of

14. *The Sermons of John Donne*, ed. George R. Potter and Evelyn M. Simpson (Berkeley: University of California Press, 1953-62), 2:222 (modernization of language mine).

15. *The Sermons of John Donne*, 2:224.

16. See Lash, "Ministry of the Word or Comedy and Philology," *New Blackfriars* 68 (1987): 472-83.

reconsideration or supplementation. Throughout the history of the church, the Bible has often been wielded as a weapon in battles both internal and external, and what I have said about the imaginative nature of the Scriptures offers one way of understanding why such usage is unethical in its treatment of both persons and the text. Moralism treats theoretical positions, not texts, as canon; thus it mutes the call to new thinking, to repentance, which the Bible addresses continually to all its readers.

One form of moralism that is prevalent in our culture is directed against the Bible itself, namely, denying the authority of those portions that we take to represent moral insight inferior to our own. This was the first heresy identified by the church, in the form of Marcion's attempted exclusion of the entire Old Testament. Preaching across the whole canon—a practice that the present volume illustrates—is the single most important practice whereby preachers can counter such moralism, in themselves and in their congregations. As I have said, coherent thinking and speaking about God requires something like the disciplines of language study, for which the Bible *in its entirety* is our primer. Truth cannot be secured by censuring the Scriptures when they do not speak as we would choose, as though they must be the last word on God or the Christian faith, rather than its first and best witness. On the contrary, it is by listening well to the Scriptures, taking seriously their perspectival character and metaphorical reticence, that we may discover in the large area of silence that surrounds them the freedom to articulate our own witness of faith.

In addition to the primary practice of preaching across the whole canon, the preacher should observe two further safeguards of ethical interpretation: historical criticism and the church's tradition of scriptural interpretation, including (and, for Anglicans, especially) the liturgy. I shall comment briefly on each of the latter two.

An imaginative approach to Scripture does not invalidate historical criticism; rather, it directs the use of historical criticism toward the end of spiritual and cognitive transformation, repentance. The agenda of ethical interpretation does not restrict investigation to only those texts or aspects of texts that are of obvious pastoral or spiritual relevance. On the contrary, the practical imagination is enriched by any study, however technical, that draws us into deeper consideration of the words, forms, and images of the text—that is, study that enables (or forces) us to read the text with care, rather than tempting us to talk around or "get behind" the text in order to reconstruct social settings or literary layers for which there is no direct evidence. Thus, study that is practical for ministry includes advanced Hebrew syntax and poetic structure as well as ancient Near Eastern agricultural and funerary practices.

Historical study of the Bible counters the impulse to moralize against the Bible, because it discourages us from imposing our cultural assumptions upon a world we do not readily comprehend. For example, the work of Carol Meyers draws on archaeology and social anthropology to challenge the view that the social role of women in early Israel was oppressively restricted.[17] By showing how economic balance was maintained in a society where the home was the primary production unit, she shows also how far from both ordinary Israelite experience and the biblical ideal is the consumer-oriented system in which virtually all North Americans participate. Again, study of ancient cultures could challenge a sense of moral superiority to the vengeful composer of Psalm 137, who longs to see Babylonian babies bashed against the rock. Opinion leaders and decision-making elements in our society (including many clergy and churchgoers) could be more readily compared to the powerful Babylonians than to the defeated Israelites to whom moralistic Christians would counsel mercy. A historically educated imagination might well consider who could (legitimately?) wish that our own empire would not last through another generation.

The third counter to moralizing against the biblical text, the tradition of premodern interpretation, may seem to sort oddly with historical criticism. A generation ago, historical criticism was regarded by many as what constituted critical biblical studies. The text's "reception history" was the ugly duckling in the nest of interpretive methods, if it was admitted at all. That situation has changed, and now serious students of the Bible recognize that premodern preachers and commentators have much to teach us about modes of interpretation that are both disciplined and imaginative. In short, "premodern" does not mean "uncritical." The ancient and medieval commentators were not naive about the complexity of meaning, however their hermeneutics might differ from our own. Further, the early Reformers reckoned seriously with the human and historical character of the Bible, even though the Holy Spirit remained for them its real author. Yet they differed from almost all modern biblical scholars in that they were essentially unconcerned about the problem of *historical* distance between the biblical world and their own. They saw (correctly, I believe) that the real problem is the *moral* distance between the world that the text calls us to inhabit and the one in which we are too content to stay. Liturgical usage, including the daily lectionary, often provides valuable clues to traditional understandings that call into question the sophistication and

17. Carol Meyers, *Rediscovering Eve: Ancient Israelite Women in Context* (New York: Oxford University Press, 2013).

adequacy of contemporary readings. Those who preach in liturgical traditions may find a previously "unpreachable" text opened up by consideration of the moral purpose that it is meant to serve at a particular time in the church year. Probably nowhere is this so true as with the Psalms.

For example, Psalm 149 seems at first to be especially ill-chosen for the Feast of All Saints, perpetuating the unhappy stereotype of the serious religious person as a ruthless fanatic:

> Let the high praises of God be in their throats
> and two-edged swords in their hands,
> to execute vengeance on the nations
> and punishment on the peoples,
> to bind their kings with fetters
> and their nobles with chains of iron,
> to execute on them the judgment decreed.
> This is glory for all his faithful ones.
> Praise the LORD! (vv. 6–9, NRSV)

This psalm might be dismissed as expressing "the spirit of the O.T., not of the N.T.";[18] yet many overtly irenic psalms were passed over in favor of this one to celebrate the glory of the saints. There must be something in the disconcerting conjunction between violence and praise that offers a key to the nature of sainthood. In fact, a regular pattern is discernible in the lives of the saints: contrition—that is, fighting the evil within—prepares the way for contending with evil in the world. Considered in this light, the psalm points—in the highly condensed and suggestive language of poetry—to the fact that the self-inflicted violence of penitence, turned against our own private empire-building, clears the way for God's praise. Augustine reads the psalm in light of Jesus's saying, "I come not to bring peace but a sword" (Matt. 10:34), and observes: "He severs from you that which hinders you."[19]

It is a useful exegetical habit, when we find ourselves feeling morally superior to the biblical text, to consider whether we might be reading too literalistically—that is, whether we do not need to exercise our imagination to discover the perspective in which the passage may speak to us as a genuinely

18. A. F. Kirkpatrick (citing Delitzsch), *The Book of Psalms* (Cambridge: Cambridge University Press, 1902), 829.

19. St. Augustine, *Expositions on the Book of Psalms,* Nicene and Post-Nicene Fathers of the Church, ed. and trans. Philip Schaff (Grand Rapids: Eerdmans, 1979), 8:679; translation modified.

new Word of God, which calls on us to repent. The interpretation suggested here takes the two-edged sword as a metaphor for the Word of God that "is able to judge the thoughts and intentions of the heart" (Heb. 4:12, NRSV; see also Eph. 6:17 and Rev. 1:16). There may be more modern utility than is first evident for Augustine's principle regarding figurative interpretation, "that what is read should be subjected to diligent scrutiny until an interpretation contributing to the reign of charity is produced. If this result appears literally in the text, the expression being considered is not figurative."[20]

The search for an interpretation that conduces to charity does not mean whitewashing the Scriptures to remove all signs of Israel's idolatry and vituperation. The writers of neither Testament were at all times successful in upholding the mystery and radical grace of God's presence, while determining concrete ways in which to live with their fears and their enemies. But in this case and many others, a figurative interpretation is on several counts preferable to writing off the text as further evidence of the primitive warlike spirit of ancient Israel. First, a figurative interpretation does not depend on a historical assumption for which there is no evidence—namely, that the Israelites were more primitive than we are in either humanitarian concern or literary usage. Second, it has the support of the explicit New Testament reading and amplification of the metaphor of the two-edged sword. Third, it follows Christian liturgists of every generation, beginning with the apostle Paul (1 Cor. 14:26), in respecting the Psalms as a witness to faith that provides the most reliable guidance for the Christian life.

The question that the preacher must continually ask is how to create an environment in which it is safe to be vulnerable to the Bible as God's Word. To call the Bible "the Word of the Lord" is to confess our vulnerability to this Word that is foreign to us, our willingness to think in radically new ways in order to receive it as gift and promise: "Thanks be to God." Refusing that effort is what the Bible calls "hardness of heart," which Paul treats as the antonym of "repentance" (Rom. 2:4–5; see also Exod. 7:13, 22; Mark 6:52; etc.). Yet acceptance may be difficult and painful, and so the assurance of safety is crucial if the congregation is to sustain the appropriate vulnerability that makes new thinking possible. The assurance the preacher must give is that listening to the text will never mean giving up one's own right to a questioning, critical voice in the interpretive conversation. The notion of "appropriate vulnerability" suggests a view of the text that differs greatly from Erich Auerbach's

---

20. Augustine, *On Christian Doctrine* 3.15, trans. D. W. Robertson Jr. (Indianapolis: Bobbs-Merrill Educational Publishing, 1958), 93.

famous dictum that the Bible's claim to truth is "tyrannical" and its stories, in contrast to Homer's, "seek to subject us, and if we refuse to be subjected we are rebels."[21] While it is true that they far more often challenge than flatter us, nonetheless the final aim of the Scriptures is not subjugation but (to use Paul's word) edification (1 Cor. 14:26). They upbuild the community of faith by seizing and stretching its imagination toward new possibilities for human life.

No one—least of all the preacher—should imagine that the church's daily and weekly work of "theologizing" can be done adequately in the pulpit, if that is the only place where it is done. Rather, the sermon should be crafted to generate around and through the text thought, prayer, discussion, argument, and action—that is, all the work that leads to true knowledge of God. The preacher's task is less to solve problems in our understanding of Scripture than to identify those problems that are most fruitful for the congregation's life. Holy preaching provides a serious introduction to the problems that should be held up for reconsideration again and again, by people striving to grow toward God.

Participating in this kind of Scripture-based conversation connects us to the past yet is never merely an exercise in archaism. On the contrary, regaining fluency in the language of the Scriptures and the long tradition of their interpretation can enrich the depleted memory of the church and bring us to new and crucial knowledge of ourselves. "The art of salvation, is but the art of memory," says John Donne—and it is scriptural memory to which he refers.[22] The Bible's language of story and symbol is the key to a store of memories that stretch all the way back to our creation in God's image, memories of ourselves as God's people, which have the power to draw us beyond the fearful and unimaginative absorption in the present that is such a strong element in the spiritual malaise of our time.

Simone Weil asked the question that weighs even more heavily now, seventy years after her death: "Where will a renewal come to us, to us who have spoiled and devastated the whole earthly globe?";[23] she answered, "Only from the past, if we love it." Because words always come freighted with history, it is in large part the work of the poet, the true philologist, to teach us to love the gifts that come to us from the past. The preacher who loves the words of the text is in the deepest sense an evangelical, out of memory bringing forth the promises that may enable us to move forward responsibly and with hope.

21. Erich Auerbach, "Odysseus' Scar," in *Mimesis: The Representation of Reality in Western Literature* (Princeton: Princeton University Press, 1953), 14-15.

22. *Sermons of John Donne,* 2:73.

23. Simone Weil, quoted by Czeslaw Milosz, *The Witness of Poetry* (Cambridge: Harvard University Press, 1983), 114.

Rock Bottom

Goodson Chapel, Duke Divinity School, Durham, North Carolina
January 27, 2011

PSALM 27

*Resisting conventional explanations of Psalm 27's curious pairing of
confidence and lament, this sermon reorients fear as a mode of faith
alongside trust. The psalmist invites this interpretation through the
grammatical consistency of naming God in all fourteen verses, thereby
revealing that total devotion to God means turning to God with "both
parts of our heart." Especially for those who have reached "rock bottom," who have endured terrifying life experiences, that God in Christ
embraces our whole heart is a solid rock of consolation.*

The LORD is my light and my salvation: of whom would I be afraid?
The LORD is my life's strength; whom would I dread? (Ps. 27:1)

It is an enduring principle of biblical interpretation that whenever God or
someone who speaks for God says there is no reason to be afraid, any ordinary sane person could see plenty to be afraid of. Take us, for instance—an
assembly of more or less ordinary sane people. I am guessing that each of us
can think of several good reasons to be afraid, and that some of us awakened
this morning with fear as our immediate companion. Maybe it's a language
test that has let fear into our hearts, or a laboratory test. Maybe it's a shaky
relationship, or a destructive one. Maybe it's uncertainty about finances, or a
job when you graduate, or admission to a doctoral program. A number of us
awakened this morning with the old familiar fear that we are "just not good
enough" (whatever that means). Some of us watch in dread as people who
mean the world to us are threatened by war, or battle with addiction . . . or

106

psychosis . . . or mortal illness. Speaking of fear—is there anyone here who does not find our national political scene scary, energized as it is increasingly by fear-mongering?

To every one of us, then, our psalmist's apparent dismissal of fear comes as a direct challenge—although we might sidestep that challenge, I suppose, by imagining that the psalmist's life has been more sheltered than our own. But for most of us here today, that would be an interpretive error. "I know what it is to have enemies," the psalmist would tell us, "crowding around, ready to eat me up." Thus this Israelite poet who knows about deadly enemies might speak for a small Sudanese boy at Kakuma refugee camp in Kenya, who lost his family when their village was destroyed in the long killing war at the end of the last century, who fled through the bush, eventually connected with other children, and then walked hundreds of miles to the camp, where in time he learned to sing and pray the psalms. And one day when a visiting minister asked him which psalm he especially liked, without missing a beat the boy named this one, because it speaks to his experience:

> Although my father and my mother left me,
> the LORD takes me in. (v. 10)

Our psalmist knows plenty about deadly enemies; but she knows also what comes of their threats:

> My adversaries and my enemies—it is they who stumble and fall.
> If a battalion encamps against me, my heart will not fear.
> If war breaks out against me, in this I am secure. (vv. 2b–3)

"In this I am secure"—period, full stop. In just a few lines the psalmist has summed up the faith dynamic of the whole Bible and of every person who tries to believe. That dynamic is this: either we see God as "my life's strength," or we are defeated by those battalions encamped around us, gradually consumed by a host of fears until we are finally undone by the fear of death itself. There is no third possibility.

I never hear this psalm without seeing in my mind the face of my student, now many years ago, who picked Psalm 27 for an exegesis paper because he had been sexually abused by both his parents. The psalm was a lifeline for him, dragging him out of the total horror of the past, every time it threatened to overwhelm him. I see his face, gentle yet at the same time intent, whenever I repeat this line: "If I were not sure of looking upon the LORD's goodness in the land of the living . . ."—dot, dot, dot. The thought remains incomplete—the psalmist will not go there, will not spend the imaginative energy even to frame what it would be to lose that firm hope of seeing God in the land of the living.

This psalmist holds on hard to hope, but that does not mean she is altogether dismissive of fear. On the contrary, the psalmist shows us precisely what she fears, namely, losing God. And so she cries out:

> Do not hide your face from me!
> . . . Do not forsake me
> nor abandon me,
> O God of my deliverance!

Now how do we make sense of that sudden shift in tone, from utter confidence—"The LORD is my light and my salvation"—to abject pleading: "Don't leave me, O God of my deliverance!"? Of course you will find commentators who tell you that this psalm was originally two different psalms, one expressing confidence, the other a strong lament. This strikes me as the kind of thing that commentators say when they don't know what else to say. The key theological insight here comes from Martin Luther, in his remarkable commentary on the First Commandment: "You shall have no other gods before me." Luther says that having no other gods means simply this: turning to the one God with "both parts of our heart," both trust and fear. And isn't that exactly what we see in this psalm: a total turning to God, who is named, what? . . . fourteen times in fourteen verses. The psalmist is showing us exactly what it is to turn and re-turn to God continually, with both parts of our heart, at one moment in full confidence, the next in a panic, or wherever we may find ourselves on that continuum between trust and fear. That is what it is to have one God, and only One.

So there is no more reason to divide this psalm in two than to divide our hearts in two, because fear is in fact indivisible from faith. After all, the Hebrew phrase *yir'at Adonai,* "fear of the LORD," is the ordinary term for faith. Fear is one of the most effective channels for deepening our faith, provided we use it well. And using fear well means asking a critical question whenever we feel that clammy grip closing around our heart and gut. This question: "Do I really need what I am so afraid of losing? What is it—rock bottom—that I really need?" A critical examination of our own fear yields deeper faith, because (as Luther saw) if we knew what we really need, then we would know precisely what we can trust God to give us.

This kind of critical assessment of fear is surely the most rigorous spiritual task we face. Listen to the psalmist as she renders her assessment:

One thing I ask of the LORD;
it is what I seek:
that I may dwell in the LORD's house
all the days of my life,
to gaze upon the loveliness of the LORD
and to frequent his sanctuary. (v. 4)

And then later on, with that intensity that bespeaks elemental need:

It is your face, O LORD, I am seeking.
Do not hide your face from me! (vv. 8–9)

I hear through this psalmist the steadying tone of my friend Julia's voice. She is an ordained minister, a very able and creative practical theologian, a young woman living in the fourth stage of colon cancer. One might say she has good reason to be afraid, although she would not. Many would say she has reason for anger, having been misdiagnosed for over a year by reputable doctors who insisted she had nothing but hemorrhoids. But Julia has no spiritual energy for either anger or fear, nor does she have time for chemotherapy that makes her ill but does not touch the cancer. "This disease is stubborn," she says, "so I have to be more stubborn. Look, living with cancer does not change my life in any fundamental way. I knew before all this that my life is for ministry, and what I want is to be free to serve as well as I can. How long my life is—that is something that has never been in my control."

Again, hear the psalmist:

One thing I ask . . .
. . . to gaze upon the loveliness of the LORD
and to frequent his sanctuary.

The psalmist, like Julia, knows that she *can* see God in the land of the living— but only if she is clear-eyed about her real need, and on that basis decides what she will do with her "one wild and precious life," to paraphrase the contemporary poet Mary Oliver.[1]

People like Julia and the psalmist ask themselves that question every single day, for they know the truth the poet tells, that everything dies "at last, and too soon." People who face that truth are challenging for us; we have a tendency to avoid them. "Most people don't want to stand too close to this," Julia says. It is

---

1. Mary Oliver, "The Summer Day," in *New and Selected Poems* (Boston: Beacon, 1992).

frightening to watch someone come down to rock bottom, to the one thing she really needs. It is scary to watch someone set aside everything else she might once have wanted and ask God for just this one thing: the opportunity to serve, to bear witness, even if it is through suffering unto death. It is scary for us, for the same reason that someone like Julia is confident: because God draws very, very close to the one who asks for only that. As the psalmist says,

> . . . he will seclude me in his shelter on a day of evil;
> he will hide me in the hiding-place of his tent;
> on a Rock he will lift me high. (v. 5)

"On a Rock he will lift me high." Whenever the psalmist says *tsur*, "rock," you can be pretty sure that "the Rock of Israel," God's own protective presence, is in view. God's immediate presence may not protect us from physical suffering or loss; life is indeed wild, as Mary Oliver says, and risky first to last. We come into this world on a venture; the birth canal is not an especially safe place. And every day that follows we are in peril, whether we recognize it or not. Everyone, "everything die[s] at last, and too soon." What then does God's rock-like presence mean for us; what on earth does it protect us from? Only one thing, perhaps: self-absorption, a small vision, a life without a view. "On a *rock* he will lift me high." Whenever we hear that word "rock" in the Psalms, we might think of Christ—God's strong protective presence revealed to the Gentiles, to us and all the world, in this Epiphany season. He is the Rock on which we are lifted high, out of our own small frightened selves.

Remember now where our psalm began: "The LORD is my light and my salvation; of whom would I be afraid?" Epiphany is the season of light, the light of Christ spreading throughout the world. So let us heed the psalmist's challenge and let the light penetrate the dark places of our hearts and minds. Let us gather up our fears, every last one, and bring them, a holy and perfect offering to our God, in perfect trust that God will give us what we really need . . . Rock bottom. That Rock is Christ (see 1 Cor. 10:4).

Amen.

Shake This Tree

Orientation Sunday, Duke Chapel, Durham, North Carolina
August 26, 2012

PSALM 34

This sermon also attends to issues of trust and fear, this time placing the hearer as a student sitting before the wise psalmist. Proceeding down an acrostic list of precepts, the teacher invites us as students to shake the tree of life, grasp its fruit, and savor the goodness of God. With our desires appropriately centered, we may drop any pretensions to invulnerability and live fully into our brokenness and fear. True fear of the Lord is the "antidote to the fear of heartbreak," but not deliverance from heartbreak itself. Nevertheless, we may live boldly in light of the fact that God enjoys the company of the brokenhearted.

People come to a place like this because they are looking for something; let's call it "the good life." Of course I don't mean a life of ease. Duke is for the most part a Type-A kind of place; only the truly insane would come here looking to kick back. What I do mean is, people come to a university like this—as a student, a staff or faculty member, a trustee or loyal friend—because they are hoping to find here something worth spending themselves on, worth their time and also their heart and mind . . . something that might be worth years of their life. A great university like this one is, you might say, a place of desire—very often, intense desire.

The church is also a place of desire. People come looking for something *more* in their lives, something more than is on offer in our culture at large, more even than in the university at large. Many of you have come this morning at some inconvenience to yourselves. You could have slept in, or knocked an item or two off your to-do list, but you came, I dare say, hoping to hear something . . . in the music or the prayers, from the pulpit, in the education hour, maybe from a friend; week after week, we all come here hoping to hear something that will feed us. Sometimes we come out of sheer desperation, hoping against hope that someone will throw out a lifeline to get us through the day, the week, the seemingly endless future. So the church, like the university, is a place of desire—very often, intense desire.

Desire is a good and necessary thing, and probably we do not speak about it nearly enough in the classroom and in the church. We let the advertising industry have the corner on desire, and that's a great shame, because their notion of desire is pretty paltry: the endless, repetitious hunger to buy more of the same stuff. But real desire is a great thing, an essential part of our humanity. As far as we know, this is something distinctively human: the yearning to realize a great dream, the passion for excellence that keeps you up at night, wakes you up in the morning, sets your heart on fire.

Desire is a necessary and good part of our humanity, but there is a catch. There's always a catch to what is good and necessary, isn't there? If there were no catch, there would be no sermons, probably no novels, and not many films either—because the human story is all about where the catch lies. If there were no catch to what is good, there would certainly be no Bible. Because the Bible is all about the desire for what is good, and how that desire so easily gets derailed, squandered, poisoned, so it becomes destructive of what is good in oneself and others. So here's the catch: because we are human, we do and must desire. And because we are *merely* human, we often desire the wrong thing, or our desire for the best is just lukewarm. Or we desire one good thing . . . and then another, and another—but we never hold steady, and so nothing good comes of our aimless desiring.

The psalmist we heard today brings us directly into this drama of desire and unfocused desire and poisoned desire. Listen again:

> Whoever is the person who desires life,
> who loves the time to see what is good . . . (v. 13)

. . . if you are that kind of person, the psalmist says, then come on over here; let's talk.

Our psalmist was a teacher in ancient Israel, well over 2,500 years ago—a teacher of young, talented, educationally privileged people, maybe even associated with the royal court (see v. 1). I'm making all this up, of course; the psalm doesn't actually tell who wrote it, when, and precisely for whom. But biblical scholars make stuff up all the time, although we don't call it that.

Rather, we say we are "offering a plausible historical reconstruction, based on the evidence available." That's what I'm doing, and here is my major piece of evidence: our psalm is an acrostic, an alphabetic poem. That's not obvious in English, but in Hebrew you can see that it has one verse for each letter of the alphabet, in order. The first verse starts with *aleph* (A), the second one *bet* (B), and so on, all the way through the twenty-two letters of the Hebrew alphabet. Alphabetic acrostics are exactly the kind of thing that ancient teachers used as school lessons, so their students could memorize the lesson and fully internalize it.

Now imagine with me that we are listening to our teacher, in an institution not unlike this one: a school for very smart people who have made it through a rigorous selection process, people who have some kind of fire lit under them; they "desire life." It might well be a school at the temple in Jerusalem, and if so, then these students attended worship or got some of their religious education in an upscale stone building not unlike this one, though smaller. But this will do nicely for the exercise of our historical imagination. So let's imagine ourselves into their sandals, with our teacher the psalmist giving us these "awesome" sound-bites to chew on—twenty-two of them in all, each verse a chewable piece of wisdom. Let's call them wisdom-bites.

This teacher of ours has several of the best lines in the whole Bible, including this one:

Taste and see—taste and see that the Lord is good. (v. 9)

It's a mind-bending idea, when you stop and think about it: the idea that the God who made earth and heaven comes so close to us that you can taste it. You might say that the whole gospel of Jesus Christ unfolds from this one line. Everything from incarnation to Eucharist/Holy Communion—everything is anticipated here: "Taste and see that the Lord is good."

Now let's put that line in context, in our imagined scenario. This teacher is talking to people just starting out on the grand tour of life, looking for something worth spending themselves on; they're so eager for a meaningful life, they can taste it. To them . . . us . . . the teacher says, "If you want something worthwhile, then come on over here and shake this tree. It's the tree of life. Taste the fruit that falls into your hand, and you'll find that it satisfies. God refreshes and satisfies the hungry. So come on over here and shake this tree. 'Taste and see that the Lord is good.' Just chew on that for a while."

And now, a few wisdom-bites later, the teacher says a second mind-bending thing. I quote:

Come on, kids, listen to me; I'll teach you . . . the fear of the LORD.
(v. 12)

"Fear of the LORD"—this is a phrase church-folks no longer use much, probably because it lacks curb appeal in our culture. But Jesus and a lot of other people in the Bible speak often of fearing God; it is the standard biblical term for what we might call "true faith"—or even, "good sense." Our psalmist-teacher puts "fear of the LORD" front and center, and the reason for that is simple: Fear is a huge part of our lives, for good and for ill. Healthy fear motivates us and keeps us moving in the right direction; unhealthy fear paralyzes us, or else it distorts our desires, so we do damage to ourselves and others. Fear of the Lord is the starting place for spiritual health and, therefore, for a life that is worthwhile.

"Tell me what you're afraid of," this wise teacher might say, "and I'll tell you the quality of your life." Here are some common options: *fear of failure*—that's prevalent enough. Not just of abject failure, washing out; even more common is the nagging fear of not being *as* good as someone else down the hallway—good but not quite good enough to come out on the very top. That's a big fear in a place like this. Or the *fear of being alone*—who isn't afraid of that? The *fear of being rejected,* judged to be uncool—young and old, we all feel that one. In the end, we know that Facebook or (for me) "Rate My Professors" will render the Great Judgment on us all. Again, the *fear of never being loved and valued* in the way we long for—by a parent or a friend, a spouse or a child, perhaps by the mentor you have chosen for your life's model. And then there are those fears that lurk at the back of our minds always, often growing greater as the years go by: the *fear of losing to death* the one who really loves me, *of losing my own powers* of mind and body. Maybe all our fears come down to this one core fear: that I might give myself totally, to some dream, some person—I might invest the whole of "my singular self," in the poignant phrase of the psalmists (Ps. 22:21; 35:17)—just to have my heart broken in the end.

Our teacher knows everything we are afraid of, and knows also that the only effective antidote to the core fear of heartbreak is fear of the Lord. Fear of the Lord is nothing other than the fear of spending your powers, your gifts, your time on what does not bring you closer to God. *That* is a good thing to be afraid of. In the end, maybe it is the only thing worth being afraid of, because being without God is the worst thing that could happen to us in this world.

Fear of the Lord is the answer to our deep fear of heartbreak. But notice, our psalmist never says: "If you are wise and fear the LORD, your heart will never be broken." To say that would be foolish; it would be a lie. What this good teacher actually says is quite different:

> The LORD is close to the brokenhearted;
> he delivers those whose spirits are crushed. (v. 19)

This skilled educator speaks frankly about broken hearts, crushed spirits, because the world is a heartbreaking place. Every heart that is not deadened will break, probably more than once. Heartbreak is the cost of being truly alive, which is to say, it is the cost of love, of investing yourself in this heartbreaking world. And so it follows that heartbreak itself is part of the cost of a good education.

On my own first day in a master's program, the dean of my seminary said to us: "If you don't shed some tears here, you will have missed the point." Maybe it is not sheer coincidence that Dean Borsch is a biblical scholar, for what he and the psalmist and Jesus and all the other voices in the Bible say, what the church proclaims through the gospel, is that heartbreak isn't something you just go through and get past; it is a lifelong learning program. The promise of God as we hear it in the Bible is not that things will always turn out as you desire, if only you are "on God's side"—whatever that means. Some irresponsible preachers might tell you that, but don't listen; it's nonsense. The promise and assurance of the gospel is no-nonsense, and at the same time it is boundlessly hopeful. Here is the real deal: when your most cherished hopes are disappointed (and this will happen), when your heart breaks, then God is right there, at your side, close to the brokenhearted. God is especially close to the brokenhearted, because God knows just what it's like to have your heart broken by the world. God's heart was broken at the cross of Christ. So God draws close to the brokenhearted, and stays with them. Funny . . . it seems that God likes the company. The brokenhearted are the kindred souls of God, and we need not fear to be among them.

Now what was it that our psalmist-teacher said a while back?

> Whoever is the person who desires life,
> who loves the time to see what is good . . . (v. 13)

. . . if that person is you, then you have come to the right place. You've come to a place where it is safe to invest yourself fully, because God satisfies and sustains through everything. Here, in the place where the gospel of Christ is proclaimed, where we try to live it out, you never have to pretend to yourself or anyone else that you are invulnerable, that your heart can never break.

You have come here, and we are glad that you have come. So be bold. Step up and shake this tree; you'll discover it is the tree of life. Taste its fruit; taste and see that the Lord is good.

Amen.

Desiring God

York Chapel, Duke Divinity School, Durham, North Carolina
January 17, 2002

PSALM 63

What does it mean to desire God, to thirst for God with our whole being, to bless God as a daily necessity? If we do not yet know, the psalmist will teach us by shaping our prayers until we begin speaking in "the grammar of heaven." In this cycle of receiving God's blessing and blessing God in return, the daily life we thought was mere drudgery becomes imbued with epiphanies great and small. The daily practice of praising God with our lips is a participation in the pattern of eternal life, and therefore reveals the language of blessing as a weapon too powerful even for death.

O God, you are my God;
urgently I seek you.
My throat, my whole being thirsts for you;
my flesh faints for you,
in a dry and weary land—with no water. (Ps. 63:2)

Do you desire God that much? Then pray the Psalms, and you will find companionship; they are all of them songs of desire. Do you wish you desired God that much? Then pray the Psalms; they will shape your desire, and rivet it on God. For desire is the note that throbs all the way through the Psalms: desire for the immediate presence of God, for that saving, comforting, exhilarating nearness. Many of the Psalms express desire that is satisfied, at least to some degree; those are the psalms of thanksgiving, the hymns of praise. But what many others, like Psalm 63, express is longing, longing so intense it hurts, like the ache you might feel, one time or another, for a lover or a child you long to hold, for a beloved parent, lost when you still needed her, or him, terribly. This is longing that drives every other need into the corner.

"My throat, *nafshi*, my whole being thirsts for you"—the Hebrew word *nefesh* is used here in its literal sense of "throat": "My throat is dry with desire for God." But in the Bible, *nefesh* most often means one's whole being, body and soul. This is thirst that consumes entirely—desert thirst, the craving for life itself, and even for more than what we ordinarily call life. "For your constant love is *better* than life" (v. 4)—so our psalmist prays.

This is someone who has learned to live thirsty—and remarkably, to turn thirst into blessing: "Yes, I will bless you [God] with my life" (v. 5). That line points to our psalmist's secret, the secret alchemy of blessing, turning painful emptiness and longing into blessing God. That is the secret of survival. In a waterless land, blessing God is what keeps the psalmist alive and more than alive:

> As with rich food, my throat, *nafshi*, my whole being is sated;
> my mouth praises you with jubilant lips. (v. 6)

Lips that bless God smack with satisfaction, although only a moment before they were cracked with thirst. Now those lips burst open in praise. The psalmist stays with the bodily metaphors of throat and lips, thirst, the palpable pleasures of food and drink; we're not talking about a headtrip. No, blessing God meets basic need; it yields satisfaction of the most elemental kind.

Strange, then, that we modern Christians speak so little of blessing God. Bruce Wilkinson's bestseller *The Prayer of Jabez* finds in an isolated verse from Chronicles a guaranteed prayer mechanism for getting blessed by God. I'll leave his exegetical method alone, but it is worth noting that in biblical prayer, the emphasis is overwhelmingly the opposite of Wilkinson's: not nearly so much on God blessing us, as it is on us blessing God. Again and again the psalmist lays hold of that lifeline:

> Bless the LORD, O my soul,
> and all that is within me, bless his holy name. (Ps. 103:1)

> May the name of the LORD be blessed,
> from now until forever. (Ps. 113:2)

> . . . I will bless your name, forever and ever.
> Every day I will bless you,
> and praise your name, forever and ever. (Ps. 145:1–2)

The psalmists claim that blessing God is a daily necessity, and if they are right, then our forgetfulness is costly. What could it mean to view blessing God as a daily necessity? We can learn something about this from rabbinic tradition, for from ancient times to the present, blessing God has been the primary and ubiquitous form of Jewish prayer. God is blessed over and over, multiple times each day, by every observant Jew—and why? Because, as the ancient rabbis taught, to use or enjoy any created thing without blessing the Creator is to steal something from God's glory. Taking for granted is just that: it's taking, not receiving. The gifts of God's love pour forth constantly toward you, abundantly and superabundantly, but the gift becomes yours only as you recognize that this good thing comes from God, and return blessing for it. So there are rabbinic blessings to recite for every event and moment of the day, most just nine or ten words long. At morning prayer, for instance, one blesses God for the strength to get out of bed today and go to the bathroom; there is a blessing for the egg at breakfast and a different one for the orange juice; there is a blessing for the privilege of study, another one for your Old Testament professor, and yet a third for the ethics department; there is a blessing for good news and even one for bad news, blessings for the sunset and for a falling star.

"For your constant love is *better* than life," the psalmist says. The work of recognizing all these many particulars of God's love toward all creation, and re-sponding with a blessing—that steady work of discernment and prayer is what makes life more than life, more than life that is, as we too often experience it, "just one damn thing after another." The truth is that this cycle of receiving God's blessing and blessing God in turn—this is the pattern of eternal life, the life of those who are wholly absorbed into God's life. "My whole being clings to you" (v. 9), as our psalmist puts it. "My whole being clings to you"—if that is eternal life, then it certainly does not begin when we die. No, we enter into eternal life as we allow ourselves to be drawn out of preoccupation with self, out of desire for anything that does not come from God or lead to God, as we let ourselves be drawn into the steady, intimate, joyous communication with God that we call, for short, "heaven."

Blessing, then, is the grammar of heaven, the accustomed way of speaking for those who dwell wholly in the light. Practicing and gradually mastering that grammar give us a foretaste of heaven's joy while we are yet in this world. We have an intimation of this at the very end of Luke's Gospel, when Jesus ascends to heaven after his resurrection appearances. What we see in our risen Lord's last moments on earth is blessing flowing at high tide, first from Jesus to the disciples. Listen:

Then he took them out as far as the outskirts of Bethany, and lifting up his hands he blessed them. Now as he blessed them, he withdrew from them and was carried up to heaven. (Luke 24:50–51)

In the very act of blessing, Jesus himself is drawn into the perfect communion, the perpetual flow of love and mutual blessing that is the Godhead. And as that happens, the disciples, too, are caught up in the flow. As Luke tells us:

They worshiped him and then went back to Jerusalem full of joy; and they were continually in the temple blessing God. (Luke 24:52–53)

The disciples watch Jesus withdraw from them, yet they do not grieve, because blessing God gives them already in this world a full share in the joy of heaven. Those short, repeated prayers of blessing God are like arrows shot through the opaque curtain that shuts us off from heaven's light, the curtain of sin and self-absorption. Each blessing tears a small hole in the curtain, and as we increase the barrage of blessings, the curtain gradually becomes tattered, and we are at last bathed in light.

On Christmas Eve I spoke with my friend Barbara, whose husband is very ill with pancreatic cancer. She told me of the lovely day they had had, with Bob home from the hospital and his pain relieved. She told me that she had said to Bob at breakfast: "You know, even in such a difficult time, I still find myself at moments overcome with joy, usually over some small thing, like a bite of warm gingerbread." And Bob answered her, "Yes, this is a time of fulfillment."

Do you recognize it? They are speaking the language of blessing, the grammar of heaven, the one language strong enough to hold us joyfully in life as we face death. "I will bless you *with my life*" (v. 5), the psalmist promises God. That promise is made in the face of deadly enemies; Psalm 63 might be David speaking, with Saul in hot pursuit. So now we can fully understand the secret of the psalmist. Blessing God as Creator and Giver of every good thing, gingerbread included, is a weapon wielded against death itself. That is why the psalmist can say,

Your constant love is *better* than life;
my lips will praise you. (v. 4)

Words of blessing slash through the heavy curtain that veils God's light. We are now in Epiphany, the season when the church especially desires light, ever more light, that our lives and our world may be illumined more and more with the light of that deathless love manifested to us in Christ Jesus. As you might have guessed, the rabbis have a blessing that is apt for us to pray in this season—a night prayer that is said just before going to sleep, but it is apt for any hour, including this one: Blessed are you, O Lord, whose majesty gives light to the whole world.

Amen.

Tough Praise

Qahal Meeting, Fort Casey, Whidbey Island, Washington
June 15, 1997

PSALM 73

The Psalms have a habit of recovering certain sayings that we might otherwise ignore as clichés. This sermon imagines how Israelite children were nurtured from birth with sayings such as, "Truly God is good to Israel, to those who are pure in heart." Yet experience often taught them the opposite: the wicked prosper, while the righteous suffer. The hard realities of life eventually lead all of us to wonder, "What distinguishes the pure in heart?" In the sanctuary of the community shaped and sustained by Israel's prayers, we discover something new about the desires of those we call pure in heart: it is "not that God pours more goodness in their direction, but that they are able to receive it."

The psalmist inhabits a world of stark alternatives:

- a pure heart, or an embittered one (Ps. 73:21)
- living near to God, or perishing far from God (vv. 27–28)
- utter spiritual stupidity, or sure knowledge that "I am always with [God]" (vv. 22–23)
- talking about how unfair life is, or talking about everything God has done (vv. 15, 28)

It is just this starkness that makes the Psalms so refreshing: like an ice cube on your forehead on a mercilessly hot day, sometimes like an ice cube down your back. The Psalms startle as well as refresh us. We are so conscious of the gray areas, and they are many. But repeatedly the Psalms confront us with those few things about which there can be no ambiguity, the few things—and I think they are no more than a few—on which all our joy depends.

What Psalm 73 clarifies, more effectively perhaps than any other biblical text, is what it means to be pure of heart—the condition that, as the Gospel of Matthew teaches, enables us to see God (Matt. 5:8).

> Truly God is good to Israel,
> to those who are pure in heart. (v. 1)

Thus the psalm begins, uncharacteristically, with something that sounds dangerously close to a religious cliché. And if the psalm stayed there, it would be of little interest to us. But in fact we follow the psalmist as she wrestles with that cliché and gradually transforms it from truism to truth. Unique among the Psalms, this one charts with care an intellectual and spiritual conversion. Looking back, the psalmist says of herself:

> I am stupid and know nothing.
> An animal I have been with you[, God]. (v. 22)

We actually watch the change take place, as the psalmist moves from bitterness and spiritual stupidity to wholehearted devotion to God:

> As for me, I am always with you. . . .
> And with you[, God], I desire nothing on earth. (vv. 23, 25)

"With you, God, I desire nothing on earth"—that is purity of heart. The heart that desires nothing but God can never turn sour, because it is set on the one desire that cannot be disappointed. Such radical singleness of desire is possible, but only for those who experience the complete reorientation of heart and mind that happens to the psalmist (as she tells us) when she enters the sanctuary of God. Exactly what happened to her there? In a word, she saw the goodness of God. For the first time, she understood the truth in the old cliché:

> Truly God is good to Israel,
> to those who are pure in heart. (v. 1)

Doubtless she had imbibed that saying with her mother's milk, and the meaning had seemed obvious enough. If you do good, if you are good, then you get good. "God is good to Israel"—that must mean that the true Israel, the pure in heart, are the special beneficiaries of God's goodness, while the wicked are designated for swift punishment and a speedy end. It makes perfect sense that God should encourage good behavior with prompt rewards and be equally conscientious in punishing the wicked. The only problem with this theory, popular among religious people of every age, is lack of evidence. As the psalmist sees, the wicked often do uncommonly well, by any objective measure: "In ordinary human affliction they have no part" (v. 5). The wicked are rich, well-placed; and, to add insult to injury, they are healthy and good-looking—whereas the righteous are poor, pale, and sickly from excessive study. This the psalmist sees, and it galls her. Following a strangled expression (*akh!*) that probably stands for some ancient four-letter word, she cries:

> In vain have I kept my heart clean
> and washed my hands in innocence. (v. 13)

If the story ended there, it would be one more instance of the falling away of the once-seriously-religious. The promising seminarian switches to a helping profession because he cannot preach the gospel with conviction. The over-eager young minister bails out when the good news seems to have failed in her own life; what assurance could she possibly give to others? What saves our psalmist from their fate is a better hermeneutic, namely, the hermeneutic of the sanctuary. For there she embraces a radically different interpretation of the old saying:

> Truly God is good to Israel,
> to those who are pure in heart. (v. 1)

In the sanctuary of God, in worship, in God's near presence, she finally gets it. This is what distinguishes the pure of heart: not that God pours more goodness in their direction, but that they are able to receive it. God is good. That is an absolute statement, true in every circumstance, in every direction. God causes the sun to shine and rain to fall on good and evil alike (Matt. 5:45). The difference between them is simply that the good receive sun and rain as blessing; they are like well-planted fields that soak up the life-giving bounty flowing continually from God. The wicked, by contrast, are like barren hillsides. God's goodness runs off them, bringing no richness, no growth. If anything, prolonged exposure to God leaves them poorer, more crusty and spiritually eroded than they were before. That, of course, is what happened to Pharaoh in the great battle of the plagues; because he could not take in God's goodness, prolonged exposure to God hardened his heart and destroyed him.

"Truly God is good *to Israel*"—we can now see this as a statement less about God's special bounty to Israel than about her special perception. The true Israel, the pure in heart, differ from others only in their ability to see that God is good. Our psalmist sums it up in the final verse: "As for me, nearness to God *to me* is good" (v. 28). That is far more than a truism. As the Bible repeatedly attests, God's immediate presence is no Sunday school picnic. Ask Abraham on Moriah, Naomi when she returns "empty" (Ruth 1:21) to Bethlehem, David weeping over his sin, Jeremiah weeping over doomed Jerusalem—ask them what the near presence of God feels like. It is pressure, excruciating in its intensity; the pure of heart have been ground and sifted like wheat (Luke 22:31). So also our psalmist felt the pressure that purifies:

> I was sorely wounded all day long,
> and my affliction was every morning. (v. 14)

It is because Israel feels the intense, often painful pressure of God's presence that their praise is so sturdy and so durable. Israel's praise is sturdy enough that God is said to sit on it (Ps. 22:4). Imagine that: praise strong enough to bear God's full weight. It is above all in the Psalms, known in Hebrew as *Tehillim,* the Book of Praises, that Israel names God as good in every circumstance. Israel's praise is durable precisely in its realism: the Psalms, the Praises of Israel, have been sung in Babylon, sighed at Bergen-Belsen; this very day they are being recited in refugee camps and at deathbeds. Israel's praise is tough enough to bear the full weight of our grief, our disillusionment, our bitter anger, and our most painful failures. The Psalms hold us up and hold us within the community that dares to call itself Israel, the congregation of those who daily name God as good and thus day by day grow to claim a desire that can never be disappointed, so at the last each of us may truly say:

> Though my heart and my flesh fail,
> God is the rock of my heart and my portion forever. (v. 26)

Alleluia.
Amen.

The Incongruity of Sin

Choral Evensong, Trinity Church on the Green, New Haven, Connecticut
January 21, 2001

PSALM 103

It is hard to imagine that God does not keep as close a record of our
wrongs as we do of others and ourselves. But this sermon describes a
God who refuses to regard our sins as the most interesting thing about
us. Our sins may be boring to God, but their "incongruity" also disturbs
God. Sin warps the image of God in us. In Jesus Christ, however, we see
a new Adam free from distortion, who reveals how fascinated God is
by our own potential for goodness.

> Bless the LORD, O my soul,
> And all that is within me bless his holy name.
> Bless the LORD, O my soul,
> And forget not all his benefits. (Ps. 103:1–2)

This evening we hear the psalmist at her most exuberant, turned almost inside
out with exhilaration: "All that is within me, bless his holy name." The cause
for exhilaration is the extravagance of God's kindness to us—most of all, in
freeing us from sin. It seems that God makes a complete break between ourselves and our sin:

> As far as East is from West,
> so far has he removed from us our transgressions. (v. 12)

But in a cooler mood than the psalmist's own, you have to ask: Really?
Has God set us a world away from our transgressions? For that claim seems

126

to contradict one of the elemental facts of human existence: our sins, once committed, are with us for the rest of our lives. The consequences of sin remain permanent facts on the ground, even though the sins themselves may be long ago regretted and forgiven. I dare say that, for every one of us, among the outstanding facts of our personal history are the consequences of sins we committed and sins by which we were victimized: a marriage was damaged or broken, a friendship lost; a child was neglected, a body abused; a good mind achieved only a fraction of its potential; years were wasted in empty pleasures or work that did not bring us closer to God.

What does it mean, then, to say that God removes our sins far from us, if we live always with their memory and their effects? This is, I think, the question that our psalm answers—not in so many words, but as the Psalms always answer big questions, in the language of poetry: in language that is metaphorical, more suggestive than explanatory, surprised and surprising language. Here, for instance, is something surprising:

Not according to our sins has [God] done to us,
and not according to our iniquities has he recompensed us. (v. 10)

It seems that God is not keeping such close score of our iniquities as we often suppose. This is a common but often overlooked error in the spiritual life: treating sin as though it were the most interesting thing about myself or any other human being, harboring guilt for my own sins and grudges about theirs, imagining that God is eternally occupied with plans to get us back for them. But, in fact, "[God] does not deal with us according to our sins." The psalm reveals that sin is essentially boring, to God as it should be to us; quite literally, it is deadly dull.

God is not interested in sin, because God is so interested in us, with the fascination characteristic of parents. The psalmist puts it thus:

As a father has compassion on children,
God has compassion on those who fear him. (v. 13)

God's parental compassion for us means this at least: our sins cause God pain. (The English word "compassion" literally means "suffering with" someone.) God suffers over our sins, probably more than we do; therefore, God has a personal interest in getting rid of them. We may understand this from family experience. The loving parent's response to the worst sins of the child is less anger than pained bewilderment: How could *you* have done this? I've seen that look on my mother's face, the bewilderment born out of bone-deep knowledge that her children were formed in the womb for goodness, not evil. Maybe that is why God has to be imaged as mother or father, because, as the psalm says, "he knows our formation" (v. 14). Only a parent has the long memory and the patience to make a firm distinction, day by day—to distinguish and separate our created selves, formed in God's own image, from our evil actions.

It takes a parent's love to do for us what we generally fail to do: to see ourselves as separate from our sins. Our confusion in this is common, but tragic nonetheless. We come to think of our sins as our real selves, and therefore we are stuck with them. We even stick up for them. Probably all of us have defended one or another damaging behavior with the remark, "That's just the way I am. . . . Sure, I have a bad temper; yes, I drink (or gossip, or flirt, or spend, or nag, or sulk) a little too much, but after all, I'm only human." Accepting our own evil with a shrug or even tears of frustration is a lie, a lie about our humanity. From the perspective of Christian faith, the incarnation of God in Jesus Christ is the definitive exposure of that lie.

The good news revealed in Jesus Christ is that we are far more like God than like our sins. No one has shown that more graphically than Michelangelo, in his Sistine Chapel painting of Adam and Eve being expelled from Eden. These are not the bewildered childlike figures who often appear in medieval art. Michelangelo gave Adam and Eve the same magnificent musculature as he painted for God, even the same gestures. He put the power and beauty of divinity into these first humans; they are truly God's image and likeness, and therefore it is especially horrible when they misuse that wonderful power to their own misery.

Christians speak of Jesus Christ as the second Adam, meaning that in him we see for once God's image without any distortion. God's purpose in showing us that perfect image was not to sink us in despair; years, or tens of thousands of years, of sin had already dragged us down into that pit. Rather, God means to draw us up into the genuinely human life that the biblical writers call "God's kingdom" (v. 19) or sometimes "eternal life"—that abundant life[1] that doesn't begin when you die but rather when you start focusing on what God is doing, living no longer out of your own whims and fears, but out of the possibilities that God's action opens up for you. That life of abundance is what the psalmist celebrates, calling forth everything she's got to bless the Lord,

> who forgives all your sins
> and heals all your infirmities,
> who redeems your life from the pit,

1. See Jesus's saying in John 10:10: "I came that they might have life, and have it abundantly."

and crowns you with steadfast love and mercy,
and satisfies you with good as long as you live. (vv. 3–5)

The work of ministry—what one person of faith can do for another person—is to make more real the possibility of that abundant life, where we are separated from our sins. One of the kindest works of ministry is to help another see that sin is not just bad (that's obvious enough). It's also incongruous. Change becomes possible when you see that your sins have no genuine place in your life; there is no real "fit" between them and you. My first confessor helped me see that. I only spoke with him once. I often made retreats at a convent where he came to hear confessions, and I asked if he would listen to mine. I am told that hearing the confessions of cloistered nuns is like being stoned with cotton balls. I was lobbing real stones, yet when I had finished he looked at me with a mildness I did not deserve and asked: "Tell me, did these things surprise you?" Up to that moment I had thought of my sins only as cause for guilt, not surprise. But now I saw for the first time how surprising sin always is, because we were made for glory. "Did these things surprise you?" Once you have seen each of your sins for what it is, an absurd accretion to your soul that defeats your deepest purposes—when you've seen that, then one by one the sins lose their compelling interest and thus the power to do real harm, through either tortuous memories or fresh repetitions.

God is bored by sin but fascinated beyond all reason by our potential for goodness; so God bends every effort to create the conditions in which that potential can develop. There is just one thing that makes human goodness possible, and that is *hesed,* the covenant love that is, to this poet's eyes, the biggest fact on the ground. God's *hesed,* steadfast love, dominates the horizon:

Yes, as high as the heavens are above the earth,
so does his steadfast love tower over those who fear him. (v. 11)

"So does his steadfast love tower over those who fear him." God's steadfast love spreads over us high and wide, like a shade tree in the summer heat. The invitation to the gospel, the good news as it comes to us in both Testaments, is to come off the long, hot road and spend the rest of your life in that refreshing shade. You are tired, for you have carried too much with you: old guilt and shame whose usefulness has passed, unhealed anger that is doing you harm, defenses and denials that offer no genuine relief. Come, the place is ready, stay here; you will find rest for your soul.

Amen.

In Memory of Joseph Taban Lasuba

St. Luke's Episcopal Church, Durham, North Carolina
June 25, 2013

PSALM 116

Joseph Taban, a Duke Divinity School graduate, beloved Sudanese priest, and Principal of Bishop Gwynne Theological College, Juba, South Sudan, died on May 21, 2013, leaving behind a wife and three children. This homily's design interweaves the psalmist's voice with Joseph's, emphasizing his faithfulness in suffering and humble service to the church. "Precious in the eyes of the LORD is the death of his faithful ones," the psalmist says. Therefore, we may proclaim that, though the dreams we had for Joseph have died, he is now alive to God and to us in a new way.

As I thought and prayed about Joseph Taban in preparation for this evening, one voice in particular emerged from the "cloud of witnesses" gathered to speak to us from the pages of the Bible. It is the voice of the poet or songwriter who gave us Psalm 116, a song of profound thanksgiving: "You rescued my life from death" (v. 8). Yet embedded within that song of thanksgiving are many memories of suffering, some of them raw:

> In my panic I thought, "Everyone is a liar." (v. 11)

These are vivid memories; whether or not the suffering is recent, it has lost none of its edge:

> The cords of death entangled me;
> the grip of the grave took hold of me; I came to grief and sorrow.

130

Then I called upon the name of the LORD: "O LORD, I pray you, save my
life." (vv. 3–4)

Joseph Taban could have written those words himself; he would often recall that his given name, Taban, means "suffering" in his native Bari language.
However, Joseph, like the psalmist, was not inclined to give a lot of details
about his experiences of suffering, such as the five imprisonments during his
fifteen years serving as a priest in Khartoum. For him, going to prison was just
part of the cost of discipleship. "I don't know any priest who was not arrested,"
he once said, "and no one who was arrested only one time." "I believed," our
psalmist says, "even when I said, 'I am greatly afflicted'" (v. 10).

In 2010, just when he was finishing his studies at Duke, Joseph was called
by Archbishop Daniel Deng Bul to leave Khartoum, and he was deeply, deeply
grateful to return to Juba, where he had lived as a child, grateful that his own
children would grow up in freedom. I hear Joseph's voice behind these words
of the psalmist:

Turn again to your rest, my soul,
for the LORD has been generous to you.
. . . .
What shall I return to the LORD,
for all his generosity toward me?
I lift up the cup of deliverance, and call upon the name of the LORD.
I shall pay my vows to the LORD, before all the people [of God]. (vv. 7,
12–14)

There could hardly be a stronger affirmation of life, of life in and with God and
among the people of God. But listen now to the very next verse:

Precious in the eyes of the LORD is the death of his saints/his faithful
ones. (v. 15)

"In the midst of life we are in death," as the Burial Office says.[1] In the midst
of celebrating life with God, suddenly the psalmist is reflecting on death, on
what death looks like to God.

For death is part of our life with God. The psalmist knows it, and so does

1. *The Book of Common Prayer* (New York: The Church Hymnal Corporation, 1979),
484, 492.

Joseph. The church knows it, and therefore so do we. "Precious in the eyes of the LORD is the death of his saints." That means that death is not just "the inevitable," one of those teeth-gritting facts we all have to face. The death of the faithful is *precious*, precious to God. Far from being a rupture in the life we share with God, death is one treasured part of it. In the midst of death, we are in life with God.

That is a crucial assurance for us now, as we grieve Joseph's death and the loss of certain hopes and expectations that we had cherished. We had hoped that he would come back here to study for a doctorate; Joseph himself held firmly to that hope in the final months of his life. Bishop Anne and others of us here in Durham had hoped to travel to Juba to work with him there; many people in the Episcopal Church of Sudan, including the archbishop, had hoped that Joseph would continue to take the lead in working for reconciliation within South Sudan, and, further, that he would gradually build a renewed theological college into a new university. Joseph and Esparanza and all of us who love them had hoped that together they would raise their three beautiful children in a more peaceful world than the one they had known as children.

None of that will happen in the way we had dared to envision it; and because we are human, we grieve the loss of all those particular hopes in which we had invested. But the words of the psalmist speak to us about what we have not lost. We have not lost Joseph. That is the assurance in those words, "Precious in the eyes of the LORD is the death of his saints." Joseph Taban's death is itself a precious event, just as precious to God as any other part of his remarkable, irreplaceable life. "Precious in the eyes of the LORD is the death of his saints." Joseph has not been swallowed up by death; he has not disappeared from our lives. Rather, he is with us in a new way, in a way we must grasp with our hearts, not (in the first instance) with our intellects. Joseph is with us even as he is now drawn closer to the God who holds all our souls in life, the God whose intentions for us are not stopped by death, the God who enfolds us in mercy and brings our lives to perfect peace and fulfillment in the glorious company of the saints in light. May it be so for us, as it most assuredly is for our beloved brother Joseph Taban, whom we are privileged to know and love, a light of the world in our generation.

Amen and amen.

Finding Strength in Praise

Vespers, Christ Church, New Haven, Connecticut
Pentecost 1995

PSALM 145; ACTS 2:1–13

The practice of blessing God through praise is "an assertion of the most profound human freedom," for it opens us to the free movement of the Holy Spirit. For the psalmist, it is also a survival instinct when facing deadly enemies. We hear in this sermon a caveat against disregarding parts of the Psalms we find offensive. "Armchair theologians" beware: praising God is not a leisure-time activity, but a declaration of God's sovereignty in times of imminent danger.

I will extol you, my God, the King,
and bless your name for ever and ever.
Every day I will bless you
and praise your name for ever and ever. (Ps. 145:1–2)

Above all days in the church calendar, this is the one devoted to God's praise. On Pentecost we commemorate not simply a simultaneous-translation event, when pious Jews gathered in Jerusalem from all over the known world and heard Jesus's disciples, uneducated Galileans, speaking in their own languages. That in itself might be regarded as one of the psychic wonders of the ancient world, but it would have been no reason for a major feast of the church. No, we remember that event because of what the disciples were saying: "They were telling the mighty works of God" (Acts 2:11). "The mighty works of God"—that is what became suddenly intelligible across the strong barriers of language and culture.

On that day, the Jews experienced the reversal of the confusion of lan-

133

guages that dates all the way back to the Tower of Babel. And for us to understand that great reversal, it is well to remember that God deliberately introduced linguistic confusion in order to hamper the Babelites in their common project of building a city and a tower whose top reached all the way to heaven. The Babelites were out to "make a name for [themselves], lest [they] be scattered across the face of the earth" (Gen. 11:4). Babel, then, represents the human attempt to stand against the vicissitudes of history by consolidating our power. Virtually every high civilization in the history of the world, including our own, has adopted the Babelites' strategy of building a tower with its top in heaven, and what the biblical story reveals is that the inevitable consequence of that strategy of self-aggrandizement is social fracture. The linguistic confusion of Babel is the beginning of the world as we know it, in which individuals and nations are separated from one another in mutual incomprehension and often hostility, each desperately trying to make a name for themselves. And what we remember today is the very first act of the Holy Spirit in undoing that ages-old legacy of Babel. The gift that the Spirit poured out on Jerusalem was the gift of mutual understanding, so that people from all over the world were again united in a common project—this time not in making a name for themselves, but rather in making a big name for God; "they were telling the mighty works of God."

It is probable that Jesus's disciples sang God's praise using some of the words we are singing this evening, from Psalm 145, which is in its entirety a celebration of the mighty works of God. From ancient times and still today, orthodox Jews recite Psalm 145 three times each day, fulfilling the words of the psalm itself: "every day will I bless you" (v. 2); and again, "One generation to another will praise your acts, and your mighty works they will tell" (v. 4). So this well-worn psalm, recited millions and millions of times within each generation, is the very essence of Israel's praise. Its daily recitation points to Israel's understanding that true praise is more than saying "Thanks" when God does something nice for you. Rather, praise is something like a lifestyle; it's a vocation. Israel knew itself as the people who were put on the planet precisely for the purpose of giving praise to God, and the Psalms are the full expression of that vocation. I believe it is exactly the vocation to praise that has given Israel's faith the power to endure through more than three thousand years—longer than any other faith in the history of the world, and many of them years of suffering. The praise of Israel's God has repeatedly transcended barriers of nationality, language, and culture. That's the Pentecost miracle, and the fact that today we Gentiles worship ancient Israel's God shows that the miracle continues to happen.

Great is the LORD and greatly to be praised;
there is no exhausting his greatness. (Ps. 145:3)

There would be nothing very interesting about Israel proclaiming the inexhaustible greatness of its God if this people were one of the big winners of history. But, in fact, the very opposite is the case. For centuries Israel was one of the pawns in the ancient Near Eastern game of empire-making, strategically located and therefore successively overrun by armies from Egypt, Assyria, Babylon, Persia, Greece, and finally Rome. First-century Jews recited Psalm 145 after Emperor Vespasian's army had killed their priests, razed their Temple, and erected one to Jupiter in its place; in the twentieth century, Jews recited Psalm 145 at Auschwitz, praying these words:

Your kingship is kingship over all worlds,
and your dominion lasts through generation after generation.
The LORD sustains all who are fallen
and raises up all who are bowed down. (vv. 13–14)

Here the psalmist flies in the face of what we would call the facts—the facts of *Realpolitik*. Think about it: a people noteworthy chiefly for their bad political luck here proclaim the absolute dominion of their God over all times and circumstances. This is an extraordinary thing, bespeaking either mass delusion (which is surely how the builders of Babel would have judged it) or else an unusually deep understanding of the nature of reality, the kind of fresh perception that comes to us only when God speaks. The essence of that new perception is this: if God's kingship is indeed over all worlds, then the way we ordinarily think about the shaping forces of our lives, of history, is woefully inadequate. If God's majesty is absolute, then the social, economic, political, and personal factors on which we spend so much energy are not determinative. They are important, and we must attend to them, in good times and bad. But if God is ruler over all, then it is God's goodness and that alone that determines the shape and quality of our lives, when viewed from the perspective of eternity. The psalmist, singing God's praise against the vicissitudes of history, throws out to the hard-pressed Israelites the lifeline of God's inexhaustible goodness. Listen:

People will celebrate the fame of your abundant goodness
and sing of your righteousness.
Gracious and compassionate is the LORD,
slow to anger and of great kindness.

The LORD is good to all,
and his compassion is over all his creatures. (vv. 7–9)

Can you hear the power in that? For it is important that we in particular do hear it—the power that can oppose, indeed transcend the hopelessness that infects so many sectors of our society and with increasing frequency erupts as terrible violence. Poverty, crime, devastating illness, addiction, cruel treatment by those we love or on whom we depend, lack of satisfactory work or any work at all—these things touch us all and dominate the lives of many in our society. These so-called facts of life threaten to destroy our humanity by blinding us to any perception of God's goodness and thus closing us in on ourselves, isolating us from one another in fear and hatred. There is an acute irony in our common life. Despite our vast wealth, our dangerously great military, and our techno-logical power, we are a society where people largely define themselves in terms of one or another form of victimization. In some cases, of course, the feeling is legitimate, and owning it marks the beginning of healing. But in every case, it is damaging to get stuck—by ourselves or others—in the role of victim, and so the question is how we move beyond victimization and lay hold of God's goodness.

The Psalms show us the one sure way, and that is by blessing God. The psalmists knew and sang plenty about suffering; they sang the midnight blues of social oppression and personal rejection, yet still they were able to make this promise: "Every day I will bless you"—an unconditional commitment to bless God regardless of circumstances, for better, for worse, for richer, for poorer, in sickness and in health. Blessing God is, like marriage, a commitment that transcends the emotions of the moment with the unconditional decision to offer steadily to another the most precious gifts we can bestow, love and respect, to offer them even in the face of the most confining external circumstances: "I will bless the LORD at all times; his praise will ever be in my mouth" (Ps. 34:1). Simply because it is an unconditional commitment, blessing God is an assertion of the most profound human freedom. Blessing God, we declare ourselves free from the tyranny of our fears and even of our preferences, which often bespeak a vision of the good life too small for the free movement of the Holy Spirit. Blessing God, we declare ourselves free and ready to direct our best energies toward realizing God's vision for this groaning and seriously ailing world.

It is in light of the power of praise to move us beyond fear that we can un-derstand the psalmists' repeatedly expressed conviction that God will destroy the wicked. This is undoubtedly the most troubling part of the Psalms (judging from the lectionary's habit of editing it out). Even a psalm as sublime as ours does not end without an assurance that the wicked will get theirs:

The LORD keeps all those who love him
but all the wicked he will destroy. (Ps. 145:20)

It is easy enough to dismiss this (and many modern commentators do dismiss it) as a sub-Christian attitude unworthy of inclusion in the church's prayers. But that strikes me as the view of an armchair theologian who has not had to reckon with what prayer is like when your back is against the wall and your enemies are looming over you, panting for your life. The psalmists always sang God's praise with that situation in mind; they knew that when you are facing radical evil, everything depends on being able to say with certainty that God's kingship is over all worlds, that finally no evil, no evil person, will be able to endure before God's triumphant goodness. Praise is not a leisure-time activity for the psalmists; it is a survival instinct, an instinct for the goodness of God, which wells up even—no, especially—before overwhelming evil. Praise of God is the survival instinct that moves us, not to violence against those who threaten us, but to confidence in the One who alone is powerful to save us.

I have the sense that you understand that here at Christ Church. I'm not telling you something new but simply underscoring the importance of what this church stands for, namely, a century-long tradition of offering praise to God daily, often elaborate praise. But praise is not a leisure-time activity for you any more than it was for the psalmists. You occupy a location where you must confront the juxtaposition of wealth and poverty and the consequent violence that troubles this city. Under Fr. Miner's leadership you have chosen to face as a community the loneliness and shame that often attend homosexuality and the tragedy of AIDS. Your common life evidences that instinct for God's goodness that develops out of the practice of praise, which enables you to stand and work in the face of both natural evil and human evil. It is a particular privilege to address you on this day of Pentecost, for I believe that as a body you are struggling to live out that freedom from fear that is an important part of the work of the Holy Spirit. Remember, the Holy Spirit was a gift given to the church in the first fear-filled weeks following the crucifixion (see John 20:19–23). God the Holy Spirit works to free us from fear of the evil we live with in this world, just as God the Son hung on a cross, died, and rose again to free us from the fear and the finality of death. Those are the mighty works of God we celebrate today, the evidences of God's abundant goodness that strengthen us to go forth from this place in the great name of God, rejoicing and working in the power of the Holy Spirit.

Amen.

Surprised by Wisdom: Preaching Proverbs

ESSAY

"They're Just Proverbs"

Why would anyone preach from the book of Proverbs? The question must be faced at the outset, because the plain fact of the matter is that not many do. (As best I can recall, I have heard only three preachers, including myself, give it a shot.) To most Christian preachers, Proverbs might well seem the *least* preachable book in the Bible—rivaled, perhaps, only by Leviticus. It offers no clear story line, the mainstay of most biblical preaching.

There is another ostensible problem with preaching Proverbs, namely, its literary form and subject matter: capsule statements about ordinary human experience. That problem was felt already in ancient times, and it nearly kept Proverbs out of the canon of Scripture. "They're just proverbs," some ancient authorities reasoned, "the kind of thing people say all the time. There is nothing sacred about that." Proverbial wisdom seems at the opposite end of the literary spectrum from "the revealed Word of God"—and isn't that what preachers are supposed to be probing and making plain for their people week by week?

For reasons such as these, I minimized Proverbs early in my teaching career, passing over it lightly in order to get on to those more unconventional and presumably more interesting wisdom books, Job and Ecclesiastes. Therefore I was surprised when my students asked for more time on Proverbs; and when I gave it to them, they invariably became excited about the punch these small poems pack. Each proverb is in fact a short poem, about the length of a haiku; moreover, like a haiku, it does not require a lot of scholarly explanation. This is precisely what appealed to my students: they recognized before I did the potential for ministry that is inherent in the biblical proverbs, a potential that

138

is quite readily actualized. Unlike some parts of Scripture, Proverbs does not seem to require that the preacher or teacher have command of a large literary and theological tradition in order to get started. All one has to *have* is some life experience, and all one has to *do* is slow down over the proverbs, savoring their words, as with any good poem.

Indeed, reading Proverbs in large chunks may be the best way to kill its revelatory potential. A friend of mine while driving happened upon a radio program that was reading through the whole Bible sequentially; that day they were somewhere in the middle of Proverbs. After fifteen or twenty minutes of listening to a string of two-liners, he had to pull off to the side of the road until he could stop laughing. Yet if we slow down in our reading and give the biblical proverbs their due, they often speak to our life circumstances in ways that are surprisingly apt, though neither predictable nor obvious.

It was my own difficult life experience that disclosed to me why Proverbs is essential for pastoral ministry. Therefore it is also essential for preaching, because the pulpit offers the pastor her most public and often her best opportunity to show how, through Scripture, God draws near to us in trouble. The year that I was writing a short commentary on Proverbs[1] proved also to be a year of family crisis, with deep division over decisions concerning the care of our elderly parents and management of their modest financial resources; the situation was explosive and possibly dangerous. Meditating on Proverbs during the worst months of the crisis, I was impressed by the fact that these sayings reflect the experience of people who knew trouble, including hostile division within the family. A saying such as this one jumped out at me:

A wise child makes a father glad,
and a foolish child is a mother's grief. (Prov. 10:1)

Proverbs is the biblical book that speaks most frequently and variously about the joys and sorrows of family life, and that in itself commends it to the preacher. But it does more than that; properly handled, the biblical proverbs can give us a profound sense of community, just when we need it most. Division within a family often generates a sense of shame and isolation; we don't speak of our trouble, believing that no decent person or family would be in such a situation. What I discovered in meditating on Proverbs is that my experience had been anticipated within the pages of the Bible; my personal story

---

1. Ellen F. Davis, *Proverbs, Ecclesiastes, and the Song of Songs* (Louisville: Westminster John Knox, 2000).

had a place within the larger experience of the faith community persisting through generations. Just because these short sayings have no explicit story line, they are inherently capacious: they make room for our many different stories and thus give us direct access to what Eugene Peterson aptly calls the "robust sanity" of the biblical wisdom tradition.[2]

Like haiku, biblical proverbs represent language in its most condensed form. Their stock characters are the wise and the foolish, those who yield to wickedness and those who practice righteousness.

> Treasures gained by wickedness bring no profit;
> but righteousness rescues from death. (10:2)

> The fool's way is straight in his own eyes,
> but the one who listens to advice is wise. (12:15)

The starkness of the sages' expression may at first seem a poor match for our most difficult experiences, which are nearly always fraught with mixed emotions and gray areas. It is not easy to dismiss as fools the people with whom we are locked in conflict, since they are often the same people for whom, in other situations, we have felt admiration, sympathy, love. Nor can we feel wise ourselves, in the midst of an ugly and debilitating situation. However, as I lived with these short sayings (a proverb can easily be memorized in the morning and carried around all day), I began to see that the wise and the foolish are not two distinct groups of people, but rather two contrasting choices that each of us may make at any moment. The proverbs were providing me, not with convenient labels for myself and the one I perceived as my opponent, but rather with points of orientation for "walking with integrity" (10:9), a central concept for the Israelite sages.

Wisdom, Knowledge, and the Information Society

The easiest way to find a preaching angle on any text is to read slowly, until you notice exactly how it challenges or even overturns the ways we ordinarily think

---

2. Eugene Peterson, *The Message: The Wisdom Books* (Colorado Springs: NavPress, 1996), 282. Peterson's colloquial translation or paraphrase of Proverbs is useful because it reminds us that proverbs belong essentially to the daily conversation of ordinary people. My translations here aim to be more transparent to the Hebrew text than Peterson's.

about things. This practice is what the monastic tradition calls *lectio divina,* "divine reading." Anyone attuned to both the text and contemporary culture might pause as early as the second line of the book, where the purpose of "the proverbs of Solomon" is stated thus: "For knowing *wisdom* and *discipline* (*musar*) . . ." (1:2). Wisdom and discipline belong together, and both are central to the thinking of the Israelite sages, but they are distinctly countercultural in our society. That may explain why some translations water down one or both concepts, rendering the phrase "how to live well and right"[3] or "for learning about wisdom and *instruction*" (NRSV). Poetry is especially tricky to translate, and so the preacher of Proverbs is advised to work with multiple translations and a commentary that yields insight into the Hebrew.

We do not speak much of wisdom in contemporary mass culture. We value people who are "smart," pursuing prestigious academic degrees for ourselves and high test scores for our children. But that is not the same as valuing wisdom, for intelligence per se is not its chief component. One can be very smart, yet not very sane, and the measure of wisdom is sanity, health of mind. It is the character of those who practice the discipline of a sober though not cheerless reckoning with the whole of reality. Wisdom denotes a way of thinking—and, equally, of living—that brings us into enduring harmony with family, with neighbors near and far, with our physical environment, and ultimately with the whole created order. That is why the biblical sages represent wisdom as foundational to God's work of creation:

> Yhwh by wisdom established the earth,
> fixing the heavens by understanding. (3:19)

In the end, our failure to value wisdom may be the most consequential difference between modern industrialized culture and the culture the Bible seeks to advance, and the difference could be deadly. This may be the most important thing for us to understand and communicate as twenty-first-century preachers of Proverbs: we are in a wisdom crisis, a crisis that is unprecedented in character and magnitude. Obviously, it is not the case that most people in the past were wise; Proverbs repeatedly says that wisdom is more rare than rubies (or "corals," 3:15; see also 8:11; 31:10). Nonetheless, no culture has been so burdened and even endangered as ours by the proliferation of knowledge that is not disciplined by the search for wisdom. T. S. Eliot's words in "Choruses from 'The Rock'" (1935) are prescient of our current malaise:

---

3. Peterson, *The Message,* 283.

All our knowledge brings us nearer to our ignorance,
All our knowledge brings us nearer to death,
But nearness to death no nearer to God.
Where is the Life we have lost in living?
Where is the wisdom we have lost in knowledge?
Where is the knowledge we have lost in information?[4]

Eliot anticipated the information age some half a century before there was a name for it. He might be dismissed as a dyed-in-the-wool traditionalist (which he was), as hopelessly unprepared for a future that has now arrived. But that would be to let ourselves and our culture too easily off the hook. In the first year of this millennium, Bill Joy, one of the architects of the electronic age, confirmed (perhaps unwittingly) Eliot's diagnosis of a disease that has only advanced steadily. In a now-famous article in the magazine *Wired,* the founder of Sun Microsystems struggled publicly with the likely consequence of new technologies such as transgenic manipulation, nanotechnology, and robotics. "Knowledge-enabled mass destruction" could come about, not only as a result of laboratory mistakes or extreme individuals gaining power (neither of which is wholly preventable), but even due to the perfection of technologies that fundamentally alter the biosphere and thus are "too powerful to be shielded against in the time frame of interest"—namely, the life of existing species. "Can we doubt," Joy asks, "that knowledge has become a weapon we wield against ourselves?"[5] An accompanying article by physicist Amory Lovins and L. Hunter Lovins, designers of ecologically inspired industrial systems, states further that, in enterprises such as transgenics and nuclear fission, "technical ability has evolved faster than social institutions; *skill has outrun wisdom.* Both have overlooked fundamentals, often from other disciplines wrongly deemed irrelevant."[6]

Certainly theology and preaching are among the disciplines that even "religious" people in our society often deem irrelevant—personally inspiring, perhaps, but finally unequal to the complexities of "the real world." This is where Proverbs challenges the preacher to take a stand and say plainly that the exercise of knowledge divorced from wisdom will kill us, because it sets

---

4. T. S. Eliot, "Choruses from 'The Rock,'" 1, in *The Complete Poems and Plays, 1909-1950* (New York: Harcourt, Brace, and Company, 1958), 96.

5. Bill Joy, "Why the Future Doesn't Need Us," *Wired* 8.04 (April 2000), found at http://www.wired.com/wired/archive/8.04/jo_pr.html.

6. Amory B. Lovins and L. Hunter Lovins, "A Tale of Two Botanies," *Wired* 8.04 (April 2000), found at http://www.wired.com/wired/archive/8.04/botanies.html. Emphasis mine.

us fundamentally at odds with the structure of the universe: "YHWH by wisdom established the earth." Moreover, probing Proverbs with imagination and depth might be the best way for the preacher to counter our society's deadly propensity to reduce religion to "spirituality," the amorphous term by which we now characterize anything that seems beneficial to the individual (and for the most part disembodied) soul. That reduction is what the acerbic modern sage Wendell Berry calls "the original and originating catastrophe."[7]

The Poetry of Acquisition

Holy wisdom itself may not be valued in our society, but, ironically, there is a form—or parody—of wisdom literature that is highly developed and well known to all of us, namely, the mock-wisdom of Hollywood and Madison Avenue. A few years ago I was invited to lead a day-long workshop at a church in Beverly Hills; to my surprise, the requested topic was Proverbs. It was early autumn, and the day dawned crystal clear and slightly cool, perfect for being in the garden, at the ocean, or on the hiking trail. I therefore expected a small and likely reluctant group to turn out for the workshop: the planning committee and a few loyal friends, perhaps. Yet, surprisingly, the room filled, and people became so engaged with the topic that I had to insist they take a break. "Tell me," I asked, "where does all this energy come from?" Immediately someone responded: "Oh, most of us work in Hollywood. We write commercials and advertising copy. And when we were in training, they told us to read Proverbs." She smiled a little self-consciously before continuing: "But now I see that most of what we write is aimed at the people Proverbs calls 'fools.'"

If more professors of Bible and homiletics had seen what the advertising industry has seen, we would doubtless hear and do more preaching on Proverbs, and it might be some of the most helpful preaching in the church. Both biblical proverbs and advertising slogans are designed to speak directly into the heart of a culture, to ordinary people in their daily lives. With just a few words, they epitomize certain core values, and if they catch on, they become a powerful way of communicating those values. They may be adapted to new contexts within the culture, some of those quite distant from a given saying's original *Sitz im Leben,* its setting in life: "Where's the beef?"

The most telling point of correspondence between biblical wisdom and

---

7. Wendell Berry, foreword to Ellen F. Davis, *Scripture, Culture, and Agriculture: An Agrarian Reading of the Bible* (Cambridge: Cambridge University Press, 2009), xii.

the advertising industry is that both are directed toward shaping and stimulating desire: more people should want something they do not yet have, or else want more of what they already possess. So a proverb and a well-crafted advertisement are both forms of the poetry of acquisition. What is crucial for the preacher is that they contrast completely on the nature of the object of desire. Proverbs such as these make it clear that *wisdom* was a reasonably hard sell, even in ancient Israel:

> Acquire [or, "Buy"] wisdom; acquire discernment;
> do not forget . . . ! (Prov. 4:5)

> The first thing about wisdom: Acquire wisdom!
> And in exchange for everything you have acquired, acquire discernment.
>   (4:7)

> Acquiring wisdom—how much better than gold,
> and acquiring discernment, choicer than silver! (16:16)

In these sayings and throughout the book, the verb *qanah* ("acquire, buy") occurs with unusual density (fourteen times in Proverbs).[8] Although *qanah* is an ordinary marketplace term, here (in all cases but one: Prov. 20:14) the thing to be acquired is intangible: variously, wisdom or discernment (see also 16:16; 17:16), truth (23:23), knowledge (18:15), skill (1:5), even "a heart" (15:32; 19:8). The sages of Proverbs are cultivating the desire for more, just as assiduously as does the advertising industry.

Not infrequently, skilled poets of acquisition play on one of the most elemental forms of desire. A Jaguar ad features a photo in which the front section of the "perfectly proportioned high strength aluminum alloy body" and the automatically adjusting headlamps—"beauty and brains"—appear at an angle that mimics a woman's full breasts and smooth belly. Lest the point be missed, inscribed over the driveshaft are the words, "sin No. 1 LUST." The caption concludes, ". . . that's not love you're feeling." Not to be outdone, Cadillac has the beautiful actress Kate Walsh deliver a soliloquy on the features of the car she is driving; she ends with "the real question . . . , when you turn your car on, does it return the favor?"

---

8. Thirteen times *qanah* occurs in Proverbs with the meaning of "buy, acquire," but there is a slightly different connotation to the verb in the one instance where God is its grammatical subject, when personified Wisdom says, "Yнwн *created* me (*qanani*)" (8:22).

Israel's sages likewise use sexual bait to stimulate desire for a nonsexual object. Some of their sayings would have been devised to amuse adolescent male students and keep them awake at their studies. So, for instance, "Lady" Wisdom declares:

> As for me, I love my lovers,
> and those who get up early for me will find me. (8:17)

And similarly:

> For Wisdom is better than rubies,
> and all other pleasures do not equal her. (8:11)

Unlike the sexual ploy of Madison Avenue, however, that of the sages is not entirely empty. For it reflects the important but often overlooked truth that strong desire is never a neutral factor in our religious development and moral character. If a preacher or teacher can awaken a craving for the things of God, and direct it in ways that are genuinely life-giving for the one who desires, then both young and old will grow in ways they never imagined possible. David Ford comments perceptively, "Desire is in many ways the embracing mood of a life immersed in history and oriented towards the fulfillment of God's purposes."[9] But much desire is unproductive or actively harmful. We waste our wanting on objects that are unworthy of our devotion, of the years we give to pursuing them—let alone of our hearts, which gradually mold themselves to fit the things we desire.

Critical questioning is essential to the "acquisition" of wisdom.[10] Therefore preachers should pay close, critical attention to the advertisements that frame nearly every piece of news we see, to the commercials that interrupt our entertainment countless times in an evening. They might ask their congregations, as I ask my students, to report on advertisements they see or hear regularly; we need to know the forces that would shape our hearts. Alyce McKenzie, certainly the contemporary scholar who has most fully explored the preaching potential of Proverbs, observes: "When a preacher knows her

9. David F. Ford, *Christian Wisdom: Desiring God and Learning in Love* (Cambridge: Cambridge University Press, 2007), 50.

10. David Ford and Graham Stanton assert that "wisdom is about trying to integrate knowledge, understanding, critical questioning and good judgement with a view to the flourishing of human life and the whole of creation" ("Introduction," in *Reading Texts, Seeking Wisdom: Scripture and Theology* [Grand Rapids: Eerdmans, 2003], 2).

own biblical proverbial heritage and is attuned to how proverbs are in constant use in her culture, she is equipped to offer the dehumanized consumers in the pews an alternative identity, worldview, and way of life."[11] There is a notable consistency to the mock-wisdom texts produced by Hollywood and Madison Avenue. All of them uphold one or more of the core values sacred to industrialized society: personal uniqueness, freedom from constraint and fear, power both social and automotive, sexual stimulation, or (for the more sedate set) exquisitely good taste. Any doubt that these values are sacred might be dispelled by the ad that features a striking ash blonde with a long stretch of exposed torso, ending in about six inches of tattered cut-offs—a promotion for True Religion Brand Jeans.

It is acutely ironic, however, that nearly every product manufacturer or credit card company stresses "your" style or story, while mounting a campaign that can be considered a success only if tens of thousands yield to the fantasy of uniqueness.

The effects of the fantasy go far beyond the immediate purchase. Norman Wirzba makes the telling observation that consumerism is

> an approach to reality that fundamentally alters the ways we engage and relate to the world around us. . . . Our engagement with an external world, now increasingly characterized in terms of commodity exchange, has less to [do] with reality itself than with marketable images that determine production and spending. . . . A consumer mentality, in other words, contributes to our overall ignorance about the truth of reality, just as it works against a life of wisdom, because we now relate to the world more ephemerally as the scanners and purchasers of it.[12]

The marketers of the Discover (credit) card put it in a nutshell: "It's like they put the *whole world* on sale."

The preacher schooled in Proverbs might counter that mock-wisdom with another saying such as this:

> Wisdom is present to the person of discernment,
> while the eyes of the fool are at the end of the earth. (17:24)

11. Alyce M. McKenzie, *Preaching Proverbs: Wisdom for the Pulpit* (Louisville: Westminster John Knox, 1996), 87.

12. Norman Wirzba, "Placing the Soul," in *The Essential Agrarian Reader: The Future of Culture, Community, and the Land,* ed. Norman Wirzba (Lexington: University Press of Kentucky, 2003), 92.

Biblical wisdom enables us to recognize that our greed is the expression and result of a deeply dangerous state of disorientation. Were we to lay hold of wisdom and grasp it firmly, as the sages advise us, then our confused minds and acquisitive hearts would be drawn back to the God who fixed heaven and earth "with understanding" (3:18–19).

Getting Real: Formation of the Self

The question that underlies the whole collection of biblical proverbs is one that occupies much attention in our own society and also within the church: What is required for formation of a healthy personality? Probably few in our congregations are so crass as to accept the simplest answer offered by consumer culture, that salvation is by shopping alone. Many more have accepted, implicitly at least, the common understanding to which the large self-help sections of chain bookstores attest: formation of a healthy self is a private enterprise, to be accomplished essentially on our own. But the biblical sages have a completely different view: we become our real selves only in community, through the demanding discipline of listening to others. As we shall see, that discipline involves listening patiently to and for two things, neither of which we are naturally inclined to hear: on the one hand, wise "reproof" (*tokhahat*, Prov. 1:23, 25, 30; 3:11; 6:23), correction of our own behavior; and on the other, the cry of the needy.

The sages' view is set forth clearly in multiple sayings such as these:

The isolated person seeks (only) gratification,
sneering at all sound counsel. (18:1)

The one who shrugs off discipline despises his own being (*nefesh*),[13]
while the one who hears correction (*tokhahat*) *acquires a heart*.
The fear of YHWH is wisdom's discipline,
and humility precedes respect. (15:32–33)

In the metaphorical physiology of the Bible, the heart is the center of the self; it is the seat of knowledge, thought, judgment, affection, imagination; the English word "character" may come closest to expressing all that the sages intend. The key insight here is that a "heart" in this sense is not innate; it is

---

13. The word *nefesh* may also be translated "life" or (sometimes) "soul"; see Prov. 24:12, cited below.

the product of years of work on the part of the one who acquires it, and also on the part of those who offer the needed discipline and correction.

The view that a healthy self is formed in response to wise criticism implies the existence of a community characterized essentially by mutual trust and commitment. The near identification between a willingness to hear such criticism and "the fear of YHWH"—a central concept for Israel's sages—implies further that some people in the community can be trusted to speak for God. They may not be "religious professionals"; in Proverbs, the chief exemplar of one who "fears YHWH" is an ordinary Israelite farmer and householder (31:30). Yet they can be trusted, because they themselves practice fear of YHWH, listening humbly for a word that comes from a Source more reliable than ego or self-interest. Therefore their words are life-giving, even though they may be harsh.

The fear of YHWH is a discipline that must be chosen by anyone who loves knowledge (see Prov. 1:29). It is the "beginning" or the "best part" (*re'shit*) of knowledge (1:7); there is no safe path to knowledge that does not begin with such fear, which is nothing other than a sane recognition of our proper human limits. Whatever facts we may learn or skills we may master are insignificant in comparison to the totality of what *is*—that is, what God has made. The fear of YHWH is the same awestruck acknowledgment of reality that T. S. Eliot calls going by "the way of ignorance." Paradoxically but quite realistically, it is the only way "to arrive at what [we] do not know."[14] By choosing "the way of dispossession" we may gain the one thing necessary:

The only wisdom we can hope to acquire
Is the wisdom of humility: humility is endless.[15]

Those who listen to the cry of divine Wisdom (1:33; 8:34) and "gain a heart" are enabled to hear the cry of the vulnerable, which is inaudible to so many. As David Ford has demonstrated, the evangelist Luke, in his "cry-centred acclamation" of Jesus, represents him as the "child of wisdom" (see Luke 7:35) whose hearing is perfectly acute in both directions. Jesus hears God's call to Israel to worship YHWH alone (see Deut. 6:4 and Luke 4:8), and at the same time he "hears the cries of the suffering and brings good news to them."[16] The sages of Proverbs point to the religious significance of the cry of the poor, no less sharply than do Jesus and the prophets,

14. Eliot, "East Coker," 3, in *Complete Poems and Plays,* 127.
15. Eliot, "East Coker," 2, in *Complete Poems and Plays,* 126.
16. Ford, *Christian Wisdom,* 20.

The one who stops his ear at the cry of the poor—
he will himself cry out and not be answered. (Prov. 21:13)

The one who oppresses the poor insults his Maker,
and the one who honors [God] is generous to the needy. (14:31)

In graphic imagery, the Dutch theologian Kornelis Miskotte draws the theological conclusion from such sayings: "The poor man is the real neighbour; the way in which he stands, or rather lies, in his life has something to do with the nature of the fear of God itself!"[17]

The ability to hear the cry of the vulnerable is the subject of a saying that is worth special attention, both because it is one of the longest literary units in the aphoristic section of Proverbs (chaps. 10–29), and also because it may be the most confrontational passage in the book. The hearer is addressed directly, as the protagonist of a small drama:

(If) you go slack on a day of trouble—your strength is so limited. . . .
Deliver those who are taken away to death,
and stumbling to slaughter! If you hold back . . .
Though you may say, "Look, we knew nothing about this . . ."—
the One who weighs hearts, will he not discern?
And the One who keeps your soul (*nefesh*), will he not know,
and requite every person according to what they have done? (24:10–12)

Thus the call to submit to wisdom's discipline becomes a call to justice. The character or self formed in community is strengthened to endure not just criticism but also danger for the sake of the weakest members of the community.

That sort of selfhood belongs only to those for whom "community" is not an abstract ideal but rather denotes particular people in particular places. Place itself, then, is a further dimension of community, and the commitment to care for our places is part of what constitutes a healthy self. It is no coincidence that shortly after this scenario that tests our commitment to the vulnerable come other teachings that test commitment to the places we inhabit. Here is a saying that urbanized readers like me might easily overlook, having no idea how to interpret it:

---

17. Kornelis Miskotte, *When the Gods Are Silent* (Dutch original, 1956; London: Collins, 1967), 249. On the religious significance of the poor in Proverbs and elsewhere in the Old Testament, see Davis, *Proverbs, Ecclesiastes, and the Song of Songs*, 94-96.

Do your preparatory work outside,
and get things ready in the field for yourself;
then, afterwards, you can build your house. (24:27)

In our contemporary setting, the best way to interpret that proverb, along
with the short narrative that follows (24:30–34), about the derelict farm of the
"slothful man," is not as advice or instruction to individual farmers. Rather,
these passages should inform a theological critique of our urban-dominated
industrial economy, which has colonized rural communities in North America
and around the world.[18] The sages' notion that the field takes priority over the
house made perfect sense to a society of small farmers, such as ancient Israel,
where everyone knew that settled life depends immediately on care of the land
as the source of food and fiber. That reality has not changed, but only our understanding of it. Therefore we North Americans are content to build developments
of "McMansions," with infertile, chemically dependent lawns, where productive
family farms used to be. We allow skilled farmers to go bankrupt—and in many
countries around the world, to starve—while the land is worked, but not cared
for, by multinational corporations whose sole goal is short-term profit. We are
willing to let our fresh water sources be poisoned by chemical run-off, our rivers
and aquifers be pumped far beyond replacement levels, our bays and gulfs be
choked into a ring of dead zones around the world. These teachings of the sages
speak to our captivity of the natural systems that sustain our life. They now rank
among the first of the "vulnerable" whose cry we must learn to hear.[19] Norman
Wirzba draws the connection between industrial society's life-destroying commitment to consumerism and our widespread willingness to practice such abuse
of people—not to mention factory-farmed animals—and living systems:

> When we are reduced to shoppers who never see the connection between
> food and habitat, or human health and soil vitality, it is unsurprising that
> as eaters we will compromise the sources of food and not see the contra-
> diction in this act. Our collective blindness and ignorance is a slow form
> of suicide that will only be corrected as we recover what it means to be
> biological beings dependent on a geo-bio-chemical world.[20]

18. For an exegetically based theological critique of the industrialized food system, see Ellen F. Davis, *Scripture, Culture, and Agriculture: An Agrarian Reading of the Bible* (Cambridge:
Cambridge University Press, 2009).
19. For the notion that nature itself is "the new poor," see Sallie McFague, *The Body of
God: An Ecological Theology* (Minneapolis: Fortress, 1993), 164.
20. Norman Wirzba, "Why an Agrarian Manifesto?" unpublished paper, August 2008.

Surprised by Wisdom

Embodying Wisdom

In Proverbs, as throughout the Bible, the preacher encounters a *possible* world—that is, a vision of our world that offers real possibilities for human fulfillment within the social and created order, possibilities that are significantly better than the practices that currently dominate and ultimately deform our lives. The distinctive contribution that Proverbs makes to the Christian canon is its detailed picture of what the practice of wisdom looks like in the course of ordinary human experience—or, sometimes, the extraordinary experience of ordinary people like ourselves. More than any other book of the Bible, Proverbs offers concrete guidance for how we may embody wisdom.

"Wisdom is justified by all her children," announces Jesus to the crowds gathered around John (Luke 7:35). Luke and Matthew (Matt. 11:19) cite different versions of that aphorism (a proverb with a known author); likely he said it more than once, and more than one way. For Luke, Jesus is the child of wisdom, "her" heir and perfect embodiment: "And the child grew and became strong, *filled with wisdom,* and the grace of God was upon him" (Luke 2:40). Tellingly, Jesus compares "the people of this generation" to "children sitting in the marketplace"—untutored children who cannot recognize Wisdom when she is before them, in the persons of John and Jesus (Luke 7:31–34; Matt. 11:16–19). If we have ears to hear, Jesus is asking us to repudiate the illusionary self that is the product of mass culture ("the marketplace"), to develop a substantial character by dwelling in Wisdom's household and learning from her.

The book of Proverbs concludes with the portrait of a person who has made that choice, the "woman of valor" (*'eshet hayil;* Prov. 31:10); the now-common translation, "a capable wife" (NRSV, NJPS), is woefully inadequate. This is the longest admiring description of any ordinary person—that is, *not* Moses or Jesus or Paul—in the entire Bible. The woman is described in heroic, even fierce terms: she is like a lioness bringing home "prey" (*teref,* v. 15), or a soldier girding for battle (v. 17) and bringing home the "spoils" (*shalal,* v. 11). She is even like God, clothed in "strength and splendor" (v. 25). Yet the scene of all her action is the household and the local community, which she builds up and makes more secure by her work. She does the concrete work of wisdom in her neighborhood: her hands are stretched out to the poor (v. 20); she cares for her land and makes it prosper (v. 16). Her words are characterized by *hesed* (v. 26), the glue of mutual commitment that binds together the members of the covenanted community.

This is an iconic portrait, a holy and vivid image of the kind of life that all the teaching of the sages is meant to inspire. But we miss the point if we dismiss

PREACHING THE LUMINOUS WORD

it (as did one preacher in my hearing) as a picture of a submissive housebound woman, a throwback to another age with no constructive challenge to address to our own. The woman of valor is a source of security for her husband (v. 11) and strength for her whole community. If the word "submissive" can be applied to her at all, it would be only to denote her proper humility before God (v. 30).

This concluding poem might in fact be the place to *begin* preaching Proverbs, for it challenges us precisely as the rest of the book does: by refusing to separate two things that most Western Christians think have nothing to do with one another, namely, wisdom and economics.[21] In other words, it reminds us that religion—a concept for which "fear of YHWH" is the closest biblical parallel—can never be an abstraction. The wisdom tradition, if we take it seriously, forces us to look at how our relationship with God is expressed through myriad daily social practices, including economic practices; it confronts us with the fact that our relationship with God is at every moment inseparable from our relation to the material world. In short, Proverbs stands within the canon of Scripture as a strong counter to the propensity, both ancient and modern, to reduce religious practice, or holiness of life, to mere "spirituality." Jesus would be the first to tell us that such a reduction is foolish and heretical, for holy "Wisdom is justified by her works" (Matt. 11:19).

21. See also my treatment of this passage (Prov. 31:10–31) in *Scripture, Culture, and Agriculture*, 147-54.

Mastering Sacrifice

"Raising Spirits" Conference of the Episcopal Church Women,
Christ Church, Raleigh, North Carolina
January 18, 1997

PROVERBS 3:11–26; 1 CORINTHIANS 1:10–31

"What would happen to us in the church if we claimed the cross as the source of our wisdom?" The question, addressed to the Conference of the Episcopal Church Women, reflects a homiletic concern that the church's present divisions result from a profound lack of wisdom. In spite of clergy and laity being more highly educated than at any time in history, "wisdom has largely eluded us." The acceptance of Christ's cross in our fellowship means letting go of our attempts to control the future. It means peace for the church and an outpouring of wisdom into the world.

[Wisdom's] ways are ways of pleasantness,
and all her paths are peace. (Prov. 3:17)

In two lectures, I have spoken at length about the dangerous condition of a world that has lost contact with Hagia Sophia, Holy Wisdom, by which, as Proverbs tells us, God founded and sustains the earth. Now, in the context of the Eucharist, I want to turn to a more intimate problem, namely, the loss of wisdom within the church. I am not here long enough to be subtle, so let me assert brashly that at this time in our church's life, wisdom has largely eluded us, despite the fact that both clergy and laity are now more highly educated than at any time in history.

I would not dare say that on my own authority, but Scripture emboldens me. Israel's sages tell us that "[Wisdom's] ways are ways of pleasantness, and all her paths are peace"—and in the modern church our peace is a rare and fragile thing. We so easily give and take offense, setting ourselves apart from one other along lines of piety, custom, sexual politics, and doctrine: charismatics vs. traditionalists, powerful women vs. powerful men, contemplatives at odds with social activists and both of those at odds with intellectuals. In places where none of these particular divisions is disabling, still many congregations suffer greatly from the perennial evil of personalities that clash and will not be reconciled. And, of course, our national church is wracked and threatens to break apart over the division between those who favor the ordination of homosexuals or the blessing of same-sex unions vs. those who do not. For many clergy, I have discovered, the peace of God begins to depart early, often while they are in seminary. Most come to seminary expecting a Garden-of-Eden experience (early Eden) and are shocked to find—I am shocked anew each year—how much anxiety, unhappiness, and anger attend the process of formation for ministry. Students worry perpetually about grades and ordination committees; faculty worry about tenure, professional stature, and whether their side is going to win in the current policy debate. You can multiply examples from your own life and experience of the church, but the point is this: the tensions and deep divisions that mark our lives individually and corporately are signs that somehow we in the church have strayed off the pleasant paths of wisdom.

As is so often the case, the apostle Paul speaks directly to the ways in which Christians lose their joy. He is writing to the Corinthians, whose church is torn by party spirit. Evidently the members are vying with one another over their baptismal credentials—whose is better, Paul's or Apollos's or Peter's. And Paul cuts through their politicking and bickering with this question: "Was Paul crucified for you? . . . Were you baptized in Paul's name?" (1 Cor. 1:13). The impatient questions are designed to reorient the Corinthians to the centerpoint of reality, the cross of Christ: "For Christ did not send me to baptize but to preach the gospel, . . . the word of the cross . . ." (vv. 17–18). "The word of the cross"—all Christian preaching must be oriented to the cross, because that is the one source of wisdom vouchsafed to the church: "For Jews demand signs and Greeks seek wisdom, but we preach Christ crucified, a stumbling block to Jews and folly to Gentiles, but to those who are called, both Jews and Greeks, Christ the power of God and the wisdom of God" (vv. 22–24).

Jesus Christ, the wisdom of God—what does that mean? Proverbs tells us that

by wisdom the LORD founded the earth,
by [God's] knowledge the clouds drip dew. (Prov. 3:19–20)

In other words, divine wisdom is what makes the world and keeps it going. Wisdom is God's vision of the world, God's provision for the world. In Jesus Christ, God made human, we see the one person who fully grasped God's vision of the world; he called it the kingdom of God. In him we see the only one who lived his life wholly in accordance with God's will, so that his life was in its entirety God's provision for the world, even unto death on a cross. Paul preaches Christ crucified—not just Christ risen and glorified but Christ crucified, against all odds the perfect image of Holy Wisdom.

With his eyes fixed on the cross, Paul comes to a new and radically simple understanding of the wisdom that founded and sustains the world. In a word, it is this: the power of willing sacrifice holds us all in life. Sacrifice, literally, is "making holy," sanctifying the world by accepting our lives as pure gift and offering back to God any and all of what God has given us. What would it mean if we really got that, if we really saw the cross as an image of perfect, holy wisdom? What would it mean for us in the church if we claimed the cross, the power of willing sacrifice, as the one source of our wisdom? Two things: it would mean peace among ourselves and an outpouring of genuine wisdom into the world.

First, there will be peace among ourselves. Paul sets the preaching of Christ crucified, the power of God, against the party politicking of the Corinthians; the implication is that when the church's attention is riveted on God's boundless self-giving, then we will be given the grace to move together beyond our sad and sometimes silly divisions. Not that we will agree on everything, even on every important thing in Christian doctrine and practice; but we will no longer waste so much of our God-given powers on disputes whose heat too often comes from love of self rather than zeal for God's truth.

Second, when the cross is accepted as the source of our wisdom, there will be an increase of wisdom emanating from the church to the world:

- an outflow of God's truth—our words will be more powerful, they will speak to the pain of the world;
- an outflow of God's love—our actions will touch and heal its aching wounds.

If sacrifice is the one thing that we in the church are really striving to master—"making holy," making God's holiness manifest—then there will be a fundamental shift in our engagement with the world, in every aspect of our lives. Our attitudes toward education and work will change. With our eyes fixed on the cross, we will be less concerned with the perfection, extension, and recognition of our personal powers than many of us feel we must be in order to survive. Professional work will be genuinely professional; it will profess faith in Christ crucified. Our attitude toward money will change. We will be less concerned with establishing ourselves in the eyes of the world, with what we deludedly call "securing our future"—as though we ever could, or need to. Our lives will no longer be shaped by anxiety but rather by an increasingly clear sense of Christian vocation. We will be able to hear God's call to us. Freed from anxiety, we will hear ourselves called into action, not by the demands and rewards of the system, but rather by the deep needs of our neighbor.

Many people feel, often early in their religious life, a desire to make a genuine, costly sacrifice for the sake of God, to give their best energies to the things of God. Perhaps you have felt that desire, and still feel it. Perhaps you see it in your child, your husband, your friend, your priest. It is a desire that is too often quenched, generally by the injunction to be just a little more practical. "Be practical"—that's good advice, if it means, "Consider the real needs of the world and how you can best prepare to serve them." "Be practical"—what that actually means, most of the time, is, "Don't frighten me, don't rattle my cage. Make your actions conform to my present desires; cut them to fit the size of my vision." But the word of the cross overturns that definition of practicality. The wisdom of the cross is in the deepest sense practical wisdom; it is realistic knowledge of the world informing sacrifice. The wisdom of the cross is non-egocentric contemplation of the world, revealing how I may best spend myself in God's service.

And if we should—imagine it—if we should manage to learn the practical wisdom of the cross, will it preach? Can it ever be heard by a world languishing for lack of the truth, unaware of the power of willing sacrifice? Paul is frank: "the word of the cross is folly to those who are perishing" (1 Cor. 1:18). But yet, some may listen to this new foolishness from the church simply because it is new, a diverting alternative to the foolishness that the church too commonly displays to our comfortably post-Christian culture. I have not forgotten the weary remark made many years ago by a close friend to whom I was defending my involvement in the church: "I'm sick of Christians doing the same thing everybody else does and telling me it's different."

The whole world is weary and sick and cannot be healed by a church that abandons itself to the folly of hypocrisy, conforming itself to the self-seeking ways of this world, doing the same thing everybody else does and calling it different. But imagine, imagine if the church were conspicuous instead for displaying the perfect folly of the cross, at the same time both reckless and knowing—spending ourselves without counting the cost, yet wisely, in obedience to God's call in response to the genuine needs of the world. May we see it in our time; may we give to it our strength, O LORD.

Amen.

Face to Face

Wedding of Meghan Feldmeyer and Adam Benson,
Duke Chapel, Durham, North Carolina
November 8, 2014

PROVERBS 27:19

Using the image of a reflecting pool as a metaphor for marriage, this sermon draws on the book of Proverbs and calls for the bride and groom to be "a deep and true source of self-knowledge for each other." Like one's reflection in a pool of water, each Christian marriage partner will be revealing, dynamic, and forgiving. Together, truly knowing each other, and being truly known, they will be a sign in the world of God's kingdom.

Meghan and Adam, when you look back upon this day in years to come, most of it will be a happy blur. Your memories will be fragmentary, probably most of them visual and tactile; you might remember something about this gorgeous dress; about seeing each other in a wholly unique way, from the two ends of this long aisle; maybe something about the rings or the joining of hands. Likely the only *words* you will remember will be your vows; yet you have placed in your program a few words to dwell upon as you look back to this day, this one verse from the book of Proverbs:

Like water, (revealing) face to face,
so the heart of one person to another. (27:19)

It's a sort of Hebrew haiku, a few syllables etching a memorable image. The poet is telling us that we may see ourselves clearly only as we are mirrored in the heart of another person: "Like water, face to face . . ." Most people in the ancient world would have had a literally hazy idea of their own appearance.

Only the very wealthy had metal mirrors. Most people would have had the chance to see themselves only if they encountered a deep, clear pool of water, and those were not common in the semi-arid land of Israel. So the poet who wrote our haiku is imagining a rare moment, when one sees oneself clearly in a reflecting pool, and that pool is the heart of another person. That is how you are giving yourself to each other now: as a reflecting pool, a deep and true source of self-knowledge for the other. In marriage you will come to know each other's heart as well as one can know another, and at the same time you will each see yourself more clearly through the other, "Like water, (revealing) face to face . . ."

As people professionally experienced in ministry, you have doubtless seen enough not to be especially idealistic about what marriage is, or what it can become. You know that some marriages are partnerships in narcissism rather than growth. Others are stunting and punishing. Tragically, the heart of a spouse can prove to be a distorting mirror, in which the other partner comes to see herself as ugly and misshapen, to believe that he is unworthy of love. But you, Adam and Meghan, are now committing yourselves to a distinctly different possibility, one that the poet of Proverbs hints is rare enough. So today we are gathered to bless and pray you toward the realization of that possibility: a marriage that will make visible, in a small but true way, the kingdom of God in our midst.

We pray that your home may be a dwelling place for God's Spirit in the world. In choosing each other, you have made the most consequential decision of your lives, from the standpoint of spiritual orientation and growth. You are one another's closest spiritual companion, until you are parted by death. What you do in that privileged position will determine very much about how each of you regards time and money; what new opportunities for ministry you will be able to welcome; how you will relate to what is unexpected and unfamiliar (the kind of thing children inevitably present); how you will deal with difficulty, and whether that itself becomes a witness to the church. In short, your growth together will determine how free both of you will be to respond to the strange call and claim that God has placed upon your life.

> Like water, (revealing) face to face,
> so the heart of one person to another.

The brilliance of the image in capturing the essence of human relationship is that a reflection seen in water is dynamic; it moves (however slightly) all the time, in contrast to the static image that appears on the hard surface of a metal or glass mirror. That very dynamism can be a source of difficulty. If the waters of your heart are churning and turbid, Meghan, then Adam will be the first to be confused. And Adam, if the waters of your heart are roiling, then Meghan will be disturbed. This will doubtless happen from time to time; marriage is, after all, for humans and not for angels. It is for humans still living and loving on this side of death, in our troubled and troubling world. So we pray now that your hearts will ever and again return to peace, that you may be to each other like clear "water, (revealing) face to face."

The biblical image suggests one more thing that is essential for any life-giving marriage. Consider: because it is always moving, a reflection seen in water is a "forgiving" image—which is to say, people tend to look a little better in a pool of water than in a photograph, which is by nature static. My husband is a photographer, and I sometimes resist and reject the pictures he takes of me: "I can't look like that!" But looking at myself through the *hearts* of those who love me best is a different experience. Yes, I can see my failings, even aspects of myself that are plain ugly, but I do not see them in a way that gets my back up—or more, drives me to despair. Seeing myself in the reflecting pool of one who loves me and loves God truly, I feel the grace of being forgiven; I am given the desire and the courage to change, and grow.

May this be your experience of marriage, Adam and Meghan: each seeing yourself truly in the heart of the other, growing side by side in faithfulness and courage, responding in freedom and joy to the often surprising, sometimes incomprehensible, and yet profoundly beautiful design that God in Christ and the Spirit is working in your life together. And let all God's people say . . .

Amen.

Wisdom and Her Works

Myers Park Baptist Church, Charlotte, North Carolina
April 19, 2015

PROVERBS 31:10–31; MATTHEW 11:16–19, 28–30

Biblical wisdom does not reside in abstractions but in "practical matters" rooted in the daily habits of a household-based economy. Despite scholarly suggestions to the contrary, the woman described in Proverbs 31 is not "submissive" but heroic in her subversive resistance to the empire's extractive economy. By joining wisdom with economics, she shows us how to recover the holiness of wholeness in our work, how to care for the material world, and how to build and sustain a healthy community.

A traditional rabbinic prayer: Blessed are you, O LORD, King of the Universe, who has given a portion of his wisdom to those who fear him. Amen.

In chapter 11 of Matthew's Gospel, Jesus is talking about wisdom—or more precisely, about the lack of wisdom in "this generation," when he compares his contemporaries to self-centered children sitting in the marketplace, who fancy that they are the ones who get to call the tune:

We played the flute for you, and you would not dance;
we sang funeral dirges, and you did not beat your breast. (Matt. 11:17)

Jesus's word to "this generation" (his own) is simple enough: life is not a game in the marketplace, and I am not dancing to your tune. And then he makes one of those carved-in-stone dominical pronouncements that you cannot forget, even if you do not yet understand it: "Yet Wisdom is justified in her works."

"Wisdom is justified in her *works*." From a biblical perspective, wisdom is

161

a profoundly practical matter; it's something you demonstrate with your daily habits, not your abstract ideas or your university degrees. Jesus, following in biblical tradition that long preceded him, speaks of wisdom in the feminine gender: "Wisdom is justified in *her* works." I am guessing that one biblical picture of Woman Wisdom he might have in mind is the one I am about to read you, the lovely poem about an *'eshet hayil,* "a heroic woman," that concludes the book of Proverbs. As you know, the whole focus of Proverbs is how we humans may live out on the ground the divine property and gift of wisdom. So listen to this poem; in the whole Bible it is the most detailed picture of what the daily work of an ordinary person might look like, when Wisdom is at work:

> **Proverbs 31:10–31**
> A valorous [or, heroic] woman—who can find?
> Her price is higher than corals.
> Her husband's heart is secure with her,
> and he does not lack "spoils."
> She renders him good and not evil
> all the days of her life.
> She searches out wool and flax
> and works with eager hands.
> She is like a trader's fleet;
> from afar she brings her food.
> She rises while it is still night
> and provides "prey" to her household and "statutes" to her young women.
> She plans a field and takes it;
> by the fruit of her palms she plants a vineyard.
> She girds her loins with strength
> and makes firm her arms.
> She judges that her trading is good,
> and [so] her lamp is not extinguished at night.
> Her hands she reaches out with the spindle,
> and her palms hold the spinning whorl.
> Her palm she spreads out to the poor,
> and her hands she reaches out to the needy.
> She does not fear snow for her household,
> for all her house is clothed in crimson [wool].
> Coverlets she makes for herself;
> of fine linen and purple is her clothing.
> Her husband is known at the gates,

when he sits with the elders of the land.
Linen garments she makes and sells;
sashes she gives to the merchant.
Strength and splendor, her garment;
she smiles at the day to come.
She opens her mouth in wisdom
and faithful teaching is on her tongue.
She is watching over the activities of her household;
she does not eat the bread of sloth.
Her children arise and pronounce her blessed;
her husband praises her:
"Many daughters have done valiantly,
but you have surpassed them all.
Charm is a lie, and beauty a vapor.
The God-fearing woman is the one who should be praised.
Celebrate her for the fruit of her hands;
and let her works praise her in the gates."

This is what wisdom looks like "on the ground"—literally on the ground, because the valorous woman is a skilled farmer. Perhaps you noticed as I read: this woman's hands are her best feature. The poet mentions them seven times: hands that plant a field or hold the spindle and spinning whorl with which she clothes her family warmly, even elegantly; hands outstretched to the vulnerable members of the community. Because her hands are busy with work that is good for everyone connected with her, good for the land itself, this woman can "smile, laugh at the day to come" (v. 25). Wisdom is living in a way that yields hope for the long-term future.

For the poet of Proverbs, as for her community, this woman is a hero, and she is celebrated here with a superb piece of Hebrew poetry. This is an alphabetic poem, with each verse starting with a different letter of the Hebrew alphabet in order; the poet is singing her praises from A to Z. No other ordinary person in the whole Bible gets such admiring attention, yet it is probably fair to say that many or most of us are underwhelmed by this portrait of Woman Wisdom at her work. One biblical scholar describes this poem as a bourgeois male fantasy of the perfectly submissive housewife.[1] With all due respect, he has not read carefully enough. The heroic woman is anything but submissive.

---

1. See Joseph Blenkinsopp, "The Family in First Temple Israel," in *Families in Ancient Israel,* ed. Leo Perdue et al. (Louisville: Westminster John Knox, 1997), 84.

The poet describes her in terms that elsewhere describe a lion bringing home "prey" to feed the little ones; or a soldier making his strong arms ready for battle and later bringing home the "spoils." The heroic woman even resembles God; she is clothed in "strength and splendor."

I am guessing that what led this scholar to misread her as submissive and housebound is likely the fact that this heroic woman does indeed work at home. "This is not the kind of woman we have been taught to admire!" exclaimed one of my students some years ago. Looking around the classroom that day, I realized that every single one of us, me included, had invested some years and tens of thousands of dollars in professional education that would "qualify" us (so to speak) to work away from home. That was one of those moments, rare enough in a classroom, when something important suddenly comes clear. We saw the gap between the value system represented in this poem and our own. We saw the difference between the Israelite agrarian economy, where the household was the center of production for the community, the most essential economic institution, and our own households, which are mostly centers of consumption, where we habitually take in more stuff than we need and eventually discard most of it, shipping it to landfills, industrial incinerators, and toxic waste dumps as far away as possible, to poor parts of the city or county, even across the state line, if there is a poorer state that will take our trash. The heroic woman is challenging to people like us, precisely because she stands for a prosperous *household-based* economy—that is, an economy fundamentally different from our thoroughly industrialized economy.

The heroic woman was challenging in her own social context, too. The poem probably dates to the fifth century BCE, when Israel/Judah was a vassal province of the Persian empire, the biggest empire the world had ever known. Doubtless many farming households were run by women, since the men were regularly drafted off the farm by the empire, for forced labor and military service, and families were struggling to stay afloat in an extractive economy, which took much of what they produced. So this poem is *resistance literature*; it shows the courage and persistence, the ingenuity and skill it takes to make it in an economic environment that is hostile to ordinary people and to local communities—an environment like the Persian empire in the fifth century BCE, or global capitalism in the twenty-first century.

As you can see, this poem of the heroic woman speaks to us of *both* wisdom *and* economics. That is hard to grasp, since we have generally put those two in different categories: our economic life is here, and our spiritual and moral life is over here. So it is interesting that Jesus compares the foolish people in "this generation" to children sitting in the marketplace—that's a telling location, isn't it?—sitting in the marketplace, distressed and puzzled that things are not going our way. Does he mean that the marketplace is where our lack of wisdom shows up first, and worst? The British economist E. F. Schumacher observed several decades ago that we could get away with the exclusion of wisdom from economics "for a little while, as long as we were relatively unsuccessful [at making the economy boom]; but now that we have become very successful, the problem of spiritual and moral truth moves into the central position."[2] Schumacher was speaking about the need for economic restraint, for wise use of what we call "natural resources," but the Bible calls them "the work of God's hands." Wisdom and economics are inseparable, if we are to survive as a culture—and maybe as a species, along with the countless other species on which human lives depend.

Wisdom and economics are inseparable; moreover, "Wisdom is justified in her works." The poem of the heroic woman shows us Wisdom at work in the maintenance of daily existence. That too is hard to grasp, because most of us have turned over to others very much of the labor that sustains us. We are more or less ignorant of what it actually takes for us to live. In the horrific drought that strangled North Carolina some years ago, the well went dry at the home of one of my colleagues. The sudden absence of water on tap came as a great shock, as it would to most of us. But my colleague was wise enough to recognize how fundamentally she was being challenged, as a theologian and as a Christian. Watching the new well being dug, she commented, "I'm beginning to see what it takes to support my comfortable professional lifestyle." With that comment this good theologian was taking a big step away from theological abstraction. Moving away from theological abstraction to a serious encounter with God and what God actually expects of us—that is what the book of Proverbs calls "fear of the LORD," and it is the beginning of wisdom (Prov. 1:7).

Moving away from an abstract Christianity into a real encounter with what God requires of us is fearsome; it involves a radical and often painful undoing of our most basic assumptions, including our assumptions about work. "The object of work is holiness," said the artist Eric Gill, who articulated a theology of work perhaps more fully than any other Christian of the twentieth century. Further, "Holiness means wholeness"[3]—the wholeness of a community living in harmony with each other and with the physical sources of our life. Knowing as we do that human work is now the chief effective cause

2. E. F. Schumacher, *Small Is Beautiful: Economics as if People Mattered* (New York: Harper & Row, 1973), 34.

3. Eric Gill, *A Holy Tradition of Working* (Ipswich, England: Golgonooza, 1983), 45.

of ecological disruption—global warming, destruction of the rain forests, soil degradation, draining and poisoning of our waterways—then surely recovering the holiness of human work is the form that wisdom must take in our lives. For "Wisdom is justified in her works."

This biblical poem about a skilled and generous woman going about her work shows us two paths whereby we might claim or reclaim holiness in our living and working: (1) we can get ourselves more deeply and genuinely entangled with matter, the physical means of life; and (2) we can let trouble lead us deeper into community.

The first of those, then: get yourself "entangled with matter,"[4] in pleasing ways. Make something that is both useful and beautiful. The heroic woman is a weaver; she clothes her household in crimson and purple wool and fine linen. This is not strictly necessary; undyed wool and coarse linen would cover nakedness, but making something beautiful is pleasing to the woman and doubtless to those she loves. Dare we believe that the care she takes with both material goods and people is pleasing even to God? Making something good and beautiful and useful with one's hands is enormously satisfying, be it a pie or a brick wall or a garden or a photograph or a painting or a dress. As children we all discovered the joy of making something that we or our parents could use, but now most of us busy professionals buy what we want, and discard it just as easily. It is a strange irony that the more materialistic our society becomes, the less time any of us is likely to spend providing for our own material needs. Or is it the reverse? The less time we spend making good things or taking care of the things we already have, the more acquisitive we inevitably become. We can say even more here, something both theological and concrete: when we care for the things that *God* has made, the creatures both human and nonhuman, we become more whole through that work. Wholeness is holiness; genuine caretaking is the source of holiness and healing in our lives and in our world. Could there be any clearer sign of the abysmal human loneliness that pervades our industrialized culture than the popularity of "virtual pets," puppies and kittens that absorb attention online, yet require no care, because they don't really exist—when we live in a world of real creatures needing human wisdom and care?

So this is the first, the easier path God offers us toward recovering wholeness in our work: caring for the material world, the creatures of God. We should take that gentler path whenever it is open to us. But the poem of the heroic woman shows us another, steeper path to wholeness, namely, letting

4. See Gill, *A Holy Tradition of Working*, 137.

trouble lead us deeper into community. The heroic woman survives and even prospers within a predatory imperial economy. So hers is a community in trouble, the perpetual trouble of the colonized and oppressed. "She opens her hand to the poor"—and doubtless there are plenty of them—"her hands she extends to the vulnerable" (v. 20). This local hero models for the church the way a troubled community can begin to heal itself from economic sickness. And this is the key thing for building a healthy local economy: the building blocks must be the things we genuinely need: food, homes, education, good work.

As one example of trouble leading the church deeper into community, I think of Anathoth Garden in Orange County, North Carolina. A murder in Cedar Grove, provoked by racism, led Scenobia Taylor, whose grandfather had been born in slavery, to offer five acres of land to Cedar Grove United Methodist, once known as "the rich white church," for the purpose of planting a community vegetable garden. Now Latinas, African Americans, and whites, poor and relatively rich, work that land together; they have weekly dinners on the ground. The older farmers contribute their local knowledge and their manure—things that no one had seemed to value before. The food goes to those who need it most; and some need it badly. A wide place in the road that a few years ago was riven by fear has grown into a small but real community, bound together by links that are material, economic, moral, and genuinely spiritual.

When a community is moving toward healing, there is a happily unpredictable flow of mutual giving between those we normally think of as having the resources to give, and those we consider to have less. A few years ago, a hurricane (Rita) had taken out the power in Nacogdoches, Texas, and hungry folks had gathered in the fellowship hall of Austin Heights Baptist. There it became clear that the people with the resources to feed others were not the "professionals." No, most of the food came from those with much smaller income levels, from their gardens and deep freezers and pantry shelves—food they had grown and prepared and "set aside for the day of trouble" (Job 38:23). That experience of feeding and being fed worked a change in how people in the church valued each other in their work. It messed with neatly drawn categories of important work—highly paid and mostly done in an office—and work that had seemed, well, less important, such as work done in the kitchen. So-called unimportant work often requires strong arms and skilled hands, and usually it involves sweat. "Yet Wisdom is justified in her works." Getting food from field and garden, freezer and kitchen to the table is justifying work.

It is realistic to say that in this generation we are facing real trouble, deep brokenness in our food system, in the earth itself. As a community we will have to get used to walking that steep path to healing and wholeness. It won't be an easy walk, and we will get tired. So it is important to remember what Jesus says just a few verses after he chides the people of "this generation" for acting like foolish children who think we are smarter than we are, who think we call the shots: "Come to me, y'all" (Jesus is from southern Galilee, so I take the liberty of adapting his colloquial Greek to Southern dialect; the "y'all" is important, because I want you to hear that Jesus addresses us in the grammatical *plural*)—"y'all who are worn out and burdened, come to me, and I will give y'all a rest" (Matt. 11:28). As far as I know, nowhere in the Bible is the call to holiness, to wholeness, formulated in the second-person *singular*. And that is the point: we'll never become holy and whole, we'll never attain to wisdom, we'll never really get a rest, if we are traveling alone. Taking up the justifying work of wisdom is a job for the people of God as a body. So come on, y'all; it is past time to begin.

Amen.

After the Rain

Wedding of Marcy Agmon and Michael Shoop, Los Angeles, California
October 10, 2004

SONG OF SONGS 2:10–12

The capacity to rejoice in love even through times of trouble is a divine mystery. In the context of marriage, it is a mystery that sanctifies us to one another in ways that draw us into the extraordinary presence of God. In this sanctified company of husband and wife, friends and family will also find a place where they are held in mutual honor. A holy marriage, then, is one that creates a haven of comfort, hope, and companionship in an otherwise broken world.

"Arise, my darling, my lovely one, and come away. For look, the rainy season is over, the storms have passed over and gone. The blossoms are out in the land; the time for singing has come." (Song of Songs 2:10–12)

Those words were written in the land of Israel, some 2,500 years ago, but they might as well have been written for this very day in California. In fact, if you believe (as I do) that the Bible has a freshness that keeps renewing itself, then those words were written for today, for you two. In the beautiful love poem that is the Song of Songs, a man is speaking to the woman he loves, a woman who has suffered greatly, and he says, "Come on now, the winter rains have passed, and spring has come again. Just look at all these flowers. Yes, it's time for singing." Maybe each of you could fittingly say those words to the other: "The hard storms have passed over us now; the time for singing has come."

When lovers marry at our age, each of them has, I suppose, been through some harsh winters. They know something about suffering and disappointment. But it is equally true that when lovers marry at our age, they are alive to joy. Strangely, they may experience joy more deeply now even than they did when they were young, before they knew grief so well. I can't explain that, but I know it's true: those who pass through sorrow yet still keep their hearts open in love, expand their capacity for joy. Passing through sorrow yet still keeping their hearts open in love, they expand their capacity for love itself. And I dare to guess, Marcy and Michael, that this is what you most honor in one another: a capacity to rejoice in love—a capacity that has grown, to some extent at least, through times of trouble. Just how that works is a mystery—yet don't we see it with surprising frequency in the lives of those we most admire? The mystery of love and joy growing deep, strong roots through the winter rainstorms—even because of them—no one can ever explain that. But the wisest people say, it is a mystery that has everything to do with God.

In a few minutes each of you will address to the other some of the most strangely beautiful words you will ever speak, in public or in private. *Harei at mequdeshet li; harei attah mequdash li.* "Behold, you are sanctified to me." What on earth can that mean—especially in the wildly secular society in which we live—"You are *sanctified* to me"? Well, when something is sanctified, it ceases to be ordinary, everyday, run-of-the-mill; when something is sanctified, it is brought into the realm of God. And marriage gives you the opportunity to do that for each other: to lift each other, moment by moment, day by day, year by year, out of the order of the ordinary. "Behold, *you* are sanctified to *me.*" Someone who is sanctified is set apart for special honor. From now on, each of you is set apart, for and by the other. It is your privilege and responsibility to show each other something of the honor in which God holds each of you. It is an amazing role in which you now stand to one another. With your words and actions, your looks and thoughts, you will be holding up for each other a sort of heavenly mirror, so you can see how you look when viewed in the light of perfect Love—which is to say, how you look to God. Marcy, you can show Michael . . . Michael, you can show Marcy something of the infinite worth each of you has in the eyes of the One who formed you in the womb of your mother, who knit your body and spirit together with exquisite care, who first dreamed each of you into being, with all your special gifts and qualities.

And there is even more to the mystery of your sanctified life. For as you two daily honor each other in the presence of God, you create—you have already begun to create—a larger circle of honor in which each of us, your family and friends, is grateful to have a place.

Our world is badly in need of places where everyone is held in mutual honor, so peace and love can grow, and your marriage gives us an opportunity to pray for that. The best prayer comes from experience, and everyone here has some experience of participating in the circle of love you have made, individually and together. It is fitting then for us to pray

- that the love you bear for one another may be a sign of God's love for this broken world,
- that your life together may continue to give comfort and hope to others,
- that each of you may be to the other a strength in need, a counselor in perplexity, a comfort in sorrow, and a companion in unending joy.[1]

And let all God's people say,
Amen.

1. *The Book of Common Prayer* (New York: The Church Hymnal Corporation, 1979), 429.

"Here I Am": Preaching Isaiah as a Book of Vocation

ESSAY

It is strange that so little attention is given to the Prophets in contemporary preaching, especially in view of the aspiration (frequently expressed among church leaders) for more "prophetic preaching." Presumably that means preaching that deepens both our comprehension of the gospel and our desire to live into it—in other words, good preaching. Were we able to ask the New Testament writers directly how to meet those goals for Christian preaching, probably a number of them would advise us to read Isaiah, since that is the book of Scripture that they cite most often as they struggle to express the new reality of God in Jesus Christ and to give definition to life in service of that reality. What Isaiah tells us is so fundamental to the gospel, so thoroughly assumed by the first Christian writers, that it is doubtful we can preach even from the New Testament with full accuracy, if we have not listened carefully to the "evangelical prophet" and digested the central theological message(s) of the book.

We need Isaiah, yet the book is daunting in its sheer bulk, compounded by its historical complexity. As modern scholarship has amply demonstrated, "Isaiah" is not so much a prophet as a whole prophetic tradition; it took shape at multiple hands over a period of more than two centuries, from the eighth century to the sixth century BCE. Although some awareness of that historical and compositional background is important for understanding the message of the three (conventionally, though debatably) "Isaiahs," that is probably not where preachers should focus their attention. What they should find compelling in the current scholarly discussion is the emphasis (increasingly pronounced in the last quarter-century) on the high degree of thematic and theological unity that characterizes the whole book.[1] Here I focus on one central element of that unity, the overarching "super-theme" of vocation, because it is especially important for connecting Isaiah's theological vision with the gospel. In the first section I establish a broad exegetical base for reading Isaiah as a book of vocation. In the second section, I identify three factors that may hinder preachers from drawing accurate connections between the prophetic message and our life in Christ: lectionary bias, theological loss incurred in translation, and the church's habit of using bits of Isaiah's language—"Immanuel," "Holy, holy, holy"—out of context, with little awareness of what they may mean for Isaiah's witness of faith.

An Exegetical Base Called to Serve the Holy One of Israel

As the New Testament writers must have seen, Isaiah is the biblical book that probes most deeply into the question of what constitutes the unique vocation of Israel. The answer is most memorably expressed in the four so-called Servant Songs of Second Isaiah.[2] For instance:

> I, Yhwh, have called you in righteousness,
> and I take hold of your hand.
> I preserve you and set you as a covenant-people,
> as a light of nations,
> to open blind eyes,
> to bring forth the prisoner from the dungeon,
> those sitting in darkness from the jailhouse. (42:6–7)

All three "Isaiahs" speak to the nature of Israel's vocation. In historical terms, this means that over a period of more than two centuries, reflection on that central question constelled in the Isaiah tradition. Indeed, all the major themes of the book can be seen as aspects of what it means for Israel to be called into God's exclusive service. Here I identify eight themes of the prophetic message, each one of which runs throughout the book. Even to identify these as separate themes is somewhat artificial, since all are interrelated, and each is essential to a full understanding and living of Israel's distinctive vocation.

---

1. In several excellent essays, Christopher Seitz treats the theological unity of the book in *Word without End: The Old Testament as Abiding Theological Witness* (Grand Rapids: Eerdmans, 1998), 113–228.
    2. Isaiah 42:1–4 or 1–9; 49:1–6; 50:4–11; 52:13–53:12.

1. The Holy One of Israel

Israel's vocation is to be understood theocentrically, in relation to the identity and nature of God. Isaiah consistently names YHWH as *Qedosh Yisra'el,* "the Holy One of Israel." Israel is called to live in perpetual, public recognition that this Holy One is "in [her] midst" (12:6). A minimal "definition" of holiness for Isaiah is that YHWH is absolutely incomparable, utterly unlike the idols of the nations. It is in Second Isaiah's polemics against the idols that the claim of divine incomparability emerges most clearly: "To whom would you liken me?" (40:25).[3] However, that claim is already implicit in the great inaugural vision of First Isaiah, when the seraphim proclaim, "Holy, holy, holy YHWH of Hosts; the whole earth is the fullness of his glory" (6:3).

The prophet's own vocation is to declare the holy God's demands among a people incapable of hearing what is clear and seeing what is obvious. With sharp irony, Isaiah is commanded to preach them into deeper stupidity: "Dull [fatten] the heart of that people, . . . lest they see with their eyes" (6:10; see also 29:9–14). The language of insentience appears elsewhere in the psalmist's polemic against idols and those who make them (Ps. 135:15–18). In other words, Isaiah's preaching will reveal the people of Judah and Jerusalem for what they are: effectively, idol-worshipers—even if their idols are not images of wood and stone, but rather wealth and military might.

This absolute incomparability is not compromised in the Christian confession of a triune God. Thus Paul, paraphrasing Isaiah, includes Jesus in Israel's distinctive confession of faith:

> . . . at the name of Jesus *every knee should bend,*
> in heaven and on earth and under the earth,
> *and every tongue should confess* that Jesus Christ is Lord,
> to the glory of God the Father. (Phil. 2:10–11, NRSV)

As the last line indicates, the confession of Jesus's name can be legitimate only if it is done in such a way as to magnify "the glory of God the Father." In other words, confessing Jesus's Lordship is a form of what Jewish tradition calls *qiddush ha-Shem* ("Sanctification of the name [YHWH]"), a witness of faith that, at the limit, takes the form of martyrdom.

The boldness of that witness is evident when one recognizes that the

---

3. See also the mockery of the nations' gods in the historical resumé of the eighth-century BCE Assyrian invasion: 37:12, 18, etc.

phrases Paul cites from Isaiah are in their original context addressed to the Babylonian idol-worshipers who hold YHWH's people captive:

> Am I not YHWH?
> There is no other god besides me,
> a righteous God and Savior—
> there is none apart from me.
> Turn to me and be saved,
> all (you) ends of the earth!
> For I am God and there is no other!
> . . . Yea, to me every knee shall bend
> and every tongue shall swear [confess]. (Isa. 45:21–23)

Thus Paul is telling the Philippians and us that God in Christ has reissued that challenge and invitation, addressed to the "ends of the earth." Will *we* hear what the once-powerful Babylonians failed to hear and heed, or will we perish, as they did, in pride and ignorance?

2. *The Justice (*Mishpat*) and Righteousness of God*

In a striking verbal portrait, First Isaiah declares that "YHWH is exalted in justice (*mishpat*) and revealed-as-holy (*niqdash*) through righteousness (*tsedaqah*)" (5:16). Throughout the book, these two nouns—*mishpat* and *tsedaqah*—denote God's characteristic modus operandi; and at the same time, they are the core human vocation, the behaviors God requires of everyone. Justice and righteousness are the substance of God's Torah, teaching, given to Israel, and to the world through Israel (2:3; 5:24). The Isaiah tradition upholds the vision that ultimately all humankind will learn justice and righteousness, when every knee and tongue submit to the One whose nature is righteousness (45:21–23).

3. *The Judgment (also* Mishpat*) of God*

One difficulty in understanding Isaiah's religious witness is that the all-important word *mishpat* does not translate fully with a single term; it means "justice" and equally "judgment," and those two aspects are related. In the immediate situations addressed by both First Isaiah (5:7) and Third Isaiah (59:11), we are specifically told that *mishpat*-justice is absent within Israel. When Israel fails to demonstrate justice and righteousness, then God's inalienable *mishpat* is manifested as judgment, as is reflected in the many harsh oracles directed against Israel that dominate the first half of the book and recur in the final section. It is not good news for the unrepentant when Yhwh is "exalted in *mishpat*" (5:16); Isaiah paints a vivid and ironic picture of a rebellious people begging seers (prophets) not to see, and above all they plead, "Spare us contact with the Holy One of Israel!" (30:11).

4. Zion

Isaiah is the most Zion-centered of all the prophetic traditions. Mount Zion, "the mountain of the house of Yhwh" (2:2), is where Yhwh is fully manifested in holiness, as Isaiah experiences dramatically in the moment when he himself is "called" (6:1–13). Nonetheless, the Zion on which Isaiah's vision centers is not a clearly visible, "present-tense" reality. Zion—the place to which the nations stream to learn from Yhwh's Torah of justice and righteousness (2:2–3), where "the house of Jacob" fulfills its own vocation to "walk in the light of Yhwh" (2:5)—this is and is not Jerusalem or any other current political or geographic entity. At the extreme, Zion is antithetical to what happens in Jerusalem and Judah; that picture of Zion is followed immediately by an extended judgment oracle against a people whose "land is full of idols" (2:8). Yhwh's just teaching and judgment both proceed from Zion; it is a place of purging (28:15) and testing: "Look, I lay in Zion a testing stone" (28:16).[4] Yet in the final salvation oracles of the book, the Zion visions come full circle: this is the place where Yhwh will be manifested as Redeemer (59:20; see also 62:12), as the Holy One of Israel (60:14), to bring comfort to mourners (61:3) and restore its righteousness (*tsedeq*, 62:1) and make its salvation known "to the end of the earth" (62:11). Zion exists and is redeemed for the sake of the whole world.

5. Vocation Fulfilled within History

Our understanding of Israel's vocation gains dimensionality, though not necessarily precision, with First Isaiah's visions of a (royal?) figure to whom cer-

---

4. The phrase *'even bohan* is normally translated "a tested/tried stone," but the combination of two nouns in construct admits of the meaning "a stone for testing." Applying Isaiah's image to Christ, 1 Peter 2:6–8 indicates that the "stone" functions as a discrimen by which God's faithful people may be identified. (See the discussion of this passage in the following section.)

tain promises attach: Immanuel (7:14), Wonderful Counselor (9:6–7), a shoot from the stump of Jesse (11:1–10). In Second Isaiah, the Servant Songs give a clear picture and even let us hear the voice of the individual (or community) who upholds and is upheld by God's justice and righteousness (9:6; 42:1, 3, 4; 53:11). It is the cumulative witness of the four Songs that divine justice is upheld through the mysterious means of exhausting labor, humiliation, death—and yet, ultimately, vindication by God. First and Second Isaiah probably identified their portraits of faithful service with particular individuals living in their own time (e.g., Hezekiah), and one of the Songs explicitly identifies the Servant with the whole people of Israel (49:3). However, the metaphorical openness of poetry in which their visions are expressed resists confinement to a single historical period or identity. It was both inevitable and apt that Christians would find in Isaiah's poetry portraits of Jesus as Messiah and Servant, yet that does not foreclose further identifications. Rather, it encourages them. Just because the Servant Songs speak to us of Jesus's labor and suffering, they also illumine aspects of our own vocation to discipleship.

6. *A Remnant Will Return* (She'ar Yashuv, *7:3*)

Every hearer of the book is addressed from the outset as part of the "tiny remnant" (1:9) of an Israel that has already experienced devastating loss (1:5–8). The First Isaiah makes it clear that further destruction is to be expected (6:11–13), a destruction that is sometimes conceived as a purging. This book does not pull its prophetic punches: our situation is grave, yet it is not finally desperate. The strong element of promise that is present in all three sections of the book draws us forward into a future where God is doing "new things" (42:9; 43:19; 48:6). By placing heavy emphasis on Yhwh's person, power, and action, Second Isaiah offers encouragement to exiles. But that emphasis is balanced, especially in the other two sections of the book, by imperatives addressed to Israel. They are to act energetically, to *pursue* their vocation to be "the ones left in Zion and in Jerusalem [who] are called holy" (4:3; see also 6:13 and 62:12).

7. *Trust and* Shalom

Along with upholding justice and righteousness, the most exacting and immediate demand that presses upon Israel is the imperative to trust (*batah*) absolutely and exclusively in the Holy One of Israel. The thematic verb *batah* occurs in all three sections; it denotes the contrast between reliance on YHWH and reliance on false sources of strength (Isa. 12:2; 36:4, 5, 6, 9; 30:12; 42:17; 59:4; etc.). Trust in YHWH manifests itself in concrete practices: in rejection first of military defenses and alliances (First Isaiah) and then of foreign idols (Second Isaiah) and syncretistic cults (Third Isaiah). This is exactly the challenge that Isaiah issues to the vacillating king Ahaz: "If you do not hold fast, you will not be held fast" (7:9). It is the practice of trust that enables Israel to receive the divine blessing of *shalom*.

Eighth-century BCE Isaiah might be seen as a radical "pacifist"; military activity and alliances are to be avoided, because they distract Israel from relying solely on God (Isa. 7:7–9). *Shalom* is a comprehensive term for Israel's experience of the blessings of salvation, renewal, unity, and safety that flow from reliance on YHWH. As Isaiah describes it, *shalom* is "like a river" (66:12)—more a natural force than a socio-political condition ("peace") that Israel might achieve through its own astute policies. It is especially powerful for a prophet to evoke the simile of the river in semi-arid Jerusalem, a city sustained only by the too-scarce rain and a small natural spring. Isaiah's vision of *shalom* might justly be called "ecological"; it draws every creature—animal, vegetable, and mineral—into relation with God and one another. The leopard lies down with the kid; the cow and the bear pasture together (11:6–7); the desert "rejoices" in bloom (35:1–2).

8. The Ultimate Fulfillment of Vocation

Israel's vocation is to orient its life wholly and publicly toward the new reality that YHWH is bringing into being. The full dimensions of that reality are visible only through Isaiah's most extravagant visions: of the nations giving up war and streaming to exalted Zion (Isa. 2:1–4), of the "peaceable kingdom" (11:1–10; 65:25), of the feast when death is "swallow[ed] up forever" (25:7), of Jerusalem free of weeping and calamity (65:18–25), of new heavens and a new earth (51:16; 66:22). Because those things are not visible to ordinary sight, trust—"standing fast" (7:9), the steadfast anticipation of what God has yet to do—must be a permanent disposition for those whom this tradition designates as "servants" of YHWH (e.g., 65:13–15). It is notable that the book of Revelation concludes with a "trustworthy" vision (Rev. 21:5), a pastiche of prophetic images drawn largely from Isaiah's visions of a "re-created" Jerusalem, fully illumined by God's glory, with the gates flung wide open and the nations streaming to it

(Rev. 21:23–26; compare Isa. 60:1–19; 65:17–19). This Isaianic conclusion to John's own "prophecy" (Rev. 1:3) suggests that the earlier vision remains relevant for the church—and not yet fulfilled. Its far horizon, the horizon of Israel's vocation, has not been reached. We are still waiting in trust for what God in Christ has yet to do.

*   *   *

The key to preaching Isaiah well is to see the *essential interrelatedness* of these various themes: God's holiness and that of God's faithful servants, justice and judgment, unwavering trust in the presence and promises of God, both now and "in that day," beyond our current capacity to see or imagine.

Problems in Hearing and Preaching Isaiah

Here I explore two factors—bias in the standard lectionaries and theological loss in translation—that shape how many or most North American Christians hear Isaiah and that may limit or even distort our understanding of its witness. Finally, I turn to the question of whether, lacking a fully integrated understanding, the church's habit of using isolated bits of Isaiah's language (e.g., "Immanuel") is an act of bad faith.

1. Lectionary Bias

For "mainstream" North American Christians, perhaps the major factor that inhibits a full hearing of Isaiah is *the general shape of the Sunday and holiday lectionary.* It is surely significant that the standard Protestant lectionaries (Revised Common Lectionary and the lectionary in *The Book of Common Prayer*) favor salvation oracles chosen from Second and Third Isaiah. The judgment oracles that dominate First Isaiah are distinctly under-represented, even though the salvation oracles make little sense apart from them. With few exceptions, the lectionary represents Isaiah as an upbeat prophet, whose messianic and evangelical message is largely fulfilled already in the life of the church.[5]

---

5. Notable inclusions of passages of judgment would be the appointment of sections of Isaiah 1 for Propers 14 and 26, Year C; Isaiah 58:1–12 for Ash Wednesday; and Isaiah 64:1–9 for Advent 1, Year B.

179

However, it is noteworthy that the evangelical passages are often oriented to the distant or indefinite future: "And it shall be, at the end of days . . ." (2:2). These future-oriented visions are throughout the book juxtaposed to judgment oracles. For example, the final vision of "new heavens and a new earth" (Isa. 65:17–25) is sandwiched between two passages that denounce the sins, first, of "you who abandon YHWH" (65:11) and then of those who "have chosen their own ways" (66:3). Thus the overall shape of the book prevents us from imagining that the prophetic message traces a clear historical progression—as though now, after the judgment on Judah and Jerusalem has been executed, the "end of days" has arrived. On the contrary, there is throughout an acute and abiding tension between the "present-tense" situation Isaiah addresses and the "future-tense" vision captured in the eschatological images.[6]

There is tension not only between present and future but also between groups of Israelites in the present, as appears clearly in the penultimate chapter, where repeated contrast is drawn between "my servants" and "you"—that is, those who have abandoned YHWH (see 65:11):

> Look, my servants shall eat,
> but you, you shall go hungry. . . .
> Look, my servants shall be joyous,
> but you, you will be ashamed. (65:13)

We readers are the "you" here; thus we are forced to recognize the fact that merely hearing the promise of newness (65:17–25) does not guarantee our inclusion in the category of "my servants," blessed participants in that new reality. Nowhere in the book of Isaiah is the small remnant preserved to date (see 1:9) clearly identified as a righteous remnant that has survived *by virtue of* its righteousness.[7] Rather, first and last, this prophetic tradition

---

6. The tension between the present and recent history, on the one hand, and God's plan for the future, on the other, is evident already in Second Isaiah's contrast between the "former things" and "new things." John Calvin highlighted the importance of verb tense in his note on Isaiah 40:1, where he stresses that the Hebrew "imperfect" is to be rendered: "'Comfort . . . ,' your God *will* say"—pointing to "an intermediate period, during which the people would be heavily afflicted, as if God had been silent." The church is still in this period of affliction, awaiting the completion of its deliverance in Christ (John Calvin, *Commentary on the Book of the Prophet Isaiah* [Grand Rapids: Eerdmans, 1948], 3:198-99).

7. The apparently (intra-Israelite) "supersessionist" statement in 60:21—"Your people are all of them righteous; they shall inherit the land forever"—does not in fact assert the righteousness of any community in the "present tense." The statement is set in a context that clearly points to an eschatological reality (see 60:20: "Your sun shall not set any more . . .").

reckons with a people who have been severely chastened and still do not turn to God.

The shape of the book suggests this principle for its interpretation: *any valid reading of Isaiah must maintain the tension between present and future, judgment and salvation, faithful and unfaithful within the community of faith.* That principle finds liturgical expression in the traditional liturgical practice of the synagogue. On Shabbat Rosh Hodesh (observed when Sabbath falls on the first day of the lunar month), the final chapter of Isaiah is read, with its hair-curling final verse, which points to the present reality of rebellion:

> And they shall go out and look
> upon the corpses of the people who sin against me.
> For their worm does not die,
> and their fire is not quenched,
> and they are an abhorrence to all flesh. (66:24)

Following that, the encouraging penultimate verse is repeated, and thus the reading concludes:

> And it shall be, new moon by new moon,
> and Sabbath by Sabbath,
> that all flesh will come
> to worship before me, says YHWH. (66:23)

Although the *canonically final* word of judgment must be heard, nonetheless, in the context of prayer, God's hope for Israel and the world is the last word heard.

By contrast, the bias against judgment in Christian lectionaries makes it altogether unlikely that we will hear and apply to ourselves Isaiah's present-tense address to rebellious Israel.[8] One must regard with deep suspicion such an artificial "deliverance" for the church. It is true that the New Testament writers apply to the synagogue *over against the early church* Isaiah's judgments of blindness, deafness, and incomprehension (e.g., Isa. 6:10 cited in Matt. 13:13–15 and John 12:40; Isa. 29:9–10 cited in Rom. 11:8–10). Yet to accept that discriminating judgment as a permanent historical fact would seem to bespeak exactly the "fat-heartedness" that Isaiah exposes in his contemporaries (Isa. 6:10).

---

8. The daily lectionary does include some such passages, but relatively few churchgoers are in the practice of reading or hearing the Daily Office.

Ephraim Radner (following Joseph Ratzinger) suggests that the contrast between synagogue and church as drawn by Paul and the evangelists is "figurally prophetic of Christian Israel too, just because of its participation in the larger christic form that allows for the initial figural transposition through the two Testaments."[9] In Christ, the church—with Israel and even *as* Israel—stands under the abiding judgment of God.

A related but more particular factor that may cause us to hear Isaiah wrong is *the shape of individual lectionary selections.* An example is Isaiah 2:1–5, appointed for the first Sunday in Advent (Year A), presumably because the picture of all nations streaming to Zion, where divine judgment will be exercised, expresses the Christian understanding of the second coming of our Lord. Yet the full reality of judgment is obscured, because these five verses have been extracted and isolated from the five chapters of (mostly harsh) judgment oracles that open the book and provide the background that makes meaningful Isaiah's call to prophesy "until cities have crashed into ruin, without inhabitant" (6:11).[10] The passage as appointed concludes thus:

> O house of Jacob, come,
> let us walk in the light of YHWH. (2:5)

Tellingly, the lectionary reading stops just short of the line that suggests a connection between present guilt and anticipated judgment. Indeed, the break comes mid-thought, if not mid-sentence; the next phrase begins, "For (*ki*) . . ." The rest of the sentence is ambiguous, since it is addressed to an unspecified "you" (singular). Is Isaiah saying to God: "For you have forsaken your people, the house of Jacob"? Or is God saying to Israel: "For you have forsaken your people, O house of Jacob"? Either is appropriate, for what follows is a lengthy litany of Israel's idolatrous practices and the punishment they may expect from God (2:6–22).

Moreover, what follows verse 5 shows that the summons to the house of Jacob is more than an evangelical exhortation. It is also, and primarily, a call to repentance. Thus the Isaiah passage *in its literary context* is more appropriate for Advent than the lectionary acknowledges. For Advent season "begins in

9. Ephraim Radner, "The Absence of the Comforter: Scripture and the Divided Church," in *Theological Exegesis: Essays in Honor of Brevard S. Childs,* ed. C. Seitz and K. Greene-McCreight (Grand Rapids: Eerdmans, 1999), 382.

10. Within the five-chapter preface, these few verses are matched by one other eschatological picture, in 4:2–6, which is explicitly a picture of Jerusalem *after* its "filth" and blood have been washed away. All the other verses bespeak Israel's guilt.

the dark," as Fleming Rutledge says in a splendid and sobering sermon (on Isa. 64:1–9); it is a time of preparation for our Lord's coming "to judge the world" (Pss. 96:13; 98:9 [98:10 Eng.]). "Advent is designed to show that the meaning of Christmas is diminished to the vanishing point if we are not willing to take a fearless inventory of the darkness."[11] It is no coincidence that the logic of the church year accords with the logic of the "evangelical prophet" Isaiah, and we need to heed both in their fullness.

2. Lost in Translation

The translation gap between biblical Hebrew and English is wide (this is what makes study of the language not just worthwhile but exciting), and widest with poetry. The "Isaiahs" were among the most gifted poets ever to compose in Hebrew, and so, for English readers, substantial aesthetic loss is unavoidable. Yet preachers would do well to recognize that the loss is also theological—and with greater awareness of Isaiah's central themes, some of it might be repaired. A good example of potential loss is found in the NRSV rendering of this familiar passage:[12]

> For Zion's sake I will not keep silent,
> and for Jerusalem's sake I will not rest,
> until her *vindication* (*tsedeq*) shines out like the dawn,
> and her salvation like a burning torch.
> The nations shall see your *vindication,*
> and all the kings your glory;
> and you shall be called by a new name
> that the mouth of the LORD will give. (62:1–2)

The Hebrew word *tsedeq* (here, "vindication") is thematic for Isaiah. In all three sections of the book, *tsedeq* and the closely related term *tsedaqah* denote the moral quality and concrete acts of "righteousness"—as the terms are traditionally rendered, for example in the KJV—that God longs to find in Israel (5:7). That Israel should seek or do righteousness is God's fundamental demand;

11. Fleming Rutledge, *The Bible and the New York Times* (Grand Rapids: Eerdmans, 1998), 26.

12. Isaiah 62:1–5 is appointed for the second Sunday after the Epiphany, Year C, in the Revised Common Lectionary; Isaiah 61:10–62:3 is appointed for the first Sunday after Christmas (each year) in the *Book of Common Prayer* lectionary.

indeed, seeking *tsedeq* seems to be virtually equivalent to seeking God (51:1; see also 64:4 [64:5 Eng.]). This passage seems to speak primarily of Yнwн's action on behalf of Zion/Jerusalem. Accordingly, several major twentieth-century translations render it with a word that has no explicit moral connotation: "vindication" (NRSV) or "victory" (NJPS). These translational alternatives raise the theological question: Can God's work of salvation or "vindication" for Israel be separated from God's demand for righteousness from Israel?

The answer would seem to be "no," since translations of Isaiah vacillate between these alternatives in different contexts. For instance, when Yнwн pronounces: "I am speaking in/with *tsedaqah*, mighty to save [Israel]" (63:1), RSV and NRSV translate "announcing vindication"; NJPS, "victoriously"; JPS, "in victory." Yet when God utters the nearly identical phrase with respect to the conversion of "all the ends of the earth," all these versions choose a translation with more overt moral content:

> . . . from my mouth has gone forth *in righteousness* (NJPS: *in truth*)
> a word that shall not return:
> "To me every knee shall bow,
> every tongue shall swear." (45:23, NRSV)

How do translators draw the distinction between "vindication/victory" and "righteousness/truth"? It seems that whenever the subject is taken to be God's redemptive action for Israel, translators choose to mute the normal connotation of moral uprightness—perhaps to avoid any connotation that "works-righteousness" is the basis for salvation. But what if Isaiah means us to see that God's work of "vindicating" Israel is of one piece with God's other characteristic actions—here, with bringing all nations into righteous relationship with Yнwн and with one another? The beautiful oracle of comfort in 51:1–11 repeatedly intertwines references to God's actions of salvation, redemption, and judgment (with respect to both Israel and the nations), suggesting that they are inseparable and at times perhaps indistinguishable.

Isaiah's total vision requires that a connection among those terms be consistently maintained, although it cannot be drawn in a single predictable way. Here, for instance, Third Isaiah asserts the connection between human and divine *tsedaqah*:

> Keep justice, do *tsedaqah*,
> for my salvation is near, about to come,
> and my *tsedaqah* is about to be revealed. (56:1)

Is it the moral rectitude of humanity (or Israel) that gives God's transcendent righteousness or vindication a point of entry into our world? Israel's obedience to the imperative "Do *tsedaqah*" gives staying power to the divine "revelation."

However, it would be too simple to say that righteousness is the moral prerequisite for which salvation is the reward. A few chapters later, we hear the rapturous divine exclamation: "And your people—all of them righteous . . . !" (*tsaddiqim*, 60:21). Israel as a wholly righteous people—that image stands in sharp contrast to the trenchant exposure of Israel's sin in the preceding chapters (57:1–21; 59:1–15). Set within an extended eschatological vision of salvation, that statement expresses a dream of God, yet to be fulfilled: "I am YHWH; in its time I will do it quickly" (60:22). Thus the literary context suggests that God's redemptive action is not the reward but rather the enabling condition for Israel's own righteousness. When "justice is lacking and [human] *tsedaqah* stands far off" (59:14), YHWH "puts on *tsedaqah* like body-armor" (59:17) and gets to work. It is only because of that aggressive divine action on their behalf that those with whom God has reestablished a covenant in Zion (see 59:21) can now strive to be righteous.

The interconnection to which Isaiah points, between humans doing righteousness and God working vindication, first came to my attention when I heard Isaiah's words one Sunday in Jerusalem, during the first Intifada. It was shortly after a rash of bombings in which a number of Israeli children had been killed. There was anger and grief among Jews, but also something more. The Intifada had precipitated a loss of national innocence; many were for the first time jolted into an awareness of the moral cost of the occupation. On a day dedicated by the Archbishop of Canterbury to fasting and prayer for the peace of Jerusalem, I attended a prayer service held by Messianic Jews at Christ Church, the oldest Anglican church in the Middle East. It was filled to capacity, mostly with locals, although many of them were immigrants gathered from "all the ends of the earth" (Isa. 45:22; 52:10). Lament and praise in many languages rose up and eddied around the dome, but we sang in Hebrew, the one language we all shared, and the words of every song were taken directly from Scripture.

Over the course of several hours, one song kept recurring, arising spontaneously out of our shared grief and passionate hope for relief. The words were just one verse from Isaiah: "For Zion's sake I will not keep silent . . . until her *tsedeq* shines forth like a beam" (62:1). That song represented an intuitive but nonetheless astute interpretation of the prophetic message in an agonized political situation, with violence and tragedy on both sides. Most of the singers were Jews living in "Zion" and committed to its well-being, even though their Christian faith distinguished (and often separated) them from the vast majority of Jews in that place. We were calling on God for the *tsedeq* of Jerusalem, and because we were singing in Hebrew, we did not have to decide if that meant "righteousness" or "vindication." Yet surely it was impossible for any of us to make a clear separation between our desire for humans to act righteously and our desperate longing for God to bring deliverance and healing for all.

3. Using Isaiah's Words in Good Faith

Up to this point I have treated difficulties that arise when passages in Isaiah are heard within the context of the book, but with insufficient attention to the message of the whole. However, Christians probably most often hear and use Isaiah's words completely outside their original literary context, namely, in the Eucharistic Sanctus ("Holy, holy, holy . . .") and the Christmas proclamation, "Immanuel." Here the question is whether we are repeating these words in good faith—in Isaiah's language, as those who "tremble at [God's] word" (66:2, 5), which would seem to be this prophetic tradition's goal for all its hearers.

As the introduction to the Eucharistic Prayer, the Sanctus is pressing for reconciliation between the holy God and sinful humanity; that reconciliation begins now, and here, with the church gathered to eat and drink. But it is a fairly safe bet that we will still be sinful when we finish, and earth will *not* be perceptibly "full of [God's] glory."[13] So if the Eucharist is neither a sham nor a failure, then the full reconciliation to which it points must be an eschatological reality. At the same time, if we are offering any meaningful sacrifice of ourselves, then reconciliation must also be a present reality, and it must cost us something. The first thing offered up for the sake of reconciliation must be whatever complacency we have brought to the table, as one form of the Eucharistic Prayer expresses it: "Deliver us from the presumption of coming to this Table for solace only, and not for strength; for pardon only, and not for renewal."[14]

The original context of the words used in the Sanctus implies both those things: the eschatological reality and the present cost of reconciliation. Thus the prophet reports his own immediate response to the seraphic proclamation of God's holiness:

13. *The Book of Common Prayer* (New York: The Church Hymnal Corporation, 1979), 362, 367, 371, 373.

14. Eucharistic Prayer C, *Book of Common Prayer*, 372.

Yipes (*'oy li*), I am done for!
For I am a man of unclean lips,
and I am dwelling in the midst of a people of unclean lips. (Isa. 6:5)

Contact with the Holy God confronts Isaiah forcibly with his own sin, and
it requires that he confront Israel's sin with equal force. Isaiah is charged to
preach God's word "until cities lie waste without inhabitant" (6:11).

A related passage reinforces the connection between YHWH's holiness and
the shattering of human pretensions to power independent of God:

YHWH of Hosts, him you shall sanctify;
and he is your fear, he your dread.
And he will become a sanctuary and a striking stone
and a stumbling rock
to the two houses of Israel,
a trap and a snare to the inhabitants of Jerusalem.
And many among them shall stumble
and fall and be broken
and be ensnared and be caught. (Isa. 8:13–15)

If Christians are to sing the seraphic Sanctus in good faith, then something
like Isaiah's view of holiness must be set forth, in teaching and preaching. And
surely that means asking some hard questions of ourselves, in light of what
Isaiah shows us about God. "YHWH of Hosts is exalted through *mishpat* (judg-
ment/justice), and the Holy God is revealed-as-holy through righteousness"
(5:16)—so is it possible to sing the Sanctus in good faith in a society in which
the economic gap between poor and rich grows steadily? Isaiah calls on Israel
to eschew military campaigns and trust wholly in YHWH—so can we sing the
Sanctus sincerely, in a fully armed society? If we are tempted to answer "yes,"
then the question of a later Isaiah challenges us:

Whom did you dread and fear,
so that you were false,
and me you did not remember
or take to your heart? (57:11)

Similar considerations apply in determining what constitutes a good-faith
proclamation that *Immanu-El,* "God is with us" (Isa. 7:14). Here it is important
to ask what is the significance of that name within the context of Isaiah, a

book in which several other names convey theological messages (e.g., *She'ar -yashuv*, 7:3; *Maher-shalal-hash-baz*, 8:3; *Heftsi-bah* and *Be'ulah*, 62:4). The best contextual clue to meaning lies, not in the elusive historical identity of the pregnant "young woman," but rather in the two repetitions of the phrase *Immanu-El*, first as a name for Judah (8:8), and then as a challenge addressed to foreign invaders (8:10). In both cases, it signifies protection for those who take the risk of trust in YHWH. But God's immediate presence constitutes a risk—or, at least, a discrimen, a test that separates the sheep from the goats. This threefold repetition of the *Immanu-El* assurance is quickly followed by the passage cited just above (8:13–15), naming God as "fear" and "dread" for Israel and Jerusalem as well as for their enemies. Indeed, *Immanu-El* captures in a single phrase what Isaiah identifies as the central paradox of Israel's existence: "For great in the midst of you is the Holy One of Israel" (12:6). Everything depends on that presence, and yet those are hardly "comfortable words." Could—should—any people ever be wholly at ease with death-dealing and ultimately death-destroying (25:7) Holiness smack in its midst? Is it any wonder that "many among them shall stumble and fall and be broken and ensnared and caught" (8:15)?

If we have read Isaiah well, then the church's proclamation "Immanuel" becomes more difficult. Any sentimental or *self*-assured assertion of God's presence becomes impossible. For, as Isaiah insists, God's presence in our midst forces us to choose between apostasy and absolute trust in God, trust that entails rejection of all penultimate sources of security. There is no middle ground. Bearing in mind Radner's notion that New Testament judgments against Jewish Israel "are figurally prophetic of Christian Israel too," we may recall that in the Gospel of John it is precisely the visible presence of God in Christ that confirms the guilt of the Jerusalemites, and especially their religious leaders. "Indeed, if it was impossible for them to believe, the reason is to be found in words spoken by Isaiah . . . : 'He has blinded their eyes and dulled their minds. . . .' Isaiah said these things because he had a vision of Jesus in his state of glory, and it was of him that he spoke" (John 12:39–41). When we Christians use "Immanuel" as a seasonal greeting that costs us nothing, then we bring upon ourselves the judgment of John's Gospel: "If you were blind, there would be no guilt in you. But you claim that you can see, and so your guilt remains" (John 9:41).

This essay began with the suggestion that if the church needs prophetic preaching, then Isaiah is a good place to start—but not because preaching Isaiah can ever be easy. On the contrary, the prophetic message stretches our intellectual powers, bruises our egos, and taxes our courage. So if any of us decides to make the effort to preach Isaiah, it can only be because of his vision. "Vision" (*hazon*) is the very first word of this book, and it aptly points to the greatest gift that Isaiah offers to preachers: a vision of God and ourselves unequaled in its scope, clarity, and depth. Probably no other book of the Bible offers such vivid images of the divine: God "high and lifted up" (6:1) as Sovereign and Judge over our sin-wracked world; God as *Immanu-El,* a sure and felt presence with us; God struggling like a woman in labor (42:14) to bring forth new life in situations that seem, to ordinary eyes, entirely hopeless. Just because his visions of God never cease to be fresh and compelling, this book continually prompts new reflection on what it means for Israel and the church to be called into God's service—precisely the kind of reflection that lies at the heart of Christian preaching.

I Saw God

Ordination of Anthony Petrotta,
St. Paul's Episcopal Church, Benicia, California
March 19, 2005

ISAIAH 6

The most crucial task for all priests is to offer the people they care for a "clear vision in the things of God." They will find their closest ally in the book of Isaiah, which provides a more multidimensional picture of God than any other book of the Bible. This sermon challenges the ordinand to continue delighting in Scripture for the pure fun of it, for the sake of sharing it with others, and, most importantly, so that he can see God, the world, and us with clarity. Through such priestly activity he will, like Isaiah, enable his people to see God more clearly, freeing them to look on the world without illusion.

From the sixth chapter of Isaiah: "In the year that King Uzziah died, I saw the LORD sitting on a throne, lofty and uplifted, and the folds of his robe filling the Temple" (v. 1).

Is there anyone else in the whole Bible who saw God as clearly as Isaiah did, that one day in Jerusalem, in the year that King Uzziah died? I don't think so, and surely it is that clear vision of God that makes it fitting for us to read Isaiah this morning, when a new priest is ordained for the church. Because it is the special responsibility of the priest to keep the vision of God before our eyes, to make the reality of God vivid for us, God's presence perceptible to us—and to do that in a culture in which virtually everything is designed to obscure that vision. Everything purports to deny that reality; everyone (ourselves included) is perpetually distracted, with the result that few of us—even (and maybe especially) those of us who are, you might say, "professionally religious"—regularly focus our full and quiet attention on the One "in whom we live and move and have our being" (Acts 17:28).

It is good, then, to dwell on Isaiah's vision of God today. And the account of his call to prophesy has a special fittingness to this ordination in particular, because Tony's journey to priesthood in the Episcopal Church began some twenty years ago in Jerusalem, no more than a mile (as the swallow flies) from the spot where Isaiah saw the Lord "high and lifted up" above the Temple. It was at St. George's Cathedral, where Tony had come to church with me—the first time, as he tells me, he had ever attended an Anglican service . . . and, well, the rest is history.

In another sense, however, this passage from Isaiah is a distinctly odd choice for an ordination. Maybe you noticed when it was read—this is hardly an upbeat forecast of the ministry to which Isaiah is called. He is charged to speak God's truth to a people who are not going to hear it. It is hard truth he is called to speak, and the more clearly he lays it out for them, the more resistant they will become. So Isaiah will preach and prophesy to a deaf and blind and fat-hearted people, until at last their world will fall down around their ears—their opulent world, which (as he sees) is a bubble in the midst of aching poverty, their world of precarious international alliances, power-brokering, war-making—all of which is contrary to the divine demand that Isaiah articulates, the demand that the king of Judah make the difficult choice to trust in God, rather than in his army. Does all this sound eerily familiar? These words from Isaiah's call to ministry are now 2,800 years old, and it is still uncomfortable to hear them, uncomfortable to hear them at an ordination. For if there is one thing they make clear, it is that standing and speaking for God in a world like ours is, frankly, about as tough a job as you can find.

Being a priest is not a matter of winning victories for God. Countless stories, movies, television, and now video games have burned into our imaginations a certain heroic plot: the brave adventurer sent forth on a Mission Impossible, and eventually winning against all odds. Yet this is not, and never can be, the pattern of Christian ministry, for the simple reason that it is not the pattern of the gospel—which, as you know, is all about human defeat, the shattering of human hope, the excruciatingly painful disappointment of human desires . . . and after all that, in spite of all that, even through all that, God's victory becomes perceptible. That is why being a priest is such a lousy job for an incurable optimist, because disappointment is so fundamentally built into the job.

But none of this is news to Tony. He knows everything I have said perfectly well, and he feels called to this job anyway. Tony is not especially young; he has seen a lot. He has been through a fair amount himself, too much to be exactly optimistic, and yet he is willing, even happy to become a priest. Now why, do you suppose? If we can figure that one out, then we will understand better what we are celebrating this day. Is it total coincidence that Tony is being ordained to the priesthood on the very eve of Passion Week, when we will as a church slowly trace one more time that utterly *unheroic* pattern of human suffering and death—and at the end, after and through all that pain, we will see and celebrate God's victory? Tony is a biblical scholar; he knows that gospel pattern well, and he knows further that every Christian life is marked with it to some degree. He knows that, as a priest, he will be called over and over to accompany us as we walk the way of the cross—to walk with us, and not lie to us that everything will turn out as we wish—but just walk with us, and tell us one more time the gospel story of human defeat and God's victory.

Now, don't you have to wonder why such an intelligent, accomplished man as Tony would train his sights on a job that has defeat and sorrow built right into it? The answer can only be that he has seen something—a glimpse at least—of what Isaiah saw. What Isaiah saw, in a word, was God, God highly exalted. "I saw the LORD, seated on his throne, high and lifted up." God lifted up over all the delusions of Isaiah's age, and our own. God exalted over our frantic grasping at various forms of false security—grasping that inevitably, as Isaiah so clearly saw, leads to war. God exalted over the pretences of the powerful to be righteous protectors (for a price, of course), with the result that urban poverty is rampant, and the poor suffer first and worst from the fortunes of war. Yes, Isaiah saw all that clearly 2,800 years ago—but the point is, over all that, high and lifted up, Isaiah saw God, the Holy One of Israel. That sight sobered him, frightened him—"'*Oy li!* Woe is me! For I am undone. I am a man of unclean lips, and I dwell among a people of unclean lips." Yet that vision of God compelled him: "Here am I. Send me!"

What is it we need most of all in our priests? This surely: clear vision in the things of God. No wonder we read from Isaiah at this ordination. I don't think any other book of the Bible shows us God quite so clearly, from so many different angles: now God high and lifted up, now God up close, deeply involved in our world. Reading Isaiah is like thumbing through the portfolio of a master photographer: one image after another, each of them clear and memorable, often surprising us with their candor. Here is God as a distraught parent, lamenting the rebellion and soul-sickness of his children. And here, God laboring like a mother, struggling to bring forth new life for a people who have gone far from God and nearly perished in their sins. And then

God nursing them, carrying them like a little child on the hip, bringing them home from a terrible exile. And again, the exalted God, creator of heaven and earth, now making new heavens and a new earth, doing something drastically creative, all for the sake of God's beloved people.

That is the vision of God that Isaiah offers. Complex and true as it is, Isaiah's vision is of course not exhaustive. Our vision of God becomes deeper, it is amplified as we as a church keep reading through the whole Bible together, over and over, week by week and year by year, so that we may grow in understanding—until one day, as Isaiah himself foresaw, "the earth may be filled with the knowledge of God, like the waters cover the sea." Today is a day of blessing for the church, for we are raising up a teacher to be our priest, a gifted and dedicated teacher, a man who has often stretched his energies and working hours far beyond what was reasonable, simply for the privilege and the plain fun of teaching, of helping others grow in knowledge of God. Today the church raises up to be our priest someone who gets a kick out of Scripture, who truly finds "his delight in pondering it day and night," as the psalmist says. Some people (even clergy) read Scripture and find it boring; some (sadly, too many) scholars make it boring for others. Tony finds interest and even humor where others see only tedium—and what is more, Tony shares his delight with others. This is a day of blessing for the church.

And what do we, the church, ask of you now, Tony? The bishop will shortly ask you several particular questions and ask you to make some particular promises, but I believe that, in the last analysis, what the church asks of you is this: keep your own vision clear.

Keep it clear *so that you can see God,* as Isaiah did, above all and in all: God exalted *above* all things, Sovereign over our world; God *in* all things, Immanuel—"God with us"—with us in our true joys, with us in the work we do that genuinely serves God and neighbor. And in our small successes, help us to see *God* working with us, and not just our own efforts and egos, easily puffed up and quickly deflated. Keep your vision clear, Tony, so that you can see, and help us to see, God with us in the places where God's holy presence is desperately needed and far from obvious: in the defeats and losses that come from war, from illness and death, from misplaced hopes, from our repeated failure to trust God more than ourselves.

Keep your vision clear *so that you can see our world* for what it is: a place, not God-forsaken, but often careless of God and the things of God. Keep your vision sharp, incisive, and critical, so that you can help the church to read our world accurately, through the lens of Scripture.

Finally, Tony, as our priest we need you to keep your vision clear *so that you can see us* as we are—not as we often pretend to be, or imagine ourselves to be, but as we really are:

> children of God, yet forgetful of our inheritance;
> blessed, yet insensible of blessing;
> lost, and in need of direction;
> bewildered, and in need of counsel;
> burdened with sin, and in need of forgiveness;
> hungry and thirsty, in need of food and drink that sustains unto eternal life.

Open our eyes, Tony, *so that we may see God* more clearly, and thus look on our world, and on ourselves, without illusion. That is why we need you and wish you to be a priest in the church. This day, we thank God for giving you the will to do that work, and we pray God to give you now enduring wisdom, strength, and joy in its performance.[1]

Amen.

---

1. See the bishop's prayer addressed to the ordinand at the ordination of an Episcopal priest: "May the LORD who has given you the will to do these things give you the grace and power to perform them. Amen" (*The Book of Common Prayer* [New York: The Church Hymnal Corporation, 1979], 532).

In Memory of John H. Davis Sr.

St. Stephen's Church, Oak Harbor, Washington
December 16, 1996

ISAIAH 42:1–9

How do we learn to die a good death? And how does our faith teach us to receive death as a friend? This eulogy for Ellen's father invites the congregation to hear how Isaiah's promise of freedom shaped a dying man's hope. As he grew in peace during his final two years, John Davis showed that "the most important work we do in this life is not done with our rational minds." When the angel of death comes as a friend, all the old fears pass away, and we receive the gift of "the peace of God, which passeth all understanding."

My father had ambivalent feelings about having reared a "lady preacher"; but I feel that for him, or for myself, I need to say something about his death. For it was a very good death, and that is one of God's gifts, to him and through him, for which we give thanks at this Eucharist.

Death is one of the proving moments of Christian faith. Contrary to the way we often think, death does not so much test our faith as confirm it. We pray that we may not die "suddenly and unprepared."[1] But that prayer does not imply that death is the ultimate final exam, for which we must have studied all the right things—never being too sure what they are—for fear of failing miserably at the last. Those Christians who have spoken most wisely about death (I think of St. Francis, among others) understand that it is not a test. Rather, they tell us that death is a trusted friend, even a beloved sister—a metaphor my

---

1. The Great Litany, in *The Book of Common Prayer* (New York: The Church Hymnal Corporation, 1979), 149.

195

dad would appreciate, for he greatly loved his sister Ina. Death is a sister who comes to help us in time of trouble, and old age is trouble. Sickness of body and mind is trouble from which we cannot, any of us, finally free ourselves.

To change the metaphor slightly, death is an angel of God, a messenger who comes to us bringing the assurance of freedom. These words of Isaiah seem most apt to express my own understanding of what my father may have heard from God's messenger:

> I am the LORD, I have called you in righteousness.
> I take you by the hand and watch over you. . . .
> To open the eyes of the blind,
> To bring out of bondage the prisoner—
> Out of prison, those who sit in darkness. (Isa. 42:6–7)

Death brings the assurance of freedom, for old age is prison. Sickness of body and mind is darkness, which God alone can finally enlighten.

Our faith tells us that death is a sister, a friend, an angel of God. But like most essential elements of faith, this is far from obvious. So we must *learn* to see death as friendly to us. The Christian life is in no small part dedicated to the befriending of death: to losing our natural and universal fear of death, so that we may go in peace into more abundant life. I believe that befriending death is what my dad did in the last two years of his life. And what I learned from him—the last thing, I suppose, he taught me—is that the most important work we do in this life is not done with our rational minds. Our greatest growth is not achieved by intellectual means—an admission that does not come easily to me, and in that as in much else I am my father's daughter.

In the last two years of his life, when his intellectual powers had failed, my father grew visibly in peace. Gradually the agitation, the restless energy that was so characteristic of him, receded. The fear also receded: the old fears of not being in control, of being abandoned if he ever should lose control; the fear of death itself. What came to the fore was his humor, his sweetness, his love—and, with that, a depth of contentment I had not known in him before.

Last August, Dad said to me, with a clarity that surprised me, "We did a good job, didn't we?" "Yes, Dad, we did." "For a long time I didn't know how it would all work out, but it worked out pretty well, didn't it?" "It's all just fine. Thanks, Dad, for everything." Of course, I did not realize that would be our last conversation, but I knew that something had changed for my dad—changed *in* him. He had, I believe, received the greatest gift with which God blesses us in this life, the gift that our liturgy calls "the peace of God, which passeth all understanding."[2] That gift of peace enabled him to receive death, when it came, as a friend, and to enter trustingly into more abundant life. May light perpetual shine upon him.

Amen.

2. *Book of Common Prayer,* 339.

The Healing of Our Flesh

Wilshire Baptist Church, Dallas, Texas
February 6, 2011

ISAIAH 58:1–12; MATTHEW 5:13–16

The pairing of Isaiah and Matthew affords a more complex reflection on what it means for the church to be a light-bearing people in a place of darkness. Attending to the subject of mission work in the season of Epiphany, this sermon calls on the faithful to be beacons of God's justice and reconciliation. However, Isaiah first calls us to come out of hiding and to recognize that we need to expose our own wounds to healing air and light. Only then may we truly befriend the poor, our flesh in Christ, and together become "repairers of the breach."

Isaiah is traditionally known as the evangelical prophet; "he" is the Old Testament prophet who most clearly articulates the good news of the God of Israel as it will in the fullness of time be revealed in Jesus Christ. Therefore Isaiah is the prophet we hear more than any other during this Epiphany season, the season when the light of Christ was first clearly manifested to the world. Isaiah uses powerful images of light breaking into darkness, God's light refracted through the people of Israel: "Then shall your light burst through like the dawn," he says. "Then shall your light shine in the darkness, and your gloom be like noonday." Hearing Isaiah and Matthew together in this late-winter season of slowly increasing light, we might well reflect upon what it is for us to be a light-bearing people in a place of darkness—or, in Matthew's language, what it is for us to have our light on a lampstand and not under a bushel basket. That is an apt question to ask on this day set aside to reflect on this congregation's ever-deepening work of missions.

"Then shall your light shine in the darkness, and your gloom be like noon-

198

day." Scholars call this prophet of light the Third Isaiah. We don't know his real name (which hardly matters), but we do know his circumstances, and they were gloomy enough. This Isaiah lived in Jerusalem at the end of the sixth century BCE. That was a generation or two after the Babylonian army had run over the city and left it for dead, having packed off most of the young sturdy survivors to labor camps in Babylon. But now the great Babylonian empire itself has been overrun by yet another empire (the Persians), and some of those Judean exiles have been allowed to return to Jerusalem. Probably for a little while they felt like they'd been sprung from prison, but now that flush of exhilaration has faded. Yes, they are back in Jerusalem, but the Holy City looks and feels for all the world like a place that God has forgotten. Now, these Judeans are religious people; they are fasting rigorously, praying every single day. Yet God does not seem to be listening to them. They are still vassals of somebody else's empire. They are sitting in deep darkness, waiting for God to show up in power and deliver them.

In fact, God does show up, speaking loud and clear through this prophet, who does not mince words. "You are kidding yourselves," God says through Isaiah, "if you think that you can have true religion without justice and reconciliation. You may be devoutly fasting, but *you fast in strife and contention*" (v. 4). Somehow all that piety and prayer are not translating into fair economic and labor relations within the community. Some folks are ostentatiously putting on sackcloth and ashes, but others are so poor they have no proper clothing (v. 7). In some cases the employment conditions are so degrading that the prophet calls them "fetters of wickedness."

We should look carefully at the profile Isaiah is presenting here. The church cherishes the words of the Old Testament prophets because they point to Christ, and we need them because they point to the conditions of the religious community in every age. So here's the profile: people coming for worship in healthy numbers, but with tension and strife among them, and gross economic inequality. It would seem that these people are trying to have piety without robust mission, without justice and reconciliation, and it's not working for them. As a result they are bitterly divided among themselves and at the same time bitterly disappointed in God.

I dare say that this set of symptoms—piety without justice and reconciliation—is so common in the church that we rarely even recognize it as a malady; that's just the way church is. So I still remember when I first heard the malady diagnosed, and also saw someone pointing to the cure. I was a theology student in England, spending a week at a school known around the world for its excellence in preparing Christians for long-term mission service. I remember just one moment from the whole week, but it continues to instruct me. We had gathered around the table for the weekly celebration of the Lord's Supper, and everyone began a Taizé-style chant, which went like this:

> We are here at the table of the Lord;
> we are not alone;
> we are here with our enemies.

That moment around the communion table at the mission college could be the foundation for a good education in missions. This is what I learned there: in the church, we come before the Lord always in the presence of our enemies—people who go to the same church we do, serve on the same board of ministry or divinity school faculty perhaps; people who belong to our denomination—or what used to be our denomination, until we fragmented. (This might be territory that Anglicans like me share with Baptists.) So this is a given of our life in Christ: we are bound in the one body of Christ with people who have hurt us, who are still hurting us, with some people we do not understand at all and others we understand well enough to wish to avoid. Here, with our enemies—that is inevitably the context in which we are called to the table of the Lord, to be fed and sent forth to mission. This is what I began to learn that long-ago day at the mission college in England. Building on that foundation today, let's see what more the prophet Isaiah might teach us—this prophet who more than any other speaks about our vocation as a people of faith.

Mission is about being healed of our wounds—that in a nutshell is Isaiah's message to the people of derelict Jerusalem in the sixth century BCE. Mission is about becoming whole; it's about being healed of wounds we did not even know we had—specifically, the wounds of separation. Mission brings us into productive relationship with those from whom we have been divided—socially, economically, politically, often theologically. We have been separated from other Christians because we live in one part of town and they in another, or we live in one country and they in another, and we have somehow come to believe that they are not our neighbors, not our sisters and brothers in Christ, not, as Isaiah puts it, "our own flesh." That misperception is profoundly wounding, but not necessarily in the way we normally suppose. Just listen again to how Isaiah describes our healing:

> When you see someone naked, and you cover him,
> and you do not hide from your own flesh—
> then your light will burst forth like dawn,
> and new skin will quickly cover your wound. (vv. 6–8a, paraphrastic)

"When you do not hide from your own flesh . . ."—notice that, as Isaiah sees it, mission is about *our* coming out of hiding; it is about exposing *our* festering wound to healing air and light. Curiously, Isaiah does not even mention what would seem to be the obvious outcome of mission work, namely, that our generosity should bring healing to someone else, presumably those we call "the poor." But with God-inspired logic, the prophet overturns completely our "commonsense" view of who is in need, and who is getting healed. We normally see the lack on their side, the empty hands waiting to be filled by those of us who have means. But Isaiah sees our own lack, our emptiness when we "hide ourselves from our own flesh." The point is that the so-called poor are our flesh; they are the part of our own body that we ordinarily neglect and mistreat. And if that does not change, then, as Isaiah memorably says in the very first chapter of that book, the whole body is sick, head to foot (Isa. 1:5–6). The breakdown in the body of faith is a kind of auto-immune disease, from which we in the church can be healed only as the relatively wealthy among us develop relationships of mutual caring and shared responsibility with those whose economic resources are smaller, as those who exercise social and economic influence work to achieve justice for those who may have less social capital, but often have depths of faith far beyond our own. We are healed as those who might have been enemies, because of our differences, become friends.

This is my experience in partnership with the Episcopal Church of Sudan to build up theological education in Southern Sudan. Our partnership began with a trip I made in 2004, to fulfill a promise to my former student, now Archbishop Daniel Deng Bul of the Episcopal Church of Sudan. He asked me to come and teach the book of Isaiah (no coincidence, probably). I intended that visit as a one-time thing, but in fact it proved to be the start of what we call the Visiting Teachers Program. We send teams of teachers and others twice a year; the program has now involved dozens of people. We work together—American seminarians and clergy, Sudanese clergy and seminarians, American, British, and Sudanese theology professors and health professionals, as well as (imagine this) farmers and gardeners. Together we are developing a holistic model of theological education, which includes not just traditional theological subjects like Greek or biblical studies, but also community health, nutrition, and sustainable agriculture. The young church leaders whom we are helping to educate will be the opinion leaders of "the new Sudan"; they will build the infrastructure in a land that was taken down to the ground over nearly fifty years of a killing war.

Those of us involved in this work are not an NGO; we are not even a church agency. We are more like a family; that is, we simply cannot imagine *not* being in each other's lives. We plan the calendar for the year around the times we can be together. We work our finances around being generous to each other—and that is a two-way street, as Sudanese hospitality stretches their resources even more than trips to Sudan stretch ours. We love each other; we get frustrated with each other; occasionally we raise our voices. When we dream of the future, those dreams involve us all: the church in Sudan, the church in the US, the church in Britain—not three different churches but one.

Those dreams are countercultural, at least for the Anglicans among us (there are also Baptists, Methodists, and Presbyterians), for we belong to a global church with deep fault lines, one that is threatening to fracture over all kinds of issues, acknowledged and unacknowledged: homosexuality and women bishops, of course; the interpretation of Scripture to some extent; and running through, beneath, and behind those arguments is the bitter heritage of European and American colonialism and the slave trade. These might divide African Anglicans from Anglicans in the West, but equally they might divide one of my Duke students from another, or one clergy friend in England from another. Moral and mortal combat now seems to be the norm in the Anglican Communion. As one friend said recently, after a depressing session of reading on the Internet, "It's war out there. People don't even seem sad about this; each side gets its energy from savaging the other side." Yet every one of those combatants is a devout Christian who "love[s] being close to God," as Isaiah (58:2) said of the folks he was addressing. The prophet would say, I suspect, that we embattled Anglicans are the walking wounded; parts of our own flesh are torn away, and we are too unhealthy even to feel it as pain.

Those of us involved in building up theological education in Sudan are finding an alternative way of being church; our shared mission based on regular shared study of God's word provides an alternative to fragmentation and bitter dispute. And we are amazed at what we see God doing among us: the beginning of healing in war-torn communities, even the healing of personal disappointments. Through the program young American and Sudanese women and men have discovered vocations to teach; older people, clergy and laity both, are finding their various Christian vocations renewed and refocused. People are getting trained as teachers and health-care workers; tuition and modest salaries are being raised to support their work. We are developing new practices of reading Scripture in community and gaining theological insights that none of us had before. In all these ways, we can see and feel new skin growing up over old wounds.

So that is some of my mission story. From the inside, being involved in this work feels perpetually fresh and amazing. But from another perspective, there is nothing at all surprising about it, since it is exactly what Isaiah promised 2,600 years ago:

> If you remove from among you the yoke of oppression,
> pointing the finger and speaking evil,
> . . . .
> and if you satisfy the need of the afflicted,
> . . . .
> then the Lord will guide you always,
> and satisfy your need in parched places
> and strengthen your bones.
> . . . .
> They will call you "repairer of the breach,
> the restorer of paths for living." (vv. 9–12)

Wilshire Baptist, I have read your website, which articulates a theology of mission; this is rare enough in my experience. I have spoken with some of you about your mission work, and there must be countless other mission stories in this church, all of them stories of new skin growing to cover old wounds. There must also be wounds still in need of healing inside the church and beyond, places where God is longing to bring wholeness, using your heart, your hands, the days and years you have to give. On this day, will you commit to sharing these stories among yourselves, to expanding and deepening your vision for mission? "Wilshire Baptist" is already an estimable name, but there is an even better one:

> They will call you "repairer of the breach,
> the restorer of paths for living."

I pray that you will claim that name for yourselves.
Amen.

Swallowing Fire

St. Peter's Episcopal Church, Salisbury, Maryland
Pentecost 1999

JEREMIAH 1:4–9

While no one would wish the particular burdens of Jeremiah's life on any priest, there is one quality unique to his prophetic ministry worth commending to new clergy: more than any other prophet, Jeremiah shows what it is like to live on the strength of God's word alone. Jeremiah embodies the patience clergy must have if they will endure the most difficult tasks of ministry. The congregation must pray, therefore, that the ordinand will have the same courage to minister with God's word at the core of her being and "to bear its incessant beating, more reliable than her own heartbeat."

May God's word only be spoken, and God's word only be heard.

From the book of the prophet Jeremiah: "And the word of the LORD came to me saying, 'Before I formed you in the belly, I knew you; and before you came forth from the womb, I sanctified you. I made you a prophet for the nations'" (1:4–5).

What are we the church doing when we read the call of the prophet Jeremiah this evening, as one of our final acts preparatory to Sheila's entry into ordained ministry? Why Jeremiah in particular? Why not Moses, say, to whom God spoke "mouth to mouth"? That would be a much more sublime example of pastoral leadership. Indeed, Jeremiah is not presented as a leader at all, and he is perhaps the least sublime of all the prophets, continually complaining as he does about how hard it is to be a prophet. So why Jeremiah? This may not be a question that has occupied you much, but once you start thinking about it the question becomes bothersome: Why Jeremiah, for God's sake? Because

Jeremiah is in some ways the very antithesis of what we all wish for Sheila in the years ahead.

Certainly, we do not wish her a ministry like Jeremiah's, long and memorable as it was. For Jeremiah is the prophet whose sad duty it was to preside over the terrible siege and fall of Jerusalem to the Babylonian army, as the just punishment for Judah's sin of forsaking God. Accordingly, Jeremiah is the most personally embattled of the biblical prophets. His denunciation of kings and religious leaders won him powerful enemies. He suffered public scorn, imprisonment, and ultimately death in exile, the most terrible fate anyone in the ancient world could imagine—to die away from home. To add insult to injury, Jeremiah was deprived of the private comfort of a family—God forbade him to marry and have children—and he had few, if any, friends. He freely confesses that, with God's hand heavy upon him, he was not very good company (15:17).

So Jeremiah's life history is not what we wish for Sheila. Nor do we wish her Jeremiah's calling from God—not really. We have read part of his call account tonight, but there are some parts the church in her wisdom chooses to omit. We stopped just short of the point where God tells Jeremiah: "See, I have appointed you this day over nations and over kingdoms, to pluck up and to break down, to wipe out and destroy, to build and to plant" (v. 10). Tearing down nations and kingdoms—this is not the sort of pastoral ministry to which any of us believes Sheila is primarily called. We in the church are not chiefly in the business of ordaining prophets to overthrow oppressive social and national systems. Yes, it happens: even in our lifetime we have seen prophetic clergy take the lead in tearing down the blasphemous kingdom of segregation in this country, of apartheid in South Africa. There is more of this work to be done, at home and abroad: pray God that the church may continue to raise up leaders with the courage to expose, oppose, and dismantle wicked social systems. Yet it is not primarily to wipe out nations and destroy kingdoms that the Episcopal Church ordains its clergy and arranges for their monetary compensation. There are relatively few salaried positions for dismantlers of social systems in the Protestant Episcopal Church USA.

So it is not Jeremiah's biography or even his calling that we anticipate for Sheila. Nonetheless, there is something about Jeremiah that makes it appropriate to begin with him this evening, as Sheila enters into ordained ministry. For there is something we see more clearly in Jeremiah than in any other ordinary person in the Bible (that is, in anyone except Jesus). What Jeremiah shows us with unique clarity is what it is like to live solely on the strength of God's word. To live on the strength of God's word—that is something we should pray for Sheila. But we can help her more if our prayers are informed, if we really know what we are seeking on her behalf, if we can begin to imagine what life would look like for a person who lives on God's word like daily bread. Jeremiah can help us imagine that. Listen, God says to him, "I put my words in your mouth." And Jeremiah tells us just what that was like: like swallowing fire and feeling it burn inside until he could no longer hold it in (20:9). Eating a steady diet of God's word is like swallowing a hammer and feeling it pound inside, hard enough to shatter rock (23:29).

So now we begin to understand what Sheila is getting into, and what we should pray for her this evening. We must pray for one thing above all: that she may have courage to live in immediate contact with God and God's word. "Do not be afraid, for I am with you," God assures Jeremiah at the time of his call. "Do not be afraid." Have you ever noticed that God says that—and God says it quite often—but only when there is good reason to be afraid? Here is Jeremiah, mouth open, with God about to drop this fireball on his tongue, and God says, "Do not be afraid; I am with you." "I am with you"—that is reason enough to be afraid right there. For if the Bible is clear about anything, it is that God's immediate presence is no Sunday school picnic. And no one knows that better than Jeremiah. Listen to how Jeremiah the priest complains to God: "I've often sat alone, feeling the weight of your hand on me" (15:17), "overpowering me" (20:7), "bending me to your will, taking away my own" (20:7).

In a few minutes, Sheila will feel the weight of hands laid upon her, as the bishop prays that God will send the Holy Spirit upon Sheila with special power, bending her life to God's will, fitting her for ordained ministry. My guess is that God will do as the bishop asks, that the Holy Spirit will come upon Sheila and make her a deacon in the church. Therefore, it is a good thing that we are here, to pray that she may have courage for this new life to which we believe she is called. She will need courage if she is to live, as Jeremiah did, with God's word at the center of her being. She will need courage if she is to bear its incessant beating, more reliable than her own heartbeat, beating like a hammer that shatters rock. It's the hammer of God's word beating against the rock of human resistance. To bear that, Sheila will need all the courage we can pray into her, for as deacon and priest she is called to be sensitive to something other people, even other Christians, often prefer to ignore. She is called to feel the terrible and frequent collision between God's word, the expression of God's will for us, and the obdurate human will. She is called to be pained by that collision, pained enough to cry out, as Jeremiah does, so that we may feel it, too, so that we may begin to face this reality we would prefer to ignore.

If Sheila has the courage to let the Holy Spirit do its full work in and through her, then she will help us see how often human will is set against

God's will. In the world, in the church, even in her own person, she will feel painfully how often we invest ourselves in what is inconsequential to God, and also in what takes us away from God. Our passions and ambitions, our habits, our possessions, even our relationships—all these may clamor for attention and shape our thinking so that we become indifferent to God; in subtle ways we may become hostile to God's hopes for us. If Sheila lets the Holy Spirit do its work with her, then sometimes, like Jeremiah, she will be stricken to the heart by the pain that God feels at our resistance. That is why she will need courage—to feel the thing that most of us dare not imagine: God's own pain and heartbroken love, in the face of the sin of the world, the meanness of the human spirit, the resistance that our hearts offer to God. Pray boldly that Sheila may have the courage to claim the role that Jeremiah models for the new deacon; that, like him, she may be a true friend to God, "ministering" to God in the strongest sense. Dare I say it?—pray that Sheila's compassion may extend even to God, that she may not shrink from feeling in her own heart the pain that God must feel, looking at our world and into our hearts.

Opening her heart to God: that deeply takes courage—this we learn from Jeremiah. Yet Jeremiah does not sound courageous, as we normally think of courage sounding. On the contrary, Jeremiah is one of the great complainers of the Bible. Yet in this, too, he is a model for Sheila. For what marks him as truly courageous is that Jeremiah complains to God—which is to say, he prays, all the time. Jeremiah gets scared, really scared; and he prays. He gets sad, deeply sad, seriously depressed; and he prays. At times, he gets angry with God, "angry enough to die" (see Jonah 4:9); and he prays. What marks Jeremiah as God's true friend is that he never grows cold with God. He burns hot, burns even against God; but he never burns out. From this it is evident that in our love for Sheila we must pray for her to learn from Jeremiah; because we all know, to our grief, that burnt-out clergy are a dime a dozen these days, and not a few of those discounted clergy are Episcopalians.

So Jeremiah burns, but he never burns out. Why? Because he is not fueling his ministry with his own vision, his own enthusiasm and creativity, with the clever answers he has devised to the problems of life. There is only one source of fuel behind every word Jeremiah utters and everything he does, and that source is God's word. Day in and day out, year after year through decades of unimaginably difficult ministry, Jeremiah keeps opening himself in prayer to God's word.

Yet Jeremiah is honest with us. There is a cost to this divinely fueled ministry. The cost is called "waiting upon God." Often Jeremiah hangs upon God, desperate for a word; and he hangs for a long time—hearing nothing, or hearing something he does not understand or does not wish to hear. Throughout Jeremiah's book, the prophet's pained cries hang unanswered in the air. Jeremiah cries out the questions any deacon or priest would cry out to God, sooner or later, if only she had the courage. How long must I look on human sin and its terrible consequences (4:21)? No answer. Why do the wicked prosper (12:1), while innocent people, good, faithful people, suffer horribly (see Lamentations)? No answer. Why is my pain unending (15:18a)? No answer. How do I get out of this thankless job (15:18b)? No answer. Why was I ever born (15:10; 20:18)? Ah, to that question God has an answer, an answer for Jeremiah and Sheila and every one of us for whom God has some use, and that is every one of us—an answer for us to cling to when the dark days come:

"Before I formed you in the belly I knew you; even before you came out of the womb, I sanctified you, set you apart." (1:5)

"Don't be afraid; I am with you, to deliver you." (1:8)

"I have saved you for a good purpose." (15:11)

"Go wherever I send you and speak whatever I command you." (1:7)

"Look, I am putting my words in your mouth." (1:9)

Pray for Sheila, and pray also for yourselves, for all of us. Pray boldly for courage like Jeremiah's, to clamor for God's word. Pray for the dogged persistence to wait for it when it seems that no fresh word, no refreshing word, will ever come. Pray for the faith to recognize God's word and hold it fast when it does come. And pray for Sheila, now particularly for Sheila. Pray that Sheila, a poet, as was Jeremiah, gifted with words—pray that she may have Jeremiah's unswerving faithfulness in speaking God's word truly to the church, that through her all of us may grow in understanding of God's aching love and hope for the world, God's promise and demand to us. God bless you and strengthen you, Sheila.

Amen.

Healing for Sin-Sick Hearts

Earth Day Service, Virginia Theological Seminary, Alexandria, Virginia
April 7, 2001

JEREMIAH 4 AND 31; COLOSSIANS 1:11–20

*Jeremiah saw in Jerusalem's destruction what no one should ever see—
the reversal of creation from harmony to chaos. The de-creation he witnessed mirrors the horrors of our own extractive economy, which turns
rich lands into wastelands and reduces mountains to rubble. But there
is reason for hope if we recall the global scope of the new covenant Jeremiah envisioned, as well as the promise in Colossians that, in Christ,
"all things hold together." Through the cross of Christ, God redeems our
sin-sick hearts, and inscribes on them a new promise of reconciliation
and peace for "every creature under heaven."*

No one should ever have to see what Jeremiah saw. What other prophets had
foreseen and warned about, and hoped against hope would never happen,
Jeremiah saw with his own eyes. He saw Jerusalem laid in ruins by Nebu-
chadnezzar's raging army; he heard her panting and moaning like a woman
in distress: "*'Oy li*, woe is me, for I am fainting before killers" (Jer. 4:31). And
he saw more. As our passage attests, Jeremiah's vision widened—against his
will, surely—and he saw the whole earth laid waste:

> I see the earth, and here—it is without form and void (*tohu vavohu*);
> and the heavens—and their light is gone. (v. 23)

"I see the earth . . . I see the mountains; *ra'iti*, I see, I see"—Jeremiah
speaks in chapter 4 as one who has learned to see as God sees. He has shed
his illusions, his blinders, his false optimism. And now, with eyes wide open,

he sees the terrible inverse of what God saw in the first week of the world. He sees the undoing of creation, step by step:

- human beings—vanished;
- birds of the air—all fled;
- fertile farmland stripped of vegetation, reverted to wilderness;
- lights out in the heavens.

Jeremiah's prophetic vision is like a film running backwards, until it gets to the very first frame—*tohu vavohu*, waste schmaste, absolute chaos—and clicks off.

No one should ever see what Jeremiah saw. Yet, as twenty-first-century Christians, we are obliged to see it. Five years ago I went to the Appalachian Ministries Educational Resources Center (AMERC) in Berea, Kentucky. I went because a friend whose judgment I trust said, "You must go. There are things you need to see." So, with a small group of faculty from various seminaries and Christian colleges, I toured the mountains. I learned a little about the culture of the mountain people—very little, I'm sure. But more importantly, in that week I learned something about my own mainstream urban North American culture. To my astonishment, I learned that the people of Appalachia pay no small part of the cost of my lifestyle. Other states pay the state of Kentucky to let us dump our garbage there. It is possible that some of the wood for my new house in Durham comes from their mountains, which are being method- ically stripped of their forests. And then the bare mountains are themselves "removed"—that is, blown to bits—to take out the coal veins that cannot be reached by conventional mining methods.

We visited the office of a mining company, heard the manager's presen- tation, and then we spoke briefly with a few miners who worked in the deep mine, with tunnels and coal carts. Then, under close supervision, we were permitted to enter the removal area. Maybe they let us in because we were professors and thought to have a detached interest, or maybe because we were church people and assumed to be harmless. Somehow I did not really get it as we rode up the mountain, until we came around to the far side—or what should have been the far side, except it wasn't there anymore. They'd blown it away completely, de-created that segment of the Appalachians—the oldest mountains on this continent, aren't they?—the place where God began work on this quadrant of the globe.

The shuddering, wordless horror I felt is what I imagine one must feel standing within the gates of Auschwitz, in the wake of an evil so absolute, it is all but unimaginable. Yet the perverted human imagination had conceived it and brought it into being; evil so stark it is in any ordinary terms unspeakable, and then I realized that Jeremiah had spoken of it:

> I see the mountains, and here they are, rocking;
> and all the hills palpitate.
> I see, and here, there is no human being,
> and all the birds of the heavens have fled.
> I see, and here, the rich land is now the wasteland. (vv. 24–26)

No one should see mountains exploding in Kentucky, so that we may defer for a few more years the inevitable, yet initially costly, conversion to sustainable forms of fuel. No one should see the hills of West Virginia blown apart, then the infertile rubble shoveled together into vast tracts incapable of sustaining any form of life—although they will do for building shopping malls. Malls in the place of mountains—no one should ever see that; but the people of Appalachia do see it, and many of them currently depend upon it for a living. They are caught up with us in an extractive economy that is increasingly tragic and desperate, for it seems to leave us, in the immediate, no choice but to destroy what God's hands have made. Of course, the destruction is not random. It happens first, and worst, not in the backyards of the powerful but in the homelands of the poor: in the hollows of West Virginia and Kentucky, in tropical rain forests, on the tundras of Alaska and Siberia. In response to the common defense that we really have no choice, God's judgment is clear:

> My people are stupid;
> me, they know not.
> They are foolish children;
> they are not discerning.
> They are wise in doing evil,
> but good, they do not know how to do. (v. 22)

It would be easier to preach on this subject if Earth Day fell during Lent. Then I might feel justified in announcing that the situation is grim, which is true enough, and be done with it. But by the providence of God, Earth Day falls within the Easter season. So my job is to consider the question, What, in this situation, does it mean for us to claim Christ's resurrected life as our own? Because this subject is so emotionally, economically, and politically charged, the danger of delusion and self-delusion is great. So I'm going to begin with what resurrection hope does *not* mean, in our present ecological crisis.

Resurrection hope does not mean that things are not as bad as they seem. It does not mean that we may expect to be shielded from the worst effects of our selfishness—although, if we are honest, probably every one of us nurtures at least some hope of that. But resurrection hope does not mean protection for us, as long as we remain committed to self-serving goals. Nor does it mean that piles, which once were mountains, will again sustain life. I do not believe that we can in good resurrection faith pray that they will, so long as we continue to show contempt for the work of God's hands. Those mountains are dead, and we killed them. If realistic resurrection hope is to take root in us at all, then it will begin with that recognition. It will begin when we admit that we see what God sees and, as a result, judge ourselves accurately.

Jeremiah's message, which accords fully with the message of the gospel, is that things are every bit as bad as they seem, and for the simplest of all reasons. As usual, the prophet puts it to us straight:

The heart is more perverse than anything,
and it is sick beyond what anyone can know. (Jer. 17:9)

The human heart is sick beyond what anyone can know. Yet, together, Jeremiah and the gospel affirm that the heart can be regenerated. That is the resurrection hope, and the source of all righteous joy—not that God will miraculously undo the destruction we have accomplished, but that, by the grace of God, we can turn back to God and never stray away again.

That hope of a thoroughly regenerated heart is what Jeremiah expresses in his vision of "a new covenant":

Not like the covenant that I cut with their ancestors in the day when I seized them by their hand to bring them out of the land of Egypt—my covenant that they broke, though I was their husband, says the LORD. For this is the covenant that I will cut with the house of Israel after those days, says the LORD: I will put my Torah *inside* them, yes, on their hearts I will write it; and I will become their God, and they shall become my people. (Jer. 31:32–33)

I propose that when God speaks here of a new covenant, the vision has the same global scope as the earlier vision of destruction. Just as Jeremiah looks back to the first week of the world and witnesses the undoing of God's whole creation, so this vision of the new covenant also looks back into primeval history. It recapitulates the moment when God made an eternal covenant with

Noah and his seed, but also "with every living thing that is with you" (Gen. 9:12) and even "with the earth" itself (9:13). In other words, just because the devastation that Jeremiah sees is total, all-encompassing, then so also must the covenantal restoration be total. We are starting over, from scratch. Therefore God can say of Israel, "I will become their God, and they shall become my people" (Jer. 31:33). The covenant written on our hearts means that God at last finds a way to overcome our sick-heartedness, so that we humans might be, for the first time in the history of the world, fully in communion with God.

Likewise, I believe that the new covenant means that we might be, for the first time in the history of the world, fully in community with the other creatures of God, even and maybe especially the nonhuman creatures whom our sin-sick hearts have neglected or despised. A new covenant written on our hearts means that we might for the first time take our proper place as fellow-creatures with everyone else whom God has made in love: with every mountain, with the soil and the trees that clothe it, with the animals and the birds that are at home on its slopes, no less than with the people who are at home in its hollows.

Jeremiah's twin visions of devastation and restoration are pushing us toward this comprehensive understanding of covenant, but it is only Jesus Christ who can bring us Gentiles into it—or more accurately, Jesus Christ brings it into us, inscribing it on hearts that without him could not receive the imprint. And in him, the universal, minutely inclusive scope of this New Covenant is fully revealed, for Jesus Christ is nothing other than "the firstborn of all creation" (Col. 1:15). "In him all things in heaven and earth were created" (1:16)—and further, "in him all things hold together" (1:17). "In him all things hold together"—the letter to the Colossians is speaking here of global reconciliation, "every creature under heaven" receiving the gospel hope (1:23) and coming together in "peace" (1:20); that is, every creature joined in community with every other creature, and all of us as one reconciled to God. That is what it means to say that God in Christ is even now "making peace through the blood of his cross" (1:20).

Jeremiah's prophetic vision and Colossians' apostolic one persuade me that the church's most important work in the twenty-first century is to commit itself fully to Christ's work of making peace among all creatures, human and nonhuman. Yet it is through the blood of the cross that peace is being made. That astonishing statement makes it clear that we are talking about sacrifice— that is, about making our lives holy, and doing it at some cost to ourselves. It's going to cost us to commit ourselves to Christ's work of reconciliation; it will cost us our false hopes, our old heedless habits of consumption. It will require from us, as individuals and even more as a society, a large investment of scientific imagination: How can we act on the world without undoing creation? It will require from us—and here, I believe, the church in industrialized regions must lead the way—restraint, a willingness to do with less, because we recognize that the gratification of our desires currently extracts too high a price from others. "Sacrifice" and "restraint" are dirty words in a culture committed to ever-more aggressive and rapacious economic strategies. My prayer is that the church will in this decade, at this crucial juncture in creation history, be the voice that articulates the blessing that always—always—attends genuine sacrifice. This we know for sure: where true sacrifice is offered—when human life is made holy, at some cost to ourselves—there God creates abundance, giving life and more life, against the odds and beyond all calculation.

That is the substance of the resurrection hope that the church is charged first to believe, second to practice, and third to proclaim in the midst of an industrial culture committed to degradation and death. May our risen Lord give us understanding and courage to hold fast to that hope in which we are, even now, being saved (Rom. 8:24).

Amen.

Learning to Lament

An Interfaith Service of Lament and Reconciliation,
on the Occasion of the Gulf Coast Oil Spill,
Immaculate Conception Church, Durham, North Carolina
July 7, 2010

JEREMIAH 14

Though Jeremiah could not have foreseen a disaster like the 2010 Gulf Coast oil spill, his prayers of lament nevertheless anticipate our modern-day sins against creation. Like our biblical ancestors, we are guilty of having cursed the soil by our sins, and we along with the rest of the created order must pay a heavy price. Is there anything we can do other than despair as the desecration of an entire ecosystem continues unabated? From Jeremiah we learn that lament is more than a cry of powerlessness; it is also an appeal to the mercy and power of God. Our lament can be redemptive if it leads us to hope in the Lord who makes everything in heaven and earth.

Since I teach at a divinity school, I go to church and chapel often, to all kinds of services, many of them quite innovative. But never have I been to a service like this one, where we gather to lament our collective sin and seek reconciliation with God . . . and it's not Holy Week; it's not even Lent. So it has to be a pretty momentous sin that brings us together this evening for a service of lament and reconciliation, so that together we may find the courage to acknowledge how we as a culture have strayed far from what is good, and so we may encourage each other to take the difficult way back to God.

If this kind of service is unprecedented in my experience, and maybe in yours as well, that is fitting enough, because we now find ourselves in a situation that is historically unprecedented. We have unleashed a monster of mythic proportions: this gushing, pluming, engulfing, mummifying monster that we have not been able to check, nor can we imagine what will be the

215

consequences if the backup technology fails, or the backup to the backup, and (God forbid) the monster gushes until it exhausts itself, two or more grim years in the future. Technologically, biologically, geologically, we are now in uncharted territory—way out beyond the reach of our knowledge, and this is bewildering, enraging, terrifying. That is why we have come together this evening to lament.

Lament is a cry of human powerlessness, but it is more than that. It is at the same time an appeal to God's power and mercy. Strange though it may sound, lament is something we need to learn how to do. As with other kinds of prayer, we need to learn how to appeal to God in good faith, how to speak to God without deceiving ourselves and dishonoring God. Scripture is altogether our best guide to prayer, but you have to ask: How can it guide us in this situation? How could an ancient text possibly shed light on a thoroughly modern oil spill?

Of course the biblical writers did not know about this particular technological disaster. However, there is one biblical voice, the prophet Jeremiah, who teaches us to lament over the suffering we have caused the earth and calls us to be reconciled with both God and the created order. Jeremiah spoke to and for God in the face of a disaster as devastating as this one: a prolonged and deadly drought, which left animals and people desperate with thirst, and ruined the once-fertile land of Judah. We would be inclined to say that drought is a natural disaster, and therefore quite unlike this oil spill, but Jeremiah would say that the earth always and everywhere suffers as a result of human sin. He would say—and this is how biblical thinking differs from the "common sense" of our industrial culture—that we cannot divide up reality into separate and unrelated realms, as though the natural world and our life with God had nothing to do with each other, as though our physical and technical actions had nothing to do with our moral actions. If we think that, we are kidding ourselves, for these are all aspects of a single comprehensive reality, and that whole reality must have integrity if we are to be saved, if—dare I say it?—if we are to survive.

So for the sake of our souls and our planet, let us listen to the words of the prophet Jeremiah, speaking for God in the midst of a killing drought. As we read, we shall pause several times to reflect on what this word of the Lord says to us as the people of God. It is a word of lament and of judgment. This is the question: Is it also a word of hope?

> Many shepherds have ravaged my vineyard, have trodden my heritage
>   underfoot;
> the portion that delighted me they have turned into a desert waste.

They have made it a mournful waste; desolate it lies before me.
Desolate, all the land, because no one takes it to heart. (Jer. 12:10–11)

This is a lament, and, strikingly, it is God's voice we hear, grieving over the desolation of the land that God once made and delighted in—God's "heritage," a precious, irreplaceable thing, a creature of infinite complexity and beauty.

The word of the LORD that came to Jeremiah concerning the drought:
Judah mourns, her gates are lifeless; her people sink down in mourning:
from Jerusalem ascends a cry of anguish.
The nobles send their servants for water, but when they come to the
    cisterns
they find no water and return with empty jars.
Ashamed, despairing, they cover their heads
because of the stricken soil. Because there is no rain in the land
the farmers are ashamed, they cover their heads.
Even the hind in the field deserts her offspring because there is no grass.
The wild asses stand on the bare heights, panting like jackals;
their eyes grow dim, because there is no vegetation to be seen. (14:1–6)[1]

The people mourn the stricken soil, and they are ashamed—but why ashamed? The answer goes back to the Garden of Eden, when God told Adam, "Cursed is the soil because of you." From the beginning of human history, as the Bible tells it, the earth has been the first to suffer whenever we have overreached ourselves—as though we were the rulers of creation and not ourselves the creatures of God. So whenever we humans act against our true nature, the whole order of creatures is thrown out of kilter. Thus Jeremiah sees baby deer abandoned in the fields, while the does run off in search of food. We see brown pelicans sheathed in oil, bluefish tuna and sea turtles poisoned by it, dolphins calving into it, breathing and swallowing it. And we are ashamed.

Now Jeremiah shows how the people pray:

Even though our crimes bear witness against us,
take action, O LORD, for the honor of your name.
Even though our rebellions are many, though we have sinned against you.
O Hope of Israel, its savior in time of need!
Why should you be a stranger in this land,

1. This is an adjusted translation from the New American Bible.

like a traveler who has stopped but for a night?
Why are you like a man dumbfounded, a champion who cannot save?
You are in our midst, O LORD, your name we bear: do not forsake us!
> (14:7–9)

Here the people appeal to God's power, call on God to act, to stand by us, "though we have sinned against you." Yet there is no word of repentance, no turning to God in humility, with a genuine desire for change. Therefore this is how God answers that empty appeal:

Thus says the LORD of this people:
They so love to wander that they do not spare their feet.
The LORD has no pleasure in them;
now he remembers their guilt and will punish their sins.
Then the LORD said to me: Do not intercede for this people.
If they fast, I will not listen to their supplication.
If they offer burnt offerings or cereal offerings, I will not accept them.
Rather, I will destroy them with the sword, famine, and pestilence.
> (14:10–12)

Ah! Lord GOD, I replied, it is the prophets who say to them,
"You shall not see the sword; famine shall not befall you. Indeed, I will
> give you lasting peace in this place."
"Lies these prophets utter in my name," the LORD said to me.
"I did not send them; I gave them no command nor did I speak to them.
Lying visions, foolish divination, dreams of their own imagination, they
> prophesy to you."
Therefore, thus says the LORD concerning the prophets who prophesy in
> my name, though I did not send them; who say, "Sword and famine
> shall not befall this land":
by the sword and famine shall these prophets meet their end.
The people to whom they prophesy shall be cast out into the streets of
> Jerusalem
by famine and the sword. No one shall bury them, their wives, their
> sons, or their daughters, for I will pour out upon them their own
> wickedness. (14:13–16)

They are being lulled by their prophets, lulled to death by their opinion leaders. This is as harsh a word as God ever speaks, and the ferocity is aimed straight at those who utter lying visions—that is, those who have every opportunity to see and speak the truth, but instead they "dream out of their own imaginations"; they prefer their convenient fantasies to reality. There are such "prophets," opinion shapers, in our culture, who speak lying visions and profit by selling them to others. We have all bought those visions to some extent, because they are convenient for us, comfortable, at least in the short term—but at what cost?

Now God tells Jeremiah what a true prophet must say in this desperate situation:

> Speak to them this word:
> Let my eyes stream with tears day and night, without rest,
> over the great destruction which overwhelms my beloved people,
> over her incurable wound.
> If I walk out into the field, look! those slain by the sword.
> If I enter the city, look! those consumed by hunger.
> Even the prophet and the priest forage in a land they know not. (14:17–18)

"Let my eyes stream with tears day and night"—in this situation, Jeremiah implies, lament is the only sane and faithful thing to do. And out of profound lament come at last words of genuine repentance:

> Have you cast Judah off completely? Is Zion loathsome to you?
> Why have you struck us a blow that cannot be healed?
> We wait for peace, to no avail; for a time of healing, but terror comes
>   instead.
> We acknowledge, O LORD, our wickedness, the guilt of our fathers,
> which we have sinned against you.
> For your name's sake spurn us not, disgrace not the throne of your glory;
> remember your covenant with us, and break it not.
> Among the nations' idols is there any that gives rain?
> Or can the mere heavens send showers?
> Is it not you alone, O LORD, our God, to whom we look?
> You alone have made all these things. (14:19–22)

"We acknowledge, O LORD, our wickedness," the sin of this generation and the one preceding it. This is the hardest thing we can imagine saying: the cultural progress of which we are so proud, on which we have all come to depend, is deadly; it is destroying our world; it has taken us away from God, so now even God looks like an enemy. And yet, even as we acknowledge that, we are turning back, we are looking to the God whose rejection we fear.

> Is it not you alone, O Lord, our God, to whom we look?
> You alone have made all these things.

The lament ends as we look to God in hope, to the Lord who makes everything in heaven and earth. The lament ends with the beginning of real hope, as we relocate our faith, not in our idols, by whatever names we call them: Progress, Comfort, Convenience, Cheap Energy. Lament ends when we relocate our hope and faith in the God who is Maker and Monarch and Redeemer of all.

May we learn to pray like that.

Amen.

Building Hope

Duke Chapel, Durham, North Carolina
Good Friday, April 18, 2014

LAMENTATIONS 1:12 AND 3:1–8, 16–24

Imagining the words of Lamentation as Jesus's own, this Good Friday sermon asks whether we have any share in Jesus's suffering. The lamenter's questions haunt us, as if Jesus had composed them from his cross: "Is it nothing to you, all who pass by? . . . Is any suffering like my suffering?" Together with a host of biblical authors, we struggle with the ways God is implicated in our suffering. But here we are given permission to respond, "Yes, Jesus, our suffering is a lot like yours." In fact, such "honest talk about God and to God in the midst of suffering is the only way to realistic hope." As we participate in Jesus's own forthright expressions of hope, with him we will find ourselves drawn steadily closer to the outstretched arms of God.

From the book of Lamentations:

> Is it nothing to you, all you who pass by? Look around and see.
> Is any suffering like my suffering . . . that the LORD inflicted on me . . . ?
>   (1:12)

That sounds just like what Jesus must have felt, doesn't it? You can imagine him framing that question in his mind, wanting to fling it at those who passed him that day in Jerusalem, as he was led through the busy streets carrying a cross, and then, just outside the walls, was lifted high—stretched out, nailed, and naked for all to see. "Is it nothing to you, all you who pass by? Look around and see. Is any suffering like my suffering . . . ?" Those words were in fact written about six centuries before Christ, by another sufferer in Jerusalem—some anonymous Jew who had survived (barely) the devastating siege and total destruction of the city by the Babylonian army. The poems that make up the book of Lamentations were composed by the shocked and awed. Those poems were ancient already in Jesus's time, and almost certainly he knew them. So it is appropriate that Christians have traditionally read from the book of Lamentations on Good Friday, as though the words came from Jesus's own mouth on this, his day of devastation:

> Is it nothing to you, all you who pass by? Look around and see.
> Is any suffering like my suffering that he dealt me,
> that the LORD inflicted on me on the day of his heated wrath?

There is a lot festering in that question. It may be the toughest question that any believer can pose or hear, because it implicates God so thoroughly in human suffering: "Is there any suffering like mine, which the LORD inflicted on me *on the day of his heated wrath?*" Today, that question equally implicates us: "Is it nothing to you, all you who pass by?" This suffering of Jesus—does it have nothing to do with you, or does it touch your life, maybe closely? That is the question for each of us this day. To hear Jesus pose it to us from the cross—that is the reason, the only reason, for any of us to stop what we were doing and sit here this Friday afternoon.

"Is it nothing to you, all you who pass by?" Jesus addresses us as busy people, just like those who bustled through the streets of Jerusalem that other Friday, getting ready for Sabbath. Sabbath preparation is always a lot of work, but this was the Sabbath that began the Passover, the high point of the whole year. It was like the last few hours before Christmas, and more, because *everybody* came to Jerusalem for Passover, thousands upon thousands of excited, insanely busy pilgrims—and now with Jesus nailed right in the midst of them, silently posing that question: "Is it nothing to you, all you who pass by?" It is really no different for us. Good Friday comes to us this year in the final week of class; we are all insanely busy, stressed about papers and exams, excited (and stressed) about graduation and summer programs and weddings and jobs. And here is Jesus in the midst of us, mounted high on the cross—a ghastly Roman-style public spectacle. In this first hour of his crucifixion, the only good news is that he won't live out the afternoon. But right now the dying Jesus has a question for us: "Is it nothing to you, this suffering of mine . . . or is it something?" Maybe we are not yet ready to answer.

There is more to Jesus's question. "Look around and see," he says, speaking through these words from the book of Lamentations, "Is any suffering like my suffering?" The obvious answer is "yes." Jesus suffers as have many humans before and since; two other men, naked and nailed, died alongside him that Friday in Jerusalem. Few of us may have witnessed executions or death by torture, but we know they happen every day in our world, even in our name. Jesus's horrible death was very far from unparalleled in the Roman world, and although we affirm in faith that he died for *us,* there is no evidence that human suffering has been on the decline in the nearly two millennia since. The meaning of the cross is that Jesus shares our suffering fully; he does not end it. So that is one part of an answer to Jesus's question: "Is any suffering like my suffering?" Yes, our suffering is a lot like yours. The deepest pain we bring into this chapel today, the agony of those we hold in our hearts as we sit before this cross—yes, Jesus, it looks remarkably like yours.

Our suffering seems always to come unexpectedly, just as Jesus's death on the Roman cross came as a bitter surprise to those who were expecting the messiah to rescue Israel from Roman oppression (Luke 24:21). Have you noticed? So often suffering comes when we are looking eagerly for something else: a new phase of life, not a terminal diagnosis; safe delivery of a longed-for child, not wrenching loss; a nurturing marriage, not an intimate form of cruelty; a happy young adulthood, not long, grinding depression; the blessings of peace, not the sudden explosion of war in the streets. One of the cruelest aspects of suffering is that it often comes when we were expecting something else, just when we were counting our blessings and giving thanks to God. That is why Jesus's question from the cross is finally a question about God:

> Is any suffering like my suffering that *he* dealt me,
> that the LORD inflicted on me on the day of his heated wrath?

Now we have come to the really tough part of this question and this day. It is tough, because religious people like us don't like to suggest that God has some part to play in our suffering. We simply don't know where to go with the thought that God has somehow allowed the worst thing we can imagine to happen. We are afraid of the overwhelming anger we might feel if we let that thought into our minds and hearts. And so, "Hush . . . , hush," we say to ourselves and each other, "Don't go there."

While we are busy banishing that thought, hushing our anger, the Bible is paying no attention to us. It is broadcasting terrible cries of anguish and

bewilderment, accusations directed against God. We hear them from psalmists; from prophets, especially Jeremiah; from Job and Lamentations. We hear
Jesus's own cry from the cross: "My God, my God, why have you abandoned
me?" Taking their cue from that cry from the cross, Christians through the
ages have not been afraid to say that these terrible words from the third chapter
of Lamentations sound just like Jesus on the cross, having his say about God:

> He has shattered my bones . . .
> He has walled me in so I cannot break out . . .
> He shuts out my prayer . . .
> He makes me the target for his arrows . . .
> He has filled me with bitterness . . .

So the biblical witness and the church's tradition together declare this
truth about the suffering of the faithful: it often feels like abandonment by
God; or worse, like God is aiming at you with a deadly weapon. This poet of
Lamentations screams out the truth that we good churchgoers try so hard not
to admit to ourselves and each other: if you have loved and trusted God for a
long time, then acute, prolonged suffering feels like divine attack.

That is part of the truth that the biblical writers dare to utter, though not
the whole truth. Suffering is one of the deepest mysteries of life with God.
The writers in both Testaments return to it again and again, because the
agony of suffering in faith—believing that God is implicated in our suffering and yet somehow not being able to give up on God entirely—this is an
abiding problem for us. It is not a problem we solve once and for all, either
as individuals or as a community of faith; it is a problem with which we are
struggling to live. Part of the honest struggle is crying out to God and others
who share both our faith and our outrage. That crying out is itself part of our
answer to Jesus's question: yes, Jesus, my sense of abandonment by God is a
lot like yours.

There is still more to the truth that the poet of Lamentations is disclosing
to us, to get us through another Good Friday, and that truth is this: honest
talk about God and to God in the midst of suffering is the only way to realistic
hope. Did you notice it in our reading? This anonymous sufferer, who sounds
to us so much like Jesus on the cross, says,

> I thought . . . my hope had died before God (3:18)

. . . and then suddenly:

This I recall to my heart—therefore I have hope:
the faithful acts of the LORD are not ended; his mercies are not finished;
they are new every morning.

And now, speaking directly *to* God for the first time:

Great is your faithfulness! (3:21–23)

Now where did *that* come from: hope in God, bursting forth out of the very ground where hope seemed to have died? Is this so-called hope just a pious scam of some ancient poet, or is it real?

We often suppose that hoping is sort of like making a bet, a bet based either on careful assessment of the odds or on magical thinking—you blind yourself to the facts and follow a lucky hunch. But hoping in God is not betting on something; it is *building* on something. The foundation for hope as the biblical writers understand it is the character of God, the ultimate Source of all that is good in this broken world. That process of hope-building is precisely what the poet traces for us. Listen again:

I thought . . . my hope had died before God.
. . . .
This I recall to my heart—therefore I do have hope:
The faithful acts of the LORD are not ended; his mercies are not finished;
they are new every morning. Great is your faithfulness!

Hope may show itself in a sudden burst, as it does here, but nonetheless, it has to be built over time. Lasting hope does not come from a cheerful disposition, an unusually high serotonin level perhaps; it comes from the steady habit of reorienting your whole self to God. Day by day, week by week, in good times and in the very worst, genuine hope comes out of turning our hearts fully toward God—whatever we may be thinking or feeling. Whether we turn to God in joy or sorrow, in anger or bewilderment or gratitude or shame, hope builds. Slowly we add to the almost imperceptibly thin layers of lasting hope each time we turn our hearts honestly and fully toward God.

It is for that reason we call this Friday "Good." Look, the nailed man is turned fully toward God. Incapable of any physical movement, bound to die in the next few hours, he is moving into the arms of God. With every labored breath, through excruciating pain, he is drawing steadily closer to the One toward whom his whole being is oriented in wild and certain hope. Jesus's hope is *fixed on God;* that is its certainty. Jesus's hope is *for us;* that is its wildness. He is there on the cross, we are here in the chapel for just one reason: that he may draw us with him straight into the outstretched arms of God.

Maybe now we are ready to answer his question. Is it nothing to you, all you who pass by, all you who have come to sit for an hour or so before this cross—is it nothing, or is it something? His suffering, his wild and certain hope for us—is it nothing to you, or could it be . . . everything?

Amen.

Making a Marriage That Preaches

Wedding of Melissa Bixler and Jacob Floret,
Truro Anglican Church, Fairfax, Virginia
January 14, 2007

HOSEA 2:16–20; PSALM 67; JOHN 15:8–17; PHILIPPIANS 2:1–11

Addressed to a couple who have given their lives to farming and the care of people with intellectual disabilities, this wedding homily depicts marriage as a workshop within the community of discipleship that specializes in the "art of cherishing." A Christian marriage of mutual cherishing creates an expansive circle of concern for everything in its vicinity, including people, animals, and land. In this way, it manifests God's promise to Israel in Hosea: "I marry you to me forever."

When Melissa and Jacob invited me to preach today, the first thing that came to my mind was, What shall I say?—which to me meant: What should I tell them to do, or not to do? What should I tell them marriage is about? Sounds like a preacher, doesn't it—a middle-aged, married preacher, who is probably just a little *too* accustomed to lecturing?

Happily, before I went too far down that road, which was bound to be tedious for us all, Jacob and Melissa sent me the Scripture readings they had chosen for their wedding. They made their own choices, not from the standard options offered by the *Book of Common Prayer*. And as I read over the texts that speak to them and for them as they begin their marriage, I saw that Melissa and Jacob had in a sense prepared the sermon. Through these passages, they are telling us what, in their understanding, marriage is about—and not just their marriage, but Christian marriage altogether. Theirs is the sermon we need to hear today, not mine. But two people plus a bouquet are a tight fit for a pulpit, so I shall try to put words to Melissa and Jacob's "implied sermon" to this unique congregation, gathered for just this day, to witness and pray for their marriage.

In a nutshell, what they have to say to us is that Christian marriage is about discipleship, as we just heard from the fifteenth chapter of John: "My Father is glorified in this, that you bear much fruit and be my disciples" (15:8). Marriage is about bearing fruit, doing God's work in and for the world. That is why in just a few minutes we shall pray, "Make their life together a sign of Christ's love to this sinful and broken world"—a public sign, visible and intelligible to all, as though Jacob and Melissa were hanging out a shingle advertising the opening of a new shop within the larger community of discipleship, a sign reading, "God's love is practiced here."

If marriage be viewed as a workshop within the community of discipleship, then you might say that it is the shop whose specialty is the craft or art of cherishing. In a few moments the bride and the groom will each make a solemn vow "to love and to cherish" the other until they are parted by death. "Cherish" is a word we don't often use, but it is essential here, for it keeps any of us from misinterpreting the overly familiar word "love"—which in this context does not mean so much an overwhelming emotion as a deliberate and repeated act. Cherishing is love that assumes the form of a steady practice, even discipline. Cherishing someone or something means noticing their special qualities, and then doing the work that is required to preserve those qualities, nurture them, and bring them to perfection. In marriage, that means honoring the special qualities of this one person whom God and I have distinguished from all others, so that my actions express my gratitude for this astonishing gift of a life in which I share more deeply than any other, a gift that is renewed to me daily, "until we are parted by death." The Jewish marriage liturgy has just the right language for this, when bride and groom each say to the other, "You are sanctified to me"—"sanctified," set apart, by God and by me, as a gift totally out of the ordinary. Cherishing is simply the active form of gratitude for the gift that never loses its capacity to surprise and delight.

The aim of this mutual cherishing within the context of Christian marriage is not that bride and groom should perfect a state of mutual self-absorption. Exactly the opposite: the art of cherishing is perfected as the circle of concern and active care is extended outward. Thus Paul instructs the disciples at Philippi: "Let each of you look not to your own interests but to the interests of others" (Phil. 2:4). All of us know something of Jacob and Melissa's already well-developed capacity to show active care for family and friends, including their vulnerable friends at L'Arche Nehalem; I have seen Melissa's remarkable ability to comfort and encourage first-year Hebrew students (the most desperate of individuals), even when she herself stood in need of comfort. But mind what they say to us today through these readings, especially the passage from

Hosea: the circle of cherishing extends beyond the Christian community or even the human community, to include also our suffering earth. The prophet articulates God's "marriage vow" to the people and land of Israel: "I marry you to me forever" (Hos. 2:21 [2:19 Eng.]), and in that wedding ceremony even the field animals, and the birds, and the earthworms and the microbes—"the creeping things of the soil," as Hosea calls them (2:20 [2:18 Eng.])—all are drawn into the circle of commitment and active concern. God marries them all. I have never before heard that Scripture passage read at a wedding, but then I have never before attended a farmer's wedding. It speaks the truth that all farmers, Jacob included, know in their bones: cherishing the fertile earth is part of the work of every good marriage, and to fail in that is possibly the worst form of ingratitude of which humans are capable, because ultimately that failure is the most destructive of everything that God has made and cherishes.

I hope I have expressed some of what Melissa and Jacob want us to understand today, as we witness their vows and share their joy. But my words are just a tiny part of their sermon about discipleship. Most of that sermon they are preaching through their actions. They began preaching about discipleship some months ago, in Portland, as they joined in the work of the L'Arche community and in the love that fills that home. They have preached on the farm, harvesting vegetables with joy and thanksgiving. In recent weeks they have preached in the homes of their families, as they prepared for this day and, more importantly, helped two families grow into one.

Jacob and Melissa, I dare say that all of us are here today, with bells on, because we believe that the sermon of your shared life speaks the truth. And that is the essence of our prayer for you, that the sermon you preach throughout your life together may be true, truer and deeper than either of you could preach alone, and so, through you, God will be glorified. Glory be to God, whose power, working in you, can do infinitely more than we can ask or imagine. Glory be to God, from generation to generation in the church, and in Christ Jesus for ever and ever (see Eph. 3:20–21).

Amen.

The Good News of Judgment

Yale Divinity School, New Haven, Connecticut
November 4, 1993

AMOS 5:18–24

The prophet Amos would be mystified by modern Christian attempts to separate judgment from justice. Both terms are translated from the same biblical Hebrew word, mishpat, *and function as interrelated aspects of God's dominion over the world. By reviving their conceptual reciprocity, this sermon reveals that God's judgment can even be an occasion for celebration, since everything in creation will finally appear in history "with the value it has in the eyes of the Creator." Though the pressure of God's nearness may be painful for us, it is finally a merciful thing, for we need the light of God's judgment to reveal the way of justice.*

Let justice roll on like water,
And righteousness like an ever-flowing stream.

It is a curious fact that the English words "justice" and "judgment" are both expressed in Hebrew by a single word, *mishpat*. It is curious, because from the standpoint of modern theology, those two concepts could not be farther apart, as is evident from the church's preaching. Preachers of judgment and preachers of justice tend to cluster on opposite sides of the theological spectrum. Judgment preachers have a strong sense of the majesty of God, and they generally envision the human encounter with God's majesty in personalistic terms; they speak of the salvation of souls, the promise or forfeit of eternal life. Justice preachers, on the other hand, tend to have a more horizontal perspective, asserting the demand for justice in terms of human systems, with only occasional glances to the reality of God's coming judgment. And, of course, the middle of the judgment-justice spectrum is occupied by those preachers (often, although by no means exclusively, Anglican) who eschew both terms as being in distinctly poor theological taste.

The wide separation of these two aspects of the single Hebrew concept of *mishpat* would have mystified Amos, for both judgment and justice appear continually together and interwoven throughout his prophecy. Amos was, as far as we know, the first to declare God's judgment upon the nation Israel:

> Woe to those who have their appetite set for the day of the LORD!
> What's this to you—the day of the LORD?
> It is darkness and not light.
> As when a person flees from the lion—and the bear runs into him;
> Or comes into the house, and leans his hand against the wall—and the
>   snake bites him!
> Is it not darkness, the day of the LORD, and not light? gloom, and not
>   radiance to him? (Amos 5:18–20)

So Amos preaches judgment; but equally, he is among the prophets the preacher of social justice par excellence:

> Woe to those who lie upon beds of ivory and loll upon their couches,
> . . . who pick tunes on the harp,
> . . . drink wine in bowls and with the finest oils anoint themselves.
> . . . Therefore they shall go into exile at the head of the exiles. (6:4–7)

For Amos, judgment and justice are two sides of the same coin—or, better, two aspects of God's dominion over the world. And if it is hard for us to see that, I suspect that is because very many of us, on both the right and the left in the church, have an inadequate concept of God's judgment, which is surely one of the central terms of the Bible. In a nutshell, judgment/*mishpat* is God's rule over the whole created order, God's exquisite, impartial attention to every single person and thing. The psalmist exults that God is coming to judge the earth; and from a cosmic perspective, that is very good news, so the fields and forests are happy about it, even if human beings have qualms. God's coming to judge the earth means that irresistibly, gradually, and maybe not slowly, all things are being drawn into immediate relationship with God. In the Judgment, everything appears for the first time in history as it really is, with the value it has in the eyes of the Creator. On Judgment Day, we may imagine that the world will be completely awash with light, just as it was in the days of creation. Mountains and hills, cedar trees, waterfalls, and wildcats will stand in sharp outline. The glory they give to God by sheer beauty of being will then be fully evident, the shadows cast over them by human exploitation finally dissipated.

For humans, also, the experience of judgment means being drawn into immediate relation to God, being bathed in that clarifying light, seeing ourselves at last as God sees us. And that is why for humanity judgment is inevitably painful. Because, unlike waterfalls and wildcats, we have the capacity to shape our lives in ways that are offensive to God. It is because of our evil that God is coming to judge the earth, and it is merciful that God is coming. For the purpose of judgment is that whatever evil we have unleashed on the world should be exposed, whatever in us is hateful to God should be opened up for healing. And the good news is that we don't have to wait to die for that to happen. Judgment is in fact an ongoing process, ceaseless as long as we are in this world. Probably for each of us there are a few memorable moments in the course of a lifetime when we are acutely conscious of standing naked and undefended before absolute Truth, although there may be no human witnesses present to testify against us. But the importance of those moments is lost upon us if we believe them to be isolated. The truth is that at every instant we are exposed to God's judgment and can be healed by it if we allow it to search us, bringing to light every habit of body and mind, every aspect of our history, sweet and bitter, every cherished hope and resentment long held. Through God's work of judgment, all that we are is brought to light and examined for its value in the divine realm. It is like the cleaning and repair of a fine watch. The thing must first be opened up and taken apart (which is why the beginning of the process is so painful), the grime cleaned off, the bent parts straightened or discarded. That is God's work of dispersion, dispersing evil; it takes time, it hurts, and we must endure it if we are indeed to be brought into intimate relationship with God and be wholly useful in God's service.

It is worth dwelling on this concept of *mishpat,* not only because it is so central to the Bible (although that is probably the best reason to dwell on it), but also because Yale Divinity School is a place where you should expect to see an outbreak of *mishpat*—in both senses, of judgment and justice—which is what makes this such a difficult and extraordinarily hopeful place to be. You might think of this as something like the house you run into to get away from the bear, after you've already had a close escape from the lion. I assume you came here and are willing to do all this work and spend all this money in order to stay, because you correctly perceive that, bad as things are here, they are worse almost every place else.

Speaking personally but perhaps not idiosyncratically, I began my own seminary study convinced, as I still am, that we face a reckoning in our destructively consumerist society, and also in a church that is on the whole distracted from the task of Christian discipleship. It was with huge relief and, if I am honest, some measure of grim satisfaction that I slammed the seminary door on the lion of rampant secularism and the bear of phlegmatic religiosity and settled down to watch the Day of the Lord come, myself surrounded by good books and kindred souls—which is to say, intelligent, seriously religious people. Of course, I was only setting myself up for the snakebite.

Now this is crucial to understand: in a place like this the snakebite is no accident; it is the point. The piercing pain of the first encounter with God's judgment, the snakebite, is the point of our coming here. Listen: every day here, in chapel, in dorm rooms, in classrooms, at meals and public gatherings, repeatedly we invoke the presence of God. If even a fraction of those prayers are answered, then we will surely feel the pressure of God's nearness; and how can we not feel that pressure as pain? For as those who are experienced in the spiritual life teach us, the pain of coming close to God is no less than the pain of alienation. It is painful to catch glimpses of ourselves as God must see us, painful to take offense at attitudes and behaviors that we formerly took for granted in ourselves, painful to take deeper offense at ourselves than we do at others. Yet we feel God's mercy precisely in the pain of self-offense, for it is a sign that God has indeed drawn near. And further, the snakebite is part of God's work in equipping us for ministry; for only those who have personally felt the pain of God's nearness can pursue justice without arrogance.

The pursuit of justice is nothing more than the flip side of the experience of judgment. Justice is correspondent living, making our lives accord with the loving, rigorous process by which everything is coming into immediate relationship with God. In other words, God's *mishpat,* judgment, finds its fulfillment in our *mishpat,* justice. So when we "do justice," we're not inventing anything, adding any new element or system to make the world run better. Doing justice is much more a matter of stopping whatever we are doing that impedes every creature from being immediately touched by God's love. Doing justice is in a sense getting out of the way, so that God's "*mishpat* may roll on like water, and righteousness like a perpetual torrent"—constant, ever-flowing, powerful to heal and freshen our world.

Doing justice then requires that we observe with care God's respectful love for the whole created order, so that gradually we may become capable of practicing such love ourselves. In other words, justice begins with contemplation, attention to the quality of God's love. It is that connection between justice and contemplation that lies behind Amos's attacks on the Israelites' insincere worship:

> I hate, I detest your holy days,
> I won't even catch the whiff of your assemblies. . . .
> Take away from me the clamor of your songs;
> I won't listen to the tunes on your harps,
> But let justice roll on like water,
> And righteousness like a perpetual torrent. (5:21–24)

Amos is often taken to be anti-cult, sort of a proto-Quaker, but I think that misses the point. It is more likely that Amos feels God's rage because he knows precisely the value of public worship: it is the time for the whole community to contemplate God's *mishpat* and together lay the foundation for its own acts of imitation. Public worship is the only fully adequate way to prepare for the public practice of justice. True worship opens a channel in our midst, so God's *mishpat* flows out through our acts of justice, our acts of respectful, loving attention to every single person and thing.

And that is the key to whether our worship is indeed working. It is a question that every worshiping body ought to be asking with regularity: Is our worship working—that is, is worship issuing in justice? It is largely because of the centrality of worship to our common life that Yale Divinity School is a particularly sensitive testing and training ground for justice. You will perhaps never again be in a situation where people are as wildly diverse in their deep convictions and commitments as we are here. This presents real problems for creating something that can meaningfully be called "Christian community." Yet at the same time it offers extraordinary opportunities for the practice of justice.

Is our worship working; are we just toward one another? On the whole, we do a fair job of practicing tolerance within this community. But the pressure of God's nearness, as it is felt painfully and joyfully within the body of Christ—the pressure of God's nearness demands much more than a cool endurance of those whom we believe to be wrong (and, if pressed, whom we frankly dislike). God's nearness demands that we search our hearts and open the locked doors that impede the free flow of *mishpat*. Is our worship working? Is the tide of prayer within these walls gradually eroding the prejudices, the pre-judgments with which we would anticipate and override God's judgment? Is worship enabling me not to look nervously past those who differ drastically from myself but rather to look *at* them, in some feeble (perhaps) but nonetheless earnest imitation of God's passionate, exquisite regard for the well-being of every child? Is our worship working beyond these walls? Is contemplation strengthening us to turn outward in costly and loving response to the whole created world? For if that is not happening, then our worship, indeed all that we do here, is nothing more than a quaint and ultimately tragic form of self-consolation. But if our worship is working, then we are surely growing toward what is coming; as individuals and as a community we are growing toward that day that is coming and maybe not slowly, when the whole world will be awash with God's *mishpat*, bathed in the clarifying and healing light of Christ. "Amen, so be it, do come, Lord Jesus. The grace of the Lord Jesus be with all. Amen" (Rev. 22:20–21).

The Compassion Architect

Yale Divinity School Alumni Convocation, New Haven, Connecticut
October 15, 2009

JONAH 3-4

Jonah's initial refusal to prophesy to Nineveh was not without reason. The Ninevites were ruthless conquerors whose enduring prosperity was due, in part, to their annihilation of ten tribes of Israel. After Nineveh repents, a resentful Jonah questions whether God has any standards of justice. God appeals to Jonah's own sense of compassion for the shade plant, in order to reveal a stunning truth: God is a "compassion architect" whose love for everything in the sphere of his creation is even more determinative for salvation than covenantal relationship.

If you've read Jonah, you have to ask: Does God have any standards at all? Standards for salvation I mean. If we are total SoBs, can we still be saved? Or more to the point, if *they* are total SoBs, can they still be saved? That is precisely what is at stake in God's acceptance of the Ninevites' act of contrition, to the disgust of the prophet Jonah. The story of Jonah may be a funny, fanciful tale, a kind of extended *midrash,* but the theological question it treats is serious and firmly grounded in Israel's historical experience, for among the several nasty enemies of ancient Israel, the Ninevites were likely the worst of the lot. As you know, the Ninevites—the great king of Assyria and his henchmen—were merciless butchers and builders of empire. They wreaked havoc on peoples and nations from India to Egypt, deporting populations en masse and importing new ones into conquered regions. Thus the great king of Assyria created empire by destroying national identity and, along with it, religious identity. The ten lost tribes of Israel were not accidentally misplaced; like countless other small people-groups, they were annihilated by the great king whose capital city was Nineveh.

To add insult to very substantial injury, the Ninevites prospered; for an excruciatingly long time (three centuries or more) they fared too well for any savvy Israelite not to wonder about the justice of God. The longstanding dominance of the Assyrian empire was, from an Israelite perspective, something that God might well be expected to answer for, and the hapless prophet Jonah is the guy who takes that job upon himself. When he sees the Ninevites successfully using sackcloth and ashes to elude the destruction that God has decreed for them, Jonah tells it like it is:

> Well, God, isn't this just what I said when I was still on my own land? That's why I up and ran for Tarshish—because I know that you are "a gracious and merciful God, patient and full of covenantal love, who changes his mind about evil." (4:2)

Any covenantally minded Israelite would hear the subtext of Jonah's objection: "They savage us, and then they say they're sorry—and you just cave, overlooking centuries of atrocities in exchange for one fancy fast. Do you have any standards at all, God?" Jonah wants to get out of God's service, for after all, what is the point of serving a God who has no standards, no justice? What is the point of Torah, of commandments, of covenant? What is the point of a lifetime of obedience, if the Ninevites' eleventh-hour repentance is effective for salvation?

That same question might occur to any one of us, even if our circumstances are less extreme than Jonah's. Your presence in this chapel—whether you are alums, current students, staff or faculty, spouses, or longtime friends—represents a commitment to long-term service, and such service is inevitably costly (if also, by God's grace, rewarding). Doubtless some of you have pretty dramatic stories about the changes and sacrifices that brought you recently or once-upon-a-time to Yale Divinity School, into some form of Christian ministry. You are preparing for or already engaged in work that pays (I dare say) considerably less than other jobs for which your brains would qualify you. You might have gotten a degree from Yale's law school or business school or medical school. If this is, say, your fifth reunion, your student loans would be paid off by now. If it is your twenty-fifth, then you could be retired by now, or donating an endowed chair. So you have a perspective that lets you appreciate Jonah's objection—although I am not of course suggesting that well-paid doctors, lawyers, and business executives are the moral equivalent of Ninevites. The crucial question is: What is the point of trying to shape your whole life in accordance with God's will, if the same end could be achieved as economically as the Ninevites did it? If it is possible to win God over with a single pious gesture, then why not serve your own interests rather than God's, at least up until the last minute?

This is the prophetic objection that God addresses when Jonah is pouting under his withered shade plant, in the memorable exchange that brings the book to a close:

And God said to Jonah, "You're good and angry over that plant, aren't you?"

And he said, "Yes, I'm good and angry, enough to die."

And Yhwh said, "*Attah hasta. You* felt protective toward that plant, though you did not labor over it nor grow it, which appeared and vanished between one night and the next. *Va'ani lo' ahus . . . ?* And *I,* I should not feel protective toward Nineveh, the great city that has in it more than 120,000 people who don't know their right from their left—plus a lot of livestock?" (4:9–11)

We always snicker at the livestock, but I want to spend a few minutes thinking about why God throws that in as a parting shot. Parting shots are important in the Bible. To urbanites like me and most of you, God's reference to livestock seems like an amusing non sequitur, but most Israelites were farmers, and I suspect they heard it differently. God talks to Jonah the way one talks to a farmer; the book of Kings tells us that Jonah was from the Galilean farming village of Gat Hepher (2 Kings 14:25). So in order to understand God's appeal to Jonah, you have to ask, What does livestock mean to a farmer? This above all: animals require care, daily care, or they die. Cows and sheep and goats are not pets, and a farmer might not claim to love them, but nonetheless they elicit a certain kind of protectiveness, even compassion. My brother has a cow, and he does not stay away from home for more than one night. He is not a particularly tender-hearted person; daily care is simply the deal he has with this cow. He feels protective toward her, exactly the feeling the biblical storyteller designates with the repeated verb *hus.* Just as Jonah is protective toward the plant, so God is protective toward the Ninevites and their livestock.

Now all this puts in a somewhat different light our question about whether God has standards. God has compassion on the Ninevites, but *not* because they meet some moral standard that is the prerequisite for salvation. No, God has compassion on the Ninevites because they are there, within the sphere that God has marked out for protection: creation itself. They are creatures, just like their herd animals, and God is hardwired for caring about the creatures—this is one thing that Jonah's story tells us about this God whom we have committed to serve.

And here is a second thing, even more important. Notice that God speaks to the disgruntled Jonah exactly the way any one of us would talk to an estranged friend. We've all been in God's situation: there has been a serious disagreement, and we are trying to explain to our alienated friend how we are thinking, hoping she can appreciate it, even if she does not agree, in order that love may continue between us.

That is how God appeals to Jonah, as a friend, and this is the crucial clue to what covenant relationship is good for. As we have seen, covenantal obedience is not what saves the Ninevites. This storyteller anticipates the apostle Paul in suggesting that covenantal obedience is not the key to salvation; God is the key to salvation. The Ninevites are saved solely because God feels protective toward them, and on that score God makes no particular distinction between them and their cows, nor even between Ninevites and Israelites. But when it comes to friendship, there God does make a distinction. Note that God never speaks directly to the great king of Assyria, nor to any other Ninevite. God speaks only to Jonah, the friend whom God has chosen. God pursues Jonah, first when he runs away in a ship and then later when he turns away and pouts. Perhaps God needs Jonah in order to reach the Ninevites—I don't know about that. But what is clear is that God wants to have Jonah as an understanding friend. So that is what covenant and a life of service are good for: they bring us into the sphere of friendship with God. "I have called you friends," our Lord said to his disciples (John 15:15). Covenantal relationship brings us into the sphere of intimacy, where God reveals something of the divine mind and appeals to us for understanding.

Curiously, the storyteller does not record how Jonah responds to God's appeal, which stands as the final word in the book. Thus, narratively speaking, God goes unanswered—unless some reader hears the appeal and offers the understanding that betokens love. So Jonah's silence puts the burden of response on us. There are as many possible responses as there are faithful servants and friends of God, and I shall point to just one that our generation of faith might offer, one possible response that reflects the challenge this story addresses to us in the twenty-first century.

Earlier this year a theologian known to the Yale Divinity School community, Dr. Aref Ali Nayed, spoke at a forum sponsored by the Brookings Institute. Asked how we might improve "the dreadful state of relations between Washington and the Muslim world," Dr. Nayed answered that we must fundamentally rethink our understanding of what constitutes security. Rather than relying on a militarized "security architecture" (in General Petraeus's phrase), we must build "a compassion architecture," a solid network of relations based on respectful and compassionate dialogue and habits of living. Such a compassion architecture must be constructed in significant part through the contributions of "religious, spiritual and philosophical communities" such as this one; local churches, mosques, and synagogues must also be engaged. Dr. Nayed observes: "Compassion architecture is built on the *theological fact* that true security can only come from God's own compassion towards humanity and the compassion of humans towards humans."[1]

"Compassion architecture"—isn't that exactly the design for the world that the book of Jonah suggests? God's own compassion, reaching to the ground and spreading through the compassion of humans toward humans—this is the theological fact underlying Jonah's call to prophesy. Later, as he sulks under the withered plant, the prophet is privileged with insight into God's heart, invited to understand and trust the God whose compassion works so largely and so strangely through human beings, including Jonah's own reluctant self.

Through Jonah we have been privileged with insight into God's heart; we know God's desire to be understood, trusted, yes, loved as a friend. God, the great Compassion Architect of our world, is even now awaiting a response. There are as many good responses as there are listening hearts in this chapel. So, in your particular circumstances, by the grace and power of God, what is the best response you can offer this day?

Amen.

---

1. "From Security to Compassion," a statement by Aref Ali Nayed delivered at the U.S.-Muslim World Forum in Doha, February 2009, emphasis added. The full text is available at http://blogs.reuters.com/faithworld/2009/02/19/from-security-to-compassion-a-needed-shift-for-obama-govt/.

Seasonal Tension

St. Paul's Episcopal Church, New Haven, Connecticut
Advent 1, December 1, 1985

ZECHARIAH 14:4–9; LUKE 21:25–31

Advent names a time of tension and dissonance, during which candles symbolizing joy and hope shine next to altars draped in purple, the color of penance. The volatile nature of this liturgical season is appropriate, for the Scriptures describe the coming of God's kingdom with violent, apocalyptic imagery. Those who submit their lives to Advent's demands should expect to experience "the hard and bitter agony which accompanies God's entry into our lives, the birth that feels so much like death." Indeed, reconciliation with God will be painful, but it is the only way to recognize the true light when it finally pierces the darkness.

This is a season of almost intolerable tension. We all feel it: the annual December time crunch, with programs and papers to complete, gifts to buy and mail, planes to catch, celebrations to plan when you're too tired even to think of having fun. For some, the tension has a sharp and wounding edge: the love and joy with which the season is supposed to abound remind us of what we've lost, of those who are no longer with us. For many of us, it is painful at this time to remember last year, or three years ago, or maybe fifteen years ago. We look back with longing at the way the holidays used to be and are stricken again with an acute sense of loss. Or perhaps we mourn what we've never had, feeling that the joy of the season is somehow reserved for other people, the ones with full and happy lives—you know, the normal people, who look ahead with expectation and eagerness.

But the tension of this season is not a personal problem belonging to us solely as individuals; it is pervasive. And while I would be glad to blame just

about anything on the distortion bred of commercial hype and the impossi-
bly diffuse demands of our culture, those also fail to account for the depth of
tension we feel now. For that tension is in no way accidental; it expresses the
essence of this Advent season. The tension we feel is, in the last analysis, a
theological problem; its roots lie in the heart of our faith. Advent is a season
of striking contrasts, of dissonance that cannot be harmonized. In Advent we
gather to light the candle of bright hope, and we drape the church in somber
purple, the color of penance. Purple is the color reserved for the church's two
great penitential seasons, Advent and Lent. It seems somehow incongruous, it
is certainly disturbing, that we wait for our Lord's birth the same way we wait
for his death, waiting in hope and in grief, enduring a season of bitter loss,
painful repentance, and wild expectation for the future.

Our lessons for today reflect that theological tension. We await the Baby
Jesus, but the scriptural images of our Lord's coming are more violent than
any childbirth. Listen again to the prophet Zechariah:

> On that day [the LORD's] feet shall stand on the Mount of Olives,
> which faces Jerusalem on the east,
> and the Mount of Olives shall be split down the middle
> from east to west by a very wide valley . . .
> and you shall flee as you fled from the earthquake in the days of Uzziah
>   king of Judah. Then the LORD my God will come, and all the holy
>   ones with [him]. (Zech. 14:4-5, emended)

This is not exactly the stuff of which Christmas pageants are made. Angels,
manger, and cotton-ball sheep are conspicuously absent. Instead the prophet
shows us the holy hills of Jerusalem, the center of the universe, bursting wide
open at the coming of God. The scene drawn in the Gospel of Luke is equally
cataclysmic:

> There will be signs in sun and moon and stars, and upon the earth anxiety
> of nations in distress at the sound of sea and waves, people fainting from
> fear and foreboding of what is coming on the inhabited world. . . . And
> then they will see "the Son of Man coming in a cloud" with power and
> great glory. (Luke 21:25-27, citing Dan. 7:13)

The Scriptures describe the dawning of a new age that looks terrifyingly
like the end of everything familiar, the kingdom of God rising out of the collapse of the world that we know. Anyone who takes that apocalyptic vision

seriously should be disturbed, shocked, appalled by it. There is nothing gentle about this coming of God into the world. "Your Kingdom come . . ."—do we know what we ask for? With those words we invite total disruption of our carefully constructed lives: we call for a new act of creation that looks from the inside very much like destruction. T. S. Eliot puts stinging words in the mouth of one of the Magi who journeyed to Bethlehem to see the infant Christ:

> . . . I had seen birth and death,
> But had thought they were different; this Birth was
> Hard and bitter agony for us, like Death, our death.[1]

The scriptural readings for Advent confront us persistently with the vision of a new world born only through radical transformation of the old, and it is impossible to exaggerate the effects of that transformation. For when God enters fully into the world, nothing, nothing remains unchanged. And there is another side to that: when we enter fully into relationship with God, everything is at stake, everything is called forth for reexamination and transformation. I'm convinced that spiritual transformation, like orthodontia, generally feels awful while in progress.

A few years ago a good friend of mine suffered a nervous breakdown. I was stunned, because she had always seemed frighteningly well-balanced. She is advanced in her profession, remodels her own home, is active in Sunday school teaching and the vestry, and, naturally, she runs. What I did not know about my friend was that she was a battered child. She herself had almost forgotten until, as she explained it to me, "I tithed to the church, and I went crazy." Through her tithing she expressed a deepened commitment to God, and that action had a bizarre effect upon her life. Suddenly childhood memories that she had suppressed for years came back with terrifying vividness. She could not control the memories; she had either to face them or to be overwhelmed. Three years of psychoanalysis have enabled her to face the terror of her childhood and the scars she still carries. It has been a hard journey of self-discovery and change; it has also been a journey of faith.

Probably my friend understands a lot about the violence of the apocalyptic vision. She has experienced the hard and bitter agony that accompanies God's entry into our lives, the birth that feels so much like death. She knows about collapse of the old order, exposure of the masks, exhaustion of the coping mechanisms, those clever stratagems for hiding from others—and from

1. T. S. Eliot, "Journey of the Magi," in *The Complete Poems and Plays, 1909-1950* (New York: Harcourt, Brace and Company, 1952), 69.

ourselves—the depths of suffering and failure. My friend has faced the bitter fact that we in the church prefer to forget, that coming close to God is deeply disruptive, that reconciliation with God is no less painful than separation.

Reconciliation with God: that is what Advent is really about, this season of waiting for God to be born in human flesh. The pain of that reconciliation, the agony of transformation that our world must undergo in order to receive God—that is what is proclaimed in the apocalyptic visions we heard today. Violent upheavals of mountains and valleys, signs in the heavens and crashing of seas—all these attest to the total disruption of our familiar order that attends the coming of God. But the end and purpose of that upheaval is a state of perfect wholeness, as Zechariah proclaims: "On that day the LORD shall be one, and his name one" (14:9). Only when the foundations have been shaken, when the familiar disguises and comfortable idols, all the sources of our alienation, have been shattered and the broken pieces of our lives gathered into God, only then is our reconciliation complete. Reconciliation with God is no less painful than separation. The pain of that reconciliation is the heart of fierce tension that grips us this Advent season.

But understanding that tension does not diminish its force. The disruption caused by God's coming and our alienation is too great for us; we cannot bear it alone. And so we gather together to light a candle in this fearsome time. We come here to find others who know something about darkness and yet dare to look for the light. We come here to wait together. The church might best be defined as the community of those who wait, who remember their losses, acknowledge their failures, their suffering, and their confusion, and yet continue to look for wholeness. I do not know a better Advent text than that written by one of the twentieth century's great theologians, Albert Einstein. He describes his experience in developing the general theory of relativity:

> the years of anxious searching in the dark, with their intense longing, their alternations of confidence and exhaustion, and the final emergence into the light—only those who have themselves experienced it can understand that.[2]

Today the church is gathered around one candle, waiting for the birth of light. Come, Lord Jesus.

Amen.

2. Quoted in Banesh Hoffman and Helen Dukas, *Albert Einstein: Creator and Rebel* (New York: Viking, 1972), 124.

Preaching in Witness to the Triune God

ESSAY

Recently, when asked how I as an Old Testament scholar think about preaching from the New Testament, I had to admit that no answer came to mind, even though I preach from the New Testament with some regularity. The reason I have little to say on the subject is that I do not consider Old Testament preaching and New Testament preaching as distinct activities. If I sometimes speak and write about "Old Testament preaching" as though it were a discrete category within biblical preaching,[1] that is for the pedagogical purpose of addressing a widespread phobia and encouraging preachers to utilize the first 75 percent of the Bible. I see no genuinely theological distinction, because, as a Christian, I necessarily read the Bible in its entirety with reference to the gospel as it appears in both Testaments. That is, I read the Bible as a single story of alienation and ultimately reconciliation between God and humanity, a story whose focal point and culmination is the full self-revelation of God in Jesus Christ. The story has a single main character, and I begin most of my sermons by naming that "character" from the pulpit, in accordance with the traditional baptismal formula: "In the name of the Father, and the Son, and the Holy Spirit."

Some of my sermons that focus on a New Testament passage follow. What strikes me most in rereading them is how closely they resemble the larger number of sermons that treat primarily an Old Testament text. All of them

---

1. See the essay in this volume, "Witnessing to God in the Midst of Life: Old Testament Preaching," and also my books *Imagination Shaped: Old Testament Preaching in the Anglican Tradition* (Valley Forge, PA: Trinity Press International, 1995) and *Wondrous Depth: Preaching the Old Testament* (Louisville: Westminster John Knox, 2005).

deal with the same recurrent themes of the whole biblical story: creation and new creation; suffering and death, redemption and resurrection; exile and self-isolation in sin; God's passionate desire to be reconciled with us; the glory of God revealed in our world. The church regards the story as complete, in the sense that it is fully written in the two Testaments. But if the canon is closed, nonetheless the biblical story is not finished; it is still being retold and enacted and commented upon, as it must be, as long as the church awaits the consummation of history. The fact that the biblical story is *complete but not finished* is the point of the Maundy Thursday sermon here ("Divine Drama"), and indeed of Christian preaching altogether.

Because the story is complete and its main lines are broadly familiar, preachers and readers of the Bible may enter at any point and start to dig down. It is neither more nor less appropriate to enter the story through Revelation than through Genesis, through Psalms than through 1 Corinthians. If we inhabit the story as a whole, then one scriptural memory triggers another. Most of my sermons delve into a single text while referencing several others, directly and indirectly. Very often these secondary references are designed to move the hearers' attention across the two Testaments. Preaching widely across the canon is necessary in order to illumine the canon's unified witness to the Triune God. Because the biblical writers themselves are continually entering into conversation with each other, consciously and unconsciously, it is the role of the Christian preacher to bear witness to that conversation as we see it within each of the two Testaments and between them.

Becoming more skilled at following that conversation should be one of the preacher's highest priorities, although developing that skill fully is the work of a lifetime of listening. We are listening to the many ways, often subtle, in which the biblical writers interact, looking for connections that may extend the theological scope of the text at hand, the main preaching text, without sacrifice of precision and plausibility. Drawing those connections precisely means becoming sensitive also to the different nuances and angles of vision that characterize each of the different parts of the canon, even sometimes within a single book. Biblical preaching of that kind—the only kind that merits the name—is an art form, which is to say that it requires imagination disciplined by knowledge and sound judgment. Practicing this particular art moderately well is a realistic goal for any preacher, and a holy obligation.

The kind of knowledge requisite to become a competent practitioner is broad and close familiarity with the Bible, with theological traditions and how they have interpreted the Bible over centuries, as well as with currents of modern theology and hermeneutics. Learning to exercise the kind of judgment that makes such knowledge useful to hearers is, like other forms of learning, largely a matter of trial and error. I recently had a conversation with a first-year divinity student in my introductory-level Old Testament interpretation class. It was five or six weeks into the fall term, and he was writing his first essay, a theological overview of the book of Deuteronomy. For the assignment I had posed the question, "How does the book represent what God is like, how God is known in the world?" "I am almost finished," he said to me as we walked in together one morning; "I just have to figure out where Jesus is in there—maybe in the blood?" The suggestion surprised me, since as a class we had not spoken about figural interpretation. I commented that preachers in the early church might well find Jesus in the blood of sacrifice in Deuteronomy, but that I would look to draw the connection in the opposite direction: Where does Deuteronomy appear in the Gospel accounts? What do the evangelists show us about how Jesus reads Torah? One answer would be, Jesus's several replies to the devil's temptations, quoted directly from "what is written in Scripture," namely Deuteronomy (8:3, 6:16, 6:13; see Matt. 4:4, 7, 10 and Luke 4:4, 8, 12). There are numerous other instances of Jesus speaking the language of Deuteronomy—for example, in the call to be "perfect" (*teleoi*), as God is perfect (Matt. 5:48; compare Deut. 18:13, where the adjective is *tamim*, "possessed of perfect integrity"), or in his warning against false prophets, even those capable of producing "signs and portents" (Mark 13:22; compare Deut. 13:2–4).

My student and I had different instincts about how to connect Deuteronomy and the Gospel accounts of Jesus, and that is fair enough; there is no single right way to read the Bible or any part of it. A preacher might experiment with these different approaches to Deuteronomy (sometimes the study and small teaching groups are better places for experimentation than the pulpit!). But the crucial point is that the preacher keep trying, with a wide variety of texts, to gain insight into how the Triune God is made known—and trying new approaches as the preacher's biblical and theological education continues through a lifetime. Looking regularly for how Jesus, or the evangelists, or Paul and other New Testament writers read the Hebrew Scriptures might go a long way toward refreshing and deepening New Testament preaching.

Preaching that probes deeply into biblical texts week after week remains a relative rarity, even though many preachers spent much time in seminary acquiring the tools to do just that. What they seem not to have acquired is the confidence that if they do that, people will be genuinely interested and edified, and so they are not motivated to hone their exegetical skills, or even to retain them. I have considered elsewhere the preacher's (misplaced) fear, a few years out of seminary, of having "forgotten too much" about the Old

Testament to say anything accurate. The counterproductive result is that many avoid the kind of regular engagement with Israel's Scriptures that gradually builds competence, confidence, and even love—the true love that one has for a friend, who is valued precisely in his complexity.[2] Here I would suggest that the greatest hindrance to deep engagement with New Testament texts is exactly the opposite, namely, over-familiarity, taking the friend for granted. Harboring the illusion that everything essential about a given passage is easily discovered and made evident, the preacher moves quickly over and past the details of the text, never to return, seeking novelty instead in a string of inspirational thoughts and stories.

I confess that my own seminary education in New Testament exegesis was cursory; it is largely through preaching that I have gained practice and interest in exploring its variety and theological depths. The literary means that guide my exploration are the same ones I often use with Old Testament texts, as evidenced in the sermons that follow here. With Matthew's story of the Magi ("Stargazers"), I notice a central element of its *narrative structure,* namely, the contrasting attitudes of the characters in the vignette: the Magi's wild joy versus the terror of Herod "and all Jerusalem with him" (Matt. 2:3). *Reading intertextually across the canon,* specifically passages from Proverbs and Romans, I discover the reason for their joy: it is anchored by hope in God.

A number of my sermons develop *a single line or image* from either a New Testament narrative or an epistle. Here the familiarity of the New Testament may work to the preacher's advantage. Preaching on the Beatitudes ("Faithful Mourning"), which have been heard countless times, there is no need for blanket coverage. Rather, the goal is illumination of an enigma, which repetition may have only made more frustrating: What basis in reality is there for the blessing that Jesus pronounces on the mournful, for those who live fully into their sadness? Again, a sermon on 1 Peter ("Easter Exiles") takes seriously its opening address to "exiles" living in Asia Minor (1 Pet. 1:1), considering what that could mean for twenty-first-century American Christians, including those at home in a beautiful Nashville cathedral. A surprising number of people embrace the image of exile when it is offered on solid scriptural grounds, starting with exile from Eden. They are relieved to have a scriptural diagnosis of their restlessness and unease, grateful to find themselves in the good company of the saints. As a preacher, I am drawn to epistles for the same reason I am drawn to psalms: they show the daily struggles and extraordinary convictions

2. Ellen F. Davis, "Losing a Friend: The Loss of the Old Testament in the Church," *Pro Ecclesia* 9, no. 1 (Winter 2000): 73-84.

of ordinary people, the squabbles and vision of the worshiping community in nearly every place and time.

In another essay in this volume, I mention the value of historical criticism for informing the preacher's imagination and countering the moralistic impulse to impose our cultural assumptions and judgments upon the Bible and the social world it ("originally") represents.[3] My own interest and competence in preaching from a wider range of New Testament texts have increased as I have paid attention to the growing body of scholarship about *the social world of the New Testament*. That work helps us see ways in which the experience of Jews and Christians in Greco-Roman society resembles that of many people in our society. It was a violent, highly militarized world in which human life and labor were often held to be cheap; an increasingly urbanized society with huge and growing economic disparities, instability, and collapse in many local communities; a culture that held the faith of Jews and Christians to be contemptible if not illegal and worked actively to eradicate it. That social situation provides a more interesting and "relevant" background than the *Left Behind* series for preaching the prophecy of John on Patmos ("Worship the Lamb"). It also means that the preacher who takes on 1 Peter's address to exiles ("Easter Exiles") cannot focus entirely on metaphorical or psychological interpretations of that experience, while ignoring social and economic forms of marginalization in our own culture.

Preaching the biblical story as a unified whole, as a witness to the Triune God, begins for most as a conscious discipline, both spiritual and intellectual. It takes work to get the hang of it, and it takes conviction to stay at the work. But in time discipline becomes habit, and conviction becomes joy. May it be so for each of us.

3. See "Holy Preaching," pp. 89–105 above.

Stargazers

Duke Chapel, Durham, North Carolina
Epiphany, January 5, 2003

MATTHEW 2:1–12

Why were the Magi so overjoyed by a birth that seemed, to ordinary eyes, to be a relatively minor miracle of God? Practiced in the art of astronomy, they were adept at looking into the darkness and centering their lives on the light that leads to God. Perhaps this small band of "stargazers" from the East already grasped the wisdom of Proverbs: "The hope of the righteous is gladness." Preached on the eve of the Second Iraq War, this Epiphany sermon introduces us to Middle Eastern dignitaries who show that we have an alternative to fear. They teach us that gladness may be the fruit of hope, not only as a reward for faithfulness in the end, but as a real possibility in the present.

"Seeing the star [stop], they [the Magi] were wildly happy" (Matt. 2:10)—but why? This is what I want to explore with you today: What lay behind the Magi's joy that night? Because, when you stop to think about it, there is no obvious reason those astrologers from the East should have been so wildly excited. They had not seen anything that ordinary eyes would interpret as a revelation of God. They had seen a star rising in the East, a tiny point of bright light. And because they were trained to take the heavenly bodies very, very seriously, they followed it, probably hundreds of miles: from Mesopotamia (the ancestral home of astrologers) across the northern edge of the Syrian desert, down into Roman Palestine, until they got to the little and not-obviously-distinguished city of Bethlehem. Then that star somehow led them through the maze of narrow streets and stopped over one particular house. (The evangelist Luke envisions a stable, of course, but for Matthew it's just an ordinary house.) And at that point those Magi "rejoiced with a really, really big joy," as the Gospel literally reads. "And coming into the house, they saw the child with Mary his mother; and falling down, they worshiped him." Those highly educated foreigners, distinguished enough to be summoned for a private consultation with King Herod—they were the very first ones to worship our Lord. "And opening their treasures, they presented him" with tribute fit for a king: gold, frankincense, and myrrh. They took that baby for the real article, "the one born king of the Jews," whose birth prophets had foretold—yet, remember, they had heard no angel choir (again, that's in Luke's Gospel). All Matthew's Magi saw was an ordinary Jewish mother with her baby. And even if we agree (as I suspect we would) that there is simply no such thing as an ordinary baby; and even if we imagine further that Jesus was maybe an especially beguiling infant (why not?)—even so, this birth would seem, to ordinary eyes, to be a small-scale wonder of God.

So my question is this: How, having seen so little that was identifiably the fulfillment of God's promises—could they feel so much joy? That may be something more than an idle question, because it seems to me that for many of us (and I include myself) joy in Christ has more the status of a pious wish than a deeply felt reality. And I wonder how those Magi—who knew so much less than any one of us knows about the life, death, and resurrection of this one born king of the Jews—I wonder how they felt something that I, with all my theological education, feel all too little: that really, really big joy in the Christ child. I think the answer must be this: the Magi had mastered the art of hoping in God. It is a saying in the book of Proverbs that leads me to draw that connection between joy and hope. I think it is the boldest teaching on hope in the whole Bible; listen: "The hope of the righteous is gladness" (Prov. 10:28). Their hope is gladness—the saying is so bold that one very popular translation changes it into something more cautious and commonsensical. The New Revised Standard Version renders it, "The hope of the righteous *ends in* gladness." Now that's a very reasonable idea; it makes sense that the righteous will *in the end* be rewarded by actually getting what they hope for. But the proverb as it stands says a lot more about people like our Magi. "The hope of the righteous *is* gladness"—already now, in the present tense. Those who train their sights on the faithfulness of God, "the righteous"—they already experience joy, even before they see their hopes fulfilled, even if they never live to see (in this world, at least) the clear fulfillment of all that God has promised. The righteous are those who trust God so much that they have learned, as the apostle Paul says, to "rejoice in hope" itself (Rom. 12:12). That is the kind of joy that burst forth that night on the streets of Roman-occupied Bethlehem, like flowers springing suddenly out of stone pavement. It was joy that takes root in nothing more (or less) substantial than hope itself.

Epiphany is the great season of the church's hope. In this season, all the prayers and Scripture readings aim at nurturing our hope—indeed, at helping us learn the art (because it is an art) of hoping in God. And so it makes perfect sense, when you think about it, that the ones to usher in this season should be Magi, stargazers, for they were masters of an art that opened their minds toward a world beyond our own. That is of course the essence of all true hope: stretching our minds and our faith beyond the confines of what we can clearly see and touch and control.

Therefore the message we get today and in the weeks to come is not one that magnifies our sense of control. The message of Epiphany is *not,* "God is born in Christ, and all's well with this old world." Thank God that's not the intended message. Looking at our world, who would believe it? The message is not even, "Jesus is born, and all's well with us who believe in him." Thank God that's not the message. Looking into our own hearts, who even among us would believe it? Rather, this is the message of Epiphany: "Jesus the Christ is born into our world, and for us who believe in him, there is a clear focus for our hope." Like the Magi who saw his star rise in the East and followed it, we Christians are stargazers, discerning a bright point of light in the darkness and following it as we travel a long and unfamiliar road, guided by the light of the one born king of the Jews.

I think of the people I know who radiate most powerfully what I see as "the joy of Christ"; all of them are, in a sense, stargazers. They are adept at the art of looking into the darkness, finding the one bright point of light that leads to God, and orienting their lives toward it. Of the two people who have been sharing their joy with me most consistently over the last year or so, one of them has been enduring rigorous treatment for cancer; the other is nursing her husband in an advanced state of Alzheimer's. In both cases their joy has much less to do with present circumstances or doctors' prognoses than it does with their continued ability to experience God as faithful, true to the promise of abundant life given in Jesus Christ. In situations that are uncertain and difficult on a daily basis, they nurture a bright hope that often bursts out as a flame of joy and laughter. Thus they attest to the truth of St. Paul's teaching that in the character of the faithful there is a real connection between enduring suffering and hoping in God (Rom. 5). Christian hope is something very different from the natural feeling of elation that comes when things are going our way. No, hope is not a feeling that ebbs and flows. Rather, it is a way of living that we choose; and gradually, day by day, we learn to be graceful in it. Hope is a way of living beyond our own limited vision and natural fears, a way of living into God's faithfulness and there finding fullness of joy forevermore.

Within his brief account of the Magi, Matthew gives us a thumbnail sketch of King Herod, and their intertwined stories show how hope opposes and ultimately, by God's grace, faces down evil—and not only natural evil, like cancer or Alzheimer's, but also the worst human evil, exemplified by Herod, who was not, you know, a real king of the Jews. He was a foreigner, a puppet-king set up by the Romans, an Idumean pretender to the throne of David. When Herod heard about the one whose star had risen in the East, "the one born king of the Jews," he felt his unstable throne shake beneath him. He could read that sign as well as the Magi; it meant that his own days were numbered. So, consumed with fear, Herod launched a desperate new security program. First he tried a closely targeted operation, a "smart bomb"; he tried to get the Magi to give him the baby's exact whereabouts. But when the Magi evaded him, then Herod settled for a general slaughter, killing every child in and around Bethlehem, two years old and under.

History remembers Herod with special loathing. He was a ruthless despot, who did not scruple at murdering his close associates, and the wife on whom he doted, and three of his own sons, because he feared they were plotting against him. It was said of Herod in his own day that it was better to be his sow than his son;[1] the pig in the royal barnyard had a better hope of survival. Yet even if Herod didn't have a friend in the world, or a trusted ally, nevertheless he had companionship in his fear. Matthew's observation is telling: "Herod was terrified, *and all Jerusalem with him.*" Herod could not have secured the deaths of all those children if he were the only one who was afraid. Matthew is pointing to the clearly documented fact that fear is contagious, and it readily crosses party lines. When fear reaches epidemic proportions, as it did that year in Jerusalem, then it inevitably unleashes destruction on a massive scale. "Herod was terrified, and all Jerusalem with him." Fear spreads like plague through an unhealthy system, infecting not only those who are powerless to defend themselves—the Jewish families in Bethlehem—but also the relatively powerful, the ruling elite in Jerusalem, who sensed (with that gut-gripping fear that comes in the middle of the night) the fragility of the base on which their power rested.

So Matthew is giving us an artful picture of two opposed entities: on the one hand, Herod and all Jerusalem; and on the other, the Magi, following the promise of God and one bright point of light as they travel in a country not

---

1. Alan Hugh McNeile, *The Gospel according to Saint Matthew* (London: Macmillan, 1955).

their own. But the Gospel story is artful—and more, it is revelatory—because both halves of the picture tell us something about ourselves. This is not a simple picture of them and us, as we would prefer to believe. Rather, if we read the story deeply and honestly, I think we will identify both with fearful Jerusalem and with hopeful Magi; for they both reveal aspects of our own situation that we have not seen clearly before.

In the fear that grips "all Jerusalem," we see an image of the fear that has grown insidiously to become such a dominant factor in our own public life. Columbine, the Washington sniper, the Twin Towers, global warming, decline in the Dow Jones, Al Qaeda, Saddam Hussein, North Korea—it is a dread litany, highlighting but not exhausting all that we as a people have come to fear, at home and abroad. Like "all Jerusalem," we are afraid even while we are still powerful. We are preparing for war because we are afraid, and because we are powerful. Yet we know that on the other side of that violence we, like Herod, will have no less to fear than we do now.

So there is judgment for us in that picture of Herod and all Jerusalem. Matthew holds it before us like a mirror, challenging us to acknowledge our fear, to recognize the violence that springs from fear and will doubtless perpetuate it. Yet Matthew does not consign us to despair. For alongside that mirror is a second one—you might call it a glass of vision, for it shows us something a little ahead of where we are now. It shows what we as a church can and will look like if we stand against the tyranny of self-perpetuating fear. We will look like the Magi. For those first worshipers of Christ are, of course, the very first biblical image of the church. Look at them: those three travelers in a country not their own, in a land literally governed by fear. Yet, in that country, they constitute a very small but powerful community of resistance. Their hope empowers their refusal to be co-opted by Herod's reign of terror. "The hope of the righteous is gladness"; having experienced the surpassing joy of Bethlehem and knowing it came from God, the Magi listened to the dream that also came from God and warned them not to return to Herod. Instead, they "departed by another road for their own country."

Matthew is showing us a way forward in this Epiphany season, this season of hope in which we are gripped by fear. He challenges us to be the community of resistance that the church has been, he tells us, from the beginning. He challenges us *as a church* to examine and deepen our understanding of the systems that generate fear for ourselves and others. He challenges us *as a church* to find ways out of those systems—not to give way to despair, though the systems are large and powerful, but to find and commit ourselves to the small steps by which we may depart from the country governed by fear and go by another road to our own country, that place we call the kingdom of God. Matthew's Gospel challenges us to live boldly in the hope of the Magi, so that, having rejoiced with them at the first coming of Christ, we may at his second coming know fullness of joy forevermore.

Amen.

Faithful Mourning

Berkeley Divinity School, Yale University, New Haven, Connecticut
February 3, 1993

MATTHEW 5:1–12

Rather than attempting to explain the perplexing Beatitude, "Blessed are those who mourn," this sermon describes two images of faithful mourning. The first description is of an Eastern Orthodox icon of Mary as the Mother of Tenderness, holding the infant Jesus up to her face in sorrow and anticipation of the Passion they will share. The second, from the poet Yevtushenko, is a description of Russian women who, despite mourning their husbands and sons lost to war, offer what little they have to a passing group of exhausted German soldiers. Both portraits exemplify mourning as an active expression of grief that transforms the pain of resentment into an abundance of compassion.

"Blessed are those who mourn, for they shall be comforted."

Surely this is the least attractive and most enigmatic of the Beatitudes. All the other blessed conditions have some romantic appeal: being a peacemaker; hungering and thirsting for righteousness; one can even aspire, somewhat paradoxically, to be meek. While no sane person would wish to be persecuted for our Lord's sake, nonetheless the possibility of consecrating that suffering is well known. But the blessing on the mournful is a conundrum, as is evident from the commentaries. Surely Jesus doesn't mean that sorrow per se is a good thing, indeed, a privileged condition—for the Beatitude could well be translated: "Privileged are those who mourn." Unable to countenance that thought, the commentators try to make sense of the blessing by narrowing its scope. So, for example, the Anchor Bible: "The favor of God does not rest upon the state of mourning *as such,* but upon those who lament the sin which mars God's choice of Israel."[1]

But the Gospel is more radical than the Anchor Bible. It doesn't say, "Blessed are those who mourn over sin, individual or corporate, their own or somebody else's." The radicality of the blessing lies precisely in its lack of specification: "Blessed are those who mourn," full stop. The Gospel implies that the task, even the privilege of the Christian life is not particularly to cheer up, but rather to embrace our sadness and learn to live well with it, live deeply in it.

I'm sure the commentators are right in part, that the blessing on mourners includes the penitent. Obviously there is a healing that comes through genuine sorrow over sin. But much less obvious is the blessing on what you might call innocent grief, in which the mourner bears no real guilt. What is the privilege of the widow; or the child stricken by his parents' divorce, or chronically deprived of attention by a parent's addiction? What is the privilege of the 35-year-old who is dying of AIDS; or the 52-year-old engineer who has been out of work now for fourteen months; or the recent graduate, well-prepared and in debt from study, who cannot find a job? It seems to me that the real test of the Beatitude is represented by these people and all the others who are more victims than perpetrators, who stand more in need of comfort than repentance. And it is worth mentioning also the less dramatic instances of loss that possibly each one of us is now experiencing to a greater or lesser degree. For every change is attended by loss—and individually and as a society our lives are characterized by nothing so much as by change. In the midst of life we are ever in death, and so we are continually charged to face the spiritual challenge of mourning. Even a happy change such as marriage, I now find, provides occasion for mourning. Anyone who knows me even moderately well is aware that my recent adjustment to suburban life is by no means perfect. In my faithful moments, when I'm ready to do some serious work, I actively mourn at least one aspect of the solitary urban life—I had a lot more discretionary time—but when I am lazy, I take the easy way out and simply harbor resentment.

My present experience of loss is relatively trivial and much outweighed by joy, but nonetheless I think it shows the clear alternatives that the Beatitude urges us to confront. On the one hand, active mourning for what is lost, what

---

1. W. F. Albright and C. S. Mann, *Matthew,* Anchor Bible 26 (Garden City: Doubleday, 1971), 46; alternatively, it is suggested that the blessed "mourn because of the power of the wicked" (Frederick William Danker, *A Greek-English Lexicon of the New Testament and Other Early Christian Literature* [Chicago: University of Chicago Press, 1979], 795).

never happened or will not happen again, mourning for ourselves and for the world; on the other hand, the easy wallow in resentment. People in the ancient world understood better than we, I think, that deep mourning is something you do, actively; it's a responsibility to be assumed. So there were rituals to be performed: tearing your clothes and heaping ashes on your head, wailing, dancing, or just sitting. Job's friends sat with him in silent grief for seven days and seven nights. Granted, that was the last useful thing they did, but it was enough to move Job out of shock and into the outraged, active grieving that would eventually lead to reconciliation with God. All these rituals of mourning are the very opposite of the stiff upper lip so much admired in our culture. From a biblical perspective, living well with sorrow means dwelling on it, lamenting it before God, allowing—no, *committing* yourself to search the sorrow, to explore every corner of it, to ransack the emptiness until it yields up its treasure, the hidden blessing on those who mourn.

That kind of mourning is a form of asceticism, and so it is useful for us to consider as we approach Lent. Living faithfully in sorrow is a form of self-renunciation that reaches to the bottom of your identity, as you learn to let go of what you could not have imagined being without: a healthy body, a marriage, a profession, someone whose life was as precious to you as your own. The asceticism of the mourner means forswearing resentment at the loss of those old necessities, ceasing to hold over God's head your idea of how things ought to be, and thus gradually becoming free to discover sufficiency, even abundance—abundance in the midst of loss.

"Blessed are those who mourn, for they shall be comforted." The comfort of the mourner is the coming into being of a new self, previously unimaginable to you—the surprising self that assumes coherence only when viewed by the light of the gospel, an unexpected new creation brought forth by God where before there was nothing but the formless waste of bitterly disappointed hopes.

The Beatitudes are more for contemplating than expounding, so let me offer for your meditation two images of faithful mourning. First, from Eastern Orthodox tradition, the icon of Mary as the Mother of Tenderness. It is a portrait of grieving love; Mary holds the infant Jesus up to her face, his cheek pressed against hers, and her face is filled with sorrow for the Passion they will both endure. In some versions of the icon, the Babe clings to her in human fear and she comforts him; sometimes the Child is an image of divine comfort, his arm wrapped gently around her neck or reaching up to touch her cheek. The calm sorrow on Mary's face reveals the quality that makes her blessed among women: her absolute humility, that is, her ability to receive every moment of love as a perfect gift. It was that humility which enabled her to hold God in her womb and in her arms, accepting grief as the necessary cost of love ("For a sword shall pierce through your own heart also"). Mary held the pain of love without resistance or defense, and therefore she is accounted "full of grace," empty of herself and powerful to bring before God in prayer the suffering of the world.

The grieving, compassionate Mother of Tenderness is one of the principal themes of Russian icon-painting. So it is probably more than coincidence that the second image of faithful mourning comes from recent Russian history. The poet Yevtushenko tells that as a child in 1944 he saw 20,000 German prisoners of war marched through the streets of Moscow. The crowd of onlookers was mostly women, all of them mourners. Probably there was no one in the crowd who had not lost a son, husband, brother, father, lover among the many millions of Russian men killed in the war. There was a low roar of hatred as the German generals marched past, chins thrust forward in disdain for their captors; police barely restrained the women from attacking them. But then came the long line of ordinary soldiers, and Yevtushenko describes the change that took place in the crowd:

> They saw German soldiers, thin, unshaven, wearing dirty, blood-stained bandages, hobbling on crutches or leaning on the shoulders of their comrades; the soldiers walked with their heads down. The street became dead silent—the only sound was the shuffling of boots and the thumping of crutches.
>
> Then I saw an elderly woman in broken-down boots push herself forward and touch a policeman's shoulder, saying, "Let me through." There must have been something about her that made him step aside. She went up to the column, took from inside her coat something wrapped in a coloured handkerchief and unfolded it. It was a crust of black bread. She pushed it awkwardly into the pocket of a soldier, so exhausted that he was tottering on his feet. And now from every side women were running toward the soldiers, pushing into their hands bread, cigarettes, whatever they had. The soldiers were no longer enemies. They were people.[2]

That crowd of Russian women, every one of them a mourner, in an instant, on a sidewalk, found the treasure hidden in her own loss and offered it up as a gift. Their extraordinary ability to give reveals the unique privilege of those

---

2. Y. Yevtushenko, *A Precocious Autobiography* (London: Collins, 1963), quoted by Jim Forest, *Making Friends of Enemies* (New York: Crossroad, 1988), 29.

who mourn. The blessing on the mourner is not when pain subsides. That usually comes with time, at least in some measure; but these Russian women experienced blessing in the midst of acute grieving. Their blessing, their comfort is not relief from pain but rather its transformation: when the hard, tight pain of resentment is in an unexpected moment touched and turned into the sweet, flowing pain of compassion, grieving love abundant enough to pour out even upon their enemies. May it be so for us.

Amen.

Offensive Faith

The Church of the Epiphany, Honolulu, Hawaii
June 30, 1991

MARK 5:22–24, 35B–43

The story of Jesus raising Jairus's daughter from death requires us to reckon with the notion that our unbelief might restrict God's power. With Jairus's daughter lying dead, Jesus's call to faith is offensive, not only because it violates our preconceived notions about death's finality, but also because it makes our faith a precondition for miracles. To be sure, if faith is a kind of love freely given, it can never be a bargaining chip. People of faith will still die and not be raised. But our daily faithfulness will enable us to discern the more uncommon miracles that do occur, and to be drawn in quiet wonder into these mysterious works of God.

It's miracle stories like this one that make it hard to take the Gospel seriously. Jesus is in his home territory of Galilee, and he is approached by Jairus, a local synagogue leader (which is to say, a member of the vestry), whose adolescent daughter is at the point of death. Jairus begs Jesus to come home with him and lay hands on the girl, and while they're on the way they get word that she has died. But of course that doesn't stop Jesus: he goes to the dead child, takes her hand, and tells her to get up, which she does, and begins to walk around. Now, how are we supposed to understand a thing like that? If you're into symbolism, you can easily see that this story of a dead girl rising and walking around is a sign of the resurrection and life in the world to come. But as far as our life in this world goes, what does this story of Jairus's daughter mean? Because in the world we live in, dead people stay that way, despite our weeping and pleading with God. A miracle story like this one seems to come from another world, where—who knows—maybe God acted more directly in people's lives; miracle stories come from another age, when—dare we say it?—people were more gullible than ourselves.

But if you listen carefully, you discover that in fact this story comes from our only-too-familiar world. "Some people came from the synagogue leader's house to say, 'Your daughter is dead. Why trouble the teacher any further?'" Jairus's friends know, as we do, that tragedy is real and permanent, that dead people stay dead, even much-loved children. And so they give him good, practical advice: "Give up your futile hopes, miracles don't happen here. This isn't the Red Sea; this is Galilee (which was, religiously speaking, the backwoods). And this Rabbi Jesus is no Moses or Elijah; he's a country preacher, not a miracle worker. Your little girl is dead; you have to accept that." But Jesus completely overrides their practical counsel, feeding those wild hopes for a miracle: "Do not fear; only believe. . . . The child is not dead but sleeping."

"Do not fear; only believe." Under the circumstances, that call to unconcerned faith is remarkable and, let's face it, offensive. The call to faith is offensive: that is the whole point of Mark's Gospel. God's way with us is offensive; it offends our common sense, it violates our notion of the way things ought to be, precisely because what God does—what God is able to do—in the world depends wholly on this mysterious thing called faith.

God's miracles depend on our faith—that's what this story is about. Modern Christians spend far too much time worrying about whether or not those remarkable outbursts of God's power that we call miracles can really happen. Of course they can. If God can create a world out of nothingness—in six days or ten billion years, it doesn't matter; if God can form a child in a womb—virgin or not, it's miraculous; if God can do that, then why can't God restore strength and health to a stricken body? The outrageous claim of the Gospel is not that God can do extraordinary things, but that our faith is the necessary condition for God to do them. Where faith is lacking, as it was in Jesus's hometown of Nazareth, then God's strong hands are bound, powerless to heal (Mark 6:5). But where faith is strong, then God's power bursts the confines of ordinary experience, flaunts all reasonable expectations, breaks the deadlock of sickness and sin with acts of healing that flow from God's relentless passion for wholeness.

Surely, for anyone who has ever seen the movie *Peter Pan,* the most memorable scene is the one in which the fairy Tinkerbell is dying. You remember, Peter—Mary Martin—is holding her, and there is only the faintest glow of light in his hands, and in a desperate move he turns to us in the audience and asks, "Do you believe in fairies? If you do, then clap!" In order to save Tinkerbell, we must believe, and so we do. Now if you've seen *Peter Pan* anytime since you were six, you probably struggled with your entirely rational unbelief in fairies; but I suspect that Peter's appeal has moved very many of us (and I include myself) to overcome our fatal unbelief and clap for Tink.

That's the same appeal that Jesus makes to the father of the dead child: "If you only believe, then she can be saved." Jairus the synagogue leader is a mature, sober man, who yet for the sake of his child must believe the impossible, that Jesus can bring her back to life. He must believe it, because his unbelief would frustrate God's great yearning to heal. And so Jesus, suspended from the fine wire of Jairus's faith, reaches down and draws the girl up out of death.

It's a crazy thing, that God's power should be restricted by our unbelief, unleashed only by our faith. If I were God, I'd make a world where I could strut my stuff, heal whom I pleased, whether anybody believed in me or not. God, it seems, can do anything, anything at all, except compel our faith, and on that everything else depends. It's a crazy setup, which makes sense from one perspective only, and that is love. For faith is a kind of love; it is the particular kind of committed love that we give to God. And love must be given freely; it cannot be coerced. Like a human lover, God can and does court us, trying to win our faith. But ultimately the commitment of faith is one that we must choose to make, for only our free choice of love can give joy to the gracious Lover of souls.

Like other kinds of love, faith achieves fullness only when it is practiced over a lifetime, with patience and persistence. The life of faith has its moments of rapture, outbursts of ecstasy and power, like this healing of Jairus's daughter. But as with every form of love, the thing that makes possible those peak experiences is the quality of daily faithfulness, continual steady attention to the things that nurture relationship. It's no coincidence that it was in Jairus's home that Jesus first burst the confines of death; for as a leader of the synagogue, Jairus went every day to the house of prayer, probably more than once. There is no point in looking for miracles, for peak experiences with God, if you are not in the regular habit of being with God, unexciting as that often is. And if you are regularly with God, and continually looking for evidence of God's action, then you will see how at every moment your life is touched and sustained, and the very act of your looking will open up the possibility for God to be present with greater and more visible power.

Yet still people of faith sicken and die; people surrounded by prayer are not always healed from their afflictions. Faith opens the door so that God's power may be released into our lives and our world, but it does not dictate the terms for the exercise of that power. Faith is a free gift of love, not a bargaining chip. If we give our faith freely, then that means recognizing that God, like ourselves, is free, free to heal or not to heal (at least in the way that we had wished). God may restore strength to a sick body, but God retains always the radical freedom to take us out of these bodies, to free us for the more abundant life that is ours on the other side of death.

Finally, and this is the sum of everything I have said or could say about faith: like all true love, faith draws us into a mystery. Faith doesn't enable us to predict what God is going to do in a situation, nor does it even help us give very satisfactory explanations of what God has already done. Faith doesn't make the world a more logical or manageable place—on the contrary, it makes it a more mysterious one, where, if you have your wits about you, you find yourself lost in ever-deepening wonder at what is really going on, that is, wonder at what God is doing in our lives. And that is why people of very deep faith tend often to talk less than other people; sometimes they don't even talk a great deal about God. For, as you know, when you love most deeply, you are little inclined to talk about it. Why should you chatter? Can you give a reason for your love? Can you explain the transformation it is working in your life?

The silence surrounding the mystery to which faith admits us is the reason for the final, seemingly strange detail in this story of Jairus's daughter: Jesus cautions all the wondering bystanders to tell no one of what they have seen. Jesus's own practicality is much deeper than that of those skeptics who doubted his power to heal. He tells the people to give the girl something to eat rather than go off preaching a miracle they don't really understand. It is better to tell no one than to speak falsely, to chatter about the mystery of God as though it were the morning news.

Jesus's warning to tell no one suggests a caution for us. Not that we should be afraid to speak of what God has done for us; that is a joyful thing, and something most Episcopalians do too little (cf. Mark 5:19). We should speak often of what God has done, but nonetheless we should be careful how we speak, careful that our speaking not violate the essential mystery of God's action. Perhaps we pray for healing for another, and our prayers are granted; we should be cautious, then, lest we give explanations that sound like a recipe for miracle. Perhaps we experience healing in ourselves—physical, emotional—that we know is the work of God; we should be cautious lest we make this present act of mercy a rule for what God will do in the future, lest we make our own healing a model for how God ought to work in the lives of others. We should be afraid to give any explanations or predictions that violate the deep wonder surrounding all God's marvelous work.

In Jerusalem, in the church that now stands in the Garden of Gethsemane, there is a sign just as you come in, saying, "No explanations in the church." The prohibition is aimed at tour guides, to keep the place quiet for prayer, but we'd all do well to heed it. We in the church have been baptized into the mystery of Christ; and so long as we attend to God, with every heartbeat we are drawn more deeply into a mystery that infinitely exceeds our understanding and power of expression, a mystery of mercy that goes beyond even our wildest hopes and imaginings. So no explanations in the church; rather, let us speak softly and with wonder, as befits a holy place.

Amen.

One More Squanderer

St. John's College, University of Durham, England
April 24, 2007

LUKE 16:1–9; ACTS 4:32–37

The manager who "squandered" his master's property and altered the books is here revealed to be a model Christian steward. By interpreting several key Greek words differently, this parable sermon reintroduces the supposedly unrighteous manager as a frugal orchestrator of an alternative economy. His actions correspond to Lukan motifs of charity, forgiveness, and resurrection—constitutive elements of Christian community that appear irresponsible in light of conventional wisdom. The steward also offers clues for how a broken church may reconcile deep social and economic divisions.

In this section of the Gospel, Luke has his mind on "squandering." Jesus has just finished the parable of that lost-and-found son, who "squandered his inheritance in dissolute living," and now he's telling another tale, this one about the steward who "squandered his master's property." The two squanderers are quite different, and the prodigal is by far the more inspiring; he is in all of Scripture the sharpest image of the sinner who, after much self-inflicted suffering, "comes to himself" (Luke 15:17). I dare say the prodigal has played an important role in the spiritual life of a number of us, who know just what it means to wander into a "far country," turn back shamefacedly, and receive a welcoming embrace you can never deserve.

But this steward is a harder case. He never abases himself, as did the prodigal. When he thinks his behavior is about to lose him his job, he doesn't repent; he just pulls off another scam. Compounding his misdemeanors, he alters the books, drastically reducing the debts people in the community owe to his boss. Now the truly surprising and galling thing is that this goes over well with the "rich man," who is surely the God-figure in this story. The steward he was ready to dismiss he now commends for acting "astutely" (*phronimōs*). That is not an ambiguous compliment (as the common English translation "shrewdly" would seem to imply); rather, it means he kept his wits about him. Apparently Jesus is offering the astute steward as a model for our imitation, even though we are specifically told that he is "a manager of *un*righteousness" (v. 8). What, then, are we supposed to learn from him?

As you know, parables are in effect poems; in highly condensed language, they sketch out the workings of the kingdom of heaven. They are like condensed soup: you need to add a tin of water to make them digestible. That is, in order to get insight into the gospel, you have to add a good measure of imagination, your exegetically sensitized imagination. You need to read very slowly, chasing down the connections the words suggest. And you must start at the beginning. Every parable, every biblical story is going to give away a lot in the first sentence or two, if you know how to read the clues. Here's the first one: "An accusation was brought before the rich man that this steward was *diaskorpizōn* his property" (16:1). *Diaskorpizō* is not a very common verb, and it is the same one used to sum up the activities of the prodigal son in that far country. "Squander"—that is what Bauer and company (the lexicon guys) say it means, and they know infinitely more Greek than I do. At least, that is what they say it means in these two parables, but everywhere else, they say, *diaskorpizō* means something entirely different: namely, "scatter," as seed is scattered (Matt. 25:24, 26), or grain is broadcast in a field (Didache 9:4). Well, if that's what it normally means, let's try it here: "An accusation was brought before the rich man that this steward was *broadcasting* his property."

Now that is a very interesting charge, especially coming through Luke's pen, because, as you know, in both the Gospel and Acts Luke gives considerable attention to the matter of how Christians handle their possessions. And the bottom line seems to be that it is not a good thing to be too particular about what is "yours."[1] Thus Luke reports concerning the community that gathered after the resurrection: "There was no one who thought anything they had was just theirs, but everything was common to them all. And with great power they rendered testimony, the apostles of the resurrection of Jesus Christ" (Acts 4:32b–33a). Anyone who owned land or a house sold it and gave the money to the apostles, who in turn distributed it to anyone in need. This should catch

---

1. "Be on your guard against every desire for 'more,' because one's life does not come from an abundance of possessions" (Luke 12:15).

our attention, especially in the Easter season: dispersing resources is a witness to the resurrection—no, not just *a* witness, but the chief witness, the clearest sign given by the new Christian community that God's kingdom already is present with power sufficient to rattle some cages.

Sharing resources shakes dominant power structures. I think of my friend Esther, a deacon who was for decades the bookkeeper at my theological college. Esther lived more simply than anyone I have known outside a religious order. She was unmarried, and she rented a bedroom and bath from a family who became through the years *her* family; Esther walked with braces and canes, so life without superfluous stuff or space to tend suited her very well. She was an accomplished bookkeeper of the old school, who kept a very clean set of books for the college. Her personal income was modest, so we were all surprised when the federal government decided to run a thorough tax investigation on Esther. The problem was her charity donations; the IRS simply could not believe that anyone would give away so much of "their own" money, year after year. Esther had rattled the US Government's cage, simply through her devotion to the few things that matter. "And with great power they rendered testimony, the apostles of the resurrection of Jesus Christ."

Now, after this detour into Acts, maybe we can begin to appreciate why the God-character in our parable approves of his steward's juggling the accounts in favor of his debtors. Notice what the rich man says when he confronts the steward: "*Render* the account of your stewardship" (16:2).[2] *Apodos*, "render"— it is the same word Luke uses to describe the Christians in Acts: "everything was common to them all. And with great power they *rendered* testimony, the apostles of the resurrection of Jesus Christ" (Acts 4:32b–33a). Like the "unrighteous steward," the apostles rendered an account of sorts; like him, they did it by giving away money that did not really belong to them. At least, these first Christians thought whatever they had was theirs only to give away. See, Luke is teasing us into thinking about money in a completely different way, according to the economics of the kingdom of heaven, and for that the strategy of the freehanded steward is just unconventional enough to be useful. Most of us Christians still are very conventional about money matters; the government has seen no need to investigate me. So in case we are having trouble catching on, Jesus ends by putting it to us straight: "My advice to you is this, make friends for yourselves by means of money, which has nothing to do with righteousness, so when it gives out, they may receive you into the eternal habitations" (16:9).

2. The verb *apodidōmi* is used in Acts 4:33 and Luke 16:2, and also in Luke 19:8, of Zacchaeus's "rendering half his 'property' to the poor."

Giving away money in a way that looks irresponsible by the lights of this world is a great way of testifying to the resurrection, as Luke says. It's not a matter of personal virtue; our steward makes no pretense of being righteous. But, being in a tight place, with no going back, he uses the resources at hand to buy or build himself a community. We are likewise in a tight place, poised now between the empty tomb and the full inbreaking of the kingdom. There is no going back and no clear way forward. Jesus's advice to us is this: get your economic practice in line with the economics of the kingdom. Start practicing resurrection now; insinuate yourself into the eternal habitations. And by the way, don't presume too much on your own personal virtue. Create a system; along with other Christians, seek out an economic structure for your life that makes broadcasting resources easier. Create a community in which having less, less to call your own, is more satisfying and less embarrassing than having a lot. Our parable of the unrighteous yet freehanded steward is the single most striking expression of Luke's countercultural economic wisdom.

I think there is even more than that going on here, and the "even more" is what lies behind the juxtaposition of these two parables, the freehanded steward and the prodigal son. Luke knows that how we deal with money is intimately connected with something else that is very big in our life with God: namely, how we deal with sin. Throughout the Gospel, Luke signals that connection by mixing the language of economics with the language of forgiveness: famously, "Forgive us our sins, as we forgive all who are *indebted* to us" (Luke 11:4). Sins are debts, not so different from other debts. Again, in his Sermon on the Plain, Luke's Jesus interweaves two teachings: "Love your enemies; forgive them," and "Lend to people who can never repay you." Jesus weaves back and forth until we see that those are not two different spiritual instructions, but one. Forgive recklessly, lend recklessly, and you will receive in the same measure, "pressed down, well shaken and overflowing, poured into your lap" (6:38). These two neighboring parables are about just that kind of reckless giving and forgiving; and by putting them together, Luke shows us that the two actions belong together. Sharing whatever we've got to an extent that is unreasonable, letting go of grudge, even for real injuries—these are the two indispensable ways in which Christians render witness as "apostles of the resurrection."

The importance of that dual witness to the resurrection becomes clear if we look from the other side, from the side of sin and death. Is there anything that so effectively blocks the free flow of God's love in the world and in the church as these two things: not sharing, together with great disparities in wealth perpetuated from generation to generation; and nursing our grudges, rehearsing steadily the benightedness of those we define as "enemy"?

By connecting these two parables, Luke challenges us to see that refusing to share and condemning the other are behaviors that often belong together, in the world and in the church. They feed into each other in ways that can never be disentangled. Reading these two parables in the midst of the agonies in our global Communion, I suspect that Luke would view our current situation with sadness, but not surprise. For along with Paul, Luke is the best biblical analyst of what makes or breaks the church. He confronts us with the awkward truth that an economically divided church is likely also to be a church broken along any number of fracture lines. Lacking sufficient stake in each other's lives and understandings, we easily become alienated from each other, mutually contemptuous and condemning.

In this sad and fearful time, it is good to recall that the church's failures do not set any of us outside the territory charted by the gospel. Later in Luke's Gospel, when the risen Lord first comes to his disciples, he is coming to those who let him down badly at the end: they slept while he wrestled alone in Gethsemane; Peter denied him three times in the high priest's court; all his followers "stood at a distance" (Luke 23:49) and watched him die on the cross. When Jesus comes to them after all that, he has a right to ask a few pointed questions, to set them straight about what they should have done. But Jesus passes up the opportunity to condemn; his first word to them is peace, "Peace be with you" (24:36). It seems he wants just to be with them, eating and studying God's word; one gets the sense that he has missed them. "Peace be with you"—with that word, the disciples' alarm and confusion begin to yield to joy. In time they will be ready for mission; they will pass on to others the forgiveness they themselves have received (24:47). "Peace be with you"—that word creates a starting place out of no place. In this season of the resurrection, let us speak that word in the church and follow where it leads.

Amen.

"Do You Have Anything Here to Eat?"

Virginia Theological Seminary, Alexandria, Virginia
Easter Celebration, April 7, 1999

LUKE 24:36B–48

Jesus so often disrupts the conventional eating practices of his day with signs of God's coming kingdom that we may rightly say, "Whenever Jesus eats, revelation happens." Even more than his stigmata, it was Jesus's breaking of the bread during a post-resurrection meal that finally enabled the disciples to comprehend the biblical witness to Christ. Luke offers this "verbal icon" of Jesus eating in order to show how fully Christ is at home in a human body. But Jesus's flesh-and-bone presence on this side of the cross also reveals the necessity of caring for all human bodies. For in seeing God as a hungry man, we may also see God with us in every hungry person, vulnerable and "burdened with the heaviness" of flesh and bone.

When Jesus eats, revelation happens, or at least so it is in Luke's Gospel. Luke shows us a Lord who likes to eat; and when he does, it is always a sign that the kingdom of heaven has come near, near enough to smell and taste its goodness. "Taste and see that the LORD is good" (Ps. 34:9); when Jesus eats, those words of the psalmist are realized.

Eating is so much a part of who Jesus is in Luke's Gospel that it even becomes a theme of the public gossip about him. Jesus knows what the Pharisees and the scribes are saying, and he confronts them thus: "The Son of Man has come eating and drinking; and you say, 'Behold a glutton and drunkard, a friend of tax collectors and sinners!'" (7:34). Unlike his cousin John, the ascetic in the family, Jesus comes eating and drinking; and everybody knows it. So they invite him for dinner, everyone who wants a taste of the kingdom of God;

271

and Jesus accepts their invitations indiscriminately. One day, for instance, he eats at the table of Levi the tax collector (5:29), who has invited all his equally disgraceful friends. And sure enough, when Jesus eats at Levi's house with tax collectors and sinners, revelation happens. Now Jesus's program is public knowledge: "I have not come to call the righteous, but sinners, to repentance" (5:32).

Some time later, Simon the Pharisee also throws a dinner party for this new religious phenomenon; and now the company is considerably more righteous. But even so, revelation happens. You recall: a woman with a bad reputation crashes the party to wash Jesus's feet with her tears even as he reclines at table with all those good religious folk, and she dries them with the towel of her hair. Revelation happens right there in Simon's dining room, when the mystified host gets a lesson from Jesus: it is the one who knows herself to be lavishly forgiven who is able to love lavishly.

Whenever Jesus eats, revelation happens. Perhaps that is why, in Luke's Gospel, the disciples do not recognize their risen Lord until they have given him something to eat. It isn't enough that he speaks—"Peace be with you"— although in the other Gospel accounts that is what convinces the disciples. It isn't even enough that he shows them his hands and his feet. Torn flesh, holes rimmed with caked blood—that was graphic enough even for Thomas, as John's Gospel tells it. But Luke says the disciples see that and still don't get it. "Look," he says, "feel me. A ghost doesn't have flesh and bones like I do." But "still they disbelieved for joy" (24:41)—it was too good to be true, "and they wondered," until finally Jesus broke the spell: "Do you have anything here to eat?"

It was only after Jesus had eaten broiled fish before their eyes that they could comprehend what had happened. Now when he spoke, all the pieces fell into place: the whole biblical witness to the Christ, in Torah and Prophets and Psalms. But just what is the connection that Luke is trying to show us, between the once-dead Jesus munching broiled fish, and the disciples' sudden comprehension of the difficult teaching about the Christ suffering and risen from the dead; between Jesus's eating, and their own commission to preach and witness to all nations about Jesus the Christ? Jesus eating after he had died—why is that the definitive revelation for Luke?

As you know, the Bible never explains this kind of thing in so many words. We are just given the image to ponder—a verbal icon, a window into the kingdom of heaven. But as with any icon, you have to look at it for a while, and dream a little before it. Only then does it become transparent, or at least translucent, to your sight.

Jesus eating broiled fish. Beginning a dream of the kingdom of God, consider this: Jesus's eating is a sign that Jesus has come home. When a child comes home at the end of a school day, when someone we love comes home from a far country, do we not always reconnect by means of food? "Do you have anything here to eat?" Probably all of us have at one time or another spoken those words, or been glad to hear them spoken, in front of an open refrigerator door. Those words say that the one we love and missed and worried about is home again, thank God. And the one who speaks those words is expressing not only hunger, but also a sense of belonging: "Hey, I'm home." In Luke's Gospel, Jesus eating is always a sign of his genuine belonging, his solidarity with his friends, with tax collectors and sinners—a sign of his utter solidarity with us in all that is human, in all the compromising situations in which we find ourselves. "Feel me and see; a ghost does not have flesh and bones as you see that I have"—this scene shows us just how fully Jesus is at home in a human body, at home with us in a solidarity that nothing can obliterate, not even death on a cross.

Not even death on a cross—that ups the stakes considerably, doesn't it? For this loved one has just come back from the far country of Golgotha and Sheol. "Do you have anything here to eat?" Uttered under these circumstances, those words say more than, "Hey, I'm home." They say also, "I am the LORD." Jesus has just come home from the far country of death safe, whole, alive. Nobody but the LORD, "the one who kills and brings to life" (1 Sam. 2:6), could accomplish that. Luke's wording in this scene earlier hints at the revelatory dimension of Jesus's speech: "Look at my hands and my feet, that I AM he." I AM, *egō eimi*, I AM is speaking to you—I AM who spoke on Sinai, I AM who commissioned Moses—I AM is speaking to you now. Read my lips. But these slow students still don't get it, until the crucified man eats in their presence.

And there is yet more to the revelation. God speaks now, in Jesus, as God has never spoken before. "Do you have anything here to eat?" That is the very last thing any Israelite would expect God to say. The counter-expectation is based on clear scriptural witness. Listen to the psalmist:

Hear, my people, and I shall speak;
Israel, I shall bear witness against you.
I am God, your God.
. . . .
If I were hungry, I would not tell you;
for the world is mine and all that fills it. (Ps. 50:7, 12)

One of the identifying marks of Israel's God, in contrast to pagan delusions, is that the Holy One of Israel has no physical needs and cannot be bribed nor appeased with physical satisfactions.

> Do I eat animal flesh,
> or drink blood of goats? (Ps. 50:13)

Of course not. Yet now Luke shows us God asking for food. God-made-flesh in Jesus of Nazareth, God crucified and risen from the dead, is asking for food. In the many pages of Scripture, surely this is at once both the least expected and the most nonchalant of all God's self-revelations.

And what are we to learn from God's new way of speaking? "Look, a ghost—a spirit does not have flesh and bones as you see that I have." Look, God has put on flesh and bones, and they won't ever go away. Incarnation is permanent, ineradicable, despite the best efforts of the empire to eradicate it. Incarnation won't ever go away, even after God-made-flesh-and-bones has been hung up to die on a cross. Flesh suffers horribly. Flesh and bones are heavy; when nailed to a cross, they sag and slowly suffocate. But once God has put them on, they do not go away. "A spirit does not have flesh and bones as you see that I have." From now on, flesh and bones are part of the permanent reality we have to reckon with as we prepare to meet Israel's God.

And this brings us one step deeper into the revelation disclosed by God incarnate, once dead, now eating broiled fish. This is the last step; we will get no farther tonight, because this is the step in God's revelation for which your work during months and years here have prepared you, and it is good to linger here. Please God, you will linger at just this point of revelation for long years of ministry. Listen again: "A spirit does not have flesh and bones as you see that I have. . . . Do you have anything here to eat?" What is God saying to us in that?

Incarnation is permanent, and it is demanding. Flesh and bones need care and feeding; they create needs that even God feels. So, dare we imagine that Jesus's asking for something to eat is more than a show of solidarity with his beloved friends, more than a strikingly vivid way of making a point about incarnation to disciples of average ability? Is it too wild to suggest that Jesus asks for something to eat because he really wants something to eat, because his resurrection body still remembers the wholly human feeling of hunger?

If this is so, then Luke is indeed offering us a verbal icon, a revealed image of the kingdom of heaven. It could only be a revealed image, because no act of human imagination is sufficient to conceive it. But if this is so, then it shows us how we must now see God, if we are to see God at all. We must see God as a hungry man or woman or child whose flesh and bones demand sustenance. It tells us how we are to serve God, if we are to serve God at all. We must give the one who is hungry something to eat. Luke's final icon of Jesus eating, always for him a sign of solidarity, shows us now, after cross and resurrection, what it means to say that God is with us, *Immanuel.* God is with us precisely as one who is willing to be permanently burdened with the heaviness of flesh and bones, willing to come to us vulnerable and in need, to stand before us perpetually, with a wholly human hunger, asking for something to eat.

Alleluia, my sisters and brothers, Christ is risen.

Do you have anything here to eat?

Amen.

Pushing toward Glory

St. Bene't's, Cambridge, England
All Saints Sunday, November 5, 2006

JOHN 11:32–44

Why is Jesus so upset in the aftermath of a death he had the power to prevent? This sermon questions translations that suggest Jesus's visceral emotions were merely expressions of compassion, arguing instead that he was "violently disturbed and troubled" by death itself. Mary and Martha have pressured Jesus to be who he says he is—the Lord of life. Now, like a distraught soldier before going into battle, Jesus must come face to face with the last enemy, Death. The story of Lazarus's resurrection gives us permission not to accept death passively, but to push against God with the expectation that God will push us to an even deeper faith.

In this week, when the church observes the feasts of All Saints and All Souls, we have the opportunity to talk about what death means to us—not primarily Christ's death on the cross, but ordinary death (as though there were such a thing), that is, death as we experience it in the loss of those whom we most love, and as we anticipate it for ourselves. Always when we come to this week, I feel the weight that has accumulated in my heart during the past year. I am sure I am not the only person here this morning who is not yet reconciled to some of the deaths that the last twelve months have brought, or the deaths that, it is now clear, lie just ahead, in a few days, weeks, months at the most. Perhaps many of us come here today bearing some deaths as a burden of unhealed grief, others as a grudge against—whom? Maybe a doctor who overlooked something. Or we might even be angry at someone we love whose life was shortened, at least in part, as a result of their own unwise choices. Or we might hold a grudge against the God who inexplicably allowed some precious life to end too soon, far too soon.

For those of us who come here today unreconciled to some death, unreconciled to God for that death, the Gospel passage we have just heard may be a gift and a revelation. For it shows Jesus visibly struggling with the violent emotion that comes upon him at the death of someone he loves, Lazarus of Bethany. In the Gospel of John, it is startling to see Jesus shaken even by death, for the evangelist's steady emphasis is on Jesus's confidence in the goodness and power of God. Jesus proclaims God as the Source of all life, powerful even to "raise the dead and give them life." Jesus shares in that power, as he says of himself: "Also the Son gives life to whom he will" (5:21). That confidence explains why, when Jesus first receives word that Lazarus is ill, he stays cool: "This illness is not leading to death; it is for the sake of God's glory" (11:4). At this point Jesus is several days' travel away from Bethany, yet he deliberately waits another couple of days before setting out, and when Jesus finally gets to Bethany, Lazarus has already been dead for about five days. Quite reasonably, Martha and Mary lay a good share of the blame at his feet: "Lord, if you had been here, my brother would not have died" (11:21, 32). Seeing the tears of friends he dearly loves, and hearing their accusations, Jesus for the first time in this Gospel becomes "violently disturbed and troubled" (11:33, 38).

The scene that unfolds in Bethany is remarkable for what it reveals about how things are between Jesus and those with whom he is most intimate—in this case, the two grieving women. As John draws the scene, there is nothing sentimental, nor even tender, about Jesus's presence to this grieving community. On the contrary, tension is thick in the air. When Mary wept at Jesus's feet, (we are told) he became "extremely upset" (v. 33). The translation in the NRSV—"[Jesus was] deeply moved"—is misleading, as it seems to suggest gentle compassion. But the Greek word normally conveys anger, agitation that is far from gentle. The onlookers read Jesus's tears as a sign of love—"See how much he loved him!" (11:36)—but in John's Gospel, anything the crowd thinks is almost certainly mistaken.

So we must try to answer this question afresh: Why would Jesus be so upset in the aftermath of this death? Did he not deliberately create this situation by his delay in coming? Did he not just say, in response to Martha's thinly veiled accusation of negligence, "I am the resurrection and the life; whoever believes in me, though he die, yet shall live. . . . Do you believe this?" (11:25–26). What happens among these three, Martha and Mary and Jesus, is quite like the dynamic any of us may experience in an acute crisis: people who trust one other enough to speak their minds fully are pushing against one another, hard. It is uncomfortable; it often generates anger. But the result of that pressure from both sides is that everyone moves forward to a new place, to a place where new possibilities begin to unfold. In this case all of them, including Jesus, move to the place where (to use John's language) God's glory can be seen.

When Mary and Martha voice their accusation—"Lord, if you had been here, my brother would not have died"—they put pressure on Jesus precisely because they believe in him. Martha goes further: "[E]ven now I know that whatever you ask from God, God will give you" (11:21–22). She is pushing her Lord to complete what he began, when he chose to wait and let Lazarus die. This deadly illness, Jesus said, was "for the glory of God, so the Son of God might be glorified through it" (v. 4). So show me, Martha says (in effect). "I believe that you are the Christ, the Son of God, the one who is coming into the world" (v. 27); so let's see some of this glory. Martha is pressing Jesus to be who he says he is, the Lord of life. And in this situation, with Lazarus's dead body lying in a tomb just at the edge of the village, they both know what that means. It means that Jesus has to take on Death, the last enemy of the One who comes into the world so that we might have life, and have it in abundance (10:10). Martha is pushing Jesus into battle with Death. That is why he feels such extreme agitation; he has come to the crisis of his life, the greatest crisis short of the cross. His is the violent emotion a soldier might feel in the hours or minutes before the heavy fighting begins. And Martha is like the Roman matron of legend, saying to her beloved son, "Come back with your shield, or on it."

This is a remarkable thing, that Jesus should let himself be pushed into redemptive action by the aggressive faith of these women. At the same time, Jesus is pushing them to even deeper faith. Especially he challenges Martha, a no-nonsense, feet-on-the-ground individual if ever there was one, to look beyond what seem to be "the facts" and to glimpse the new reality that faith makes possible. When she accuses him of culpable negligence, Jesus responds, "Whoever lives and believes in me will never die. *Do you believe this?*" That is not a throw-away question. Martha knows how dead Lazarus is. That is why she objects to the rolling away of the stone from the tomb: after four days, there will be a terrible stink; do we really have to endure this indignity? And again Jesus puts pressure on her with a question: "Did I not tell you that *if you would believe* you would see the glory of God?" (11:40).

Those words go to the heart of all that John wants to say about God. "[I]f you would believe you would see the glory of God"—our faith and God's glory exist in dynamic relationship. When John speaks of faith, he means a single-minded concentration on the goodness and power and faithfulness of God. Unless we have cultivated that kind of attentiveness, we will see nothing glorious in this world. It is as though I were to go hunting wildflowers or mushrooms in a dim wood with my glasses off; I would distinguish nothing, see nothing of beauty or value. Without that clear focus on God, we will mistake worldly prestige for glory—and of course there is a lot of deceptive glory in a place such as this one, as there is in every great center of power, of whatever kind.

So faith is the prerequisite for seeing the glory of God. At the same time (and more strangely), faith seems to open the way for more evidences of divine glory to appear in our world. I don't pretend to understand why this is so, but John on more than one occasion indicates that it *is* so. Those who love Jesus—the sisters Mary and Martha, his mother Mary—all these women who believe that the power of God is in Jesus push him toward manifesting that power more fully. This happens first at the wedding in Cana (John 2), when his mother Mary notices that the wine has run out and pushes Jesus, evidently against his inclination, to do something about it. It happens now a second time in Bethany, when Lazarus has been four days in the tomb.

Insistent, persistent human faith elicits God's manifestation in glory. Whether or not I understand it, the Bible insists repeatedly that this is so and gives multiple instances of it—one of the most dramatic being the story of Job. As we have read in recent weeks, Job in his desolation insists on seeing God. He keeps pushing at God to show up, and when at last God speaks from the whirlwind, of course there is push-back. God pushes Job to a deeper and less self-centered faith, just as Jesus pushes Martha: "Did I not tell you that if you would believe, you would see the glory of God?"

The vision of God's glory that Mary and Martha are privileged to see is frankly way ahead of our experience; we have not yet seen our dead walk out of their tombs. But still the story of these women tells us something about how it is between God and ourselves as together we confront death. Their story gives us permission not to accept death resignedly, not to swallow the indignation that is in fact born of our faith and love: "Lord, if you had been here, my brother—or my young husband or wife or child or parent—would not have died." Martha and Mary give us permission to push for a sign of God's glory, to demand that some sign of God's ultimate triumph over death should be made visible to us even now. Our Gospel tells us also and truly that if we push against God, God will push back. If we open ourselves to God, even in our indignation, then God will push us to a deeper faith, to fuller concentration of heart and mind on the goodness and power and love that flow from God.

So, pushing against God as God pushes against us, we move forward together to the place where true glory is manifest as light entering into our darkness.

"Did I not tell you that if you would believe, you would see the glory of God?" May it be so for us.

Amen.

Learning to Believe

Duke Chapel, Durham, North Carolina
April 11, 2010

JOHN 20:19–31

The Sunday following Easter is disappointing for many, for it exposes the gap between the joy of promised resurrection and the reality that graves still hold the dead. Standing in this gap with Thomas, our identical "twin" in doubt, we discover a more reliable way of experiencing Easter than merely seeing and touching Jesus's wounds. Just as God once breathed into Adam's nostrils, John tells us that Jesus breathes the Spirit of forgiveness on the disciples. In the wake of this "second creation story," the work of forgiving sins can be shared in ways that bring life out of death, and encouragement to those slow to believe.

It's "low Sunday," the Sunday after Easter. "Low Sunday"—the term supposedly refers to church attendance: presumably, everyone who is not here today exhausted their religious energy last week. But there's got to be more to it than that. If people stay away from church in record numbers after Easter Sunday, then you have to wonder if it has something to do with the fact that for many, even some of us here today, Easter season is a disappointment. A week ago we proclaimed that Christ is risen, triumphant over sin and death. Yet today the graves of those we love so dearly are not empty, nor does the news of the past week indicate that sin has been eradicated from our world. But we don't need the mass media to tell us that; our own hearts and homes and workplaces offer abundant evidence that sin has not loosened its grip since last Sunday. Some years, for any one of us, there is a huge gap between the Easter proclamation of joy and the felt reality of grief, guilt, chaos, hopelessness—a gap that threatens to swallow us and our fragile faith.

That is why it is good to have the Gospel of John in the Bible, because John takes on directly the disappointment of Easter, the real difficulty of believing two things: first, that Jesus has risen from the dead, and second, that anything has really changed as a result. John writes, he tells us, so that we may learn to believe these things that are hard to believe, and our lives may be changed as a result. "I write these things," John says, "so that, believing, you may have life in [Jesus's] name" (20:31).

In John's Gospel, Thomas is the one who flagrantly calls attention to the gap between the Easter proclamation and our present experience. Thomas is stuck in that gap. He wasn't there when the risen Jesus appeared to the other disciples, but he has heard that Jesus is alive, and he's not buying it. Disappointed, heartbroken by the death of his Lord, Thomas now just wants to get on with his life; he was off somewhere else, on his own, when Jesus showed up in that locked room. "Doubting Thomas," we call him, but John calls Thomas "the Twin," and that nickname may tell us something important. If Thomas has a sibling, we never hear anything about it, so why does John make a point of naming him (three times) as the Twin? I need to tell you something about John's mind: he thinks like a poet—suggestively, always choosing words that point to meanings he does not directly name. So maybe John is dropping a hint here, and his point is that Thomas is *our* twin brother, embedded within the story of Jesus's resurrection. He is our identical sibling, articulating our disappointment and doubt that anything has changed, absolutely and forever, with Jesus's death on the cross.

How Thomas finally comes to believe is one of the most familiar scenes in the Gospel; countless artists and musicians have taken it as their theme. "Come on, thrust your hand into my side," Jesus says. The instant Thomas touches the raw wound, he blurts out, "My Lord and my God." We all remember that single moment, but we forget what Jesus says next, though certainly the evangelist John means us to ponder these words: "Because you have seen me you believe? Blessed are those who have not seen and yet have come to believe" (20:29). I hear some impatience in our Lord's voice, as though Jesus were saying to Thomas and all subsequent doubters, ourselves included: "Look, I will not continue to do this. There is a better way to learn to believe than sticking your hand in my side. There's a better way to feel the truth of the resurrection."

Jesus has already shown his other disciples that better way, when he breathed into them the Holy Spirit. Jesus breathed the Spirit into them—think about that, recalling John's habit of suggesting meanings he does not spell out. John is telling a second creation story. Just as God once breathed life into Adam's nostrils, so now Jesus breathes new life into his disciples, saying, "Receive the Holy Spirit. Whenever you forgive the sins of any, they are forgiven them" (20:23). Through the Holy Spirit, Jesus is granting humans a power that previously belonged to God alone: the power to unlock the death-grip that our sins have on our souls, to erase them from the cosmos. The power to forgive sins is the mark of a new creation, of a profoundly changed life, not just for this small group of disciples, but potentially for humankind altogether.

Now how does that work? Think for a moment about the old creation story, in Genesis. Already in Eden, human lives came to be governed by shame and blame, anger and fear; the man turned against the woman, the woman turned against the snake, and all of them turned away from God. But now the risen Jesus comes to the disciples when they are locked away in fear of their enemies, and he offers them a completely new version of the human story, in which forgiveness and freedom in the Spirit replace the old constraints of bitterness and blame. Jesus comes to that fearful community, tottering on the verge of collapse, and he breathes into it the Spirit that does not condemn, the Spirit of God that works in and through us for peace and wholeness. The disciples are to carry that Spirit out into the world: "As the Father sent me, so I send you. . . . Whenever you forgive the sins of any, they are forgiven them" (20:21, 23). The forgiveness of sins is the foundational mission of the church, as John conceives it. That is how we, Jesus's disciples, are to practice resurrection, the new life that began with his victory on the cross. Practicing the forgiveness of sins is practicing resurrection; that is how we may come to believe that, in the crucified and risen Lord, everything has changed.

"I was sixteen when my mother left our family," my friend said to me. This wise friend in Christ was telling me a story from many years in the past, after I had wondered out loud how it is that forgiving those who have sinned against us leads us deeper into faith. She went on: "I was convinced that she had ruined my life. What I lost when my mother left were things I really needed: the happiness I felt in our home, the special intimacy between the two of us; I even lost my picture of what I might be like as a woman. Sometimes I imagined that my hands were around her neck, and I was screaming, 'You owe me!'

"My loss felt like a huge debt that was overwhelming us both: I could not live without what was missing, and of course there was no way she could pay it back. People in my mother's past owed her debts they could not pay. It just seemed to go on and on, an endless chain of unpaid debts, with the deficit always getting bigger. But then gradually, over years, I came to realize: that is what the cross is about—Jesus paying off all those debts we owe to each other, which we can never pay.

"And this is the strange thing: once I knew that, that the debt had already been paid, then I could feel all my pain. We cannot be whole unless we go all the way into the depth of the pain and the wrongdoing. But to go all the way down, we need the Holy Spirit within us, giving us strength. Then we can be healed."

My friend's story of her young self suggests why Jesus might have been impatient with Thomas the Twin. Thomas wanted to believe, but in his pain and disappointment he got the learning process the wrong way round. Until he had thrust his hand into Jesus's gaping wound, he refused to believe that there could be life beyond his loss. But my friend did the opposite, something more difficult and more hopeful: she exposed her own wound to Christ. She opened herself to the probing touch of God's Holy Spirit and asked for healing.

"*Shalom*," Jesus says to his disciples. "Receive the Holy Spirit," the Spirit of *shalom,* of wholeness and peace. God's Spirit within us frees us from the fear that there is no bottom to our loss, that the hole in our lives can never ever be filled. It frees us from all our vain attempts to fill the emptiness with sex or status or stuff—something, anything that will plug the hole that finally only God's love can heal.

As my friend's story shows, forgiveness is not so much a feeling as it is work—very often the work of years. "Forgiveness has many levels," another wise friend once told me. "We have to work our way through them one by one." Probably in every case the holy work of forgiveness challenges our natural feelings, and especially the instinct for justice. When I am suffering, I want the one who has hurt me to suffer—what wronged child or spurned lover has not cried out for that? An innocent life has been taken; the killer must die—what society, including ancient Israel, has not thought for a time that "a life for a life" was the best justice it could execute?

In fact, that does represent a form of justice. Ethicists call it retributive justice: the one who has inflicted suffering must pay with his or her own suffering, measure for measure. Retributive justice is useful in many situations; our courts use it, and on the whole we are grateful that they do. But that kind of justice should be recognized for what it is: a zero-sum game; it assumes that every loss is final and permanent. The gospel, however, offers a vision and mandate for an altogether different kind of justice: restorative justice. The assumption here is that the God who triumphs over death is powerful to heal every wound, to grant new life where we can see only death and destruction. This is the justice of the resurrection, of the new creation in the risen Christ.

So Jesus comes to his disciples, locked away in fear of "the Jews," as John says. In John's Gospel, the word "Jews" is code for "the religious authorities"; of course they were all Jews, followers of Jesus or not. Jesus shows his anxious and probably embittered disciples that they have a choice about what kind of justice they will work and pray for. "If you forgive the sins of any, they are forgiven them; if you retain the sins of any, they are retained." Forgiving the sins of others—that is restorative justice. In the power of the Holy Spirit, we, the disciples of Jesus, can put our best energies and creativity into the slow work of opening a space in our personal lives, our families, and our communities for God's work of bringing life out of death, reconciliation out of alienation. Or we can choose to retain sins, seeking not erasure but punishment, not embrace but exclusion. The choice is real in any given instance, and it is ours to make.

Restorative justice, the forgiveness of sins, is the child of faith. It is born of the belief that, beyond my suffering, God is at work, working through us for healing. The forgiveness of sins is an expression of faith, however inarticulate, and it can also generate new faith. My own faith comes largely out of the experience of being forgiven, over and over again. But one experience in particular was formative.

It was 1969, and I was a teenager, spending the year at the Hebrew University in Jerusalem. My roommate was also an American, from a family of Hungarian Jews, most of whom had died at Auschwitz, including my friend's older brother and sister. The survivors had settled in the United States and in Israel, and so on Sabbath my friend would visit her aunt and uncle on the coast south of Tel Aviv. One weekend she asked me to come. This was not exactly a routine visit home with the college roommate, since this Hungarian-Israeli family had had no contact with Christians since the war, when their trusted Christian neighbors had betrayed them to the Nazis and sent them to the death camps. Later my roommate admitted that her aunt and uncle had not been eager to welcome me into their home. But all they showed me was the warmest hospitality and, as the year went on, genuine love. They made me, a Christian, a member of the family.

This was my first profound experience of being forgiven. They forgave me for my religious identity—hardly my fault, you might say, but six million European Jews had been murdered simply for their religious identity. The experience of receiving their forgiveness was life-changing for me, at a time when I was just beginning to ask what it might mean to be a Christian. In countless ways, I am still learning to believe out of what I experienced that year, now more than forty years ago, spent almost entirely in the company of Jews.

Today, viewing my Israeli family through the lens of John's Gospel, I understand better why the forgiveness of sins is the very first work the risen Jesus assigns his disciples. They were hiding in fear, because of their religious identity, and Jesus calls them to set that fear aside and go out in the power of the Holy Spirit. He empowers them to turn hatred and fear into genuine relationship, even into love. Isn't that just what my Jewish family did? Setting aside their natural feelings toward a Christian, feelings born of betrayal and unthinkable suffering, they redefined me not as enemy but as their own. These Hungarian Jews were not consciously following Jesus. Yet in modeling the forgiveness that Jesus taught his disciples, they taught me to believe.

It is low Sunday. Low-spirited or not, we have come here, each of us hoping to believe that Jesus has risen from the dead and that something, everything has changed as a result. And look, each of us has valuable experience that can help us believe: at some time, someone has forgiven us; at some time, we have forgiven. May knowledge of forgiveness be for us a source of mutual encouragement and hope, so that together we may learn to believe this hard thing—that there is life abundant beyond sin and death—and, believing that, we will have life in Jesus's name.

Amen.

Divine Drama

King's College Chapel, Cambridge, England
Maundy Thursday, April 1, 2010

1 CORINTHIANS 11:23-26

This Maundy Thursday meditation asks the audience to view the Pas-
chal Triduum as theater, but listeners soon find themselves pushed onto
the stage and into a seat at the Lord's table. Here Jesus demonstrates
the risky, self-giving love of God with the words of institution, "This is
my body, broken for you." We also hear the voice of Paul telling us that
Jesus's death was not in vain, but rather the purest form of God's love
for us. As we dine surrounded by these voices, we find the "gap" closing
between past and present. Just as Jesus spoke to the disciples at the first
communion, "So, then, Jesus is speaking to us here."

Think of this as theater. That may be the best way to take in the three-day drama that begins this evening, as we watch Jesus walk with certain knowledge into a death trap. If we think of this as theater and not just church, then we may see that, like all great dramas, the one being enacted here is meant to give us a certain perspective on our world. Ordinarily, when we watch a drama, we more or less consciously ask the question, What does it say about the way things are in this world—and in my own life? But we may be less inclined to ask that question of this particular drama, which suffers greatly from over-familiarity. Regular churchgoers or not, we all know the plotline, and so—especially if we are regular churchgoers—we may fail to ask the question that anyone coming to this story for the first time surely would ask: What is the point of Jesus's death on the cross? Or is it pointless, just another random act of violence, like so many deaths in our world?

That question must be faced by anyone who takes seriously what the Bible says about Jesus's death. As the evangelist Luke tells the story, it was just one technicality removed from a lynching. Pontius Pilate was ready to release Jesus; the Roman governor knew he had done nothing wrong. But the crowd cried out, "Crucify him! Crucify him!" and so Pilate the Roman governor signed off on the killing. You could easily conclude that the whole thing was a senseless tragedy; it doesn't mean anything at all.

Yet from the beginning the church has said the opposite: this is the event that enables us to make sense of everything else in our world. Therefore we shall "proclaim the Lord's death until he comes," as St. Paul says (1 Cor. 11:26). Christians even claim that Jesus's death is the source of all our hope. But how can that be? If Jesus was really the Messiah, the anointed of God, King of the Jews, then wouldn't it have been better for him to use his power and connections to save himself, just as those mockers at the crucifixion said? Pinning our hope to a death that came from mob rage—can this be anything other than a prolonged case of mass delusion?

It can, but only if Paul is right that Jesus's death on the cross is God's supreme act of love for the world. That is the central claim of the gospel, a claim that is thoroughly counterintuitive yet not crazy. However, in order to understand it, you have to think seriously and unsentimentally about what it is to love. Think of the strongest and purest love you know: for a child perhaps, or a parent, a friend, or a spouse; for an animal who has wordlessly yet deeply shared your life, teaching you gentleness and devotion; for the work that gives meaning and purpose to your life. To any or all of these we give ourselves without stint—foolishly, in a sense, because in every case we pour ourselves out with no assurance of a good result. For it is the very nature of loving that we give up control over the beloved, just as St. Paul taught: "Love does not insist on its own way" (1 Cor. 13:5). We might experience great joy as a consequence, or great sorrow, and chances are we will experience both, every time we give ourselves in love. Paul knew that, too: "Love bears all things" (13:7). Any of a thousand or ten thousand things can turn the lover's story into a tragedy, as every dramatist is keenly aware, and every lover also. Yet as long as we are emotionally and spiritually healthy, we will choose to love, this time and the next and the next, even knowing that our hearts will ache and break over and over again. Our hearts will be broken by pain, but unless they are twisted, distorted by it, then we will remain fools for love, as long as life endures.

Strangely, it seems that God loves exactly the same way we do: incautiously, even foolishly. Love by its nature is risky; it does not control its outcome. And God's own nature is boundless, self-giving Love. The only difference between God's loving and ours is that God is wholly Love, and so it follows that God is wholly at risk. The most risky *and* the most loving thing that God has ever done is becoming flesh and blood in Jesus Christ—a supreme venture in love, which can end only in death.

This evening begins the climax of the divine drama, as Jesus utters these words at the Last Supper: "This is my body, [broken] for you" (1 Cor. 11:24). He is speaking to his disciples, of course, but also to every Christian since. At the Last Supper Jesus speaks the words that will be spoken at every altar or communion table, day after day and week after week, as long as the church exists. So, then, Jesus is speaking to us here. It's like a fantasy we have all entertained as children: imagining that the characters on the screen or the stage might actually speak to us. One day they might just turn their faces and see us, sitting in the audience, full of interest and empathy, eager to enter their story. Who knows? They might invite us in, just as Jesus does when he says, "This is my body, which is [broken] for you."

With those familiar words, Jesus answers our question—Does this death make any sense?—answers it by saying in effect, "My death may be horrible, but it is not a senseless tragedy. No, I tell you, I would do it again in a heartbeat. I *am* doing it again, day after day and week after week until time is no more. This is my body, that is [broken] for you. Remember this; remember me." Do you hear? Jesus is speaking to us as a lover speaks. Isn't this just what each of us hopes to hear from our beloved and say to our beloved, when death is near: "Knowing everything I know now, I would do it all over again, for you"? At the Last Supper, knowing his intimate friend will betray him this night, Jesus reveals himself to be the perfect Fool for Love. "This is my body . . . [broken] for you."

Think of this evening as theater, improvisational theater. Ready or not, you are being called onto the stage, into the drama of God's love for the world. Now here is your scene: It's Thursday evening. Knowing he will die tomorrow, Jesus has just thrown himself at your feet with these words: "I would do it all over again, for you." Now, warm to your part. How does it feel to hear that from the One whose love can never die? God in flesh and blood is at your feet. As this three-day drama unfolds, how will you respond?

Amen.

The Secret of Community

Union Theological Seminary, New York
October 17, 1988

EPHESIANS 4:1–7, 11–16

For Paul, "diversity" is far more than an end in itself, or even a guiding principle for Christians. Rather, the church presumes heterogeneity as a starting point for the discovery of our shared identity in Christ. The secret of this community's life is not tolerance but humility, which entails the ability to receive other's strengths and weaknesses as gifts. Risking vulnerability as members of the body of Christ, we will publicize a way of life that startles others, makes them envious, and finally draws them into our expanding community of peace.

Have you ever noticed how difficult it is to read Scripture while riding your favorite hobby horse? Let the reading distract you from the riding for just a moment, and it's as though someone had slipped a thorn under the imaginary saddle, and suddenly you find that you've lost your comfortable seat and landed, sometimes pretty hard, on the ground. The biblical writers seem to make a regular game of unseating us in this way: we continually find that they challenge not only our unconscious assumptions but also some of our deepest convictions, turning horses whose habits we thought we knew into bucking broncos.

Today, the name of that suddenly feisty horse is "Diversity." I expect you know it. We in the church have ridden Diversity hard in recent years, and in some unlikely places, such as seminaries and religious orders and bishop's palaces. In those venerable halls where they used to talk about Tradition, Church Order, Creeds, and Catechisms, now they're talking about Diversity. And probably no place has committed itself more strongly than this seminary to maintaining the diversity that is essential to the church's life. Union has focused its mission on asserting to the church at large how costly is the systematic attempt to mute any of Christianity's multiple voices, how we are all impoverished and endangered when any of our number cannot, will not be heard.

Diversity is a value we are working hard to establish and live by, and so it may be unsettling for us to notice that the first Christian theologian spends so little time and passion on the celebration of difference. It's not that Paul opposes the diversity of the church; on the contrary, he assumes it as foundational: Christian diversity is a natural reflection of the universality of the gospel. Indeed, Paul's own missionary work was the force that first realized that universality. Through his efforts, the church ceased to be a small, homogeneous sect of pious Judeans and came to include people from every ethnic group and social stratum in the Mediterranean world: Greeks, Romans, Africans, and Asians; pagans and Jews; slaves and slave owners; soldiers, artisans, aristocrats.

But if Paul is responsible for the church's heterogeneity, nonetheless he places surprisingly little emphasis on its advantages. According to Paul, diversity is the starting point for the church: we are called from our different backgrounds, with our different skills, to follow Jesus Christ. But the church's real business is to move beyond that initial diversity, beyond the separate identities of its individual members, so that together they may claim a new identity as Christ's body in the world. Paul conceives the church as a single living organism, whose distinct members, as he writes to the Ephesians, are "joined and knit together," so that each part works properly only as it works in concert with the other parts. Yes, Paul says, don't be afraid to acknowledge your differences—but don't idolize them either. Accept your diversity, welcome it, and then get on with your real business, the business of discovering a shared identity richer than any of us could claim on our own.

When we talk about the church in those terms, as a unified body, we're making a faith statement. That is to say, we're talking much more about what we hope for from God than what we already see in ourselves. The church as the body of Christ is God's creation among us; it is the perfect expression of the life God intends for us: a life of total shared commitment, whose single purpose is to grow in love. That is the full humanity to which God calls us, but it is not the way most of us have learned to live in the world. So we need to be trained, actually retrained, in order to be effective members of this body of Christ. The letter to the Ephesians sets forth the elements of that training program. As with any form of fitness training, those who undertake this body-of-Christ-building program should be prepared for some hard work; for the program that Paul outlines treats the two most fundamental aspects of our lives: the way we regard ourselves, and the way we treat one another.

First, with respect to ourselves, Paul calls us to an attitude of humility: "I beg you to lead a life worthy of the calling to which you have been called, with all humility and courtesy." Now, as it is commonly practiced among Christians, humility could hardly be considered a virtue. Often we act as though humility means denying our own worth and talents, which then makes us humble Christians perfect candidates for resentment of those who also fail to acknowledge them. But in reality, humility is the very opposite of angry self-denial. Humility means full acceptance of your own talents; and the key word is "acceptance": that is, recognizing those talents for what they are, a gift from God, God's gift to the world through you. Humility demands that we nurture our talents—slowly, as they grow to fullness; nurture them patiently, not quite knowing what their full growth will look like. Thomas Aquinas taught: "Humility is nothing other than the patient pursuit of your own excellence." "The patient pursuit of your own excellence"—*your* excellence, the fullness of being that God particularly intended for you; yet the fruits of that excellence must finally be offered as a gift to the community. Living together with humility and courtesy—that means listening to others, letting them call forth in you that excellence which the community needs for its health, listening as they help you name your place in the body of Christ.

Humility, then, is more than a way of regarding ourselves. Humility is essentially a public virtue; it calls us out of ourselves, beyond a concern for the development of our own gifts, and into active regard for the good of others in the community. Paul calls this public exercise of our humility "forbearing one another in love." Now, on the face of it, forbearance doesn't sound like much of a challenge. Most of us are pretty good about putting up with one another, shoring up our good manners with wry humor and a fair measure of emotional distance, making up in wry humor for what we lack in understanding. But Paul is not going to let us get away with that kind of mutual avoidance. Remember, this guy is going for gold: the whole point of our forbearance is to bring the church to perfection, that is, to perfect unity. As Paul instructs the Ephesians, we are to show ourselves "eager to maintain the unity of the spirit in the bond of peace." And forging that bond of peace requires more than a grin-and-bear-it tolerance that is hardly distinguishable from indifference. For we are to forbear one another in love; and the kicker there is "love." Paul calls us into passionate engagement with one another, into hot pursuit of our common well-being. Our common well-being—that is the peace that holds us together: not the absence of conflict, but rather peace in the sense of wholeness, well-being, *shalom*. Forging the bond of peace means promoting the health of other members of the body, knowing that we can achieve our own health in no other way, that how I'm doing as the left foot depends very much on how you're doing as the ankle, and this one can't fully enjoy being a healthy hip if that elbow over there is in pain.

So that's it, the one simple secret of community life: your being fully who you are is essential to my well-being. And the charge to forbear one another in love does not mean only receiving each other's strengths and admirable qualities. The full measure of our humility is whether we can also receive weakness as a gift. Vulnerability—and by that I mean weakness that is freely named—genuine vulnerability is a gift to the community; we find a focus for our common life only when we know where each member is struggling to grow. We've all experienced the gift of vulnerability in a home where there is a baby: the one whose weakness can be named binds us together, reminding us of our commitment to nurture one another, teaching us that it is not power that secures us a place among the people of God, but rather our capacity to respond to love.

Like all forms of countercultural living, what I am describing is risky— actually, more than risky: if you commit yourself to the public exercise of humility, then you should expect at times to feel uncomfortably exposed, to be asked to give more than you want to, and, more painfully, to have the gifts you offer refused. Yet Paul assures us that if we as a community commit ourselves to this lifestyle, then together we can grow into the full measure of our perfection, into the "stature of the fullness of Jesus Christ." We won't finish that growth in this life. Perfect humanity is a heavenly reality; we will achieve it fully only in the resurrection. But living together in humility and courtesy, forbearing one another in love, we can catch a glimpse of our final perfection. More importantly, we can offer a glimpse of heaven to a world straining after a reason to hope. For that is finally why we are called together into this body of Christ: to open a window into heaven, by the quality of our common life to offer others a new vision of their God-given humanity.

So what should people see when they look at us? They should see something a little startling: they should see a place where the defense walls are coming down, a place where people have begun to cultivate a taste for vulnerability, to enjoy being free from a constant fear of exposure. Perhaps no one is impressed with the extravagance of our gifts, yet they are struck by the way we put them at one other's service. They notice how we care for each other, listen to each other, find healing, comfort, joy in each other's presence.

Brothers and sisters, we should be living in such a way as to excite envy in others, envy so intense that we must continually expand the bounds of this unwalled city, so that they, too, can enter in and share in the bond of peace that unites us.

So be it.

Amen.

Being Perfect

Yale Divinity School, New Haven, Connecticut
Baccalaureate, May 26, 1996

PHILIPPIANS 3:4B–4:9

Paul provides three directions for a perfect ministry: "Don't be anx-
ious; be gentle; keep your mind on what is good." Each direction is
simple enough, and yet each one presents a challenge to our natural
inclinations toward anxiety, severity, and despair. Originally a source
of encouragement for those embarking on lives of service to the church,
this sermon's exploration of Paul's wisdom is relevant to all Christians.
We see how each of his three prescriptions may be a means of grace for
all Christians to grow into Christ-like perfection.

"Let those of us then who are mature be of like mind . . ." (Phil. 3:15). Thus Paul
calls the Christians at Philippi to advance in the thinking that belongs to faith.
But the translation is not entirely satisfactory; it's more than maturity to which
he calls them. It's perfection. The word is *teleioi*, complete, perfect. Of course,
Paul knows that nobody, including himself, is a perfect Christian in this life. But
he has a particular fondness for these Philippians, who supported him, as he
says, "in the beginning of the gospel" (4:15) and support him now in his present
need. So to these trusted friends Paul opens his mind fully, so that they may
strive with him toward the perfection to which he aspires, namely this: "To know
[Christ] and the power of his resurrection and the fellowship of his sufferings."

"To know the fellowship of Christ's sufferings—*koinōnian*, the community
of Christ's sufferings—becoming like him in his death." To our still-imperfect
ears, that statement of the goal sounds grim, but behind it lies the wildest hope,
which bursts from Paul like a once-in-a-lifetime Christmas wish from a child:
"if only somehow I may attain to the resurrection from the dead!" (3:10–11).

The full opening of Paul's mind is a daunting experience. He is so far ahead of us: an athlete of the gospel (4:3), going for the gold, straining every fiber—moral, physical, and spiritual—to win a prize that most of us, if we are honest, cannot claim even to desire. Consider: you have to be very close to perfection to want a share in Christ's sufferings. You have to be in better spiritual condition than most of us to face squarely and cheerfully the clear message of the gospel, that the only way to attain the resurrection from the dead is to achieve a resemblance to our crucified Lord—"to become like him in his death." If you cannot yet desire that resemblance, don't despair. This occasion is properly called "commencement" and not "the grand finale."

Fortunately for the Philippians and for us, Paul is not only a nearly perfect athlete; he is also a wise and surprisingly gentle personal trainer. The whole of Paul's letter is a careful instruction to those who still need basic training in the practice of Christian perfection. To them—to us—Paul gives three simple directions: "Don't be anxious; be gentle; keep your mind on what is good" —instructions so simple they hardly seem right. And in fact, each of them is completely counterintuitive. Each of them pushes us to act in ways that are unnatural to us, in our present state of sin. In other words, each of them pushes us to act less like our fallen selves and more like Christ.

Yet the instructions really are simple. Paul does not compromise the goal of perfection, full resemblance to Christ; compromising on that would be delusive and ultimately cruel, for it would keep us from attaining to the resurrection from the dead. Nonetheless, he grades the learning curve, so the goal becomes realistic for us. Moreover, the goal is realistic just because it is Paul who sets it forth, this man whom we know so well. We know his grim past history, his continuing struggles with himself and with others. His disappointments, his occasional harsh words and his blind spots, if so they be, are permanently recorded. What Paul's letters reveal is a remarkable and difficult personality, who has moved from enmity to the gospel to a faith in the power of Christ's death and resurrection as close to perfect as we may expect to see in this life. This is someone from whom we can—and must—learn.

First then, "Do not worry about anything, but in everything by prayer and thanksgiving let your requests be made known to God" (4:6). "Don't worry about anything"—coming from a laid-back person, this advice would be suspect, at least to the Type-A personalities among us, and our name is Legion. But certainly no one could accuse Paul of being happy-go-lucky, this zealot who now "chases" after the heavenly prize as he once "chased" after Christians to exterminate them (*diōkō*, 3:6 and 12). Moreover, Paul knows deep anguish. Even now, he writes in tears as he remembers how many still live as enemies of the cross of Christ, whose "god is the belly, [whose] glory is in their shame, [whose] minds are set on earthly things" (3:19).

It is a curious thing: Paul strives mightily and grieves deeply; yet he is untouched by the anxiety that plagues most of us. Which is to say, he is not anxious for himself. This is unmistakably clear earlier in the letter, when Paul wonders whether his present imprisonment will end in execution or release. He weighs the alternatives as you or I might debate purchasing a navy blue sweater or a charcoal gray one. Listen to him: "Christ will be exalted now as always in my body, whether by life or by death. For to me, living is Christ and dying is gain. . . . I do not know which I prefer. I am hard pressed between the two . . ." (1:20–23). This would not be a tough choice for most of us, and so it is hard to believe Paul's indifference is sincere, until we recognize that he is speaking here, as he so often does, from the perspective of eternity. He speaks as one who lives perpetually in the presence of God, for that is what eternal life is, living continually with God, in this world on into the next. Eternal life, then, does not begin when we die, but rather when all the distractions that keep us from God are finally overcome, when nothing we desire or value or fear is outside our relationship with God, so that we may "in everything by prayer and thanksgiving let [our] requests be made known to God." In that condition of uninterrupted blessedness, even the choice between life and death is a choice between two great goods, two different ways of exalting Christ in our flesh.

"Do not worry about anything." It would be well if this commencement marked a significant step toward your freedom from anxiety about yourself. I think it is fair to say that perpetual anxiety goes with the territory of student life. Here you are continually judged for "how you are doing"; and because all of us are sinful—professors and administrators and church officials as well as students—that judgment sometimes produces as much anxiety as growth. As you now end your student career, or in some cases move to a higher state of "perfection" as a student, it is timely to pray for deliverance from anxiety. It is fitting that you should grow in trust that another intention and action underlies yours and will bring your efforts to a fruitful conclusion. For until you claim that freedom from anxiety, you will be hampered in the work for which your education here has prepared you.

I discovered this during my first year of full-time teaching. Everyone had said it would be the hardest working year of my life, and I certainly brought that prophecy to fulfillment. Each class represented an agony of preparation and worry about whether my ignorance was showing. It was not until the eighth week of the second semester that I finally got my eyes off my own feet, stopped worrying about how I was doing, and thought hard about my students—what was their experience of the class, were they learning as much as they could? Which is to say, it took me eight months to think like a teacher instead of a student. When I finally made that adjustment, I experienced no blinding illumination, but something must have perceptibly changed, for immediately after the next class a student said to me: "You were different today." The obvious implication is that I was pretty bad before. Nonetheless, "forgetting what lay behind" (3:13), I heard that remark as encouragement. I heard in it what Paul would call "the upward call of God in Christ Jesus" (3:14). At last I had made the first small step toward my own perfection, toward maturity in the form of Christian service to which I am called.

A second instruction: "Let your gentleness be known to everyone. The Lord is near." The gentleness of which Paul speaks is "a willingness to yield in matters that are not essential";[1] the word (*epieikes*) is sometimes translated "moderation, forbearance." Such gentleness proceeds from a desire for unity over purity of opinion and motive within the body of Christ, for many of the things that divide us most bitterly within the church are not in fact essentials of faith in Christ crucified. The gentleness that tolerates differences is not an easy virtue for us to appreciate. Yale Divinity School is a place where we all value a sharp critical edge; indeed, we sometimes regard moderation as an enemy of truth. But we may be less sensitive to the fact that the truth of the gospel is inevitably compromised by personal animosity.

Again in this matter, Paul is an extraordinary teacher. The gentleness that he commands entails a willingness to shrug off personal injuries for the sake of unity in the body, and here Paul instructs us out of his own experience. Even within the small circle of the early church, Paul had professional enemies. Some were only too glad to take advantage of his imprisonment to promote themselves in his stead as preachers of Christ crucified, as Paul says, "supposing to add affliction to my bonds" (1:17). It is hard to think of anything more hurtful: Paul must have been a teacher to some of these supplanters. Yet his magnanimity defeats their cruelty; he welcomes his would-be rivals as colleagues. He rejoices, he's genuinely happy at what they are doing; for Christ Jesus is preached, the gospel is proclaimed, even if the preachers themselves are interested chiefly in their own advancement.

Paul's freedom from rancor is as extraordinary as his freedom from anxiety, and it is crucial for us to understand; for some of you also will have professional enemies. "Let your gentleness be known to everyone. The Lord is near." "Oh," we might say, "no wonder Paul can afford to be cavalier. He

1. A. H. McNeile, *Discipleship* (London: SPCK, 1924), 87.

expects Christ's imminent return, that within a few years his enemies will be standing before the judgment throne." But that line of reasoning misses the point. It doesn't matter if Paul's schedule for the Second Coming does differ from ours, because, as we have seen, he speaks from the perspective of eternity. "The Lord is near." Is that any less true for us than it was for the Philippians some nineteen and a half centuries ago? God forbid.

The point is this: gentleness proceeds from the perception of our Lord's nearness. If I experience that nearness and can refer everything in my life to God, including my injuries, then I can believe that my rival, my enemy, this person with whom I disagree also stands near God. Indeed, she cannot stand anywhere else. So we stand together, each of us with our highly mixed motives, awaiting God's judgment. In this situation, I can afford to be gentle. Indeed, I must be. "The Lord is near"; we have urgent need for repentance and cause for bursting hope. "The Lord is near"; and are we to waste our energies in bitter rivalries among ourselves?

A third instruction: "Finally, brothers and sisters, whatever is true, whatever is honorable, whatever is just, whatever is pure, whatever is pleasing, whatever is commendable, if there is any excellence and if there is anything worthy of praise, consider these things" (4:8). From someone else, in other circumstances, we might dismiss such counsel as hopelessly naive, a denial of how hard life really is, an escape into cloud-cuckoo land. But Paul is the consummate Christian realist, who has suffered repeatedly for the gospel and even now writes in chains (1:13). So we must recognize this advice for what it is: a call to rigorous discipline of our attention in the face of adversity. Riveting our attention on what is good and true even in the midst of our sufferings—this is indispensable if we are to have the joy on which Paul so strongly insists. And again, Paul is his own best example. He writes jubilantly that because of his present imprisonment the gospel is now known among the Roman guards, and most of the Christians have grown bolder in proclaiming their faith (1:14).

Fixing your mind on what is good does not mean ignoring the evil in the world and in yourself. Rather, it means refusing to let evil be the determinative factor in the human situation, refusing to let it kill the joy of the gospel. You have in fact been committed to that refusal ever since baptism, and the work you have done here should have greatly reinforced your commitment and your ability to refuse evil. You have honed your skills for studying the works of the Lord, which, as our psalmist says, are "to be scrutinized in their every detail" (Ps. 111:2). And that is finally what it means to refuse evil, for yourself and for the people whom you will serve. You are charged to scrutinize the works of the Lord in a world ravaged by evil, both natural and moral evil.

In other words, you must discover whatever God is doing for which we can return genuine thanks.

This is the first and most exacting responsibility of pastoral ministry. It will take all your learning and your probing prayer to discern what is good and praiseworthy, when evil seems to have triumphed. What is still true, when love has been betrayed? What is just, when a child has been abused or killed or born greatly handicapped? What is noble, when UN refugee camps have been bombed or peacemakers murdered? What is pure and lovely, when we of the industrialized nations have in our greed savaged the whole globe—earth, water, and air even up to our tattered ozone layer?

The answer to these questions is in every case far from obvious. But if the answer is "nothing—nothing lovely, nothing praiseworthy," then we are of all people most to be pitied, for our faith is in vain (1 Cor. 15:14–19). So you must find answers. You must search and help your people find whatever God is doing to raise up those who are bowed down, to comfort those who mourn, to open the eyes of the blind, to sanctify God's own holy name. It will take courage to stay in that search, to look squarely at evil and not turn away to some pleasant distraction, but rather to look on until you see signs of resurrection life bursting forth even in the midst of death. It will take great sensitivity to discern the possibility for more perfect Christian faith that comes only through doubt, disappointment, bitter loss. Yet you must keep looking for it. That ceaseless search is necessarily part of what it means for each of you to participate in the community of Christ's sufferings. By virtue of your gifts, your education, and your upward call, you are privileged to make perspicuous God's marvelous works, ancient works and astonishing new ones, to make them shine forth, points of light in our deeply shadowed world, marking the way into the kingdom of our God, to whom be praise, glory, honor, and every blessing, for ever and for evermore.

Amen.

The Table of Creation

Grace Cathedral, San Francisco, California
Earth Day, April 25, 1999

COLOSSIANS 1:15–29

We cannot be healed of our estrangement from and hostility toward creation until we realize the twofold nature of our invitation to the Lord's table. That is, the invitation to the feast of reconciliation is also an invitation to sacrifice. Christ's sacrifice does not preclude our own; rather, "Christ's sacrifice makes ours possible." Our visible witness of an ethic of sacrifice will be a genuine disclosure to the world of "the mystery hidden throughout the ages." This mystery is the blood of the cross, by which we are made able to participate in Christ's restoration of our ecological devastations.

The Bible is not an early ecological tract. Although ecological devastation was a known phenomenon in the ancient world—devastation on a local or regional scale, not a global one—"sustainable living" was not a primary concern of the first Christians. For, as you know, they were waiting on tiptoe for the Second Coming, for Christ to come in glory, bringing an end to this world and ushering in the next. Therefore it comes as a surprise to hear, in the letter to the Colossians, words that seem to reflect what we would today call a "deep ecology" perspective. "Deep ecologists" are those who believe that the ecological crisis is not in the first instance a crisis in technology, but rather that the root cause lies in the human heart. In a word, deep ecologists believe that the ecological crisis stems from what Christians call "sin," above all the sin of isolating ourselves from the rest of the creatures, preferring the immediate advantage of the privileges of our species over the well-being of all creation. Conversely, deep ecologists believe that humans must reconnect with the rest of the creatures, if this wounded yet still lovely planet is to be a livable place for us all.

That is what modern deep ecologists think. The surprising thing is that the apostle Paul (it may have been a disciple of Paul who wrote the letter to the Colossians, but I am going to say "Paul") seems to share this perspective on the need for humans to make a profound (re)connection with the rest of the creatures, if our world is to be healed. Of course, Paul understands that the first and greatest need is for us to be reconnected with God, from whom, as he says, we were "once estranged and hostile in mind, doing evil deeds" (1:21). That reconnection is what the gospel is about; the whole New Testament proclaims that Christ Jesus has come that we may no longer be estranged from and hostile to God. Yet each book of the New Testament has something particular to tell us; each one has a somewhat different angle on Christ's work of reconciling us to God. And it happens that Colossians' angle helps us especially *this* day, when we pray to be more responsible in our relationships with every other creature God has made, including that most complex and glorious of creatures, the earth herself.

Listen to the promise of reconciliation Paul holds out: you can come before God "holy and blameless"—that in itself is a remarkable promise, considering how deep Paul knows human sin to be. Nonetheless, you can be "holy and blameless and irreproachable before [God] *provided*—*provided* that you continue securely established and steadfast in the faith, without shifting from the hope promised by the gospel that you heard, [the gospel] which has been proclaimed to every creature under heaven" (1:23). "The gospel . . . which has been proclaimed to every creature under heaven"—that is the wildest evangelical statement in all of Scripture. Think about it—"every creature under heaven." If taken seriously, that would suggest that the good news is meant not just for "every family, language, people and nation" (Rev. 5:9; cf. Dan. 7:14), but also for rock badgers and rocks, for fruit bats and giant sequoias—every creature under heaven. Even at the end of this designated "Decade of Evangelism," that scope for gospel proclamation far exceeds anything our church has yet imagined.

But if this statement is so far beyond where the church is, this wild statement that the gospel is proclaimed to every creature under heaven, then why should we take it seriously? Because in all the New Testament, this is, I believe, the most important clue to how we humans can reconnect with our fellow creatures. What the letter to the Colossians is laying before us is a comprehensive ecological vision. Ecology is the study of relationships, and the insight Colossians offers us is that everything in the world is related to everything else

302

precisely in Christ Jesus. In him, everything that is, is related to everything else that is now, ever was, or ever shall be. Listen again to Paul: "*All things* have been created through Christ and for Christ . . . , and in him *all things* hold together" (1:16–17). "*All* things"—that phrase is repeated five times in the space of a few sentences—all things hold together in Christ. And what's more, through Christ all things are being reconciled to God. I don't pretend to understand that. This is mystical insight that exceeds my grasp. But this I understand: it is for the sake of reconciliation that the gospel has been proclaimed to every creature under heaven, so that everything created in Christ and for Christ—every person, every stick and stone and stallion and seahorse—everything can claim its place in the reconciling work of Christ Jesus.

Okay, so what does all this mean on the ground? What possibility does Colossians open up for us that would not otherwise be obvious? We do not really need the Bible to tell us that every created thing is related to every other created thing on this "small blue dot" of a planet. The essential unity of all inhabitants and elements of the earth—this is now accepted as a given in scientific reports and in the news media. And frankly, it does not sound like good news. If the ship goes down, we all drown—a possibility we cannot discount, if you are reading the same reports I am. So what difference does the biblical witness make on this matter? What is the *good* news about the fundamental relatedness of all creatures that Paul says he is "toiling and struggling" with all his energy to convey to us (v. 29)?

This: what Colossians shows us, and the scientific reports do not, is the unity of the creatures *under the universal Lordship of Christ*. It shows us all things held together, not in bondage to a single threatening fate, but *in Christ*. The difference the biblical witness makes is the difference between accepting a sober fact—our common danger—and accepting an invitation to a party. The Christian participates in the solidarity of the creatures as one who is responding to an invitation to a gala banquet. That is how the German Swiss theologian Karl Barth describes what it means for the Christian to accept the fact that she is a creature, no more and no less, present in this world simply as an honored guest of the sovereign Lord of all the worlds. If we accept God's invitation to the banquet of the creatures, then, Karl Barth says, we take our "place at the table, in the company of publicans, in the company of beasts and plants and stones, accepting solidarity with them, being present simply as they are, as a creature of God."[1]

But let's be honest. This is a vision of the kingdom of God we do not

1. Karl Barth, *Church Dogmatics* III/3 (Edinburgh: T. & T. Clark, 1958-61), 242.

easily accept. It sounds flaky, vaguely sub-Christian, even though it comes from so respectable, even formidable a theologian as Karl Barth. Christians partying with plants and stones?! Our imaginations do not readily stretch so far; certainly the evangelistic vision of the church does not stretch so far, despite Colossians' witness that "the gospel . . . has been proclaimed to every creature under heaven." But why is it hard for us to claim this vision of solidarity with all the creatures? Could it be that we are afraid? Afraid to sit down at the banqueting table and open a conversation with the nonhuman creatures? Afraid that if we once open that conversation in the presence of God, the other creatures will find their voice and cry out against us? Afraid that the rivers we have dammed, drained, and poisoned will accuse us of culpable negligence? Afraid that the soil we have stripped of its hardwood forests, the seas we have drag-netted and depopulated will cry out against us for our greed? Afraid that the mountains we are literally taking down to the ground, scraping out veins of low-grade coal and leaving behind vast piles of infertile rubble—are we afraid that the mountains of Kentucky will testify against us, that we have undone the work of God's hands, misused our God-given powers for evil, to satisfy our own selfish whims?

That would be an intelligent fear, informed not only by the news media but also, and more importantly, by the Bible, which tells us that things we call "inanimate" do, in fact, have a voice in the presence of God. Remember those psalms where the mountains and hills ring out for joy, the sea shouts, rivers clap their hands, when God comes to "judge the world with righteousness, and the peoples with his truth" (Ps. 98:9)? The nonhuman creatures clamor at the good news that their Lord is coming in power and justice to judge the world. They are ecstatic at the prospect of being delivered at last into God's hands, delivered from our doubtful mercies. If all the abused creatures we call "dumb" find their loud voices in the presence of God, then maybe that is why we don't envision ourselves sitting at God's table with them. Who wants to be lambasted at dinner? Better to stay away, even if that means missing the meal that God has laid for all the creatures.

However, we may sit at the table without fear of humiliation if we will accept this one thing about the rules of this house: the wine served here is the blood of sacrifice. Christ's blood poured out for the life of the world is the wine of fellowship that unites all the creatures. In stunning terms Paul sets forth the sole basis for reconciliation, after all the harm that we have done: "through [Christ] God was pleased to reconcile to himself all things, whether on earth or in heaven, by making peace through the blood of his cross" (Col. 1:20). "Making peace through the blood of his cross"—those words confound our rationalism; and, if we can hear them, they draw us deep into what Paul calls "the mystery hidden throughout the ages . . . [that] has now been revealed to [the] saints" (v. 26).

This mystery: through the blood of the cross, Jesus Christ is healing a breach that dates back nearly to the beginning of world history. The first chapters of Genesis disclose that humanity's dangerous self-isolation originated, not in twentieth-century technology, but rather in the fallout from the first human disobedience. As soon as human beings had begun to seek their own way in the world, apart from God, the peace of Eden was shattered, and we fell into total alienation on the planet. It's all in the third chapter of Genesis; snakebite and weeds choking out the garden are the signs of our alienation from the nonhuman creatures. But now Christ offers to make "peace through the blood of the cross." From the cross, the centerpoint of all creation, Jesus Christ reaches out to embrace all things and reconcile them to God. Christ the firstborn of all creation, the most privileged of God's children, dying to draw the rest of us back to God—that is an image that has power to heal us from our profound estrangement and hostility of mind, if we can grasp just this one thing: the invitation to the feast of reconciliation is an invitation to sacrifice.

Sacrifice—literally "making holy," sanctifying the world by accepting our lives as pure gift and offering back to God any and all of what God has given us. Strange and sad to say, it is easy to miss or misunderstand the power of Christ's sacrifice. It's easy to think that Christ did it so we don't have to; his sacrifice makes ours unnecessary. But the gospel teaching is the opposite. Christ's sacrifice makes ours possible. Christ bids us follow him without fear in the way of the cross. He teaches us the strange inverse economics of the kingdom of heaven, where wealth is measured by how much you can afford to do without, where comfort level is measured by your ease in giving up.

Sisters and brothers, beloved in the Lord, we are invited now to the feast of reconciliation. If we speak with integrity and eat to our salvation, we commit ourselves to an ethics of sacrifice. What can we do, what can we give or give up in order that our words and even more our lives may become a genuine and persuasive proclamation of this mystery long hidden that has now been revealed, the mystical solidarity of all creatures, held together in Christ, reconciled to God and one another through the blood of the cross? In our time may that mystical solidarity be made manifest, to God's eternal glory, to the welfare of every creature under heaven.

Amen.

Easter Exiles

Christ Church Cathedral, Nashville, Tennessee
May 5, 2014

LUKE 24:13–35; 1 PETER 1:1–2, 14–23

What might it mean for us to claim our identity as exiles? While striving for superficial forms of community will leave us lonely and undisciplined, a full recognition that we are in some way marginalized, alienated, and reeling from loss can propel us into the real community called "church." As we share in God's holiness, we may recognize each other as gifts of grace, and discover in the light of this grace that we have finally found our true home.

Lord Jesus, stay with us. Make us holy, make us your church. Amen.

Greetings and the joy of Eastertide to you, the exiles in Nashville, belonging to the church of Jesus Christ dispersed across the globe. I bring you greetings from the Christian exiles in Durham, North Carolina. That is how the author of our epistle reading this morning (we'll call him Peter) would have us greet each other, as he greeted the so-called exiles in Galatia, Cappadocia, and other places in the region we now call Turkey. Welcome home on this Eastertide morning to the worldwide church into which we have been baptized—the company of exiles who have been chosen by God and sanctified by the Spirit (1 Pet. 1:2). It is good to spend the time of our exile together, worshiping God and honoring one another (2:17).

The people to whom Peter is writing are not literally exiles, any more than we are. The reason he names them and us thus is to bring us right into the heart of the biblical story, which is mainly a story about exiles, almost from the beginning. Think about it: Adam and Eve are the first exiles in the Bible; expulsion from Eden is exile. As the Bible tells it, we were made for intimate companionship with God; that's what Eden symbolizes. Yet almost from the beginning we got in our own way. Perhaps you know from experience how that goes: you didn't mean to get out of touch with God, not at all. But you had something in mind; it was compelling, at least for a little while. So you followed that up and the next thing you knew, you were, well, in a different place, spiritually speaking—and it was hard to get back to feeling close to God. You were in exile.

The Bible has many different stories about exile, because so much of the human experience can be described as a kind of exile: being displaced, marginalized, dispirited, with no control over what is happening to you. We have just heard about Jesus's disciples, walking sadly along the road to Emmaus, after their rabbi had been crucified. Remember what they said: "We had hoped that he was the one to redeem Israel" (Luke 24:21). Losing your dearest hope: that is exile—losing something that gave meaning to your life, gave you a vision for the future. But then the risen Jesus came to these exiles on the road. He stopped with them, perhaps at some roadside inn; he made himself "known to them in the breaking of the bread" (v. 35). This story in Luke's Gospel points to one of the great biblical insights about exile: it can be a place of revelation, precisely because exile is a place of radical uncertainty, where our own vision fails. In the no-place of exile, where all ordinary hope is lost, God may give us a new and stronger hope, grounded not in our plans and preferences, but in the new thing that God is doing. That is the kind of hope that came to these exiles on the road to Emmaus. They were still marginalized, still not in control of their future, but now they were exiles living in Easter hope. "That same hour" these disciples went back to Jerusalem to tell what they had seen. They rushed back after dinner, in the dark, to tell others *whom* they had seen (v. 33). Thus they became the first of the great community of the marginalized known as the church, the community of Easter exiles.

We are not accustomed to thinking of ourselves as exiles—and that label does seem incongruous, gathered as we are in this beautiful church. But that is how Peter would see us, so we need to consider what it might mean for us to claim that identity. Perhaps you know what it is to lose something, or the hope of something, that once seemed to be the unshakable center of your existence: a strong marriage; good health, physical or mental; a job or a sense of vocation; the person you could hardly bear to live without. A loss that severe is a kind of exile; you recognize that you have no control over what is happening to you; you feel like a stranger in your own life—not recognized, loved, and valued for who you are, or who you used to be. When you are in exile, there is a strange relief in naming that experience for what it is.

It is not just individuals who experience exile. The Bible speaks of Israel and Judah going into exile, and I am guessing that Peter has something like that in mind when he writes to the exiles scattered all across Asia Minor; it's a whole culture of exiles. The situation of those first-century Christians was in many ways similar to ours in the twenty-first century. Theirs was also an age of massive social upheaval and cultural change, with traditional communities coming apart, traditional values eroding, people in vast numbers losing jobs, losing family land, often moving to a new place to try to get life going again. If they had had a newspaper in the first century, it would have read like ours. Peter is addressing people at or below the economic waterline: slaves or serfs, the unpaid or low-paid laborers on whom what we call "civilized life" has always depended, from ancient times to the present.[1] Think factory workers and un-documented farm or domestic workers; think sanitation workers, caretakers for the elderly; think (dare I say it?) sex workers—the people we see every day, or maybe we look past them, but as a society we depend upon them nonetheless.

The truth that Peter tells us is that all of us are in exile, be it emotional or social and economic; all of us are longing for a place to belong, for a community of substance. And the sooner we acknowledge that, the sooner we can get down to the real work of being the church, a place where all of us can come home. The church is or should be a community of substance, where we who are marginalized, alienated, reeling from loss and bewildering change can be recognized and respected for who we are. "Honor everyone," Peter says (1 Pet. 2:17); "love one another deeply from the heart" (1:22).

There is a strange irony in our culture. We don't see ourselves as exiles, yet that is exactly how the advertising industry sees us. Don't most advertisements appeal to our unsatisfied longing for belonging? "Join the *community*"—have you noticed how often that word "community" shows up in ads?—"join the community" of those who drive a certain car or drink a particular Scotch or wear this brand of whatever. And if we do pay the price and join the community, the advertising legend goes, then we will be at the center and not on the margins. We will have a recognized and respected identity; we will not be exiles anymore.

---

1. The *paroikoi* ("exiles") were often serfs, slaves, tenant farmers, lower-class artisans. They were not citizens and were regarded as foreigners, although they might be born, live, and die in a given place (John H. Elliott, *A Home for the Homeless* [Philadelphia: Fortress, 1981], 68). The Hellenistic Roman era was an age of anxiety, geographic and cultural displacement, and turmoil. Political leaders and religious leaders alike might promise a home to the homeless (221). "The Christian gospel and the Christian community, according to 1 Peter, are a response to the predicament of strangerhood" (232).

The author of the letter of Peter knows this line of reasoning; there was a prestige industry in the ancient world, too. His answer to the hype is clear and direct. "Be serious" (1 Pet. 4:7), he says. You could also translate that: "Get real." And then he tells us exiles how to get real, and how to get a real community at the same time. This is Peter's essential word to Christian exiles: you will never have a real community, and you will never have a lasting hope, if you focus on what you don't yet have, what someone would like to sell you. No, community happens wherever exiles see themselves, not as needy, as lacking something essential for a complete life, but rather as gifted. Hope begins to grow whenever exiles recognize in their own lives something of the abundant grace of God and look for ways to share that grace with others, with their neighbors in exile. That is what it means, Peter tells us, to be holy, as God is holy (1:15). Being holy means putting aside all those phony needs generated by the ad industry, and getting real. Being holy means living out of the knowledge that everything we are and have is gift. Everything of real value, everything that genuinely satisfies, is the grace of God, poured out in countless ways, big and small: here a great shaft of light, here perhaps only scattered drops. Being holy means turning away from the Madison Avenue glitz and facing up to the darkness of exile—and then looking for the real light of God's grace, and pointing others toward it, the light that will lead us home.

"Get real, be disciplined," Peter says (4:7; see 1:13). Community such as this does not come easily, even by the grace of God. "Be disciplined . . . , serv[ing] one another with whatever gift each of you has received" (4:7–10). Peter is giving us, a motley bunch of Easter exiles, a discipline, so that we can grow to be a church. Now is a good time to begin, or begin again.

Now in a moment of silence, name before God a gift you have received, however small it seems to you at this moment, a gift that can be shared.

And now, consider your neighbors in exile, within these walls and far beyond them. Bring them before God in your imagination. Imagine what word you might offer today or this week that could bring a little ease in exile, what small act of thoughtfulness that could strengthen hope.

As I end this sermon, we'll take a moment of silence for this, our Eastertide discipline. I urge you to do it again tomorrow, and the day after. Maybe find someone to partner with you in this Easter discipline, to challenge and support you as you stretch your Christian imagination. What a good way to spend this time of our exile (see 1 Pet. 1:17).

Amen.

Worship the Lamb

Church Street United Methodist Church, Knoxville, Tennessee
April 25, 2004

JOHN 21:1–19; REVELATION 5:11–14

The book of Revelation presents us with two options for worship: we may worship God, or we may go "wondering after" the Beast—the empire. Yet, Revelation expresses in vivid imagery that only the Lamb who was slaughtered is worthy of worship. This Lamb is Jesus Christ our Lord, who, time and again, wins only by seeming to lose. Recalling Bishop Desmond Tutu's repeated call for the white South African government to "Come over to the winning side!" in the struggle against apartheid, this sermon invites our total confidence in God's power to triumph over evil. Such a life of worship will entail selfless striving for reconciliation with enemies, so that we may all finally walk together into the open arms of God.

Then I looked, and I heard the voice of many angels surrounding the throne and the living creatures and the elders; they numbered myriads of myriads and thousands of thousands; singing with full voice, "Worthy is the Lamb that was slaughtered to receive power and wealth and wisdom and might and honor and glory and blessing!" (Rev. 5:11–12)

For sheer fanfare, there's nothing quite like it in the whole Bible, this scene from the book of Revelation, when we actually see Jesus Christ the Lamb of God receiving the worship of the entire cosmos. It's a total contrast to the intimate scene from John's Gospel that we just heard: Jesus's last breakfast with his best friends, a post-resurrection breakfast, when Jesus asks his old sidekick the question that should touch us all: "Simon son of John, do you love me?" The passage from Revelation is equally affecting, but in a completely different way. It's an epic scene; you have to imagine it in wide-screen Technicolor with wrap-around sound. For the biblical writer known as St. John the Divine is catching us up into his own overwhelming vision of the risen Christ as the Lamb upon the throne, surrounded by the entire population of heaven: angels, cherubim and seraphim, redeemed human souls by the tens of thousands. And not just them. *Every* creature we could name or don't know how to name, in heaven, on earth, in the soil, in the sea, right here in the Tennessee River, earthworms and daisies, river oats and snails—every single creature of God finding a voice we never knew it had and belting out a song: "To the one seated on the throne and to the Lamb be blessing and honor and glory and might forever and forevermore!" (5:13). And then the heavenly creatures shouted, "Amen!" and the vast ranks of redeemed souls fell on their faces and worshiped. It was some revival.

I'm not from a revivalist worship tradition myself, so I was surprised to find myself drawn to preach this passage today. It seemed oddly familiar—probably because my own Anglican worship tradition draws fairly heavily on the book of Revelation for its hymnody, even if we don't preach from it a lot. Some of us perhaps instinctively avoid this book just because Christians have so often used—or misused—it to predict when and how the world will end. Tim LaHaye's best-selling *Left Behind* series[1] is just the most recent in a long line of attempts to decode Revelation and pinpoint Armageddon, an approach that has been wildly popular at least since the Middle Ages. But I think there is good evidence that St. John was doing something more important and more urgent than encoding information on the end of the world for Christians two thousand or more years in the future. He was writing to keep the church alive in his own troubled time. John was writing as a pastor, determined to reinvigorate the faith of his people, when everything in the surrounding culture was aiming to kill it. Does this sound familiar to you? If so, then John can minister to us as well, although some of the people for whom he wrote were in a situation more obviously desperate than ours. Probably none of us has been socially ostracized or prevented from holding a good job because we are Christians; certainly I have never feared for my life because I worship Jesus the Christ. In John's world, not worshiping the Roman emperor was considered "atheism," and atheism was a capital offense. Nonetheless, we are like John's people in this sense: we live in a highly sophisticated culture that conspires in many ways, maybe not to kill Christians, but to kill faith, to make faith in Jesus

1. The *Left Behind* series of novels is based upon Tim LaHaye's reading of the book of Revelation.

Christ seem puny, unrealistic. So maybe we, too, can be helped by the vision John offers his congregation, to strengthen them against the seductions and coercions of a powerful, impressive, and faith-killing culture.

It was near the end of the first century, about the year 90; the church was then some sixty years into its fragile existence. In that year, in Ephesus, an important eastern outpost of the Roman empire, they dedicated a temple to the emperor Domitian. John never mentions that temple, but he probably knew about it, because he knew the church in Ephesus well. As best we can tell, John was something like a district superintendent, a circuit-riding teacher and preacher who had responsibility for seven congregations in Asia Minor (the western coast of modern Turkey). John had a gift for prophecy, and that was enough for the imperial officials to banish him to the small island of Patmos, where, it seems, he wrote the book of Revelation. It's really a long pastoral letter, encouraging the churches in his care to resist the official and cultural pressure on Christians to be sensible, to make life easier for everyone and just go ahead and worship the emperor instead of Jesus the Christ.

The book of Revelation is entirely about worship. Whom will Christians worship? That is the big question for John, not, When is the world going to end, and how? And John shows graphically that the church then and now has only two options: we can worship God in Christ, or we can take the more popular route and worship the culture, the empire; John calls it "the Beast." For he is a poet as well as a visionary. Probably you've noticed: this book never says anything in plain language. John sees things in images, and he speaks in symbols. And maybe that is exactly why the book of Revelation has to be in the Bible. It takes the essential message about Jesus Christ that we find in the Gospels and in Paul and re-presents it—vividly, dramatically, imaginatively. If it weren't for the book of Revelation's way of presenting the gospel, *The Lord of the Rings* never could have happened. Because St. John the Divine, like Tolkien long after him, knew that the best way to strengthen faith is to get Christians' imaginations fired up. He understood that God works through our imaginations to touch our hearts. So John gives us powerful verbal images— not empty fantasies, but true symbols that guide us as we probe the world with our imagination. Isn't that why God gave us an imagination anyway, so we could look with eyes of faith beyond surface impressions, and see what is really going on in our world?

So John shows the two options for worship that are available to Christians in every age. There is always "the Beast," the empire, the apparent source of all power and safety. So, as John puts it, the whole world went "wondering after" the Beast (Rev. 13:3; see 13:4, 8), awestruck at its political, economic, and military might. People don't just submit to the Beast's power; they *worship* it. "Worship" literally means to give someone or something ultimate worth, and every great power creates and sustains for a while the illusion that it is worthy. Whether it be the Roman empire or the numerous other superpowers that have ruled the world since, the Beast always seems for a while to have God in its corner and the good of all in its heart. Therefore it seems for a while to be worthy of all the adulation it demands. Because the Beast seems to guarantee our well-being, it is worthy also of the sacrifices it requires from its countless worshipers.

The alternative to worshiping the Beast is worshiping Jesus Christ. And John shows us what that ultimately means with an image that is the most striking in the whole book: the Lamb that was slaughtered, the quintessential sacrificial victim of the ancient world, its throat slit from ear to ear, now standing on the throne of God, receiving the homage of the whole cosmos. Probably no one before John or since has captured the gospel in such a condensed image; this is biblical haiku. And the beauty of haiku is that once you have seen the picture with your mind's eye, it is with you forever: "Worthy is *the Lamb that was slaughtered* to receive power and wealth and wisdom and might and honor and glory and blessing!" With those few words, St. John gives the church the unforgettable mental picture we need in order to stand firm against the dazzling power of empire.

"Worthy is the Lamb that was slaughtered"—the Bible could not end without that image, because it tells us just what it means to worship God in Jesus Christ. It means accepting the gospel truth that God is indeed of ultimate worth; God is to be worshiped as the One who wins the cosmic battle against evil and death; but . . . *but* God wins only by seeming to suffer total defeat. The image of the slaughtered Lamb on the throne of heaven drives home the reality that when we look at God in Jesus Christ, suffering, defeat, and death are a big part of what we see. The gospel shows us God's glory for what it really is: a glory that survives disaster. All the agony we humans suffer and the agony we inflict—it is God's glory to endure that and transform it. We would, of course, prefer a somewhat different version of the good news; we'd rather that God be *immune* to disaster, so we might hope to share in the divine immunity. But the hard gospel truth is that God wins out over suffering only by first seeming to lose, and those who choose to worship God truly often lose, for a time, right along with God. St. John knew that well; after all, wasn't he banished as an enemy of the empire? Giving glory to the God who refuses to turn away from suffering and death but walks right into them, stumbles and falls into them, and *only then* rises to eternal life—giving glory to the real God gets you into trouble, because it invariably means detracting from the Beast some of the glory it demands.

Time and again, God wins only by seeming to lose. That is the gospel truth that the church at its best proclaims. The church has survived because in every age and throughout the Christian world, there have been some who made that gospel truth plain, proclaimed it joyfully and with full voice, and then willingly paid the price the Beast extracted from them. My Duke colleague Peter Storey served as a Methodist pastor and later bishop of the Conference of Southern Africa during the long struggle against apartheid. Peter often marched with the black Anglican Bishop Desmond Tutu, and often went to jail with him. And one of the most memorable images he carries from those years is of Bishop Tutu in his public addresses, with arms outstretched and a broad smile on his face—Bishop Tutu, who is about my size, calling out to the white South African government, "Come on over to the winning side, come on over before it's too late!" The government officials hated it when he said that.

Now hold those two images together in your mind—the Lamb that was slaughtered receiving all the worship of the saints, and Desmond Tutu inviting his white brothers over to the winning side. Can you see that those images are perfectly matched? They capture the same gospel truth that God wins; finally, invariably, God wins—yet only by first seeming to lose. It is good to hold those two together, because the real historical image of Desmond Tutu demonstrates that John's vision of heaven is something more than pie-in-the-sky-when-you-die. John is giving us an imaginative yet realistic picture of the divine glory in all its fullness. The *fullness* of God's glory we will see only on the other side of death. But we can glimpse some of it now, as we do in this picture of Bishop Tutu. By the grace of God, we are privileged to see some of God's victories over evil in real historical time. Many of us personally recall the wonder with which we watched God win what looked for so long like a losing battle against apartheid in South Africa. Christians need to hold in mind images of such victories.[2] We need to tell them to each other, encouraging one another to believe that God does indeed enter into the disasters we experience and sometimes make for ourselves and others. God enters into all the tragic situations that so badly deform life in this world. The picture of Tutu is valuable because it reminds us that God is present and active even in our political life, in this nation and around the globe. God is present in situations of which many of us frequently despair, calling us—sometimes visibly in the

2. This sermon was preached the week of the tenth anniversary of the end of apartheid in South Africa.

person of someone like Desmond Tutu—to experience God calling us over to the winning side before it's too late.

That image of Bishop Tutu helps us to identify exactly what in John's vision of heaven is essential for us to grasp now. In both Tutu and the book of Revelation we see total confidence in God's power to triumph over evil, and further, confidence that we can have a share in God's triumph. But it's not that confidence in itself that is compelling—at least, not to me. For across the world today many people are overconfident about getting themselves lined up with God in a war against evil, and the outcome is always violent. Depending on how much power a given faction commands, the outcome of that overconfidence is terrorism, counterterrorism, war against terrorism. And the idea behind all that violence is that God's triumph over evil means blessing and prosperity for me and mine, and death and destruction for someone else. In other words, that vision of God's triumph is shaped by exclusiveness; it necessarily excludes the one I call my enemy. By contrast, what is so compelling about Bishop Tutu is that in him we see total confidence in God *without* the exclusiveness. Through him we see God in Christ reaching out to embrace the one who is called an enemy—even a lifelong, implacable, death-dealing enemy. A black South African priest extending his arms to the white government officials and police lines: "Come on over to the winning side!"—that in itself is a vision of heaven, for it shows the utter self-forgetfulness that is surely one of the major ingredients of heaven's joy. The saints in heaven are not thinking about themselves; they can't think of anything but God. Heaven is the place where everyone is completely freed from fear and self-concern. John shows us kings taking off their crowns and throwing them down at God's feet, myriads of myriads falling down on their faces, laughing and singing and praising the God who is "all in all" (1 Cor. 15:28).

We might say that the saints in heaven can afford to forget themselves and we cannot, living as we do in this world of competition, strife, and terror. But those who have the most to teach us about what Christian life must look like in a dangerous world—and I would include Anglican Bishop Tutu and Methodist Bishop Storey in their number—those teachers would tell us that the exact opposite is true. Not only can we afford some measure of saintly self-forgetfulness; we cannot afford anything else. We cannot afford our personal and national habits of keeping ourselves front and center, and excluding so many from our circle of love and concern: the poor in our own country and around the world, those who differ from us in color and language and the name they use for God. Most of all, perhaps, we cannot afford to think about ourselves, our own generation, to the exclusion of our grandchildren and their children. We cannot afford to insist on winning our own small temporary "victories," securing present comfort on terms that guarantee incalculable suffering and loss for others, including those not yet born. Such exclusive victories can never be God's victories. On this the judgment of the gospel is clear: if we are "winning" now on terms that keep others from experiencing the blessing of God, then we will not in the end find ourselves on the winning side.

Yet the invitation of the gospel is just as clear, and it is repeated over and over to the last page of the Bible: the invitation to a life of worship. I don't mean just going to church a lot; for that, sadly, does not always bring us closer to God. No, a life of worship means living wholly out of the reality that God alone is the source of power and safety, of all that is truly worthy of my trust and devotion. Choosing a life of worship means accepting God's invitation to dare to forget myself, to lay aside my fear of those I have come to think of as "the enemy," to reach out and invite her, him, them to come with me, so that together—this is a move we can only make together, we cannot do it alone—we may move over to the winning side, where God is even now waiting to embrace us all.

Amen.

Afterword

"Do you know why she's my favorite preacher?" a divinity student asked me, having just heard Ellen Davis preach. "She never wastes a word." The tribute struck me as the perfect compliment for any preacher, especially one who proclaims God's mission to redeem the world in this time of unprecedented profligacy. To hear Ellen Davis preach is to be drawn into a meticulously worded, Scripture-based world of uncommon eloquence and transformative potency. In her pulpit, language is restored to its primordial, creative function. The source of her elegance is a rhetoric that dovetails with the love of God and God's creation for the gospel's sake. We see an "ecological homiletic" at work in Davis's preaching, one marked by radical care for the planet and all things living upon it. But by "ecology" I also mean to evoke her presumption that preaching shares in creation's materiality, and also aims to participate in its new creation in Jesus Christ. Her sermons reveal how church and world, Scripture and tradition, past and present, even friends and enemies are all included and interconnected within the divine economy of God's imagination.

Ellen Davis never wastes a word, thanks be to God. Now, after combing through over thirty years of her sermon files, accompanying thank you notes, and encomia from appreciative congregants, I remain confident that no single compliment more fully captures the preaching wisdom in this volume. What remains to be seen is how a new generation of preachers may communicate the gospel with such clarity, attentiveness, and imagination. My sincere hope is that this book will be not only a collection of great sermons and essays to savor and enjoy, but also a demonstration of homiletical habits and practices worth imitating. With this afterword, I aim to commend to the reader four particular elements of Davis's preaching that distinguish her homiletic approach: (1) theological exegesis, (2) prophecy, (3) elegance, and (4) prayer. My purpose in doing so is not to help anyone duplicate Davis's style, for that would be impossible. Rather, I wish to draw attention to her style in a way that enables other preachers to strengthen their own craft. Even if we do not identify as clergy, we all have much to learn from Davis's work.

The Fecund Word

Ellen Davis esteems Scripture the way Wendell Berry does soil.[1] For this reason, her sermons have "the kind of taste of the earth that floors you."[2] Like an enchanted gardener, Davis kneels down upon the written word, sinks her fingers into it, and luxuriates in its textures, hues, smells, and tastes. With a hermeneutic of trust, she puts her faith "in the two inches of humus that will build under the trees every thousand years."[3] This is the first element that distinguishes Davis's preaching. She does not blast the meaning out of a passage. Rather, she cultivates her speech to grow organically from the fecund word of Scripture, focusing always on the God it reveals. Davis preaches in the hope that the Word of God may constitute a community of faith just as humus constitutes every human being. Thus, she endeavors to ensure that her text and message match one another at a molecular level. Her sermons are no more independent from their texts than an heirloom tomato is from its garden plot. We would be supremely challenged to find one paragraph in this collection that does not derive its essential content from both the given lectionary texts,

---

1. I mention Berry to draw attention not only to Davis's friendship with him, but also to the ways her work draws from and complements his. See, for example, Berry, "'And the Land I Will Remember' (Lev 26:42): Reading the Bible through Agrarian Eyes," in *Wendell Berry and Religion: Heaven's Earthly Life,* ed. Joel Shuman (Lexington: University Press of Kentucky, 2009), 115-30. See also an interview of Ellen Davis, with poetry readings by Wendell Berry, on *Speaking of Faith,* with Krista Tippett (aired June 10-16, 2010), transcript and audio link available at: http://www.onbeing.org/program/poetry-creatures/transcript/4426.

2. As columnist Mark Bittman described a meal at Berry's farm in the *New York Times,* April 24, 2012. Available at: http://opinionator.blogs.nytimes.com/2012/04/24/wendell-berry-american-hero/?_r=0. For Ellen's own perspective on the relationship between Scripture and soil, see Ellen Davis, "The Soil That Is Scripture," in *Biblical Authority: Perspectives on the Bible as Scripture,* ed. William P. Brown (Louisville: Westminster John Knox, 2007), 36-44.

3. Wendell Berry, "Manifesto: The Mad Farmer Liberation Front," in *The Mad Farmer Poems* (New York: Counterpoint Press, 2009), 12.

and also related passages throughout the canon.[4] This high view of Scripture's authority frees her (and likewise the congregation) to be "an astonished child in a wonderful garden."[5]

Reading Scripture theologically allows Davis to employ modernist interpretive methods in service to a more determinative, traditional approach. Take her sermon on Genesis 1, for example. In "Being a Creature Means You Eat," she places the commentaries aside and plunges directly into the text. The scholarly literature is "of no real help" because its modern worldview, in contrast to the biblical one, has yet to fully recognize eating as an essential theological concern. From her careful exegesis, she produces a bounty of revelation about God, Scripture, and our current situation. Ironically, the relevance of her message derives its persuasive power by reading Genesis with an agricultural lens. Upon entering the text through such an antiquated imagination, she comes in contact with the real world, where to be a creature "means eating within the limits that God has set in the design of creation." Without assuming this so-called primitive scriptural worldview, she likely would not have noticed Genesis' literary shift toward verbose delight as it describes the food supply on the fifth day.

Because Davis is so captivated by the text's richness, which continuously points to God, she cannot help but keep God at the theological and rhetorical center of the entire sermon. As God is the central player in Genesis 1, God is also the main character in this congregational address. Even when the sermon is about "us," it is so only by way of our relationship to God. Beginning with her introduction, where she invokes God's providential character in Psalm 50, Davis claims we can know our true identity and vocational duty to creation only after we know who God is and what God calls us to do. From there, the only sermonic move she makes without mention of God or drawing on a specific biblical verse is, in fact, a thoroughly scriptural demonstration of what *anti*-creation looks like. She gives us a dystopic vision of creation in reverse. Through this haunting interpretation, Davis emphasizes our distance from God by omitting any mention of God or Scripture from her descriptions of environmental degradation. Only a preacher who is convinced that "God is the primary agent revealed in the biblical narrative"[6] could craft such a potentially

---

4. Davis usually preaches from the lectionary, though there are exceptions. The Genesis 1 sermon I cite below, for example, "Being a Creature Means You Eat," was not on the lectionary text for that day.

5. Karl Barth, *Homiletics* (Louisville: Westminster John Knox, 1991), 128.

6. Ellen F. Davis and Richard B. Hays, eds., *The Art of Reading Scripture* (Grand Rapids: Eerdmans, 2003), 1.

powerful homiletic maneuver. Consequently, she does not begin with a rhetorical technique in mind. She begins with the hard work of exegesis, remembering always that God is the subject.[7] Only then does the captivating rhetoric ensue.

The Prophetic Word

Of all the senses, Ellen Davis is most partial to sight. She so often calls us to envision the dramatic narrative of a passage of Scripture, a particular person or metaphor, or a description of the very presence of God. Her proclivity toward vision and perception is due in part to her deep knowledge of the Old Testament, brimming as it is with signs and wonders. Biblical authors continually prompt us to "Look! See! *Behold!*" But Davis's tendency to kindle the visual senses is rooted in her conception of biblical prophecy. Most of us have been taught to think of prophecy as a means of predicting future events, or as "speaking truth to power." Prophetic preachers are those who, with passion and conviction, take a courageous stand on a difficult contemporary issue, perhaps even putting their own lives at risk. While she would not discount that such preaching can be prophetic, Davis believes biblical prophecy is a more expansive and complex theological category. Prophecy is primarily a work of radical perception, of seeing what is really true about God and the world. It is not so much an adjective for a powerful sermon as it is a way of being attentive to God's presence. Biblical prophecy names the persistent practice of discerning the will of God on behalf of God's people.

In the ordination sermon "I Saw God," Davis describes the call to prophesy as a "lousy job for an incurable optimist." It is so difficult because the work of prophecy involves drawing everyone's attention to the pattern of the gospel in their lives and accompanying people as they walk the way of the cross. The ordinand could only "train his sights" on this job by drawing strength from a vision that transcends the power of his own faculties. That is, "he has seen something—a glimpse at least—of what Isaiah saw" . . . "God highly exalted." Davis focuses the congregation's gaze on a most humbling and compelling part of ministry: the ability to see "God exalted over the pretenses of the powerful." This "clear vision in the things of God" will accompany the young priest throughout his ministry as he delights in reading Scripture and shares his

---

7. See, for example, Davis's discussion of the relationship between exegesis and rhetoric in *Wondrous Depth: Preaching the Old Testament* (Louisville: Westminster John Knox, 2005), 70-71.

delight with his people. Despite the difficult and unrelenting work of prophetic discernment, the fruit of such labor will be a blessing for the whole church.

One of the blessings in this sermon is Davis's artful use of metaphor. The book of Isaiah becomes "the portfolio of a master photographer," offering one striking image of God after another: a distraught parent, a mother in labor, or a nursing mother. The captivating idea of Isaiah as photographer is designed to be an invitation for the ordinand himself to follow in Isaiah's vocational footsteps. It matters little whether the ordinand's community recognizes him as prophetic in the conventional sense. It is, however, a matter of life and death whether the young priest seeks to dispel the illusions that otherwise captivate our age. Davis shows us that a preacher is not necessarily a prophet who provokes the ire of the powers and principalities with soaring oratory. Rather, a true prophet enables people to see that, while the world is "careless of God and the things of God," God's love for and sovereignty over the world remain steadfast.

The Elegant Word

A student once said to Ellen Davis, "Your sermons are like an Armani suit. The design seems so simple, at first you think there is nothing to it. And then you look at it hard and see how it has been put together." This is an excellent, if surprising, definition of elegant preaching. While Davis's sermons are never simplistic, they do have a beautiful simplicity. They are refreshingly free of the intellectual gymnastics one often associates with scholarly preaching. There are no intrusive moves in her content, and no trace of histrionics in her demeanor. Davis tells the truth gracefully refined, a third distinguishing mark of her preaching. Using such elegance is also one of the most difficult habits for preachers to develop, caught as we often are in the search for "relevance." How we flail about in the pulpit from one clever story to another, hoping to craft a message that will keep people's attention. Scripture gets lost in the pursuit of new and interesting content. The elegant word is Davis's gift for pastors trapped in the exhausting, weekly hunt for "illustrations."

In her 2014 Good Friday sermon in Duke Chapel, Davis interweaves the Lamentations text with glimpses of the Passion narrative. But she does not force Jesus into the Old Testament. Instead, she positions the poetry of Lamentations alongside the narrative of Luke's Gospel, enabling the texts to illuminate one another. She offers no additional illustrations to make points. She makes no moves that one could use interchangeably with other sermons.

Rather, she develops all of her content from the fertile ground where the texts overlap, with the result that Jesus illustrates Lamentations, and vice versa. She draws the hearer into a hypnotizing interplay between the wisdom of lament and its hopeful embodiment in Jesus. She challenges our reluctance to implicate God in our suffering, and asserts that while we repress our anger at God "the Bible is paying no attention to us." Jesus's terrible cry of abandonment from the cross is not only the incarnate crescendo of Lamentations, but also an invitation for every Christian to confess, "Yes, Jesus, my sense of abandonment by God is a lot like yours."

To preach with such elegance is to preach with a confidence that the text will give rise to the sermon's most interesting content. Elegance is, therefore, an expression of patience. The patient preacher has mastered anxiety and has developed the humility to wait for the Holy Spirit to open the Scriptures. Impatient preachers want immediate gratification, as if they have power to produce fruit before the bud flowers. They force extraneous matters upon a text in an attempt to control it. If they were mining coal, instead, they would think nothing of blasting the tops off mountains. But elegance recalls Joseph Sittler's favorite translation of Matthew 5:5: "Blessed are the debonair." We should say this alternative interpretation of the Beatitude depicts the elegant preacher, not trampling and gouging, but walking lightly upon the earth, pausing often to savor the sacred places.

The Prayerful Word

If you could see Ellen Davis's homiletical life's work arranged canonically, you would be struck by the size of the "Psalms" file. She has preached more from the Psalms than from any other book. I suspect the majority of preachers today gravitate toward other texts—the Gospels, the Epistles, and the grand Old Testament stories, for example. Narrative has outrun poetry as the literary preference among preachers, since the former seems to be more conducive to storytelling. When you are grazing through the lectionary options, why would you select the psalm when you could preach from the parable of the prodigal son instead? Davis reverses this logic: Why would you preach these other texts when you could preach the psalm?

Her fascination with the Psalms coincided with the genesis of her preaching talent as she read the sermons of John Donne. Though remembered mostly for his poetry, Donne is arguably the church's greatest preacher of the Psalms. He is without question the greatest influence on Davis's preaching. She claims in her introduction that Donne captivated her with his steadfast focus on a particular text—usually one verse—and his ability to "enter fully into the textual world of the Bible." But I suspect there is a deeper connection at work. Both Donne and Davis stand out among their peers for preferring above all other modes of discourse the psalmists' visceral language of prayer. They would rather be caught in the bewildering vortex where the human heart clashes with the heart of God in linguistic versions of interstellar cataclysms. When the stardust settles, a sermon is born.

You might have noticed that whenever Davis does apply anything like an illustration, she does so by highlighting a single person or community that epitomizes a psalm. We hear particular names, like David, Israel, and the church, or Julia, Dean Borsch, and Bishop Daniel. Davis sees the Psalms dramatically unfolding in the lives of real people around her because she is paying attention to them. To pray for someone means giving a person your undivided attention before God, to meditate on the ways God might be present in that person's life, and even to speak with God on that person's behalf. Davis's sermons abound with such prayerful curiosity about specific people. Let this be a lesson for preachers: if we are ever short on "illustration" material, let us meditate upon the Psalms, and watch as familiar faces rise up from the ancient depths of Israel's and the church's prayer book.

The Luminous Word

Even if Ellen Davis "never wastes a word," we Westerners are still a wasteful lot. This is a hard truth Davis has preached with both judgment and grace since well before it was in vogue. We waste food, fuel, and time. We lay waste to creation, to the mountains and the seas, to the creepy, crawly things under our dominion. We lay waste to one another with the industrial efficiency of modern violence, fattening ourselves in a new century of slaughter. We are also surrounded by the noxious fumes of chatter, both vicious and affable, which have their own warming effect on the globe. "The tongue is a fire," the letter of James reminds us. Even more, James says, careless tongues are toxic. Every beast and bird "has been tamed by the human species, but no one can tame the tongue—a restless evil, full of deadly poison" (James 3:7–8). Davis believes our destructive relationship with land bespeaks our impoverished speech. It follows, then, that the source of her passionate concern for ecological waste springs from her understanding of the Word of God. Her preaching shows that the root of ecological devastation in all its forms is our habit of wasting words.

We know from Genesis 1, however, that on the first day of the week God speaks a good creation into existence through words. *Words create.* That any shimmering, preached word may carry the same creative power as God's word means all preachers may share in the refashioning of the world, beginning with their own particular people and plot of ground. Whenever this happens, it is a miracle. Ellen Davis's ecological homiletic challenges a new generation of preachers to recognize that consecrating the raw materials of language is a solemn task. When we stand on the first day of the week to preach the gospel, we are always saying in a sense, "Let there be light." May we stand, then, convinced that the God who never wastes a luminous word rests in the pleasure of every ensuing new creation.

AUSTIN McIVER DENNIS

Acknowledgments

The sermon "All That You Say, I Will Do" was originally published with the title "'All That You Say, I Will Do': A Sermon on the Book of Ruth," in *Scrolls of Love: Ruth and the Song of Songs,* edited by Peter S. Hawkins and Lesleigh Cushing Stahlberg (New York: Fordham University Press, 2006), 3–8. Reprinted with the kind permission of Fordham University Press.

The sermon "Healing for Sin-Sick Hearts" was originally published with the title "Costly Vision," in *Touching the Altar: The Old Testament for Christian Worship* (Grand Rapids: Eerdmans, 2008), 103–11. Reprinted with the kind permission of Wm. B. Eerdmans Publishing Co.

The sermon "I Saw God" was originally published with the title "I Saw God: The Ordination of Anthony Petrotta," in *Preaching from Psalms, Oracles, and Parables, Sermons That Work XIV,* edited by Roger Alling and David J. Schlafer (Harrisburg, PA: Morehouse Publishing, 2006), 91–113. Reprinted with the kind permission of Morehouse Publishing (Church Publishing Incorporated).

The sermon "Stargazers" was originally published with the same title in *Sermons from Duke Chapel: Voices from a "Great Towering Church,"* edited by William H. Willimon (Durham, NC: Duke University Press, 2005), 337–41. Reprinted with the kind permission of Duke University Press.

Versions of the sermon "The Table of Creation" were previously published as "And in Him All Things Hold Together," in *Preaching What We Practice: Proclamation and Moral Discernment,* ed. Timothy F. Sedgwick and David J. Schlafer (Harrisburg, PA: Morehouse Publishing, 2007), 142–47, and in *Earth and the Word: Classic Sermons on Saving the Planet,* ed. David Rhoads (New York: Continuum, 2007), 127–34.

The essay "'Here I Am': Preaching Isaiah as a Book of Vocation" was originally published as "Christians Hearing Isaiah," in *Preaching from Psalms, Oracles, and Parables, Sermons That Work XIV,* edited by Roger Alling and David J. Schlafer

325

(Harrisburg, PA: Morehouse Publishing, 2006), 91–113. Reprinted with the kind permission of Morehouse Publishing (Church Publishing Incorporated).

The essay "Holy Preaching: Ethical Interpretation and the Practical Imagination" was originally published with the same title in *Reclaiming Faith: Essays on Orthodoxy in the Episcopal Church and the Baltimore Declaration,* edited by Ephraim Radner and George R. Sumner (Grand Rapids: Eerdmans, 1993), 197–224. Reprinted with the kind permission of Wm. B. Eerdmans Publishing Co.

The essay "Surprised by Wisdom: Preaching Proverbs" was originally published with the same title in *Interpretation* 63, no. 3 (July 2009): 264–77. Reprinted with the kind permission of Sage Publishing.

The essay "Witnessing to God in the Midst of Life: Old Testament Preaching" was originally published with the same title in *Expository Times* 124, no. 1 (October 2012): 1–8. Reprinted with the kind permission of Sage Publishing.

Index of Scripture References